DEMOCRACY
IN THE
CARIBBEAN

A World Peace
Foundation Study

DEMOCRACY IN THE CARIBBEAN

Political, Economic, and
Social Perspectives

Edited by
Jorge I. Domínguez, Robert A. Pastor,
and R. DeLisle Worrell

The Johns Hopkins University Press
Baltimore and London

AOA 4746-0/3

GIFT
5/18/93

RECEIVED

JUN 9 1993

Kennedy School
Library

The Johns Hopkins University Press
2715 North Charles Street
Baltimore, Maryland 21218-4319
The Johns Hopkins Press Ltd., London

Library of Congress Cataloging-in-Publication Data

Democracy in the Caribbean : political, economic, and social
    perspectives / edited by Jorge I. Domínguez, Robert A. Pastor,
    and R. DeLisle Worrell.
        p.   cm. — (A World Peace Foundation study)
    Includes bibliographical references and index.
    ISBN 0-8018-4450-9. — ISBN 0-8018-4451-7 (pbk.)
    1. Caribbean Area—Politics and government—1945– .
2. Democracy—Caribbean Area.   3. Caribbean Area—
Economic conditions—1945– .   4. Caribbean Area—Social
conditions—1945– .   I. Domínguez, Jorge I., 1945– .
II. Pastor, Robert A.   III. Worrell, R. DeLisle.   IV. Series.
JL599.5.A91D46   1993
972.905'2—dc20   92-28447

A catalog record for this book is available from the British Library.

Contents

Foreword

Books on the Caribbean typically fall into two categories. One category is aimed primarily at specialists who wish to broaden or deepen their understanding of the region. The second is directed to those concerned with the Caribbean's role in the international system. Books in the first category look at the Caribbean from the inside; the region's international relations are of interest to the extent that foreign influences and events shape the area's societies, but the focus is on domestic matters. Books in the second category look at the region from the outside; for their audience, the Caribbean is of interest as one arena for the larger game of international politics. For books of the first type the Caribbean is the subject, while for those of the second type it is the object.

This volume tries to combine both points of view. Its authors believe that for both those who live in the Caribbean and those who are its neighbors, it is no longer adequate to see the region in one-dimensional terms. For the United States, the Caribbean can no longer be viewed as simply a battleground in a struggle with a threatening extracontinental power, whether it be Germany under the Kaiser and Hitler or the Soviet Union during the cold war. For those living in the Caribbean, the rest of the world can no longer be simply the place to escape to or the place whence occasional bonanzas or, more often, disasters arrive.

The interest of the United States in the Caribbean has always been geo-political. Since the earliest days of the republic, U.S. leaders have been sensitive to the encroachments of rival powers in the region. Once the United States laid claim to great-power status by driving Spain out of the Caribbean, the area became one of vital strategic importance. The chief concern of U.S. leaders has been that political instability in a Caribbean country might lead to its becoming an outpost for a hostile power. It is this fear that has triggered sporadic U.S. intervention in the region, from the taking over of the customs houses of Santo Domingo in the administration of Theodore Roosevelt to the invasion of Grenada during Ronald Reagan's presidency. The geopolitical importance of the Caribbean to the United States was dramatically underlined by the Cuban missile crisis of 1962, when the Soviet Union placed nuclear weapons in Cuba and the worst fears of U.S. policymakers became a reality.

Except for periodic crises arising from these strategic concerns, how-ever, the United States traditionally has paid little attention to the course of events in the Caribbean nations. This is hardly surprising given their small size and insignificance for the giant U.S. economy. In addition, the majority of the English-speaking nations of the Caribbean, which com-prise twelve of the sixteen independent countries of the area, have been stable democracies since their beginnings of self-government in the middle of this century. For most Americans, the Caribbean is a place for winter vacations, a source of big-league baseball players, and the home of reggae and salsa music. One might conclude that with the passing of the cold war, Washington will pay even less attention to the region. This is unlikely, however. The same characteristic that has made the Caribbean important to the United States in times past—its geography—will make it impossible to ignore in the future, but not just for reasons of military security.

The Caribbean is no longer the passive actor in its relationship with its giant neighbor: for some time, it has had an impact on the United States in the most direct manner possible—by penetrating American society with its culture, its people, and even its politics. This has happened because modern technology, and the revolutions it has wrought in communica-tions, information, the organization of the production process, and pat-terns of consumption, has made all countries, no matter their size or their power, vulnerable to the rest of the world. Borders are now porous, and people, goods, and ideas move across them with relative ease.

Americans, accustomed to thinking themselves distant from other peoples, now find that not only is the world at their doorstep but it has moved inside the house. By virtue of the new wave of immigration that has been underway for the last several decades, American society is being transformed, just as it was by the influx of Europeans around the beginning of the century. In this latest mixing of the American stew, the Caribbean peoples have been an important ingredient.

Miami has long been a Caribbean metropolis, but the tide of Caribbean immigration has spread far and wide. The Puerto Ricans, with some 3.5 million on the island and another 2.3 million on the mainland, make up the largest group within the U.S. borders.[1] They are followed by the Cubans: an estimated 778,000 foreign-born Cubans resided in the United States in 1988. The figures for other Caribbean-born peoples in the United States are also impressive: an estimated 380,000 Jamaicans, 313,000 Dominicans, 189,000 Haitians, and 105,000 Trinidadians.[2] New York and Miami are meccas for the majority of these newcomers, but there are significant Caribbean communities in other cities as well. In the Boston area, for example, there were an estimated 32,000 Haitians in 1990.[3]

These immigrants require expanded educational facilities and other services, which must be adapted to their linguistic and cultural differences, and their assimilation into the larger society is not an easy one. Nevertheless, as producers and consumers, these recent arrivals from the Caribbean strengthen the U.S. economy, and their cultures and literature are enriching the communities where they settle and the nation as a whole. As they become citizens, they will become an important political force, as have other ethnic groups in the past.

Caribbean immigration should bring net benefits to U.S. society. There is, however, another import that frequently arrives via the Caribbean, one that is now widely held to be as much of a threat to U.S. security as Soviet missiles used to be: illegal drugs. The drug dealers also have found a number of havens in the Caribbean for laundering money.

Immigration, and to some extent drug trafficking, reflects the poor state of Caribbean economies. The stresses put on these societies by their long economic crisis have also taken a toll on their political systems. As a result, the area's proud tradition of democracy can no longer be taken for granted. If democracy fails in the Caribbean, the social and economic ills of the region are likely to worsen and the United States will feel the spillover effects.

For these reasons, the U.S. government is unlikely to be able to ignore events in the Caribbean in the years ahead. Yet, that does not necessarily mean that Washington policymakers will act in the larger interests of either their own constituents or the peoples of the Caribbean. It is just as possible, and even likely in the U.S. system, that actions taken by U.S. officials and lawmakers in response to the impact of events in the Caribbean will be reactive and narrowly focused on the immediate problem at hand. That has often been the case in the past. What is needed when two societies interact with each other as intimately as do those of the Caribbean and the United States is a strategic vision of how the individual problems relate to one another and what needs to be done to resolve them.

For the people of the Caribbean, their interdependence with the United States is not news. Also, it is a mixed blessing. Take immigration. The flow of people from the Caribbean to the United States is a social safety valve, but it also means a loss of workers with badly needed skills. In addition, these small and fragile economies, heavily dependent on tourism and the export of raw materials, are highly sensitive to the ups and downs of the U.S. economy, as well as to the vagaries of the U.S. political system. An example of the latter is U.S. sugar policy. In a move designed to benefit its small group of domestic sugar producers, the United States drastically cut the quotas for sugar imports during the 1980s. Simultaneously, the United States was attempting to boost the economies of the Caribbean through the Caribbean Basin Initiative (CBI). Yet the region's loss of income from sugar was greater than the increase in its exports to the United States that resulted from the lowering of trade barriers under the CBI.

The Caribbean's vulnerability to the outside world raises a more fundamental question, namely, whether small states can ever hope to be masters of their destiny. In the 1970s, some tried to achieve a measure of economic independence by using the power of the state to protect domestic markets and to offset the power of foreign corporations. These experiments in statism failed. In addition, a number of Caribbean governments have tended to rely heavily on official loans from the developed countries and the international financial institutions for the capital and know-how needed for development, while pursuing policies that discourage private investment and exports. It is now generally recognized, even by some Caribbean leaders who were proponents of the failed policies of the past, that a totally different strategy has to be attempted, one that encourages private entrepreneurship, is open to the world, and is able to compete aggressively in it—as the small exporting states of East Asia have done, for example.

The conclusion of our study is that both the United States and the Caribbean nations need a new strategy for dealing with the area's problems. The United States needs a *Caribbean* policy that attempts to weigh a sugar policy, a drug policy, or an immigration policy against its larger interests in the region. The Caribbean nations need a *global* policy to meet the challenge of making their way in an increasingly competitive world economy. It was to help those who must craft those policies—leaders and people alike—that the World Peace Foundation undertook the study that culminated in this volume.

One of the first problems faced by anyone who wishes to study the Caribbean is to answer the question, What is "the Caribbean"? In recent years the U.S. government has used the notion of the Caribbean Basin to define the scope of its initiative to create special trade and investment preferences for the area. But in addition to the island Caribbean, the Caribbean Basin includes Central America, Mexico, Colombia, Venezuela, and, indeed, the United States. The countries that make up the basin are too heterogeneous to make the concept a useful analytical tool, except for quite limited purposes.

At the other extreme is a tendency to use the term *Caribbean* to mean only the English-speaking countries of the region. Because of their common language, history, culture, and economic and social characteristics, this is a convenient category for analysts who wish to make generalizations about the area. The problem with this approach is that it omits three countries and a commonwealth that contain more than four times the population of the English-speaking nations: Cuba (10.5 million), the Dominican Republic (6.7 million), Haiti (5.7 million), and Puerto Rico (3.5 million). From the point of view of the United States, these latter islands are at least as important as the Commonwealth Caribbean; indeed, historically, they have been the source of most of the U.S. interest in the region.

To include both the Latin and the English-speaking countries in the analysis presents some difficulties, however. While they share some common characteristics, particularly their dependence on a single power (the United States for all except Cuba), the two groups have much less in common with one another than they have differences. One is struck by how little Jamaicans, for example, know, or seem interested in knowing, about the Dominican Republic, and vice versa. Nevertheless, there seems to be a growing acceptance among the English-speaking Caribbean that regional institutions, such as the Caribbean Common Market (CARICOM), should be expanded to bring in the other countries (with, for now, the exception of Cuba).

In the end, the organizers of our study opted to include in their definition of the Caribbean the Commonwealth countries, Cuba, the Dominican Republic, Haiti, Puerto Rico, and Suriname but to focus more attention on some of these non-English-speaking countries than on others. Thus, there are chapters on the Dominican Republic and Puerto Rico, which, in the near future at any rate, seem to have the most potential for playing important regional roles, but not on Cuba, Haiti, and Suriname.

Some years ago a volume of this kind would have required a discussion of Cuba's role in the region as a possible alternative model of development, but statism has proven itself no more effective in Cuba than elsewhere, and as a result of the deep crisis into which Cuba has now entered, interest in the Cuban model has shrunk almost to the vanishing point. On the other hand, if there were to be a regime change in Cuba leading to the island's reentry into the global market system—which no longer seems as remote as it did a few years ago—the impact on the rest of the Caribbean could be profound. Cuba has one-third of the population of the Caribbean, the largest arable land mass, a skilled and literate work force, and a potential pool of expatriate capital and entrepreneurship currently located in southern Florida. However, given Cuba's current isolation from the rest of the region and the uncertainty about its future, we did not feel that it would be useful for the purposes of our study to attempt to deal with Cuba in detail. Similar circumstances caused us to omit separate chapters on Haiti and Suriname.

As noted at the outset, this study is an attempt to provide both an analysis of the origins of the region's current strengths and weaknesses and a basis for meeting the policy challenges of the future. Accordingly, the volume is organized in three main parts. The first, "Politics and Societies," examines the interaction between the area's social evolution and its politics. Jorge Domínguez points out that the English-speaking Caribbean's dedication to democracy was in no way preordained simply because the area's colonial master, Great Britain, was democratic or because the countries have enjoyed a relatively high per capita income. He points to the unhappy history of high-income developing countries elsewhere and former British colonies in Africa to prove the point. Domínguez explains why the Caribbean managed to preserve and strengthen its democratic institutions after independence but, in so doing, reminds us that these democracies are not invulnerable to the adverse effects of the economic deterioration and growing crime that are at work in the area. Franklin Knight describes the forces that have molded Caribbean societies and given them their unique characteristics, making a case for heavier investments in education as a key to building on the societies' strengths. Anthony Maingot describes the threats to which these societies are now being subjected from corruption and violence arising from international crime and argues for a new definition of national security for the region and for a Caribbean security system. On a more positive note, Anthony Payne shows how the English-speaking Caribbean peoples adapted the Westminster model of democracy to their peculiar needs and, in so doing, created a strong polity that should stand them in good stead in the face of the serious challenges

they now face. Evelyne Huber ventures to look at the prospects for democratic government in the region in three categories of countries: (1) established democracies like Jamaica, (2) fragile democracies like the Dominican Republic, and (3) nondemocratic regimes like Guyana. Weaving
together democratic political theory and the specific circumstances of the
Caribbean countries, Huber draws some policy implications for those who
would strengthen democracy in the region, emphasizing the need for the
nations of the area and their neighbors to make the strengthening of democracy a self-conscious collaborative endeavor.

The second part of this volume presents four cases that address common problems as well as national idiosyncrasies. Vaughan Lewis describes
the precarious situation of the tiny states of the Eastern Caribbean in the
face of an increasingly fluid and competitive international environment
and argues for hastening and deepening the process of integration among
these countries that has already begun as the only sure way to successfully
meet the challenge—a prescription that he points out as holding for the
larger states of the Caribbean, as well. Selwyn Ryan shows how attempts
at major reform of economic structures in Trinidad and Tobago and Guyana have exacerbated the ethnic cleavages between blacks and Indians in
those two countries and have produced political instability of a systemic
kind. Ryan advocates the use of some sort of power-sharing formula
among political parties to give each group a stake in the policy process.

Jonathan Hartlyn traces the surprising evolution of the Dominican Republic in recent decades from a classic Latin American dictatorship to a
democracy, albeit a fragile and "uninstitutionalized" one. There has been
an evolution as well in the society from an isolated, mostly rural country
of 3 million inhabitants to "a vibrant, internationally connected, mostly
urban country of 7 million." Yet the verdict is still out as to whether democratic institutions will survive the severe economic crisis the country is
undergoing and its legacy of "cynical, distrustful, and conspiratorial politics." Hartlyn sees neither the best nor the worst scenarios but, rather,
the survival of democracy, albeit under unstable economic and social
conditions.

Juan Manuel García-Passalacqua shows us the excruciating dilemma
that it has been the fate of the Puerto Rican people to live since the con-
quest of their island by the United States in 1898. Torn between their consciousness of themselves as a nation with its own cultural identity and
unique history and their feelings of dependence for their economic well-
being on their association with the United States, the Puerto Ricans have
been at an impasse for decades as to the political status of their island.

Until this impasse is broken, Puerto Rico's role in the Caribbean, which García-Passalacqua argues could be significant, will be only *in potentia*. He sets forth the steps that should be taken to cut the Gordian knot.

The third, and final, section of this volume addresses the questions for policymakers posed in the preceding chapters. The first two chapters serve as background to the economic challenges that the region faces. DeLisle Worrell analyzes the evolution of the economies of the English-speaking Caribbean since the early days of independence, showing how misconceived economic policies over the last ten years have produced slow or no growth, high unemployment, and declining or stagnating living standards in most of the countries. Then he sets forth the policies that he believes are needed to put things right. Stephen Quick complements Worrell's analysis with a picture of the dramatic changes that are now transforming the international economy and what that means for the vulnerable nations of the Caribbean. Like his colleagues in this section, Quick sees an urgent need for the Caribbean countries to take bold measures to be able to survive in the fierce new world of a global system of production and consumption.

The next two authors deal with specific threats to the area's democratic institutions described earlier in the volume, namely, the drug trade and other new challenges to the region's security. In addition to the predictable noxious effects of the drug traffic, Ron Sanders sees a threat to the sovereign authority of the Caribbean states by the well-meaning but pervasive efforts of the U.S. government to combat the drug trade throughout the region. Sanders argues that the only way to ward off this intervention in their internal affairs is for the countries of the area to mount a vigorous collective effort, which can only be fully effective if carried out by a regional authority that can deal with all aspects of the drug problem.

Neville Linton looks at the whole area of security threats. He describes the halting efforts in the 1980s to create a regional security system and the impact of the U.S. invasion of Grenada on the Caribbean elites' view of this question. He reviews the variety of "new" security problems facing these countries, ranging across crime, civil unrest, terrorism, natural disasters, and environmental degradation, as well as more traditional security problems, such as armed attempts to overthrow governments. Rather than seeing the recent efforts to cope with all this as "militarization" of the Caribbean, Linton sees the danger as stemming from inaction on the part of governments in the face of increasing vulnerability of these small islands to external forces, whether they be conspiracies of criminals and political fanatics or predatory enterprises seeking to exploit the area's natural resources. Linton sees an urgent need to build a regional system that, in turn, would be backed up by more powerful democratic states, preferably through multilateral òrganizations, such as the United Nations or the Organization of American States. Such a system should develop contingency plans and procedures that would provide a quick reaction to crises such as the attempted overthrow of the Trinidadian government in 1990.

In the final chapter of the volume, Richard Fletcher and Robert Pastor set forth a strategy and a program to be undertaken by the nations of the Caribbean to deal with the range of political, social, security, and economic problems described in the study. Fletcher and Pastor emphasize that this effort must be one that is home-grown, that is, conceived and initiated by Caribbean leaders and accepted by the Caribbean people themselves. If the Caribbean shows that it is willing to make the hard choices and bear the burdens that such a broad program of self-help requires, then the United States and other outsiders should be willing to take steps to provide the effort with significant political and economic support.

The World Peace Foundation and the editors wish to gratefully acknowledge the financial support of the Andrew W. Mellon Foundation for this study.

Richard J. Bloomfield

DEMOCRACY
IN THE
CARIBBEAN

1 The Caribbean Question: Why Has Liberal Democracy (Surprisingly) Flourished?

Jorge I. Domínguez

In *Society and Democracy in Germany*, one of the more influential books published about Germany after the Second World War, Ralf Dahrendorf began by asking what the "German Question" was.[1] For Germans, Dahrendorf suggested, the German Question was one put to foreigners: Why was Germany divided and how could it be reunited? Many Germans thought that the German Question focused on the role of the German people in international affairs. For Dahrendorf and, he said, for many non-Germans, there was a different German Question: Why had liberal democracy (surprisingly) not flourished among Germans?

In the nineteenth century Germany had seemed to be very much a part of the "culture of the West," which had given birth to liberal democracy in Western Europe; Germany's economic resources were at the forefront of Europe. Germany's transition from the empire to the Weimar Republic seemed at the time no more traumatic than other European transitions to democracy; the Weimar Constitution seemed to enshrine many of the West's values of liberty and democracy. Dahrendorf's own German Question, therefore, sought to understand why liberal democracy had not taken root under the empire, why it failed so spectacularly in the 1930s, and why this happened among a people once seen as good candidates for liberal democratic politics?

There is, perhaps, a Caribbean Question, and to its exploration I turn.

As for the Germans in their history, so too for many in the Caribbean (the islands, the Guianas, and Belize)[2] the Question has been and remains at the international level: Why is the Caribbean so divided and above all why has there not been a better integration? In this book, for example, Vaughan Lewis (chapter 6) assesses the role of the Eastern Caribbean states in their international environment, giving special attention to integrative efforts among the member countries of the Organization of Eastern Caribbean States (OECS). Neville Linton (chapter 13) discusses regional security in the Caribbean. Anthony Maingot (chapter 3) reflects on the internationalization of corruption and violence in the Caribbean. And Ron Sanders (chapter 12) considers the international dimensions of the drug-traffic problem in the Caribbean. There are many differences between the German and Caribbean cases, even beyond the fact that the OECS does not threaten to conquer the world; above all, this book's authors do not insist on political unification but focus, instead, on pragmatic questions for which regional policy options are reasonable and appropriate.

Many outside the Caribbean also consider the Caribbean Question from an international perspective. This is the way in which the major powers and, above all, the U.S. government have thought about this region; at times it has seemed as if the region's sea lanes mattered more than the region itself. Across the centuries, for the major powers the Caribbean has been an arena for competition. In a similar spirit, DeLisle Worrell (chapter 10) and Stephen Quick (chapter 11) shed light on the impact of the international economy on the Caribbean, and Pastor and Fletcher appropriately focus on international issues (chapter 14).

The Caribbean Surprise

From a comparative perspective, however, there is another Caribbean Question: no other region in what has been called the Third World has had, for so long, so many liberal democratic polities. Huber defines democracy by its free and fair elections, held at regular intervals, in the context of guaranteed civil and political rights, responsible government (i.e., accountability of the executive, administrative, and coercive arms of the state to elected representatives), and political inclusion (i.e., universal suffrage and nonproscription of parties). A somewhat longer definition, as Anthony Payne makes clear (chapter 4), would also specify that the elections be competitive and that the guarantees of rights be embodied in what he calls the convention of constitutionalism, that is, the presumption that political change should only occur in accordance with rules and precedents.

The Caribbean's capacity to sustain liberal democratic polities is impressive. Since independence (beginning with Jamaica and Trinidad and Tobago in 1962) ten of the twelve (Guyana and Grenada excepted) Anglophone Caribbean countries have consistently held fair elections and have been free from unconstitutional transfers of power. Also since independence a majority of the ten consistently constitutionalist Anglophone Caribbean countries have witnessed at least one election as a result of which the governing party peacefully turned power over to the hitherto opposition party; in Barbados and Belize this democratic achievement has occurred twice, and in Jamaica, thrice. Since 1978 the transfer from government to opposition has occurred twice in the Dominican Republic, where there have been no unconstitutional transfers of power since the key 1978 election.

This Caribbean achievement is far superior to that of Latin America and also to that of the countries of Africa and Asia that acquired their formal independence from European powers after the Second World War. Some have noted that former British colonies have had a better record than the former colonies of other major powers at sustaining liberal democracy.[3] It is noteworthy, however, that the former British colonies in the Caribbean have also had a far superior capacity to sustain liberal democratic polities than most former British colonies in Africa and Asia and have done so with much lower levels of violence. Nigeria and Uganda, plagued by military coups and civil war, became independent within the same time span as Jamaica and Barbados, which have suffered no coups and no civil wars. There is no Caribbean analog to Sri Lanka's sustained ethnocommunal violence. And in the Caribbean, too, the Dominican Republic's transit to democratic politics in the late 1970s preceded most of Latin America's democratic transitions of the decade that followed. Thus even from a comparative perspective it is a "surprise" that the Caribbean has so many liberal democracies.

The surprise goes beyond such international comparisons. As Jonathan Hartlyn shows (chapter 8), the Dominican Republic's transit to democracy occurred after the decades-long rule of Rafael Leónidas Trujillo, a type of despotic experience that has not elsewhere fostered liberal democracy. Puerto Rico's domestic democratic institutions, as Juan García-Passalacqua reminds us (chapter 9), have been refreshed by twenty-four uninterrupted elections in the twentieth century. Moreover, the level of electoral participation by Puerto Ricans in Puerto Rico puts to shame the level of electoral participation by U.S. citizens on the mainland. The engagement of Puerto Ricans in the politics of their island resembles electoral participation in Europe far more than it does that in mainland United States. The vigor of

political competition among Puerto Rico's principal parties may be unsur-
passed anywhere.

Thus, some favorite explanations for the flourishing of democracy in
the Third World do not explain these cases. The Dominican Republic's
liberal democracy is not the mature fruit of decades of cultural-historical
nurturing. Nor is Puerto Rico's vigorous, electorally participative liberal
democracy to be explained as derivative from politics in the United States.
Nor can one explain the practice of liberal democracy in the Anglophone
Caribbean merely as to be expected among former British colonies. Why,
then, has liberal democracy (surprisingly) flourished in the Caribbean?

Economic Arguments

One longstanding explanation for the consolidation of liberal democracy has been the level of economic development. As Evelyne Huber notes,
for the world as a whole that argument has always been somewhat useful
because highly economically developed countries are, indeed, much more
likely than poor countries to have consolidated liberal democracy. But the
argument has also been somewhat problematic; the Caribbean experience
illustrates why. For the sake of standardization, let us rely mainly upon
data for the World Bank's 1990 report.[4]

At first blush the Caribbean confirms the proposition that wealthier
countries are more likely to have liberal democratic regimes. In 1988 U.S.
dollars, the gross national product (GNP) per capita of every Anglophone
Caribbean country but Guyana was above $1,000; Guyana remains the
only Anglophone Caribbean example of sustained authoritarianism since
independence (Payne, Selwyn Ryan [chapter 7]). Moreover, as compared
with the Anglophone Caribbean, Nicaragua, El Salvador, Honduras, and
Guatemala all had lower GNP per capita levels, again illustrating that the
prospects for stable liberal democracy are poorer for poorer countries.
Moreover, with one of the world's lowest GNP per capita levels, the poorest Caribbean country is Haiti, which is also the one country in the region
with the longest experience of authoritarian rule.

The relationship between levels of economic development and liberal
democracy in the Caribbean is much weaker than the above facts suggest,
however. The Dominican Republic's GNP per capita was about the same
as that of Guatemala. Jamaica's GNP per capita was only slightly above
that of Guatemala. Though in the late 1980s Guatemala took some important steps toward democratization, Jamaica has never experienced the grip
of military power that Guatemala has, nor has the Dominican Republic
since the late 1970s; nor has either experienced the thirty years' civil war
that Guatemala has suffered. In the same vein, St. Lucia, Dominica, and

Grenada differ little in their GNP per capita, yet only Grenada experienced the authoritarian episodes of Eric Gairy's latter years in power and of the New Jewel Movement. Suriname is much more economically prosperous than St. Lucia, Dominica, or St. Vincent and the Grenadines, but only Suriname experienced nearly continuous military rule in the 1980s.

What, then, of the effect of economic growth rates on the endurance of liberal democracy? As Worrell makes clear, in the 1970s and 1980s the economic growth rates of the Anglophone Caribbean were not good. Guyana, Haiti, the Dominican Republic, Suriname, and Trinidad and Tobago had a lower gross domestic product (GDP) per capita at the end of the 1980s than at the beginning; Jamaica's GDP per capita at the end of the 1980s was lower than it had been in 1970.[5] Thus it may be argued that faltering rates of economic growth could "cause" regime changes or at least extensive political violence. For example, Jamaica's 1980 election was marked by high levels of political violence, in part in response to a deteriorating economy. Guyana's economic decline was associated with its trend toward further authoritarian rule. The fall of the Duvalier dynasty in Haiti could have been related to faltering economic performance. In the early 1980s riots in the Dominican Republic were related to austerity measures adopted after negotiations between the International Monetary Fund (IMF) and the Dominican government. Suriname was governed mainly by its military during its decade of economic decline. And the government of Trinidad and Tobago was nearly overthrown by a mutiny in 1990.

And yet the relationship between trends in economic growth as "cause" and "democratic stability" as effect is muddled at best. The governments of the Dominican Republic and of Trinidad and Tobago were not overthrown despite their economic troubles. If economic explanations for political stability were dominant, the Trinidadian government should have fallen in 1983 or 1984, when GDP per capita fell massively and abruptly. In 1980 the opposition's victory in the Jamaican elections was recognized, and despite continuing economic troubles in the 1980s, Jamaica's levels of political violence declined over the decade. Military government began in 1980 in Suriname after a decade of economic growth.[6] Nor was the government of Barbados overthrown in 1974, when, as Worrell shows, the inflation rate seemed to spiral out of control—an acceleration of the rate of inflation as statistically worrisome as that which preceded the 1964 military coup in Brazil. Nor were some of the better economic performers among the OECS countries free from political violence.

A final illustration of the insufficiency of economic arguments is to compare the political regimes of countries at comparable levels of GNP per capita: the Dominican Republic and Egypt, Jamaica and Cameroon, Trinidad and Tobago and Gabon. Though Egypt, Cameroon, and Gabon have been among the more open political systems in the regions in which they are located, for the same level of economic development and even in some ways comparable kinds of economic activity, the countries of the Caribbean are much more liberal democratic. Thus we should remain surprised that given the Caribbean's levels of economic development, liberal democracies have flourished as much as they have.

Though he made only passing references to the Caribbean, perhaps Samuel Huntington has characterized best the relationship between economic performance and political regime as it bears on the Caribbean: it is indeterminate. Most Caribbean countries have a level of economic development in or near what Huntington called the "transition zone," in which high enough "economic development compels the modification or abandonment of traditional political institutions; it does not determine what political system will replace them."[7] By Huntington's assessment of the economic argument, among the Caribbean's independent states only Barbados and the Bahamas appear wealthy enough to be considered "safe" as liberal democracies. More generally, the Caribbean's comparatively high level of economic development by Third World standards seems to make liberal democratic politics more likely than, say, in Africa and even in much of Latin America (although the GNP per capita level of several OECS countries, Belize, and Jamaica is below that of South American countries), but one cannot explain the marked success of liberal democracy in the Caribbean just in such economic terms.

The Armed Forces

In order to ponder why liberal democracy, surprisingly, has flourished in the Caribbean, let us turn to consider the role of the armed forces. As Huber notes, the military has played a major role in preventing the installation and consolidation of democracy in the Third World; in the Caribbean, the military apparatuses were small upon independence and typically remained so. Anthony Payne notes as well that one feature of the "Westminster model," which has played such a key role in the Anglophone Caribbean, is civilian supremacy. This is an important institutionalist point (to which we shall return in a later section).

A related but different argument—that big armies undermine democracies—does not find enough support, however. Consider the evidence from the U.S. Arms Control and Disarmament Agency about "militarization" measured as armed forces personnel per one thousand people.[8] At first blush there appears to be a clear relationship between high rates of militarization and the probability of dictatorship. In the mid-1980s only the three Caribbean countries under sustained authoritarian rule had more than five soldiers per one thousand people: Cuba, Guyana, and Suriname. All the liberal democracies had lower levels of militarization.

And yet the relationship between militarization measured in this way and the nature of the political regime is muddled as well. One of the Caribbean's most stable liberal democracies has been Barbados, which did not have armed forces (only police forces) upon independence. In 1979 the Barbados Defense Force was founded.[9] In the first half of the 1980s the Barbadian rate of militarization rose to between three and four soldiers per one thousand people—a rate about the same as that of Chad and higher than that of Haiti or Ghana, none of which is an example of democracy or stability. The Barbadian rate was also twice as high as those of Jamaica and of Trinidad and Tobago, both of which experienced higher levels of domestic political violence. Jamaica and Trinidad and Tobago increased slightly their rate of militarization from the 1970s to the 1980s, reaching levels comparable to those of other former British colonies such as Ghana and Uganda, neither of which exemplifies democratic order. Militarization so measured does not distinguish countries in terms of the likelihood of democracy or stability.

Consider other examples. From the mid-1970s to the mid-1980s the Dominican Republic and Haiti had stable rates of militarization, but the Dominican rate was three times as high as Haiti's. And yet it was the Dominican Republic that made the earlier and smoother transition to democratic politics.

The cases of Guyana and Suriname are interesting. Suriname's rate of militarization was stable (about 2.8 per 1,000 people) for the years prior to Desi Bouterse's coup. The rate of militarization doubled only after the coup; thus the increase in the rate does not "explain" the prior coup. Guyana's level of militarization jumped from below 3 in 1975 to above 9 since 1977, but that was in response to Forbes Burnham's choices, not the result of a coup. As Payne aptly notes, the militarization of the Guyanese system of government under Burnham ultimately reflected the corruption of a civilian system rather than its displacement by military rule.

In brief, higher rates of militarization accompany the consolidation of dictatorships in the Caribbean (except in Haiti), but the origins of Caribbean dictatorships must be found in factors other than the relative size of the armed forces or the change in their size.

Overthrowing the Government: Unconstitutional Attempts

Have any attempts been made to overthrow these liberal democratic regimes by force? Liberal democracy might have endured in the Caribbean because no one had bothered to try to seize power. And yet Caribbean constitutionalism has been tested all too frequently. Maingot's chapter presents a partial list of security threats; Linton's supplements it. In 1969 there was a black power uprising in Curaçao that led to the dispatch of Dutch marines. In 1970 there was a black power uprising in Trinidad (see also Ryan's chapter, 7) in which parts of the army were included. In 1976 Sidney Burnett-Alleyne attempted to invade Barbados with forces organized in Martinique (where French authorities arrested and convicted him); in 1979 Burnett-Alleyne made a second attempt to overthrow the Barbadian government.

Also in 1979 the New Jewel Movement seized power in Grenada, combining aspects of a putsch with those of a popular uprising (as Payne notes). In that same year St. Vincent's Prime Minister Milton Cato requested and received Barbadian military support to repel an invasion of Union Island by a group called the Movement for National Liberation. There was also a coup attempt in Dominica in 1979. In 1980 sixteen noncommissioned officers, led by Desi Bouterse, seized power in Suriname. As already mentioned, the level of political violence that was a part of Jamaica's elections in 1980 (and some of the political rhetoric during that contest) raised real doubts whether Jamaica's democratic regime was in peril.

In 1981 two separate coup attempts were made against the government of Prime Minister Eugenia Charles in Dominica; these were defeated in part thanks to the dispatch of Barbadian military forces. (As a result of these coup attempts, Charles's government abolished the standing army.) In 1983 a military coup overthrew Prime Minister Maurice Bishop's government in Grenada—technically, the only successful military coup ever in the Anglophone Caribbean—and this was followed by the invasion of Grenada by U.S. and some Anglophone Caribbean forces.

In July 1990 an uprising by the Jamaat-Al-Muslimeen kidnapped Trinidad's Prime Minister A. N. R. Robinson and many of his ministers and nearly toppled the government (Ryan, Linton); Trinidad's army overcame the uprising and defended the constitutional government. In December 1990 a military coup overthrew Suriname's weak civilian government. From 1986 to 1991 considerable political instability, punctured by military coups and other violent uprisings, marked Haitian politics.

Moreover, the Caribbean has been the one area in the Americas most marked by frequent international, conventional military confrontations since the Second World War. Leaving aside events pertaining mainly to U.S.-Cuban relations, the United States invaded the Dominican Republic in 1965 and (together with several Anglophone governments) Grenada in

1983. Guyana and Belize have faced serious attempts by Venezuela and Guatemala to lay claim to much or all of their national territories. In 1980 a Bahamian coast guard boat was attacked by a Cuban air force plane, which killed several crew members (the only conventional military attack ever by Cuba on one of its neighbors).

The record is discouraging: is the Caribbean, but for the grace of God, not unlike Latin America and the rest of the Third World? Why has liberal democracy (surprisingly) flourished in so many of these islands?

Toward an Answer

Habits of Societal Resistance to Centralized Power

The Caribbean is the only part of the world (with the partial exception of Rwanda) where the descendants of slaves govern sovereign countries. Payne argues that for the Commonwealth Caribbean, this legacy may have placed a premium on freedom in the emergent political culture. For those who may have heard at home stories from their grandparents about the consequences of highly concentrated power, the arguments on behalf of freedom may not seem abstract; the distrust of political claims that would install illiberal regimes is marked.

The abolition of chattel slavery elsewhere in the Americas did not, however, much alter the racial identity of rulers even a century after abolition. As García-Passalacqua notes, even today Puerto Rican elites have difficulty coping with the country's Afro-Caribbean legacy. Hartlyn notes as well a lingering racism in Dominican political life, often expressed as a distrust of "Haitians"; Hartlyn has also noted the efforts by Dominican President Joaquín Balaguer to assert his country's Spanish heritage by making a major effort to celebrate the quincentenary of Columbus's voyage. Fewer changes occurred, therefore, in the social structure of the Hispanic than in that of the Anglophone Caribbean to foster the distrust of centralized power, and it is in Cuba and in the Dominican Republic where the harshest dictatorships have been founded.

Outside of Haiti and the Hispanic Caribbean, the pattern of resistance of Caribbean societies against slavery may also have contributed to a social structure more enduringly resistant to centralized rule. In the densely forested Guianas and in mountainous Jamaica, slaves escaped from their masters and formed communities that did not recognize central power. The ever-present trickster figure of Afro-Caribbean folklore and the extensive use of humor through musical and other forms of expression stand out as living symbols of resistance against those who have too much power.

The slaves brought from Africa had no common language. They combined European and African languages to give birth to the French-based Creole languages of Haiti, Martinique, Guadeloupe, and Dominica; the English-based Sranan (or Taki-Taki) and Djukatongo of Suriname; the English Creole of Jamaica; and the Portuguese-based Saramakatongo of Suriname and Papiamentu of the Netherlands Antilles. These languages did not belong to the elites, even if they learned them. In the Hispanic Caribbean the only analog is the endurance of Spanish as Puerto Rico's nonimperial language.

Africans and their descendants were equally creative in adapting European religions, and in this regard the Hispanic Caribbean was no exception. Afro-Caribbean religiosity today is strong and complex. In contemporary Cuba Afro-Cuban religions probably command greater fidelity than any other system of belief. In the English and Dutch Caribbean a wide variety of Protestant denominations, many indigenous religious communities, Roman Catholicism, Hinduism, and Islam have all taken root; probably no comparably small part of the world is so religiously pluralistic as well as so intensely religious. These are among the dimensions of what Maingot has called "conservative societies," which value the right to one's own beliefs and also the ownership of private property—for a house lot or to raise food.[10] These habits of thought and behavior with regard to religion and property are inhospitable to the ambitious plans of dictators. As Franklin Knight puts it (chapter 2), this Caribbean social structure is especially receptive to challenges from below (not necessarily in a revolutionary sense) to affirm the worth of religion, culture, and social mores in the face of state power.

In contrast, ethnocommunal pluralism in the society may be as adverse to liberal democracy in the Caribbean as it is worldwide. Studies from many countries indicate that the likelihood of consolidating liberal democracies is much greater in societies with a low degree of subcultural pluralism and much lower in societies with marked or extreme pluralism.[11] The latter have often been marked by civil discord (as in Lebanon or Cyprus) or by authoritarian rule to control such pluralism (as in the Soviet Union from the 1930s to the 1980s). Among the independent countries in the Caribbean, the societies with the most extreme ethnocommunal pluralism have been Guyana (Ryan) and Suriname, both under authoritarian rule for many years. And as Ryan shows also in his chapter, over the years race has explained a great deal about political behavior in Trinidad and Tobago; until the 1986 election very few blacks felt that it was legitimate for them not to vote for the Peoples National Movement (PNM), founded and led by Eric Williams until his death.[12] The ethnocommunal constraints on

Trinidadian politics have made change and accommodation harder. On normative grounds, the case on behalf of liberal democracy as a preferable system for the management of such ethnocommunal cleavages is of course strong, but that is not to say that this is a frequent outcome.[13]

In sum, the Caribbean's habits of societal resistance were generally favorable for liberal democracy, but the experiences of the largest islands and of the Guianas indicate that such societal factors do not suffice by themselves to establish and to consolidate liberal democracy.

The Statist Bargain

For Karl Marx, John Stuart Mill, and Alexis de Tocqueville, among others, capitalism and full democracy were at best an odd couple, if not strongly contradictory. In fact, the wedding between capitalism and universal and equal suffrage under representative government is at the heart of liberal democracy as it has come to exist. One explanation for this outcome has been the Keynesian welfare state.[14] Labor accepts the logic of profitability and markets as means to allocate resources in exchange for a sustained rise in living standards, along with the exercise of political rights. Business supports the welfare state to buy peace. Keynesianism becomes a positive-sum game of economic growth with economic security in which capitalists and workers acknowledge that they need each other. Profits are needed for investment, which is the guarantee of future jobs and future income, which will enrich makers of goods and increase demand, which will yield greater profits.

This welfare state was an aspect of the economic success during the 1960s, described for the Caribbean in Worrell's chapter. Thanks mainly to factors external to the Caribbean, the region's economies grew and were able to benefit the elites and the masses. (In this way, this particular economic argument helps to explain the timing of Caribbean democratic consolidation.) Some of these gains are ably summarized in Knight's chapter: building on trends begun during the Second World War, primary and secondary education expanded in the Anglophone, Francophone, and Dutch Caribbean, in Cuba, in Puerto Rico, and somewhat later in the Dominican Republic (Hartlyn). The levels of literacy, and of schooling beyond literacy, achieved in many of these countries are impressive.

One way to assess the Caribbean's record is to compare some of the welfare achievements of Caribbean liberal democracies with those of non-democratic regimes at comparable levels of economic development. For example, the Ivory Coast is somewhat wealthier, more populous, and larger than the Dominican Republic, but both are small primary goods–

producing countries with about the same GNP per capita, vulnerable to international price fluctuations in very few products. In the mid-1980s the rate of illiteracy in the Dominican Republic was less than half that in the Ivory Coast, and the life expectancy of Dominicans was thirteen years more than that of Ivoiriens. Trinidad and Tobago and Gabon have comparable populations and about the same GNP per capita; both are oil producers, and neither had a good economic growth record from the mid-1960s to the mid-1980s. And yet in the mid-1980s the rate of illiteracy in Trinidad and Tobago was one-tenth that of Gabon, while the life expectancy of Trinidadians was fourteen years more. Jamaica's level of GNP per capita is comparable to Botswana's, another former British colony and one of Africa's few democratic regimes. At the end of the 1980s Jamaica's infant mortality rate was one-quarter that of Botswana. Though Colombia is a bit wealthier than Jamaica and has had a much higher economic growth rate, in the late 1980s Jamaica's infant mortality rate was also one-quarter that of Colombia's.[15]

Caribbean states invested the income derived from favorable international circumstances (high prices for commodities, new investments in tourism and other sectors, and foreign aid) to improve the standard of living for many Caribbean citizens. The Caribbean state was the midwife: economic growth gave birth to social welfare. Because this practice continued in the 1960s even after independence in the larger countries of the Anglophone Caribbean and in the 1970s in the Dominican Republic (high sugar prices, high foreign aid, high remittances from emigrants) as it democratized gradually, the allegiance of citizens to democratic states was enhanced: democracies delivered material gain.

In this way the political economy of Caribbean states differed from that of the small states in Western Europe.[16] Small European states fashioned domestic political and economic arrangements, including creation of a welfare state, to maintain social peace but also to ensure their ability to survive on their own in the international system (from which they could not expect financial donations and which could even engulf them in war) by means of the cohesion of their polities and the competitiveness of their economies. Small Caribbean states began with the premise that their economies were uncompetitive (except for primary products) but that their strategic location would generate the protection from friendly major powers to spare them the costs of defense as well as generate the funds to pay for their welfare states.

There was, however, a less happy but equally important face to the welfare state in the Caribbean. As Worrell, Quick, and Hartlyn indicate, with their externally originated resources Caribbean governments also

THE CARIBBEAN QUESTION I 13

built an apparatus that protected their economies from international competition while using both subsidies and government jobs to distribute income and employment broadly in the societies. In some cases, as Hartlyn
notes for the Dominican Republic, the result was a massive but irrationally
constituted state apparatus. In other cases, especially Puerto Rico in the
1940s, a strategic design for the state's role was in greater evidence. The
consequences for economic policy and performance are enormous. Because these are discussed in the Pastor-Fletcher chapter, I focus only on
the consequences for liberal democratic politics.

This corruption of the welfare state was necessary for the kind of democratic politics built in the region. Joaquín Balaguer's presidencies have
been the hallmark of pork-barrel "machine" politics (Hartlyn). Machine
politics can function in democratic or authoritarian settings, but the latter
are typically neither totalitarian nor among the harshest bureaucratic-
authoritarian regimes. Machine politics is inherently distributive, seeking to include, albeit with unequal gains, the many people needed to
build political support. Machine politics was one key factor in the Dominican transition from Trujillo's monopoly of resources toward democratic politics.

As Huber and Ryan make clear, so too in the Anglophone Caribbean:
political parties have traditionally maintained the loyalty of their supporters in large part through patronage. That patronage has often benefited
poor people. And in racially divided societies such as Trinidad and Guyana, parties were avenues for jobs and contracts for those associated with
victorious parties.

Patronage did not just benefit the poor, as Payne, Huber, Ryan, and
Hartlyn make clear. It often benefited the business community, which was
the direct beneficiary of the structures of protection against imports and of
direct subsidies to their operations. In the agricultural and livestock sector,
the state created the conditions for legal, successful business cartels.[17]
Moreover, by relying on relatively high commodity prices in the 1960s and
early 1970s and on foreign aid in the late 1970s and early 1980s (net
external transfers to Caribbean countries rose from U.S. $542 million in
1978 to $1,142 million in 1982),[18] the liberal democratic states were able
to tax business less than would otherwise have been necessary to pay for
education and health services, for the costs of import-substitution and
cartel-fostering protection, and for patronage of various kinds and for various beneficiaries.

Another feature of the statist bargain that obtained the allegiance of
Caribbean business elites to the newly independent liberal democratic regimes was that many firms did not have to work so hard to be profitable.[19]

The Caribbean states built walls around their economies to guarantee profits higher than justified by competitive efficiency. For somewhat more venturesome firms, CARICOM (the Caribbean Common Market) provided a slightly wider market that was still highly protected. Liberal democracy was good for business: politicians sought to include everyone.

Even in Puerto Rico the state government is big. Puerto Rico's government was designed in the early 1940s by U.S. and Puerto Rican social democrats; it is the only place under the U.S. flag where the state has had such a large role in the economy. In more recent years, as García-Passalacqua notes, new ways have been designed to use state power to foster the allegiance of Puerto Ricans. For those who support statehood, votes are to be found among those who hope that the U.S. federal government will bankroll the Puerto Rican welfare rolls (especially through food stamps) indefinitely. For those who support commonwealth, the complex financial provisions of Section 936 of the U.S. Internal Revenue Code represent the most recent attempt to harness the state's power for the sake of economic growth.

From the 1960s to the mid-1980s the statist bargain on behalf of democracy sought to provide gains for the great many, the worker and the business owner, while exporting the costs of running such states to the international economy via commodity prices or foreign aid. Parties were the institutional brokers for such distributive politics; allegiances to them depended to a large degree on the expectation of particularistic benefits. These states by and large did not threaten the society's habits of resistance in religion, language, or property ownership. They could be big because they were not lordly. They had to be big and capacious to construct democratic politics. By the late 1980s commodity prices were down; net external transfers to the Caribbean had turned negative (Quick). The Caribbean's liberal democracy had flourished, not surprisingly, thanks to what economists call "inefficiencies." Liberal democracy as it has been built in the Caribbean had depended to a large degree on the kind of state that, many chapters in this book suggest, the countries can no longer afford.

The Institutionalist and Leadership Arguments

Perhaps most important of all to the establishment and consolidation of liberal democracy, this book's chapters suggest, has been the intersection between political institutions and political leaders. As noted above, the statist bargain could also buttress certain kinds of authoritarian rule, and the habits of resistance in the society could be overcome under certain conditions, as they were in Haiti, Suriname, and Guyana. The simple form of the international argument—British legacies—was insufficient to explain why liberal democracy was more enduring in the Anglophone Caribbean than in Anglophone Africa or Asia.

The argument begins, Huber, Payne, and Maingot suggest, however, at the international level, but with a special focus on the impact of the international system on institutional development in the Caribbean. As Huber indicates, in the 1930s there were mass uprisings in Central American and Caribbean countries. In Central America (except in Costa Rica), in Cuba, and in the Dominican Republic, dictatorships emerged (at times with U.S. acquiescence or even explicit support) as a response to the crisis. In the Anglophone Caribbean, British colonialism opened up the political system instead; the process of decolonization was long and deliberate but also democratic in its direction. Thanks to the British empire, the Anglophone Caribbean successfully handled in much less repressive ways problems that some Central American countries have yet to settle.

A second dimension of the connection between the international system and local institutional development has been highlighted by Maingot: the role of political leaders and of available international ideologies to fashion the new institutions in the context of imperial decolonization.[20] For the French, decolonization meant even fuller Antillean assimilation into France; in 1946 the French Antilles became French departments. Political leaders in the French Antilles thus proceeded to reconstruct the political parties of metropolitan France, responding in part to the ideologies prevalent on the French mainland, including those of the Communist party.

For the Dutch, the important thing was to allow for various forms of voluntary choice, which nonetheless retained the tie to the Netherlands. Dutch elites and the elites in the Netherlands Antilles and Suriname worked hard to forge consociational agreements, that is, agreements among elites of the various ethnic and religious communities that sought to establish democracy and to guarantee certain rights and privileges to all while constraining some features of mass democracy.[21]

For the British, decolonization was motivated in part by the desire to reduce the costs of empire. Institutionally, the Westminster model—the subject of Payne's chapter—was already in place and working toward a political opening. Certainly attractive were its constitutional guarantees of government by rule and precedent but also civilian supremacy (given that local politicians had no military experience) and bureaucratic neutrality (at least until politicians could get a better grip on administration). The analysis of the Westminster model suggests that what matters for stable democracy is less the size of the armed forces and more the institutionalized pattern of civilian elite supremacy over military elites. And as Maingot also makes clear, the political ideology that West Indian politicians most readily picked up in Britain was Fabian: promote social welfare and redistribution through a state built on a democratic process via competitive elections.

Anglophone Caribbean politicians learned as well that defeat in elections, and the turnover between government and opposition, while never pleasant—no politician likes to lose an election—was not necessarily life-threatening. The concept of the official, loyal Opposition (with capital *O*) may have been among the United Kingdom's most valuable institutional legacies to these colonies. The Opposition was honored for its necessary and constructive role; its leaders were not killed—they were paid to do their job. Even many of the programs politicians might have implemented while in government survived their election defeat. The norms of democratic competition were learned.

The institutions and procedures could take root in part because of the very long tradition of British rule. Unlike in Africa and in Asia, British rule in the Caribbean had been uninterrupted for centuries. The colonies of exploitation founded by the British empire in the Caribbean had deracinated the African population and created new Caribbean peoples that were themselves products of empire. There was no preimperial society to overcome; that had been done centuries before by means of the slave trade and the cruelty of slavery, the past's bloody legacy to the constitution of liberty today.

For the United States, the shift toward a commonwealth in Puerto Rico was bolstered by the belief that Puerto Ricans wanted it. Puerto Rico's new institutions were not just a replica of those of states in the United States; they were also a policy legacy from the New Deal's ideology. Luis Muñoz Marín's Popular Democratic Party, Maingot reminds us, shared many of the political attitudes then prevalent in the British West Indies. The developmentalist state flourished more in Puerto Rico in the 1940s than in the U.S. mainland under Roosevelt in the 1930s because Rexford Tugwell and Muñoz Marín, colonizer and colonized, agreed on it more than the U.S. Supreme Court agreed with Franklin Roosevelt.

A third feature of institutional development has been the democratic role of labor unions especially in the Anglophone Caribbean, as Huber notes. Labor expressed mass rage in the 1930s, but labor unions channeled protests through more peaceful channels in later years. The connection between the labor unions and many political parties on various islands provided the foundations for both democratic transition and consolidation. To some extent, the development of trade unionism and its connection to a political party was the particular contribution of the British Labour party's active engagement in support of Caribbean democracy. At independence the Anglophone Caribbean's party-union complex was firmly established in terms of electoral effectiveness and as one pillar of the democratic order.

More generally, in some countries social-class cleavages played a constructive role in the establishment and consolidation of Caribbean liberal democracy. The existence of such cleavages facilitated the creation of competing political parties, while the ideological convictions and leadership skill of key politicians contained the potentially too-divisive effects of such class cleavages. In ethnocommunally divided societies, of course, many parties were founded and operated on such societal segmentation. In other countries still, political leaders built multiclass coalitions, often around patronage, that set the foundations for political competition. In any case, moderate but effective party competition became the norm, except in Guyana.

In short, the disposition of the United States and especially of the United Kingdom to grant substantial autonomy and eventually independence to many countries was manifest in an institutional, ideological, and leadership context, from elite to mass, that strengthened the foundations of liberal democracy. Leaders discovered that they could accomplish their welfare goals by democratic means through institutions that had proven democratically resilient in other international settings. These leaders acted through political institutions that did not threaten the society's own religious and cultural institutions, which, as Payne notes, were themselves vigorously pluralistic. Unions and parties tied citizen allegiances to the newly independent democratic states at moments of world economic expansion. For various reasons, including but not limited to the articulation of social cleavage differences, leaders founded and led competitive parties that for the most part were politically moderate. The statist bargain brought business, initially distrustful of the experiment, into the democratic coalition.

The point is not that the Caribbean's political leaders were born democrats (though, as we will see, many have indeed been convinced democrats). It is that the international and institutional factors—even in an authoritarian international setting such as that of colonial empires—set constraints that made domestic authoritarian outcomes less likely while inducing political leaders to learn about democratic politics.

Consolidating Democratic Politics

The consolidation of democratic rule followed mainly from the combination of these institutional and leadership factors, but other factors became important as well. First, the international system came to play a new, different, ultimately constructive role. One reason why the many violent and unconstitutional attempts to overthrow various governments failed is that at key moments international actors intervened in time on democracy's side. This has happened so often that it can no longer be described just as good luck; it is a pattern of international behavior in this subsystem.

Prime Minister Charles's government in Dominica owes its survival more than once to timely arrests or weapons seizures by the U.S. Federal Bureau of Investigation (FBI). The Barbadian government was assisted at one moment by similar timely action by French security forces in Martinique. Barbados itself has given military help to Dominica and St. Vincent and the Grenadines. The government of Trinidad did not request foreign military intervention in 1970 or 1990, but it certainly received ample and public political backing from its various neighbors. In this context, the most controversial international intervention—the 1983 invasion of Grenada—is consistent with the norms that had evolved in the Caribbean international subsystem to privilege democracy over nonintervention (the opposite of the more common norm in Latin America).

This democratizing role for the Caribbean's international subsystem is also an essential explanation for the Dominican Republic's democratic transition in 1978 (Hartlyn). As the counting of the ballots stopped, the U.S. government made it clear that it expected the results of the election—an opposition victory—to be honored. The participative effects of machine politics, under U.S. pressure, completed the transition toward a fuller democratic opening.

A less dramatic and less discernible probable international effect has been emigration. As Knight reminds us, the Caribbean has a long history of migration—among the islands, to the European metropolis, and to the United States. Emigration might also have been a way for the countries to export without coercion some of the social basis for an opposition that might have placed even greater strains on the system. Emigration in fact has made democratic politics more difficult to mount in Cuba; in general, emigration helps to explain order more than competition. But the maintenance of political order in a region where liberal democracy is the norm has as an indirect effect the fostering of a democratic order.

Apart from such international factors, the Caribbean has been blessed with remarkable political leaders.[22] It must have been difficult for Michael Manley in 1980 and for Edward Seaga in 1989 to acknowledge defeat, but they did. In Barbados, too, leaders of both major political parties have had to accept electoral defeat at least once. It must have been difficult for Trinidad's PNM in 1986 to acknowledge defeat for the first time since independence, but it did. So too have political leaders in the Eastern Caribbean time and again. Most impressive of all was Puerto Rico's Luis Muñoz Marín, who in the mid-1960s, in order to bring about a leadership transition beyond the party's founder, had to impose his will on the Popular Democratic Party so that it would *not* nominate him again.[23] Moreover, the parties in the larger countries—Trinidad and Tobago, Jamaica, Barbados, and Puerto Rico—have all witnessed a transition of power within the party at least once since independence (or, in Puerto Rico's case, since commonwealth). In the larger islands only the Dominican Republic has been stuck with two powerful octogenarian leaders, Balaguer and Juan Bosch.

Parliamentary institutions have also served the Anglophone Caribbean well. A relatively smooth political transition has occurred upon the prime minister's death twice in Barbados and once in Trinidad. The new prime minister in each case was, in turn, politically strengthened by having to form his own government, not just inheriting the mantle of the deceased predecessor. Perhaps an even better test of the utility of parliamentary institutions occurred in 1982 in St. Lucia. In January the prime minister resigned under pressure from a heterogeneous coalition (which even included the chamber of commerce and middle-class groups) that accused the government of corruption and abuse of power; Parliament was dissolved. The caretaker government was led by a member of the smallest of St. Lucia's three parties, a politically radical party, in part because this party had not been the source of the government crisis. In the end, the moderate parties won the election.[24] In Latin America this scenario might have led to a coup. Or an embattled president might have stayed in office, presiding over policy drift. Few might have trusted the most politically radical party to play the caretaker role and then to turn power over peacefully to its ideological opponents.

On the other hand, some Caribbean countries might have been less well served by the first-past-the-post (or single-member-plurality) system of electoral representation typical of Anglo-American electoral law (Payne). Parties at times win too many seats relative to their share of the electorate. In countries that are ethnically deeply segmented this can present serious problems of citizen allegiance. In 1986 in Trinidad, for example, the PNM won nearly one-third of the votes but not quite one-tenth of the seats (Ryan). The opposite, of course, had often been the case. For different reasons, the Jamaican Labour Party swept the 1984 parliamentary elections; had the electoral rules been closer to proportional representation—something like the German two-vote system—the willingness of Jamaica's opposition (which had boycotted the elections) to participate in the elections might have been greater.

Finally, mass-media institutions and key intellectuals have played important roles in defending freedom of expression. Though the personal and institutional behavior of some intellectuals and of some mass-media institutions may be subject to sharp criticism, and though some of that behavior may at times have been self-serving and even abusive, and though the printed press in much of the Caribbean has had a marked probusiness predilection (Payne, Huber), freedom of expression, including freedom of the press, is essential to liberal democracy. Important examples, therefore, of the decline of democratic liberty were the murders of Rupert Bishop in 1974 in Grenada and of Walter Rodney in 1980 in Guyana. And an equally important example of the preservation of democratic liberty was the decision of Michael Manley's government, in the late 1970s, not to shut down the *Daily Gleaner*, while the *Gleaner* itself stood up for its own pluralistic vision of Jamaica's polity.

Austerity, Insecurity, Democracy, and Markets: New Questions

As the 1990s began, the international economic situation was adverse to most of the Caribbean. In 1990 a recession began in the United States and in the United Kingdom. It was triggered in part by the sudden rise in the price of petroleum, which benefited Trinidad and Tobago at a critical moment after the July 1990 attempt to overthrow its government but which hurt most of the region. Recessions typically lead to reduced spending on Caribbean tourism, as U.S. consumers cut back on nonessentials, and to decreased international demand for various products exported by Caribbean countries (including lower industrial demand for bauxite and alumina), hence depressing prices.

Even before the beginning of that recession, the economic outlook was problematic. Net external transfers to the Caribbean had fallen steadily from a high of $1,142 million in 1982 to $15 million in 1988. Net transfers from the United States alone fell from a high of $353.5 million in 1984 (the aftermath of the intervention in Grenada) to a low of $−44.5 million in 1988.[25] Given the constraints of the U.S. budget deficit and the demands for economic aid to democratize Eastern Europe, rebuild Panama and Nicaragua, and fight Andean drug trafficking, the United States is not likely to make large, new commitments of economic assistance to the Caribbean. In 1992, moreover, Caribbean banana producers are likely to lose their preferred access to the U.K. market when the single European market is completed (Lewis, Quick). In short, the economic constraints on the Caribbean are likely to worsen in the short term.

Insecurity, Democracy, and Drug Traffic

With declining domestic and international economic resources available to Caribbean states, will they be more vulnerable to attacks connected to drug traffickers? Will their politicians and government officials become even more vulnerable to the lure of corrupting drug money? Can liberal democracy survive these threats?

Drug-traffic operations already threaten the Caribbean's security, society, and political order (Maingot, Sanders, Linton, Huber). In 1984 a commission of inquiry in the Bahamas concluded that at least one minister had "corruptly accepted funds from known drug smugglers." In March 1985 the head of government of the Turks and Caicos Islands and two of his ministers were arrested in Miami for facilitating the transshipment of drugs to the United States. In 1990 a commission of inquiry in Antigua-Barbuda heard evidence alleging that Prime Minister Vere Bird's son, Vere Bird, Jr., himself a government minister, had facilitated the transfer of weapons to a Colombian drug-traffic organization. Among the threats earlier in the 1980s against Dominica's stability was the possibility that the island might be seized to serve as a drug haven. Thus the problems range from the possibility that a country might be seized by force to facilitate future drug traffic, to normal corruption, to the "purchasing" of a government such as that of the Turks and Caicos.

One Caribbean response to the drug-traffic threat has been the development of a regional security system. Neville Linton, Anthony Maingot, and Vaughan Lewis argue for the need for such a system, while Evelyne Huber worries about the potential for militarization. At issue between them is not the need for some means to enforce law and order but the particular configuration, size, command structure, and sovereign authority for the force. In addition, there are two connections between this problem and the Caribbean's worsening economic difficulties: (1) how can the incomes of politicians and government officials rise to make them less subject to the temptations of drug corruption and (2) how can these countries pay for any kind of regional security force?

The Caribbean's New Question: The Effects of the New Economic Strategy on Democracy

In the Anglophone Caribbean, one general response to the grim economic agenda has been to attempt to shrink the size of the state and its role in the economy and to rely more on market forces and on the role of private business. Apart from the issues of economic policy, domestic and international, considered in the Pastor-Fletcher chapter, let us focus on some consequences of this new strategy for the survival of democracy in the Caribbean.

The Caribbean's emerging strategy depends on the entrepreneurship of its business firms to rely upon international markets to generate growth and on the toughness and skill of its politicians and administrators to cut back on government expenditures and subsidies, so that the country can afford the state, and to create a regulatory environment conducive to market-led economic growth. To put it differently, the new strategy requires terminating the "statist bargain," discussed earlier, because Caribbean countries can no longer export its costs to foreign consumers and to foreign governments. But can Caribbean societies and political institutions preserve liberal democracy while terminating the statist bargain? This could be the Caribbean Question for the 1990s.

The behavior of Caribbean business firms does not augur well for the prompt ending of the statist bargain. There is pessimism about the current capacity and skill of Caribbean business firms to compete in global markets.[26] Anglophone Caribbean business firms remain attached to protected markets; so too does Puerto Rican business. Are Caribbean capitalists afraid of capitalism and all too eager to continue to seek the state's protection as they did under the statist bargain (Payne, Quick)? But given budget cuts and patronage reduction, such business political action would mean not just participation in distribution, consistent with aspects of the old system of patronage, but redistribution on behalf of business.

The behavior of some politicians in the Hispanic Caribbean seems no more hopeful. Joaquín Balaguer won reelection as Dominican president one more time in 1990, Hartlyn reminds us, by running a government based on personalist, pork-barrel politics. All major Puerto Rican formal status options seem also to be connected to policy hopes that seek to make even more use of the state for the sake of economic welfare.

In the Anglophone Caribbean, however, politicians and government officials have been taking more vigorous steps to terminate the statist bargain and to behave in ways consistent with the new economic strategy. If these politicians are to succeed in a liberal democratic setting, they need political support. Stable democracies everywhere require strong political parties. And yet many political parties in the Caribbean have relied on patronage in exchange for electoral support (Hartlyn, Huber, Ryan, Payne). As politicians cut back on patronage as required by the new economic strategy, what will be the new bases for voter loyalty and party organization?[27] Huber cites Carl Stone's study of the elections in Jamaica as showing the decline in the proportion of loyal party voters: if there is less patronage to distribute, it is more difficult to retain voter allegiance.[28] Can democratic regimes survive if the partisan institutions that have been at the heart of politics can no longer provide organized political support and opposition?

Moreover, many political parties in the Anglophone Caribbean historically had relied on labor union support to generate more general political support. And yet labor union militancy and power have weakened, too; whatever their ills, labor unions have been one of the foundations of Caribbean democracy (Huber, Payne). With weakened labor unions, what will channel into peaceful avenues the discontent that is a normal part of politics and that could become abnormally severe if economic circumstances deteriorate?

The Caribbean's demography, Knight reminds us, is still characterized by its youthfulness: the average age is still generally in the midteens. This exacerbates problems of high social expenditures, unemployment, underemployment, and political disenchantment. It was precisely young and underemployed people who were involved in the 1969 and 1970 black power uprisings in Curaçao and Trinidad. Demography cannot be remade overnight. Will such people threaten the stability of Caribbean democracy again and even more because the parties and the unions can no longer channel protest as effectively as they did in the past?

Ryan's chapter details the consequences for racial politics in Trinidad and Tobago of the efforts to reduce government patronage in a society where citizens have expected their parties to favor their ethnic community with government jobs and other forms of economic support. The government's economic austerity policies have already resulted in severe ethnic dislocations, including an attempt to overthrow the government. (Ryan made this warning in this project's first conference; the subsequent July 1990 attempt to overthrow Trinidad and Tobago's government is consistent with his argument.) Similar violence, protesting against economic austerity measures, had occurred years earlier in the Dominican Republic. The government of Suriname actually fell in December 1990.

Even the possible valuable economic contributions of private direct foreign investment (Quick) may present some problems for liberal democracies under economic stress. Such foreign firms may choose to invest in the Caribbean because they find labor markets attractive; if so, they may prefer even weaker labor unions with even fewer connections to political parties. Some Anglophone Caribbean business sectors may fear the coming of such foreign firms, either because they worry about direct competition or because they fear that foreign firms will soak up all the investment incentives that Caribbean states can now afford.[29]

Foreign firms tend to be large; Caribbean countries are small. Under these conditions, Quick reminds us, the countries could become vulnerable to the "Dutch disease" problem, that is, the successful development of one sector that pushes up island costs to the point where other industries are rendered uncompetitive. The political analog of the "Dutch disease" problem is the "company town"—the overwhelming political dominance of a single firm on the affairs of the community and the combination and concentration of political and economic power to the detriment of democracy.

What, then, could be a new bargain between politics and markets? The Caribbean's new economic strategy rests on according a "privileged position" to business.[30] While such an outcome is at odds with the Fabian traditions common in the West Indies and with the New Deal statist traditions of Puerto Rico, as we have noted, business has already been greatly influential in all of these countries as well as in the Dominican Republic. The new strategy seeks, however, to tilt further toward business.

The legitimization of business power will require, in due course, the generation of economic growth. Local business elites need to prove that they can generate economic growth. But the legitimization of business power cannot await some hypothetical economic boom of the twenty-first century. A new political bargain is required to enable liberal democracy to survive while the new economic strategy is at work. The chapters in this volume suggest three foundations for such a bargain.

1. The shrinking of the state, Worrell reminds us, has been occurring in a capricious and cavalier fashion, giving priority to sustaining current expenditures and cutting capital expenditures instead. Maintenance has been neglected; supplies to deliver government services are insufficient, and thus the quality of services and of infrastructure required to resume economic growth has eroded. There is a need to increase the government's capital expenditures to improve services and infrastructure that benefit economic reactivation as well as the population as a whole.

2. For the public at large, such improvements would represent an early benefit of the new strategy and thus would increase the likelihood of the public's continued support of the parties committed to it. But as Knight reminds us forcefully, the new strategy must also focus on one of the Caribbean's premier assets, namely, its people, and their level of education. To be consistent with the new strategy, educational policy needs to be refocused to stimulate training in skills for which there are jobs, because

there are business needs for those jobs; such a refocus of policy also requires increased investment in university education. Increased investment in education thus not only would continue to garner political support and be socially appropriate but also would contribute to the new economic strategy.

3. To finance these increased expenditures consistent with an export-promotion strategy, governments need to reform their fiscal strategies to provide inducements for the growth of exports in goods and services, while raising revenue by penalizing the diversion of resources away from export-oriented investments toward nontraded activities such as real estate (Worrell, Quick).

Politicians and government officials should reorder their priorities accordingly; national and international business, and foreign governments and international financial institutions, should also support increased government capital expenditures, a different as well as a renewed commitment to education, and fiscal reform.

At issue is the need to recognize that liberal democracy cannot survive if all of the pillars on which it was built are destroyed without replacing them with new foundations. The society's habits of resistance to dictatorship could turn against the liberal democratic order. In the Anglophone Caribbean the public's impatience became evident in the second half of the 1980s as government after government on island after island was defeated in elections. The institutions and procedures on which Caribbean liberal democracies have been built would not withstand much greater levels of hostility in the postpatronage, poststatist circumstances unless new, palpable gains were evident.

For business and for political elites, the challenge is to find how to legitimize an even more privileged position for business, as other democracies elsewhere have. That requires efficient economic growth and also establishing the foundations of an efficient and capable state that delivers quality services and generates and maintains a necessary infrastructure to serve not just economic growth but also the public as a whole. For the production of these public goods, the democratic state receives and deserves the allegiance and support of its citizens.

1 | POLITICS & SOCIETIES

2 The Societies of the Caribbean since Independence

Franklin W. Knight

The decade of the 1960s constituted a major turning point in the history of the Caribbean. It represented the beginning of some fundamental restructuring of the politics and society of the Caribbean region. In many ways it could be regarded as the start of a new era, the birth of a new consciousness among the elites and the masses. The remarkable changes were most manifest at the superstructural level of political operation and political form, but they were not confined to this arena.

In the British West Indian colonies a wave of political independence engulfed the far-flung islands and territories, ushering in the twilight of internal self-government and externally directed colonial rule. Complete self-government produced a new rhetoric, new rituals and new local responsibilities, and greater international visibility with the new status. In Cuba, the mostly bearded young rebels that captured the state in early 1959 rapidly set about dismantling the entire structure and replacing it with a uniquely personalized socialist model in the 1960s.[1] In Puerto Rico the charismatic, able Luís Muñoz Marín left the political scene, and the island began to reevaluate the long-term implications of their decade-old accomplishment under the Associated Free State.[2] Even in the French departments of Martinique and Guadeloupe and in then coequal Antillean branches of the Kingdom of the Netherlands, centrifugal forces awakened newly articulated sensibilities and self-identities that demanded urgent attention. Politically the Caribbean entered a period of intensified restlessness.[3] For the British Caribbean political independence became the order of the day.

But the restlessness was more than mere political ferment. It reached down and across all sectors of the local economies and cultures caught up in the tantalizing upsurge of rising expectations after the Second World War only to be suddenly overwhelmed with the disappointments and explosive despair that afflicted the entire world in the 1970s and 1980s. In trying to come to terms with itself, the region has always had to deal with the prevailing extraregional powers and forces. For the Caribbean that has been a problem as old as colonialism itself, dating from the entry of Christopher Columbus and the permanent settlement by Europeans after 1492. Political independence, however, accentuated the influence of external forces in the reality of Caribbean daily life.

In looking at the various complex societies of the Caribbean since their independence two factors must constantly be borne in mind. The first factor is the prolonged process of the legal acquisition of independence by the various states. The second resides in the profound commonalities that characterize the region as a whole, ranging from history and demography to limited natural resources.

The Process of Independence

The process of independence began nearly two centuries ago with the impromptu and destructive revolution that created the state of Haiti. The French revolution in its tropical colony of Saint-Domingue inadvertently produced the independence of Haiti in 1804. That was the first colony to gain its independence in the Caribbean, and the second anywhere in the Americas. It was also the only case of spontaneous political independence in the Caribbean.[4] In all the other cases independence resulted from a long-term process of negotiation with the metropolis, or the metropolitan withdrawal of empire. The Dominican Republic, after fits and starts, finally achieved its freedom in 1865. Almost a century after the independence of Haiti, the Cuban–Spanish-American War resulted in the eventual political independence of Cuba in 1902, and the quasi incorporation of Puerto Rico with the United States of America. The third stage of political independence began in the middle of the twentieth century with the independence of Jamaica as well as Trinidad and Tobago in 1962 and continues with active discussions of the status of places such as Montserrat and Aruba.

Between the resolution of the political status of Cuba and Puerto Rico

TABLE 2.1. Caribbean Political Divisions, 1991

Independent	Associated	Dependencies
Antigua/Barbuda [1981]	Aruba	Anguilla
Bahamas [1973]	French Guiana	Bermuda
Barbados [1966]	Guadeloupe	British Virgin Islands
Belize [1981]	Martinique	Cayman Islands
Cuba [1902]	Netherlands	Montserrat
Dominica [1978]	Antilles	Turks and Caicos Islands
Dominican Republic [1865]		U.S. Virgin Islands
Grenada [1974]		
Guyana [1966]		
Haiti [1804]		
Jamaica [1962]		
St. Kitts and Nevis [1983]		
St. Lucia [1977]		
St. Vincent and the Grenadines [1979]		
Suriname [1975]		
Trinidad and Tobago [1962]		

Note: Dates in brackets indicate year of independence.

at the beginning of the twentieth century and the constitutional adjustments in the British West Indies in the 1960s and after, the process continued elsewhere. In 1946 the French converted their Caribbean colonies into integral parts of France, administering them as overseas departments. Similarly, in 1954 the Kingdom of the Netherlands granted autonomous status to its Antillean possessions Aruba, Bonaire, Curaçao, Saba, St. Eustatius, and St. Martin. In 1986 Aruba chose to leave the Netherlands Antilles and seek total independence—a course it has been pursuing on its own. The general Caribbean political configuration in 1990 comprised independent states, associated states, and dependencies (see table 2.1).

A second observation is worth bearing in mind. The chronology of independence has not substantially affected the present political, social, and economic conditions of the contemporary Caribbean. The timing of the acquisition of independence did not, by itself, present inherent advantages or disadvantages to the recipient. Haiti's chronic poverty can no more be connected to its early achievement of independence in 1804 than the relative prosperity of Barbados can be linked to its belated independence in 1966. The superficial differences in formal political status, linguistic boundaries, geographical size, or populations do not substantially affect the basic commonalities of the region. Differences in the Caribbean remain more variations of degree than fundamental distinctions of kind. That is extremely important in understanding the basic reality of the Caribbean.

Commonalities and Differences

The Caribbean region is perhaps more fractured and fragmented than any other in the world. Its largest state, Cuba, has slightly more than 10 million people. The population of the Turks and Caicos Islands numbers slightly less than 10,000. The legal distinctions of independent states, associated states, and dependencies—colonies having lost respectability in the current political lexicon—do not indicate intrinsic distinctions in the way domestic politics or social organizations operate. Form seldom defines function. The challenges of the present, as they invariably have from time immemorial, constantly undermine the valuable legacies of traditions and experience. While the political culture may be different, political stability is no greater among the former colonies of the British West Indies than elsewhere in the former Spanish, French, and Dutch Caribbean. The political culture cannot be divorced from the social culture.

Indeed, the most serious recent threats to constitutional democracy have been in Grenada and Trinidad and Tobago, while the practice of constitutional democracy can hardly be said to have taken hold in Guyana. All three states retain political traditions of the British imperial system. Race and ethnicity have been exceedingly strong throughout the region, but never as strongly designated and invidiously defined as in the United States, Africa, or Europe. Nevertheless, the general observation that the masses throughout the region are predominantly nonwhite as well as poor bears some validity and historical provenience. The Caribbean demographic reality is an inescapable result of its unfortunate history of colonialism.

Whatever the negative consequences of colonialism might have been, however, it is interesting that the higher per capita incomes in 1985 were found among the dependencies and associated states: Bermuda ($13,421), the Netherlands Antilles ($6,600), Puerto Rico ($4,301), Martinique ($3,717), Guadeloupe ($3,151), the British Virgin Islands ($3,561), and Montserrat ($3,127). The highest per capita income among the independent states was found in the Bahamas ($7,600). This was considerably higher than the others, whose ranges varied between $1,534 (Cuba) and $2,865 (Barbados).[5]

Economic constraints have seriously handicapped the societies of the Caribbean since independence. The economy, after all, has been a constant determinant of the Caribbean experience. Engineered primarily as colonies of economic exploitation, the societies of the region have endured a fluctuating, opportunistically contrived dependence on the wider world.[6] As a result, they have been structurally linked to the outside world and so have been more sensitive to the vagaries of international relations than most other newly independent societies.

The changes that have occurred since independence have resulted in the continuation of processes that, more or less, have been characteristic of the entire period of the twentieth century. In most cases the problems have become exacerbated with time. The declining economic situation throughout the region cannot be easily exaggerated and throws a long shadow over most other domestic problems. Since the 1970s the economic situation has deteriorated increasingly overall with steady declines in the real gross domestic production in almost all the states.

According to figures produced by the Inter-American Development Bank in May 1989, using 1987 as the base year for calculation, the declines in per capita gross domestic product were quite sobering. Guyana and Haiti had declined to levels they had already attained as far back as 1960. Jamaica had fallen to its 1965 levels; the Bahamas, to 1968 levels; and Trinidad and Tobago, Barbados, and the Dominican Republic had fallen to levels reached in 1976, 1979, and 1980, respectively.[7] In the smaller Caribbean islands the situation varied along the spectrum represented by the larger ones indicated above.

Another consequence of the Caribbean's structural linkage to the outside world has been the historical restlessness of the population of the region. Migration—both immigration and emigration—remains a constant feature of the Caribbean, a characteristic indelibly embedded in its history. The Caribbean peoples have a deep-seated penchant to move from one place to another.[8] After the abolition of slavery and during the early decades of political independence, migration had a strong economic incentive. Jamaicans, Haitians, Barbadians, Grenadans, and others sought better economic opportunities outside their native states, and often outside the region.[9] *Target migration,* the deliberate migration to seek specific employment to attain a particular goal, has always been a viable option for the upward economic status seeker. But other forms of migration have also been present. Disturbed political conditions have produced successive waves of political exiles from Cuba, the Dominican Republic, Haiti, Guyana, and Trinidad. Restrained domestic economic and intellectual opportunities have encouraged a steady stream of intellectuals to abandon the region too.

Migration, however, does not represent a net loss for the region. Emigration provided—and continues to provide—a safety net to the explosive forces of overpopulation. Monetary remittances from emigrants constitute an important component of the gross national product of a number of states, especially Puerto Rico, Barbados, Jamaica, the Dominican Republic, Haiti, and the smaller Eastern Caribbean states.[10] And despite occasionally muted local concern, the Caribbean has not so far experienced any pronounced brain drain with deleterious economic, political, or social consequences.[11] The salient factors that shape, and have historically shaped, Caribbean migration rest more in the region's changing relationship with the "outside world" than in more narrowly understood demographic factors. Nevertheless, the local demographic features are of increasing concern.

The decade of the sixties saw a vigorous spurt in the population throughout the region. While some of this population increase represented a recurring universal generational phenomenon, the inescapable regional consequence was a problematic general youthfulness exacerbating seriously the problems of high social expenditures, unemployment, underemployment, and political disenchantment. Throughout the Caribbean the average age of the population in 1985 was approximately eighteen years.[12] In Jamaica almost 37 percent of the population was under fourteen years of age. By contrast, in Japan persons under fourteen years made up about 21 percent of the population; in West Germany, 15 percent; in the United Kingdom, 19 percent; and in the United States, 22 percent.[13]

Caribbean population growth between 1970 and 1985 fell into three discernible categories: (1) low growth rates of less than 1 percent per annum; (2) medium to high growth rates of between 1.5 percent and 3.8 percent per annum; (3) and abnormally high or low rates. Barbados (0.3 percent), Cuba (0.9 percent), Guyana (0.3 percent), and Suriname (0.4) belong to the first category. These states have the least pressure from rapidly increasing populations, since if the present trend continues, they have the better part of a century before their populations will double in size.

The intermediate group can be divided into two subcategories: the faster growers, such as the Dominican Republic, St. Lucia, and St. Vincent (each increasing at an annual rate of 2.5 percent) and Belize (2 percent); and the moderate growers, such as Jamaica (1.5 percent), Puerto Rico (1.25 percent), Trinidad and Tobago (1.4 percent), Haiti (1.8 percent), and Grenada (1.8 percent). These states should see their populations double in size in twenty-eight to forty-five years. The higher the population growth rate, the shorter the period in which the society has to make the adjustments necessary to cope with the normal incremental demands of that burgeoning group. This invariably strains the local resource base and undermines proper planning and implementation of policies.

The third category of abnormal growth rates also can be divided into two subcategories: those experiencing a net population loss of approximately 0.5 percent per year—Montserrat, Guadeloupe, and Martinique; and those with an extraordinarily high rate approaching 5 percent, indicating a doubling of the population within twenty years—Dominica and the Cayman Islands.

These population growth rates, as with so many other aspects of these societies, manifest the dovetailing of local and external factors. The low Puerto Rican population growth rate has been achieved by occasionally heavy out-migration to the United States, especially in the early 1980s.[14] Similarly, the French Antilles, as functionally bureaucratic internal departments of France, find that the European mainland has become a veritable mecca for its citizens. Where population outmigration has not enjoyed such structural facilities as in Puerto Rico, or the French Antilles, or the British West Indies before independence, the impact of migration—or the lack of it—has had more far-reaching consequences for the state. The ability to export people has always been an important economic and political concern in the Caribbean.[15]

Changes in Culture and Society

Political independence arrived in the British West Indies while the region was experiencing some profound social and cultural changes. By the 1960s significant changes had already occurred, and were continuing to occur, in the availability of primary and secondary education, in the proportion of women in the workplace in general and in the professional occupations in particular, as well as in the impact of technology on the dissemination of culture (both local and imported) among the masses.

Since the Second World War the Caribbean states have all placed uniformly great emphasis on education, greatly expanding the facilities at the primary and secondary level and promoting full attendance at the primary level. Based on their resources, the improvements have been dramatic in terms of those formally educated and certified as well as in the overall literacy rates of the respective states. School enrollment in Jamaica, a rather perfunctory affair before 1945, reached impressive levels of 98 percent at the primary level and 58 percent at the secondary level in the 1980s, and the literacy rate increased during those same years from about 67 percent of the adult population to more than 85 percent.[16] Trinidad and Tobago as well as Barbados (acknowledged as having the best system of public education anywhere in the Caribbean) had managed, by the early 1980s, to enroll virtually all their primary-school-age populations and had increased the proportion of their secondary-school attendees. While less dramatic than in the larger islands, primary and secondary education also expanded under government and religious auspices in the smaller islands.

Public education is recognized as a great lever for upward social and economic mobility. Besides, individuals and government place great premium on the availability of schools and teachers. In the early 1970s the government of Jamaica spent nearly 20 percent of its budget on education, a proportion that fell to just over 11 percent in the difficult economic climate of the 1980s.[17]

The smaller units have never been able to place as much of their resources, measured as a proportion of the national budget, into education as the larger units, and there has been much internal debate everywhere over both the structure of the educational system—whether too few of the products at the lower level are making it to the tertiary level—and the aptness of the curricula for the needs of the region. One thing seems certain, however: the number of local secondary graduates entering the universities locally or abroad is quite small.

While it is hard to ascertain the graduation figures for actual secondary and postsecondary education, the circumstantial evidence suggests that the falloff between primary and secondary education in the Commonwealth Caribbean is startlingly low. By contrast, the falloff between secondary and university education is startlingly high. In Jamaica in the 1982–83 school year the secondary schools enrolled 163,882 students while the university had an enrollment of 4,798, and all postsecondary local enrollment (including technical colleges and other vocational training institutes) was only 13,920. If we use the secondary enrollment as the base (and neglect those who went abroad for education), only 2.93 percent of graduates entered the university, and only 8.4 percent found places in all postsecondary institutions.[18] The proportions for Barbados and Trinidad were slightly higher, but not by much.[19] The 1989 report of the vice-chancellor of the University of the West Indies gave university enrollment figures of 5,444 in Jamaica, 2,185 in Barbados, and 4,209 in Trinidad.[20] With a combined population of about 3.6 million then, the three units had slightly fewer than 12,000 students enrolled at the university level. By contrast, Puerto Rico, with just about the same population (3.59 million in 1990), had more than 200,000 students enrolled at the university level.

Women were major beneficiaries of the economic expansion that took place in the postwar economic boom years leading up to 1960. Since there is a tendency to underreport female economic activity, the data on female employment should be considered conservative, provisional, and merely illustrative. After 1931 the proportion of women in the emigrant stream

TABLE 2.2. Percentage of Female Labor Participation, 1950–2000

State	1950	1990	Projected in 2000
Barbados	42.6	47.4	47.1
Dominican Republic	9.0	15.0	17.9
Guyana	18.0	25.1	25.9
Haiti	48.8	41.6	39.2
Jamaica	36.4	45.7	46.0
Suriname	21.1	29.6	30.5
Trinidad and Tobago	26.0	29.6	30.1

Source: Inter-American Development Bank, Economic and Social Progress in Latin America, 1987 Report (Washington, D.C., 1987).

increased significantly, and as elsewhere throughout Latin America, women moved into the labor force in ever greater numbers. In 1950 the highest proportions of female participation in the labor force in Latin America and the Caribbean were found in Barbados, Haiti, Jamaica, and Trinidad and Tobago—all exceeded 25 percent. The 1987 Inter-American Development Bank Report considered "the most important factor in the past twenty years [to be] the rapid increase of participation by women in the labor force."[21] In 1990, when twelve countries exceeded the 25 percent mark, the English-speaking Antilles seemed to be again at the forefront. In Barbados and Jamaica women account for nearly one out of every two jobs, with the prospect of increased proportional representation should the general economic situation continue to deteriorate (see table 2.2).

The social and economic implications of this labor force sectoral differentiation might very well be more important than initially presumed. With economic opportunities for females expanding more rapidly than those for males, the repercussions on family life and male-female relationships could be quite significant. Most female employment is in domestic service and other service industries notorious for their low wages and minimal working conditions.[22] In any case, increased female employment might not result in an overall proportional increase in capital accumulation given the lower earnings of women in general and the possibility that female dominance in certain new jobs, such as at free ports, hotels, and data-inputting services, might indeed result in depressing these wage rates. One area on which the impact of greater female participation in the work force has not been measured is that of the family. Whether the rapid increase in single-parent, female-headed families has much to do with increased opportunities for work cannot be ascertained at this time.

The postindependence populations of the Caribbean have been not only better educated formally but also been more politicized as a result of the technological advances of mass communication. The new mechanical devices of media dissemination—transistor radios, televisions, telephones, telefax and Walkman-type portable machines—have inundated the region as they have anywhere else in the Third World. The Caribbean people, then, have been technically integrated into the wider world and bombarded by the alluring appeals of mass consumerism common in wealthier societies. At the very least this integration has accentuated their consumer expectations beyond the capacity of reasonable satisfaction. Economic discontent therefore is both real and imagined, with the perceptions often as important as the reality.

Yet another post-Second World War development—and this is not peculiar to the Caribbean—is the increased urbanization, as well as the rise of a chaotic urban culture challenging the social values and physical property of the political, social, and economic elites. In relatively small places such as these Caribbean countries (excluding Guyana, Cuba, and the Dominican Republic), formal distinctions between rural and urban or town and country do not accurately convey today, as they did not so long ago, an almost visible difference in manners, values, and views of the world. Facilitated by the expansion of electricity, running water, education, and the various media, the differences between rural and urban have been collapsing rapidly. Residential density and administratively defined spaces do not characterize a sharply differentiated urban culture. Dominica's claim, therefore, that "the entire island is considered urban" appears less eccentric when regarded in this light.[23]

The contemporary Caribbean, less a melting pot than a mélange, remains a strangely fascinating fusion of race, ethnicity, class, and cultures. The arrival of new immigrants—East Indians, Chinese, Lebanese, Syrians—and the inescapable legacies of slavery and the plantation system have enormously complicated the social stratification of the region. No single organizing principle determines definitions of race, class, status, or high and low culture. So while the societies may be regarded as "plural," the social cleavages are not neatly mutually reinforcing, with the result that social designations often appear irrelevant, contradictory, or ambiguous.[24]

This can be seen most clearly when one looks at the general labels imposed on certain groups. All groups reflect a variegated spectrum. The term *white* in the Caribbean is not reserved exclusively for people of European descent, even though that sector constitutes the most important component of whites. Jews, Syrians, Lebanese, and Chinese are also considered white. And while white people make up a significant majority in Cuba, Puerto Rico, the Dominican Republic, St. Bartolomew, and a few other small islands, in the modern Caribbean the whites are politically and socially on the defensive.

As a group, blacks are the most diversely segmented. While prominently represented among the lower orders of all the societies, they nevertheless span class lines, and they are integrated in all economic and social groupings. They are particularly dominant in the political structures of the French and English Antilles—even in Trinidad and Guyana, where they may not form the absolute majority of the population.

East Indians, while considered an ethnic group, are split along religious as well as socioeconomic lines. Their group cohesiveness is most pronounced in Trinidad and Guyana, where they constitute a significant critical mass and exert a pronounced political self-consciousness.

Before independence came to the British Caribbean the metropolitan power imposed a rough corporate order on the society and invested power disproportionately in the numerically smaller group of white descendants of the former plantation owners. A subtle and not so subtle form of periodic cooptation of talented nonwhites was designed to placate the general aspirations of the nonwhite orders. The British tried to accentuate ethnic identity, often with strong overtones of an anachronistic nineteenth-century Social Darwinism, as a form of "divide and rule" politics. It did not work well, however, and the inexorable disintegration of the colonial system accelerated the movement toward self-government that grew out of the discontent of the 1930s.

Political independence changed the conventional relationships between ethnic groups, in some places drastically, both by politicizing the previously nonrepresented masses and by forcing groups to move beyond their ethnic base (at least in public rhetoric) in order to capture a majority of votes and to form or influence the government in an open political system. With their modest critical mass, the white sectors rapidly lost political control—having long before lost both their self-confidence and their political credibility.[25] How well the system has worked, and whether it is truly democratic and open, is subject to considerable debate. What remains clear is that everywhere the entire political system is being impatiently challenged from below.

And the Caribbean social structure is especially receptive to challenges from below. Political participation and the implementation of public policies have encouraged and provided opportunities for the reappraisal of traditions and an active integration of the popular and the elite. The result has been a blurring of the distinctions—some would say a reduction to the lowest common denominator—in aspects of religion, culture, and mores. In a way this has been a legitimizing experience for the nonelites. Nowhere was this more marked than in the decision of the Jamaican government to recognize the then socially marginal Rastafari group in the 1960s and to sponsor officially their demanded trip to Ethiopia.[26] Official recognition of the Rastafari marked the beginning of a wider acceptance of the African element in Jamaican society and coincided with a new redefinition of Caribbean nationalism throughout the region. Under the sponsorship of the various ministries of culture, the African and folk dimensions of the society are being widely inculcated and legitimized.

But while the African influences remain strong and pervasive, the rhetoric about Africa and the African dimension of Caribbean societies betrays an uneasiness or insecurity about the complex African legacies—understandable in such a polyglot, pluralistic, and artificially constituted society. Like most new societies, the Caribbean units remain conscious of their distinctiveness but not altogether comfortable with their identities. That they are political states is certain. Whether they constitute cohesive nations still remains in doubt. Certainly their symbols, their traditions, and their identities have yet to be fully accepted and internalized, and that is part of the tension that spills over into the contemporary political and economic atmosphere.

Conclusion

What, then, can the leaders do about this situation? Economic concerns, as other chapters in this volume acknowledge, loom large in the contemporary Caribbean. That is perfectly understandable. But the macroeconomic problems should not gain exclusive attention. Despite the overwhelming intrusion of economic considerations of a major order—trade balances and imbalances, debt servicing and interest rates, foreign currencies and exchange rates, inflation and stagnation, resource development and allocation, industrial production and productivity—one item that should remain a high priority is education.

The Caribbean states all have a basically good system of public education, despite the limited university opportunities in the English-speaking area. And public education has served these societies well. The policies of education implemented and pursued in the early 1950s and 1960s did bear some fruit and made substantial positive changes in the societies. The educational infrastructures require maintaining, and the curricula should always merit close attention. Education still remains a very good investment for the Caribbean, even if the calculation made in North America that every invested dollar yields five in return is optimistic. Given the limited natural resources and the complexity of the problems that continually surface, investment in human resources offers a magnificent opportunity. An educated society is not only the best hope for maintaining democracy but also the best and cheapest way for small countries to fashion and maintain equitable and just societies. Education demands their attention.

3

The Internationalization of Corruption and Violence: Threats to the Caribbean in the Post–Cold War World

Anthony P. Maingot

In many ways Robert Vesco is prototypical of the modern-day pirate operating in the Caribbean. A fugitive from United States' justice, his status as a "felon in flight" in no way prevented him from establishing the closest of relationships with political elites, first in Costa Rica, then in the Bahamas, Antigua, and finally as a guest of Fidel Castro in Cuba. Clearly, aside from money, Vesco has talents and skills that a variety of elites of diverse ideologies find useful. There is—in the Caribbean Basin and elsewhere—no shortage of sovereign states ready to give such pirates safe haven. Indeed, there are even states that purposely encourage and facilitate the granting of a safe haven as a significant source of income in convertible currency. Panama under the Noriega dictatorship was one such case. Citizenship, passports, and visas all were for sale, and governments in countries as diverse as the United States and Cuba found the Panamanian "arrangement" quite suitable to their wider geopolitical goals. It is now revealed, by the director of Panama's Technical Judicial Police (PTJ), that fully 75 percent of the criminals sought by Interpol entered or settled in Panama at some point.[1]

It was the awareness of this reality that led newly elected Jamaican Prime Minister Michael Manley to tell the United Nations that drug traffickers and criminals "have the globe to play with. . . . You are dealing with a level of international criminal organization that is probably without precedent. Those who manipulate production, transport, distribution and marketing operate in a global framework."[2] What Manley was addressing was the internationalization of corruption that made such a "global framework" possible. What makes this corruption international is the fact that it invariably involves actions and transactions in more than one national jurisdiction. A whole series of actions, generally referred to as "layering," make the tracing of money flows and principal actors virtually impossible. This type of corruption is beyond the control or supervision of any one state. Manley's concern was, of course, with how this process would affect his native Jamaica. "I certainly can't conceive," he told the press, "of what kind of Jamaica our people could build on the basis of a drug culture or a society massively corrupted by drug trafficking."[3]

Neither traditional (viz., nepotism) nor bureaucratic-administrative (viz., jobbery) corruption is new to the Caribbean. From the Bahamas through Cuba, all the way down the island chain to Trinidad, the region has had a reputation for both. Nor is the region necessarily more corrupt than other areas. When Walter Lippmann noted that in the United States corruption was "endemic," he could well have spoken for many another country.[4] Lippmann also made a universally valid point when he maintained that no history of corruption was possible, only the history of the exposure of corruption. Exposure, he maintained, invariably was merely one sequence in a cycle that alternated between "unsuspecting complacency and violent suspicion." Clearly, however, empirical and conceptual elusiveness should not deter attempts at a more systematic understanding of the phenomenon. It is the central argument of this paper that the greatest menace to the security of the states in the Caribbean Basin stems from a new level of corruption that should best be called the internationalization of corruption and violence.

The Caribbean Sea acts both as a barrier and as a bridge. Both functions favor the new internationalization of corruption and violence. By balkanizing the region into relatively weak nation-states while at the same time facilitating the flow of international commerce and transnational activities of some of the world's great producers and exporters, this sea puts many an international activity beyond the reach of nation-states. The result is often an asymmetry in maneuvering capabilities between national and international actors. This asymmetry is augmented and perpetuated by the technical and electronic revolution, which gives even private parties enormous capacities of communication, including the electronic transfer of capital. The international cartels tend also to have preferential access to human talent. Indeed, as former President Lopez Michelsen of Colombia has noted, the transferability of skills and technology from legitimate industry to the drug trade has made the latter a truly modern and transnational industry.[5] Not only does the Caribbean provide the bridge between the producer and the consumer in that industry but its modern banking system provides virtually impenetrable shelter to its profits.

The importance of all this is that the drug trade both contributes to and is facilitated by widespread and enduring corruption that permeates key (though certainly not all) elements of both the public and private sectors. Combating specific aspects of the drug trade (cultivation, transportation, distribution), difficult as that is, is a great deal simpler than uprooting corruption. The problems are both conceptual and practical.

Forging a New Conception of Security

The central methodological difficulties in discussing security in the post–cold war era are two. The first is that the bulk of the literature has concentrated on cold war issues, that is, the threats from Communist subversion. The role of Cuba in highlighting cold war issues has been amply covered. The second difficulty is that the tendency of the behavioral sciences to "measure" and quantify behavior leads necessarily to a focus on discrete events, or "incidents," that fit into fairly clear conceptual categories. As such, the coup d'état (an internal action to overthrow a regime) and the *coup de main* (an overthrow attempt by invasion or, at least, by external forces) lend themselves very neatly to quantification. Once the incidents have been quantified, social scientists can "measure" degrees of instability.[6] Using the coup d'état and the *coup de main* as the dependent variables, for instance, the first major study of security in the Eastern Caribbean concluded that population size is "the best explanation of how size affects the probability of security incidents occurring." The smaller the population, the greater the instability. Destabilizing incidents in small states, however, tend to be over quickly. The minuscule size of the political, social and economic institutions in microstates "simply makes it difficult to sustain prolonged divisions in the body politic."[7]

Neither of the above approaches, however, adequately explains the *ongoing* threats to the security of small Caribbean states. Neither versions of a communist menace nor enumerations of discrete (and short-lived) incidents of violence address the true nature of the contemporary threats. Much more promising is the approach of Peter Calvert, who divides the threats to small states into four categories: (1) attack by external forces, including mercenaries; (2) coups d'état; (3) subversion by narcotic traffickers; and (4) generalized corruption in government and/or the private sector.[8]

The displacement of the threats of the cold war by a new type of threat did not go unnoticed. Note the exchange between Senator John F. Kerry (D-Mass.), chairman of the Subcommittee on Terrorism, Narcotics and International Operations of the Senate's Committee on Foreign Relations, and Nestor D. Sanchez, former deputy assistant secretary for Latin American Affairs, Department of Defense:

> *Senator Kerry:* You are familiar with the assessments that General [Paul] Gorman made . . . that the national security of the United States was threatened by Latin drug conspiracies dramatically more successful at subversion in those areas than the subversion efforts from Moscow.
>
> *Mr. Sanchez:* Absolutely, it's a national security threat to one country, because of the countries and individuals involved.
>
> *Senator Kerry:* Now, General Gorman also testified that if you want to move weapons or munitions in Latin America, the established networks are owned by the cartels.[9]

Senator Kerry could have mentioned that the cartels control not only gun-running networks but also networks of illegal aliens. While the vast majority of illegal aliens are law-abiding,[10] the cartels use key "pipelines" to bring distributors, "enforcers," and others into the United States. Much attention has been focused on the Jamaican "posses" (called "yardies" in Great Britain), but the so-called Sandoval Pipeline brought into South Florida some 175 illegal aliens a week, at U.S. $1,700 per head, via Panama, Nassau, and Bimini.[11]

The critical methodological point, however, is that events in the Caribbean demonstrate that hardly ever do Calvert's four points operate as discrete, or "independent," events; they are interconnected, to be sure. Nevertheless, it is the assumption here that they all have to be understood in the context of a widely practiced type of corruption: a corruption that is "functional" to the internationalization of capital, labor, and labor movements that characterize the region's (and the world's) economy. In other words, a corruption that suits the logic of the marketplace. "A corrupt civil servant," writes Jacob van Klaveren, "regards his public office as a business, the income of which he will . . . seek to maximize. The office then becomes a 'maximizing unit.' The size of his income depends . . . upon the market situation and his talents for finding the point of maximal gain on the public's demand curve." The definition is similar to that of Robert Tilman, which sees corruption in terms of a rational choice, a "free market" type of calculus: the corrupt individual may "decide that it is worthwhile to risk the known sanctions and pay the higher costs in order to be assured of receiving the desired benefits."[12] It should be evident that in the context of a new corruption, fostered by the enormous amounts of drug-related monies, the concept of "maximization," or any other utility function, cannot be measured in "normal" terms. Even if historical standards of corruption are incorporated in the calculation, the phenomenon defies measurement. Robert Klitgaard's sound recommendation that administrative corruption be combated through material and other incentives clearly fails on the material (i.e., wages) side; and up to now, no one has figured out which "other" incentives will work.[13]

Interestingly enough, the "rational" corruption of the individual civil servant operates with the same logic as the foreign policies at certain periods of major state actors. What else—if not the maximizing of geopolitical advantages—would lead an administration to "marry" a corrupt dictator such as General Manuel Antonio Noriega?[14] Again, the calculus might not be financial gain but rather an attempt to avoid the discomfort of being called "colonialist" or "imperialist" by a corrupt Third World tyrant such as Suriname's Colonel Desi Bouterse.[15] What, then, do we know about Caribbean Basin elites' perceptions of threat?

Caribbean Realities

The decades of the 1970s and 1980s were convulsive ones for the then–newly independent countries in the Caribbean. An array of violent challenges to legitimate authority seemed to find, if not direct causes, at least fertile ground in the area's propensity to both traditional and bureaucratic corruption. In the process, the nature of both corruption and violence changed.

There can be no doubt that the present attempts to "structurally adjust" the various economies of the Caribbean Basin have put these governments under tremendous strain. The pressures are all the more threatening because these attempts at creating "open" economies follow decades of centralizing tendencies and growth in the public sector. Pressures from the newly enfranchised masses and formerly marginalized elites forced the state into the economic field. A 1972 Trinidad white paper made government's role in promoting jobs quite clear:

1. The public sector must be expected to play the role of a prime mover in the economy.
2. It is important to make optimum use of private foreign capital to develop the country in a manner consistent with the emergence of local initiative and local enterprise.

3. A complex of financial and nonfinancial corporate bodies under public control is being progressively developed, each with terms of reference which give it greater opportunity and facility for participation in the equity of private enterprise in order to stimulate new activity.[16]

Indeed, given Trinidad's oil resources and the jump in revenues from the "OPEC shock" of the 1970s, the island's government had the wherewithal to enter into a state-led development program. The other societies in the Caribbean had no such source of wealth, but their expectations of jobs and "localized" development were equally strong. This was the impetus behind the calls for a "mixed economy," which were particularly well articulated by Michael Manley and the Peoples National Party (PNP) in Jamaica. With governments throughout the region involved in negotiating contracts on ventures from oil refining to tourism and casino gambling, it is not surprising that opportunities for malfeasance increased. The commission of enquiry into this or that "deal" became a fixture of West Indian political life.

By the end of the 1970s there was a clear perception in some quarters that the threats to national security were related to more than just the cold war. Indeed, the geopolitical perceptions of some Caribbean elites were being shaped by a series of events, many not directly related to the basic structural problems of the society (see table 3.1). During this radical decade, it was this array of events, rather than apprehension over mass revolutionary movements, that generated the local perceptions of threat.

The differences can be appreciated in the changing nature of the declarations of Barbados's Tom Adams. In 1976 he visualized no threats and thus no need to establish an army or enter into any foreign defense pacts. By 1979 he had established the Barbados Defense Force, and what became known as the "Adams Doctrine" was fully developed. Adams's Barbados Labour Party Manifesto for 1981 made it clear that events "within Barbados and the Caribbean" made it necessary to create "a limited defense force with a capacity to withstand the immediate assault of potential marauders, terrorists and mercenaries." The language was similar to that of the 1979 Memorandum of Understanding between Barbados and Trinidad, which spoke of the threat of "terrorism, piracy, and the use of mercenaries." In the face of such a variety of threats, Adams believed that a policy of "wait and see" was akin to a policy of no assistance. The Adams Doctrine called for good intelligence so that the small but well-trained defense forces could nip conspiracies in the bud.[17]

As is evident in table 3.1, the threat did not come from one country or

TABLE 3.1. Specific Events Leading to a Caribbean Sense of Threat, 1969–1983

1969	Massive urban riots in Curaçao.
1970	Black power movement and mutiny of the army in Trinidad.
1975	Transshipment of Cuban troops (to Angola) through Barbados.
1976	Bombing (by Cuban exiled terrorist group) of Cubana Airlines plane out of Barbados.
1976	Barbados Prime Minister Tom Adams reveals that mercenaries under Sidney Burnett-Alleyne (and supported by South Africa) are preparing to invade. French in Martinique intercept Burnett-Alleyne, and he is convicted of smuggling arms out of Martinique.
1978	SRC corporation, operating out of Barbados and Antigua, found to have links with Israel and to be shipping arms to South Africa through Antigua.
1978	British intelligence reveals a second Burnett-Alleyne attempt to invade Barbados.
1979	Marxist coup in Grenada.
1979	St. Vincent's Prime Minister Milton Cato requests (and receives) Barbadian military assistance with an invasion of Union Island by a group called Movement for National Liberation.
1980	Coup d'état in Suriname by 16 noncommissioned officers.
1980	Cuban air force MiGs sink Bahamian coast-guard cutter.
1981	Two separate coup attempts against government of Eugenia Charles in Dominica. The recruitment of mercenaries in the United States is revealed by French intelligence in Martinique.
1982	Regional Security System created in the OECS.
1983	OECS requests and receives U.S., Jamaican, and Barbadian military intervention in Grenada.

Source: A. P. Maingot, *Some Perspectives on Security of Governing Elites in the English-Speaking Caribbean,* Essays on Strategy and Diplomacy, 4 (Claremont, Calif.: Claremont McKenna College, Keck Center for International Strategic Studies, 1985).

one ideology. "In 1982," wrote Prime Minister James F. Mitchell of St. Vincent, "although the U.S. might be single-minded in its position, the Caribbean with its political diversity cannot agree on a common enemy." Not that West Indian leaders were innocent about Cuban actions, wrote Mitchell, but there were other threats. Those who disparaged the menace posed by the Mafia, he noted, "are already victims." And then there was white-collar crime: "In St. Vincent's case, more money is swindled through our offshore banks from U.S. accounts than our total annual budget."[18]

Prime Minister Mitchell's description of one of the shady sides of the growing offshore banking industry was a rare official Caribbean statement about that business. Easily one of the fastest-growing sectors in the Caribbean, the offshore tax havens have attracted increased attention from British and U.S. law enforcement authorities.[19] The upshot of this series of concerns was that by the early 1980s the leaders of the small states of the Eastern Caribbean had concluded that security was to be found in collective action.

On October 30, 1982, the governments of Antigua, Dominica, St. Lucia, St. Vincent, and Barbados created the Regional Security Systems (RSS). At this point the Caribbean leadership's perceptions of threat were more in line with those of the Reagan administration. The alignment was not total, however. While the actions of Marxist-Leninist Grenada and its Cuban ally certainly were instrumental in giving shape to the new Caribbean geopolitical perspective, this was only part of the story. Many (though certainly not all) Caribbean leaders emerged from the radical period fully aware that "pirates," "mercenaries," and "terrorists" responded to more than just Marxism-Leninism, that the issue of security was broader than the North-South confrontation that had taken up so much intellectual attention and energy in the Caribbean.

The fact is that Caribbean leaders' perceptions of threat were not grounded in any broad ideological or theoretical conception of national security, but on hard experiences. None of the important politician-writers of the Caribbean in the 1960s, 1970s, and even early 1980s had even intimated that the threat to Caribbean security would come largely from corruption, internal and external. Even the prolific Michael Manley was totally absorbed by the North-South issue.

Elected in 1972, Manley published a book in 1973 in which he advocated national control of the "commanding heights of the economy" plus a "non-aligned" foreign policy; and in 1975 he took an even more strident "democratic socialist" stance.[20] In the decade out of power, Manley published an explanation of why the PNP lost the 1980 elections (U.S. "destabilization" was a major cause), a new call for his idea of "self-reliance" through a "New International Economic Order" and South-South cooperation, plus a monumental book on cricket, A History of West Indian Cricket.[21] Nowhere is the issue of a criminal threat to Jamaica seriously discussed prior to his return to government in 1989.

Academic scholars tended to follow suit; their concern was with issues of "revolution" and dependency. Even one as moderate and well-informed as Carl Stone refused to confront the issue of the international criminal threat. As late as April 1988, Stone wrote that he found it distressing that in a year when Jamaicans were electing a new government, "we are spending as much time agonizing over petty U.S. gossip about supposed mafia-type links between local politics and drug dons." He called for a discussion of "the real issues."[22]

Exactly one year later, after the Jamaican electorate had elected a new government without any serious debate or discussion of the Jamaican drug problem, Stone demonstrated a dramatically changed perception of threat. The drug dealers, he wrote, were "crippling" Jamaica; "the very future and livelihood of this country and its people are at risk." Such was his sense of threat that he urged that steps be taken "in a hurry" to stop this trade, including "any constitutional changes necessary."[23] What had happened, and how does it illustrate the nature of the threat to the security of Caribbean countries?

The Drug Trade and Violence

Between 1987 and 1989 several major shippers stopped shipping goods out of Jamaica. Evergreen Lines had already paid U.S. $137 million, and Sea-Land Services, U.S. $85 million, in fines to U.S. customs; the Kirk Line had one of its ships confiscated in Miami (released after the payment of a fine); Air Jamaica was suffering from constant fines; and the Free Zone manufacturers were said to be in a "tailspin" because of the use of the port by drug lords.[24]

The discovery on January 6, 1989, of a container in the port of Kingston holding U.S. $8 million in arms illustrated that the problem had wider ramifications. Of West German manufacture, the weapons were shipped from Portugal on a Panamanian registered ship and were destined for an unspecified group in Colombia. It took a joint effort of Jamaican, British, U.S., and Colombian intelligence to break the Jamaican link of what was described as "an international network of drug traffickers and terrorists."[25] The Panamanian ship was owned by Bluewater Ship Management, of Panama. Both the company and its British (naturalized Panamanian) president had previously been tied to illegal arms shipments, cocaine distribution, and the laundering of drug-related monies.[26]

What was happening in Jamaica was symptomatic of a regional crisis. The regionwide alarm over the links between the corruption wrought by the drug trade and violent threats to the region was heightened by three events in 1989 and 1990 that put a frightening new gloss on the region's problems. By far the most dramatic was the mid-1989 trial of Cuban General Arnaldo Ochoa and thirteen high-ranking codefendants. The most serious of various charges was "engaging in hostile acts against a foreign country" through involvement in the drug trade. Ochoa and three codefendants were sentenced to death on the basis of the prosecutor's arguments that their involvement in the drug trade had resulted in Cuba's humiliation: "The shower of insults, infamies, and slanders that are currently falling upon our country is basically motivated by the imperialist press agencies, using as an excuse the actions perpetrated by the accused."[27]

Following the trial and execution, the minister of the interior, José Abrantes, and numerous other high-ranking officers of the ministry of the interior were either arrested or reassigned. It was by far the largest purge in Cuban revolutionary history. Certainly no other country in the Caribbean Basin had ever confronted a drug-related crisis as deep as this one. The self-congratulatory, not to say self-righteous, tone of the Cuban media reflected the severity of the crisis:

> It would be difficult to find a country in the world where a vice-president [Torralba] is sent to prison for corruption . . . where a man with a distinguished record such as Arnaldo Ochoa's is the subject of a trial . . . or where a group of relatively high-ranking officers of MININT also is sent to trial . . . and where the crime of drug trafficking is exposed in front of national and world opinion. . . . To do this requires a great deal of moral fortitude, honesty, and political integrity.[28]

It might very well be, as Enrique Baloyra has indicated, that in that trial "no son todos los que están, ni están todos los que son."[29] One does not have to accept the Cuban version of the trial; General Ochoa's guilt is certainly much in doubt.[30] The important point is that the United States had long been accusing Cuba of being involved in the trade.[31] Cuba's admission that not only were the accusations correct (despite the shift in characters involved) but the involvement went to the highest reaches of the government was startling.

The critical question for leaders in the Caribbean was, If a tightly controlled society such as Cuba could be so deeply penetrated and threatened by the drug cartels, could any society in the Caribbean be immune? The various testimonies presented before an increasingly alarmed U.S. Congress indicate that few escaped the reach of the cartels.[32]

Further evidence of the difficulties facing the region was provided by two other dramatic events that shook Caribbean leaders and their societies. The first was the taking as hostages of the prime minister of Trinidad and much of his government by a group of black Muslims in July and August 1990. According to their pronouncements, they were motivated to combat the "rot" that rampant corruption had engendered in the society. Here, then, was a case—not unknown in the Caribbean—where alleged corruption was used as a justification for disrupting constitutional government. And yet the very preparation and execution of this plot demonstrates the intimate links between the labyrinthian world of international finance, the world trade in weapons, and violence. The fundamental aspect of this event, from the point of view of security, is the realization of the ease with which a terrorist group, regardless of "cause," can carry out a military operation in the Caribbean. Neither Trinidadian nor U.S. authorities appeared to have learned much from the already well-developed concern with threats to existing democracies. In the U.S. case, the Trinidad incident appears to demonstrate a feature evident in the past: lack of preparation and even basic information about the Caribbean.[33]

Since 1983, Trinidad papers had been reporting that Muammar Ghadafi's money was splitting the Muslim movement on the island, as well as on the purchases of weapons by the Ghadafi-supported group, Jamaat-Al-Muslimeen.[34] An offer to the Trinidad government to sharpen its intelligence skills with the assistance of Scotland Yard was rejected as "too colonial."[35] From the U.S. side, there appeared to be no intelligence failure but a very evident failure to take action on the known intelligence. Between April 7, 1990, and October 21, 1990, U.S. agents in Miami recorded all the purchases of assault rifles and ammunition, their storage, and the purchase of a large shipping container. They recorded the tens of thousands of hundred-dollar bills used in the purchases, brought into Miami (and declared to U.S. customs) from Trinidad or in traveler's checks from a Bahrain bank. The terrorists did not assume false names; they even shipped the container directly to the Jamaat-Al-Muslimeen headquarters in Port-of-Spain, a location that had been placed under "surveillance" by the Trinidad Special Branch since 1986.[36]

The capacity of the terrorists to collect weapons, train their men in Libya, and in broad daylight capture a whole government leads to several conclusions. First, Miami, not Moscow or Havana, is today the center of subversion of Caribbean states. The flows of illicit drugs and monies and the freedom of the arms market combine to make it an ideal city in which to plan terrorist actions. Second, despite the heightened perceptions of threat with which they emerged from the previous phase, there is no evidence that all West Indian governments have taken the necessary precautions to safeguard their national security. There is, in fact, a certain reluctance to accept foreign assistance in the area. Criticisms about the "militarization" of the Caribbean—often terribly superficial and naive— may have contributed to that sensitivity.[37]

As grave as the Trinidad events were, they pale in comparison to the implications of the second event, which came more fully to light in 1990: the Antigua guns scandal. The fundamental difference between that and the Trinidad case was that while the guns in Trinidad were privately bought for domestic terrorist use, the Antigua guns were purchased by the government for international terrorist use. In the latter case the state borders on being an agent of international terrorism. The Antigua case, as revealed by the official commission of inquiry, exposes the depth and spread of corruption, indeed, its internationalization.[38] It also clearly reveals the links between internationalized corruption and violence.

The charges were that ten tons of arms were bought in Israel, the end user to be the Antigua Defense Force (fewer than one hundred men already armed by the United States), but the weapons ended up on the farm of Medellin Cartel henchman Jose Rodriguez Gacha. It was proven that some of the guns were used in the assassination of popular Colombian presidential candidate Luis Carlos Galán. Among the many terrifying details revealed by the commission of inquiry, the following are central to the issues of this paper:

1. While Antigua had "a heavy moral duty" to Colombia and the world to pursue this matter, because of its meager diplomatic and police capabilities, it could not alone pursue the investigations, which had to cover "over four continents."

2. Despite the wider conclusion that small Caribbean states cannot confront the cartels on their own, "Intellectual collaboration to elicit the truth about Israeli firearms finding their way into the hands of Colombian drug barons was not to be easily achieved" (p. 40). The British government, said commissioner Louis Blom-Cooper, Q.C., "have turned a blind eye" to evidence that their nationals, operating as skilled mercenaries, "turned untrained killers into trained killers" (p. 34).

3. On the central role of the city of Miami: "This conspiracy was, in my judgment, hatched in Miami and developed from that city" (p. 37).

4. On the role of the banks: "I find it wholly unacceptable that banks in America, whose services were used to facilitate, what can without exaggeration be described as a crime against humanity, should be permitted through the inaction of the American authorities to hide evidence of that crime behind the cloak of confidentiality" (p. 37).

5. Finally, and critically, the report called attention to the role of wider, more enduring corrupt relationships between the principals in the scheme and high officials of the Antigua government, which called for "further investigation" (p. 83). Two questions in particular required urgent investigation: (1) What, if any, were the roles of Israeli and British mercenaries in establishing a training camp for terrorists in Antigua? and (2) Were there plans to train Tamil guerrillas in that camp in exchange for access to the East Asian heroin trade?

These questions were answered by an investigation undertaken by the Permanent Subcommittee on Investigations of the U.S. Senate. In hearings held in February 1991 the subcommittee established conclusively that (1) British and Israeli mercenaries, under contract to Colombian drug cartels, had been operating in Colombia since 1988; (2) because of pressure from the Colombian government, they had decided to shift operations to Antigua; (3) Antigua would serve both as training base and conduit of guns for the cartel; and (4) the Antigua deal was only one part of a much deeper and wider operation. As the subcommittee noted:

> This transaction provides a case study of the multi-national nature of arms trafficking. In this case, we had weapons made in Israel purportedly going to a Caribbean nation which wound up with the drug cartels in Colombia, financed through banks and individuals in Panama, the United States, Israel, Antigua and, probably, Colombia.

The Subcommittee was adamant that any effort against such international networks had to be multinational in scope. It was no surprise, then, that by the 1990s there were few who doubted that the most serious threat to the security of the Caribbean stemmed from the drug trade and its links to violence. Those who formerly had ignored it or had regarded it as merely a local nuisance now raised voices of alarm. Michael Manley, who had spent little time on the drug threat up to that point, declared that combating the drug mafias would be one of his top priorities upon taking office in 1990. "We are threatened," he told an audience in Toronto, Canada, in April 1990, "by an international criminal network in drug trafficking that has no precedent in history." Manley's words were being thoroughly corroborated by investigators and by events in the Caribbean.[39] Not only did Manley make the war on drugs the first priority of his administration but he carried his call for collective action to the United Nations. Similarly, Trinidad's Prime Minister A. N. R. Robinson called for the establishment of a special international court to try drug dealers. Unfortunately, not everyone was ready for Manley's or Robinson's ideas on how to combat the trade: traditional conceptions of sovereignty had still to be overcome in the Caribbean.

Conclusion

That world awareness about the threat posed by the drug trade and the internationalization of corruption and violence has reached new levels is evident in the language of the 1987 U.N. Draft Convention against Illicit Traffic in Narcotic Drugs and Psychotropic Substances, a multinational agreement designed to increase the effectiveness of law enforcement efforts against illicit drug trafficking. That convention's language showed that the threat is perceived in quite broad terms. It calls for seven areas of action:

1. Eradicate illicitly cultivated narcotic crops
2. Monitor chemicals and equipment used in the processing of drugs
3. Identify, seize, and forfeit illicitly generated proceeds
4. Improve international legal cooperation by such means as extradition, mutual legal assistance, and exchange of information relating to trafficking activities
5. Improve "controlled delivery" procedures (a term referring to law enforcement cooperation whereby the movement of an illicit drug consignment can be monitored so that arrests are made at the time of ultimate delivery)
6. Require commercial carriers to take reasonable precautions to avoid use of their facilities and means of transport for illicit trafficking
7. Prevent illicit traffic by sea, through the mails, or by abuse of special rights prevailing in free trade zones and free ports

As broad as these seven areas are, they do not fully address the problem. In fact, they omit any reference to the underlying structures and practices that make the drug trade possible: corruption, nationally and internationally.

Quite evidently, as aware as the leaders of the world are of the threats posed, they still resist any outside "interference" with "internal" political and administrative affairs. Any suggestion that extraterritorial jurisdiction be located in an international body is stiffly resisted. It is still regarded as an absolute precept that each nation should be left to govern its own territory and apply its own laws within that territory, never outside it. Corruption, to the extent that it is so regarded and punishable by a nation's laws, is clearly a national matter. And yet, can any major inroads against the cartels be made without effective, and worldwide, sanctions against it? It is to the credit of the U.S. Senate's Caucus on International Narcotics Control that they believe not. Their report on the U.N. Draft Convention notes the absence of any charge on corruption is a major weakness:

> Official corruption and complicity in the drug trade by some governments, particularly the laundering of illicit drug profits, has been one of the biggest obstacles to effective bilateral and multilateral drug enforcement efforts. The draft Convention, however, contains no language addressing this aspect of the international drug control problem, nor have any proposals been seriously discussed by any par-

ticipating nation. There are several options that could be considered to address the gap in the draft Convention's language: (a) including sanctions similar to those included in the 1961 Single Convention and the 1971 Convention on Psychotropic Substances against governments found participating in the drug trade, and (b) prohibiting any such government from participating in cooperative drug enforcement efforts with all signatory countries. While this Convention may not be the most appropriate vehicle to address the corruption problem, *international narcotics control efforts will never adequately attack the trafficking problem until official government corruption in the drug trade is eliminated,* so that the efforts of the international community can be focused solely on prosecuting the criminal syndicates directly involved in the international drug trade.[40]

The United States, for instance, wants money laundering to be considered as serious a crime as narcotics trafficking. In a region where offshore tax havens are thriving, and where their fastest growth is in still colonial or semicolonial territories, there is great resistance to any such suggestions. In short, the Caribbean—like much of the rest of the world—knows what the poison is and many have ideas about what a possible antidote might be; Caribbean leaders are not yet prepared to take the full dose of any remedy.

While solutions to the new threats to small Caribbean states appear nowhere in the offing, there is no reason for total despair. These are not what Gunnar Myrdal called "soft states," where corruption, brigandage, and venality are parts of a total way of life. The profoundly conservative nature of most Caribbean societies means that there are deep sources of moral indignation ever ready to flow. This requires democracy, however, and democracy means accountability. Where democracy flourishes there will be an opportunity for moral indignation to express itself. As case after case shows, "throwing the bums out" is an integral part of Caribbean history. The "Le Lavalas" (massive cleansing) campaign in Haiti demonstrates that there is a "logic" to a democratic system. Because the internationalization of corruption means that so much occurs beyond the national jurisdiction, national actors will have only limited scope over its elimination. But since any corruption involves a giver and a taker, national actors can at least hold the local takers accountable. The rest will require international, collective action, which all nations should encourage.

4 | Westminster Adapted: The Political Order of the Commonwealth Caribbean

Anthony Payne

In a helpful review of comparative approaches to the study of Caribbean politics written some years ago, Patrick Emmanuel began by citing a preindependence identification of the principal features of the politics of the English-speaking, or Commonwealth, Caribbean. These were deemed to be "colonial status, economic dependence, racial and cultural heterogeneity, dependence on British institutional models, social pluralism and malintegration, histories of slavery, monoculture, and frequent transfers between European powers in the seventeenth and eighteenth centuries."[1] Emmanuel noted that this list, except for one feature, could equally well have described the socioeconomic history of the non-Commonwealth Caribbean, indeed of plantation societies at large. He went on to aver that the indicative political characteristic of the English-speaking states in the Caribbean context was "the nature and relative durability of their constitutional regime."[2] The general point being emphasized was the existence in all societies of a political order that not only can be separated analytically but also actually exists separately from the social and economic orders with which it is, of course, connected in all manner of ways.

In this chapter I build on this argument and analyze the contemporary political order of the Commonwealth Caribbean. I take as my theme the notion of "Westminster adapted," focusing attention upon the nature and extent of the adjustments that have been made in the region to the classic

Westminster system, as set out in British constitutional theory.[3] More specifically, I assert (1) that the historical legacy of British colonialism shaped the emergent forms of politics in the postindependence Commonwealth Caribbean; (2) that this inherited political order has been adapted to Caribbean conditions in a creative and distinctive way; and (3) that the resulting system, which can be described as democratic,[4] offers the region a workable, although far from flawless, basis on which to defend its political practice into the 1990s and beyond.

The Colonial Crucible

The first part of the argument can only be made in outline. Britain's colonial connection with the Caribbean goes back to 1625 and only began to be released in 1962, with the independence of Jamaica and Trinidad and Tobago. There is too much history to review in detail. Nevertheless, the particular significance of three phases of that history should be highlighted. Firstly, the era of slavery, which lasted until 1834, served to place a premium on freedom in the emergent political culture of the Commonwealth Caribbean and invested that concept with a positive association with the ownership of property and the free expression of speech and worship.[5] Secondly, the era of the "old representative system," which held sway across more or less the whole region until the Morant Bay uprising in Jamaica in 1865, laid down many of the mechanisms of the Westminster system, albeit on a narrow and highly restricted basis, and established the habit of devolving responsibility from the imperial center to the colonies.[6] Thirdly, the era of "constitutional decolonization," which effectively began with the general rise in the political temperature of the region after the First World War, tied people and politicians into an evolutionary process by which the territories of the region were slowly graduated, albeit with occasional setbacks, along a series of stages toward greater self-government and eventual independence.[7]

The legacy of these phases was cumulative and self-reinforcing and has been noted by many observers, although few have put the point as trenchantly as Major E. F. L. Wood, Britain's under secretary of state for the colonies, in 1922. His visit to the region was occasioned by the growing demands for constitutional advancement being made by representative government associations (precursors of the modern political parties and trade unions formed in the 1930s and 1940s), and he reported as follows:

> The whole history of the African population of the West Indies inevitably drives them towards representational institutions fashioned after

the British model. Transplanted by the slave trade or other circumstances to foreign soil, losing in the process their social system, language and traditions and, with the exception of some relics of *obeah*, whatever religion they may have had, they owe everything that they have now, and all that they are, to the British race that first enslaved them, and subsequently to its honour restored to them their freedom. Small wonder if they look for political growth to the only course and pattern that they know, and aspire to share in what has been the particularly British gift of representational institutions.[8]

These were strong words, marked by the self-confident tone that characterized the British colonial stance toward the Caribbean before strikes and political violence, engendered by economic depression, spread across the region in the second half of the 1930s. Yet, even after these events, Wood's analysis still broadly applied. The political energy of the disturbances, which at least one historian considers could have become a genuinely revolutionary assault upon the derelict edifice of British colonialism in the Caribbean,[9] was channeled and controlled without too much difficulty. Constitutional advances followed, but always at a pace dictated by Britain, not forced by the Caribbean. The precise direction of progress was marked, in typically British fashion, by much that was ad hoc. The point with the greater subsequent relevance, however, was that every step—adult suffrage, the committee system, the ministerial system, the transformation of the executive council into a more representative council of ministers, the establishment of cabinet government, and so on—took on the character of a generous gesture by the benevolent colonial master rather than a victory on the part of indigenous nationalism.[10]

This is important not because Britain left behind in the Caribbean a perfect set of liberal, representative institutions. After all, institutions are only institutions: they can be as easily abandoned as preserved. Similar institutional inheritances collapsed quickly enough in other ex-British colonies, notably in Africa. Rather, it suggests that in the Caribbean, Britain inducted successive generations of political leaders into the ethics of the Westminster system. As this author has asked of the Jamaican leadership that took that country into independence, "English-speaking, colonially educated, the recipients of elite scholarships from Jamaica College to Oxford, Cambridge and London, the beneficiaries of other training programs in Britain—what else could the Jamaican elite become but would-be parliamentary democrats, especially since they grasped the fact that political independence granted on these terms would not bring them down from the top of the tree socially and economically?"[11] What applied to Jamaica applied broadly to the whole of the Commonwealth Caribbean. Norman Washington Manley, the founder of the Peoples National Party (PNP) in Jamaica, may best embody this type of middle-class leader, but he had his counterpart in Barbados in Grantley Adams and in Trinidad in Dr. Eric Williams. Even those new political leaders who came to the fore via trade union activity quickly acquired the habits, attitudes, and limitations of the British labor movement. The result was that, with some important exceptions, notably the avowed Marxist, Cheddi Jagan, in Guyana, the leading political figures who contested power in the Commonwealth Caribbean at the time of independence possessed values that were more deeply rooted in liberal democratic politics than in any other ideology. Moreover, so natural had the process of acculturation been that the whole apparatus of the Westminster system was widely regarded as autochthonous, not externally derived.

The Core Elements of the Contemporary Political Order

The second part of the argument I advance in this chapter suggests that these inherited values have not been abandoned in the Commonwealth Caribbean during the course of the first generation of political independence. They have not been adhered to in every respect, and they have unquestionably been adapted to local circumstances, but they have survived, and have done so in recognizable form. A political order has emerged that is based on the working of practices and commitments that manifestly have as their inspiration the Westminster system. The latter is, of course, an ideal type not necessarily in existence in Westminster itself. Indeed, even as an ideal type, no standard formulation exists. Drawing on the literature on Britain, however, we can identify several core elements, such as the convention of constitutionalism, the doctrine of civilian supremacy, the presumption of bureaucratic and police neutrality, the habit of competitive elections, and the practice of pluralist representation. For want of an agreed definition, these particular features of liberal democracy can be deemed to constitute the Westminster "model." They are thus the basic ground rules against which the reality of postindependence Commonwealth Caribbean politics can be evaluated.

Constitutionalism

The Westminster system does not depend on the existence of a written constitution, but it is associated strongly with the convention of constitutionalism, that is, the presumption that political change should only occur in accordance with rules and precedents. The Commonwealth Caribbean can certainly be said to be characterized by the culture of constitutionalism as defined in this way. This is something that becomes particularly apparent when the Commonwealth Caribbean states are compared either with other parts of the island Caribbean (Cuba, Haiti, and the Dominican Republic), or the wider Caribbean Basin (El Salvador, Guatemala, and Nicaragua), or with a number of states formerly under British rule (Nigeria, Uganda, Aden, and Pakistan). In contrast to the political experiences of these countries, most Commonwealth Caribbean states either still operate the constitutions they were given at independence—the predominant pattern—or have conceived of constitutional change as an incremental process of adjustment.

The details of the changes are reviewed by Sir Fred Philips in his survey of constitutional reform in the region.[12] For example, in Jamaica the manifesto on which the PNP won its second term of office under the leadership of Michael Manley in 1976 promised to put constitutional review on the agenda and made specific reference to the creation of a republic, the public financing of political parties, and the extension of "integrity-legislation" to include senior public officials. The left in the party, in fact, had an even more radical review in mind, but in the event nobody was able to give priority to the issue in the context of deepening economic crisis. Although a package of reforms was agreed upon in August 1979, the PNP's electoral defeat the next year prevented its implementation.[13] Similarly in Barbados, although a comprehensive constitutional review was published in 1979, it was never carried into being. Several of the smaller eastern Caribbean islands, to which Britain granted Associated Statehood (rather than full independence) in 1967, enjoyed an interim opportunity to adjust their constitutional arrangements—mostly to accommodate the demands of outer islands such as Barbuda in the case of Antigua and Anguilla and Nevis in the case of St. Kitts—at the time of their final passage to independence in the late 1970s and early 1980s, thereby reducing their appetite for constitutional change as independent states.

As Paul Sutton has noted, "This leaves Trinidad and Tobago as the state attempting the most comprehensive reform within the Westminster system."[14] It has involved the establishment of a republic in 1976, the provision of several new posts such as an ombudsman and a director of public prosecutions, the creation of an integrity commission, and in 1980 the devolution of a measure of self-government to Tobago. Indeed, the country's predilection for constitutional reform continues to the present, with the report of a new commission being made public as recently as May 1990. Yet all of these changes can be construed as modernizations and modifications of the basic model: they certainly do not disturb the essential formulation of the British constitutional inheritance. Indeed, Sutton quotes a speech by Trinidad's first prime minister, Dr. Eric Williams, in 1980, a year before his death, in which he advised his party that "if the Westminster model has helped Trinidad and Tobago in not producing our own barbarities and monsters, then we need not be too perturbed about the non-uprooting of our colonial structures." [15]

This observation provides a reminder that the postindependence Commonwealth Caribbean has witnessed two attempts to uproot the inheritance of colonialism—by the Peoples Revolutionary Government (PRG) in Grenada between 1979 and 1983 and by the Peoples National Congress (PNC) government in Guyana between 1978 and 1980. The former came to power by nonconstitutional means and based its claim to legitimacy on a theory of "people's power," supposedly to be institutionalized by means of the interlinked work of parish and zonal councils on the one hand and mass organizations on the other. However, a constitutional commission was not set up until June 1983, a matter of only months before the revolution imploded in bloodshed as a result of a quarrel conducted secretly within the ruling party's central committee.[16] The experiment in Guyana did result in the promulgation of a new "socialist" constitution in 1980, ostensibly expressive of the favored new doctrine of the paramountcy of the party. Under its terms, Forbes Burnham became the country's first executive president, with dictatorial powers. He was immune from prosecution, he could dismiss Parliament, he could delay elections for up to five years, and he could even appoint the official charged with determining the validity of his own election.[17] Barbarities and monsters indeed!

From a constitutionalist perspective, the best that can be said of both the Grenadian and Guyanese cases is that the two regimes did belatedly attempt, each in its own way, to create an alternative constitutional apparatus. Putting the point in reverse, they realized that in the Commonwealth Caribbean they could not hope to defend their politics by reference to a revolutionary, insurrectionary, or *caudillist* political tradition. The region has always been uncomfortable with these tendencies when and where they have occurred, and neither of the two nonconformist models proved to be at all attractive to other Commonwealth Caribbean states. Rather, the reverse was the case. It is true that more political pressure was imposed on the revolutionary regime in Grenada (largely because of greater external prompting from the United States) than was ever brought to bear on the PNC administration in Guyana. There is no doubt, however, that the excesses of the Burnham era in Guyana were genuinely embarrassing to most Commonwealth Caribbean governments and peoples and that the revulsion felt across the region at the brutal murder of Maurice

Bishop and others in Grenada in October 1983 by their political enemies was both spontaneous and intense. Such reactions reveal the depth of the commitment to constitutionalism in the region's political culture.

Civilian Supremacy

The Westminster system is a civilian system. It subscribes to the doctrine of civilian supremacy, which requires that the military be subject to civilian control and remain outside the formal political arena. These are standards that Commonwealth Caribbean countries have maintained quite successfully since their independence, certainly if they are again compared with countries in other parts of the developing world. No country in the region has experienced a successful military takeover of government in the classic sense of such an event, and for the most part the military in the Commonwealth Caribbean is characterized more by its weakness (indeed, its nonexistence in some territories, such as Dominica and St. Kitts) than by its predatory instincts. For this reason it cannot easily be used, as it sometimes has been in Latin America, as a last resort for failed politics of the right. Nevertheless, the picture is not entirely without blemish, and some of the difficulties the region has experienced in handling the military do need to be noted.

For example, political crises have occurred where the military has sought to push its way openly into the political arena. In Trinidad and Tobago in 1970 an army mutiny combined briefly with a wider black power revolt to threaten the Williams administration (although in 1990 it was the army that helped to rescue members of the elected government held hostage by a Muslim terrorist group). In Jamaica in 1980, during the course of the highly charged few months leading up to the election, a coup was apparently planned by some officers in the Defense Force, only to be discovered, stopped, and admitted by the army's own command. In Dominica in 1981 a series of attempts were made to bring down the government of Miss Eugenia Charles, all involving disaffected members of the Defense Force and ultimately leading to the force's abolition. These were incidents in which, in the end, military intervention was rebuffed and the doctrine of civilian supremacy in government preserved. But events could have turned out differently in each case, there being no immutable law of Commonwealth Caribbean politics dictating that coups cannot succeed. Indeed, some have referred to the process by which the New Jewel Movement (NJM) took power in Grenada in 1979 as a coup.[18] Such a designation oversimplifies the politics of what certainly was a violent, unconstitutional act unprecedented in the region's history. It was the case that some fifty or so lightly armed party members mounted an attack on the army headquarters at True Blue, just outside St. George's, in which two soldiers were killed, but it is also relevant that the news of Eric Gairy's overthrow was greeted with delight on the part of many ordinary people. This was the factor that broke the political resistance of the Gairy regime and made the event as much a popular insurrection as a coup. In many ways, the murder of Bishop in October 1983 is better described as a coup, since it was effected by a unit of the Peoples Revolutionary Army under military command and led directly to the formation of a Revolutionary Military Council, headed by General Hudson Austin. But even this bloody event has to be more properly understood as the outcome of a bitter internal struggle within the governing party in which the army was largely on one particular side. It was certainly not a conventional coup, and, of course, it did not bring down a conventional Westminster regime.[19]

Revolutionary Grenada, both before and after the October 1983 crisis, does certainly represent a case in the Commonwealth Caribbean where the line between civilian and military control was blurred. So too, although in a very different way, does Guyana, the other exceptional case in the modern politics of the region. The structure of rule assembled by Forbes Burnham contained a distinct military dimension. In addition to the Guyana Defense Force, which was inherited at independence in 1966, various other watchful and suspicious paramilitary forces were created—the police itself, the National Service, the Peoples Militia, and the National Guard Service. By 1984, according to one calculation, the number of men in arms in the country had reached 15,373, a process of militarization which not only commandeered over 10 percent of recurrent expenditure on published figures but represented an extraordinary increase of 673 percent on the figure twenty years earlier, when Burnham first came to office.[20] As potentially threatening as these forces were to the notion of civilian supremacy, they remained under Burnham's control. No general or captain ever rivaled Burnham, and no military takeover of government ever took place, despite predictions to this effect at various times over the last decade of his rule. The militarization of the Guyanese system of government under Burnham thus ultimately reflected the corruption of a civilian system rather than its displacement by military rule. Since Burnham's death in 1985, his successor as president, Desmond Hoyte, has slowly set about the difficult task of returning Guyana to the democratic fold, most recently making important changes to the electoral system. Nevertheless, the full test of the degree of demilitarization in the country will not be seen until Hoyte's ruling party fights, loses, and concedes defeat in a free and fair election.

Lastly, in connection with the general theme of civilian supremacy, it is necessary to comment briefly on the more general militarization of the Commonwealth Caribbean that several analysts claimed to detect in the mid-1980s.[21] The argument was developed in the aftermath of the United States' invasion of Grenada in 1983 and pointed to the expansion in security personnel at the disposal of regional governments in the eastern Caribbean and to their new involvement in military maneuvers with U.S. and other external forces. A debate about "who guards the guards" was initiated in the Commonwealth Caribbean, and for a time critics feared that one or two political leaders, notably perhaps Tom Adams in Barbados, were beginning to sense the additional power an expansion of the military apparatus of their states could give them. However, the election victories of James Mitchell in St. Vincent in 1984 and Errol Barrow in Barbados in 1986 altered the political mood in the eastern Caribbean and effectively brought the debate to a conclusion.[22] The level of armaments and equipment possessed by the military in the region remains very limited, and doubts about its technical weaknesses and inability to combat the new drug threat can fairly be put. It is the case that since 1983 the Commonwealth Caribbean has been more fully incorporated into U.S. security planning vis-à-vis the Caribbean Basin as a whole, but there is no reason to conclude from this that the basic commitment of regional elites, inside and outside of the military, to the broad notion of civilian supremacy in political life is any the weaker.

Bureaucratic and Police Neutrality

The Westminster system is organized on the presumption that the state machine behaves in a neutral manner. In other words, the bureaucracy is not theorized as the representative of a particular class or race but rather in quintessential pluralist fashion as a neutral broker to which contending interests can make representation and from which some enunciation of an overarching national interest can be expected. The existence of this presumption constitutes the Whitehall dimension of the system, and it has been a totem to which the Commonwealth Caribbean has paid homage since gaining independence. The church and the judiciary, for example, have everywhere been formally separated from the state, and with the exception of Guyana, where the doctrine of the paramountcy of the party was officially adopted in the Burnham era, the convention has been that the leaders of victorious political parties take over the stewardship of the state for strictly limited periods of time only. Their civil servants are expected to owe allegiance as firmly to them as to either their predecessors or their successors; this is in effect what displaying neutrality means under Westminster conventions.

Such arrangements have manifestly worked better in Commonwealth Caribbean countries where there has been regular party interchange in office (such as Barbados and Jamaica) than in those (such as Belize and Trinidad and Tobago) that for long periods of their postindependence experience were virtual one-party states. In these latter cases, doubts about the political neutrality of top bureaucrats, associated with the former regime by longevity if nothing else, did emerge when political power eventually changed hands in Belmopan in December 1984 and Port-of-Spain in December 1986, although it should be said that no purges took place. Generally, the ethic of presumed bureaucratic neutrality is deep-rooted, even in the expectations of politicians. It can be challenged in periods of ideological polarization, as when the Manley government in Jamaica attempted to move in a sharply leftward direction in the mid-1970s: it turned to a number of young political advisers outside the bureaucracy (the "tampack," named after their favored headgear) for ideological inspiration.[23] Yet even in Grenada between 1979 and 1983, ministers in the PRG, although drawing on political guidance from nonofficials, still assumed that they would receive objective advice from their permanent secretaries and other senior officials, and there is no evidence that they did not.

This has meant that across the Commonwealth Caribbean one of the most striking features of political life has come to be the existence of an elite civil service still organized along British lines. The University of the West Indies school of public administration, exemplified by, among others, Paul Robertson (now a minister in the post-1989 Manley government), G. E. Mills, and Edwin Jones,[24] has brought to light many aspects of the functioning of this service. Their findings confirm the "gentleman amateur" tradition associated with Whitehall, as well as the relatively narrow class base from which senior officials have typically been drawn (again a British inheritance); they also pay tribute to the competence and administrative capacity of public agencies in the region. At the same time, the analysis has turned up specific problems. It notes that the divided ethnic compositions of the populations of Guyana and Trinidad and Tobago have created tensions in the civil services of both countries, particularly the former, and that the extensive institutionalization of party clientelism in Jamaica cannot but have had implications for considerations of fairness and merit. In the very small islands of the eastern Caribbean, civil servants operating in such an intimate environment cannot but be exposed to the political arena, and in the worst cases they may be persecuted, almost terrorized, by unscrupulous politicians.[25] By contrast, in the immediate aftermath of independence well-educated officials tended to be contemptuous of governments led by uneducated men from lower-class social backgrounds. The problem is less marked today in countries such as Barbados and Jamaica, where the majority of cabinet members are university graduates. Senior civil servants are now more likely to complain of their low level of influence on policy.[26]

The difficulties that derive from such attitudes pale into insignificance, however, when they are set against the problems of corruption in public life, which is beginning to infect the Commonwealth Caribbean. As yet, the most flagrant abuses have involved political figures rather than civil servants, although it is at the bureaucratic level that the problem threatens to become endemic. The growth of corruption derives from a combination of factors—the extension of the state's regulatory functions into a range of new areas, the stringencies under which public officials live in societies with underdeveloped economies, and the increasing deployment of the vast financial resources at the disposal of external agents in the business world, notably in the drug trade. The scale of the temptations that have come to exist is revealed in the contrast between the monthly salary of a junior customs officer or a police constable in, say, Antigua and Barbuda, which is approximately $400, and the value of a load of Colombian cocaine carried in a light aircraft, which is approximately $1.5 million.[27] It is clear that Commonwealth Caribbean countries—like all countries for that matter—cannot presume to command the loyalty of any of their officials (or, even more worrying, their military officers, however senior), when bribes and financial offers of such magnitude can be routinely made. The extent to which bureaucratic systems in the region have already been corrupted varies, the most marked problems occurring in Antigua, which has recently been the scene of a major political scandal involving the provision of guns to Colombian drug runners; the Bahamas; and increasingly Jamaica, all of which not insignificantly are on the main drug routes. The real worry is that nobody knows how widespread or deep-seated the problem of corruption has become in the region. The evidence is, by its nature, concealed as much as possible. There is, nevertheless, genuine cause for concern that one of the associated features of the state's presumed political neutrality under the Westminster system—the reputation of the bureaucracy and the police for impartial administration of the law—may be in the process of irretrievably breaking down.

Competitive Elections

The Westminster system also critically depends on the existence of regular, competitive elections fought freely and fairly by rival political parties. They are the lifeblood of the system. Accordingly, the vitality of electoral politics has long been the most visible and most widely acknowl-edged characteristic of the postindependence political order of the Commonwealth Caribbean. Detailed evidence of the frequency and pas-sion of most regional elections is widespread, as testified in the writings of Carl Stone on Jamaica, Selwyn Ryan on Trinidad and Tobago, and Patrick Emmanuel on the eastern Caribbean.[28] The few cases of major electoral malpractice are equally well known, the most notorious without doubt being the step-by-step destruction of the electoral system in Guyana wrought by the Burnham administration. This began with falsification of the electoral lists in 1968, proceeded to the stuffing of ballot boxes with illegitimate votes in 1973 and the announcement of an absurd 97.7 per-cent turnout in a referendum on the new constitution in 1978, and cul-minated in massive malpractice in "elections" in 1980.[29] Guyana is, how-ever, as so often, the exceptional case in the region. In general, it is worth noting that elections have been validated by a change of government ev-erywhere else in the Commonwealth Caribbean at some time in the last twenty-five years, apart from, unexpectedly, the Bahamas, where the Pro-gressive Labor Party, led by Sir Lynden Pindling, has triumphed in every poll since 1967.

As a consequence of this overall record, competitive elections have come to enjoy unchallenged ideological legitimacy in the region. Yet this was not always so. The emergent radical intelligentsia of the region in the late 1960s and 1970s tended to dismiss electoral politics as superficial and discredited. They crudely associated the Westminster concept of elections with the general economic, social, and psychological dependency they deemed to be at the root of the region's continuing underdevelopment. This critique was picked up by the NJM in Grenada, whose leaders argued that "the type of democracy where people walk into a ballot box and vote for five seconds every five years is not real democracy at all."[30] In office, Maurice Bishop dismissed Westminster parliamentary democracy in Gre-nada under Gairy as "really Westminster parliamentary hypocrisy."[31] But his regime failed to implement its alternative notion of "people's power" in any meaningful way.[32] (It should be said in defense of these ideas that it was not ridiculous per se to claim that more participatory mechanisms for choosing leaders and taking decisions could be found in a small island with a population of only some 100,000 people.) In the end the NJM fell prey to the very authoritarianism it purported to oppose. Indeed, the fact that the whole experiment foundered in this particular way has strength-ened the popular appeal of competitive elections not only in Grenada but across the Commonwealth Caribbean.

Elections are typically rough and rumbustious affairs. Malicious gossip, the famous Trinidadian *mauvais langue;* personal abuse; sexual innuendo; the buying of votes; intimidation and casual violence—all have been commonplace, especially in the smaller islands, the general mood brilliantly depicted by V. S. Naipaul in his description of *The Suffrage of Elvira.* Certainly, the scale and the level of organization of the political violence that took place in Jamaica in 1980, when some eight hundred people were killed in the runup to elections, was unprecedented in the region. That only thirteen people died in the February 1989 election was regarded as a substantial achievement. Nevertheless, the deployment of armed gangs by both major political parties has now become a standard feature of elections in Jamaica. Indeed, some limited disruption of a small number of polling stations in every recent election, local as well as national, has become the new norm, although no less unacceptable for that.[33] In short, when the leaders of the NJM in Grenada railed against "oldstyle rum–and–corned beef politics, the politics of bribery and corruption . . . a process that consciously sought to divide the people into two warring camps, the 'ins' and the 'outs,'" they did not do an injustice to their target.[34] Some of the more old-style of these unattractive features have been ameliorated lately in some territories, but others have been exacerbated by the new money that has spread into the election process as United States campaigning techniques have begun to be imported into the region, as has been the case particularly in Jamaica. The deeper point, however, is that with the exception of the violence, this is the manner of electioneering the people have come to tolerate and quite like. As Gordon Lewis said of the region many years ago, "The society is a popular society."[35]

One final feature, almost a technicality, of the Commonwealth Caribbean's electoral system that should be noted is the continuing attachment displayed to the "first-past-the-post" model, which, as in Britain itself, has tended to create excessive support in Parliament for the winning party. This has had several implications for the nature of politics. Parliaments have been rendered vacuous as arenas of political conflict. Parties have been inclined to be "center-hugging," the largest loser often being rewarded almost as much as the winner because it is immediately established as the likeliest nucleus for a future opposition victory.[36] Governments, for their part, have been the more easily turned into forms of "elective dictatorship" between elections, with worrying implications for the preservation of civil and political rights. On this point, Anthony Maingot has argued that "first-past-the-post" does not promote the concept of citizenship in the region as effectively as it ought and has proposed a change to proportional representation.[37] The British government introduced such a system in Guyana in 1964 as a means of removing from office the Peoples Progressive Party, led then as now by Cheddi Jagan, an avowed Marxist.[38] The reputation of proportional representation was damaged within the region by this piece of manipulation, and not until the last few years have its merits and demerits begun to be debated again. Some attest to its suitability for racially divided societies such as Trinidad and Tobago and Guyana itself; others take the view that it would frustrate and ultimately paralyze political action.

Pluralist Representation

The Westminster system is rounded off by the operation of mechanisms for pluralist representation of the various interests that compose civil society. There is an understanding that the organizations, associations, and institutions formed by these interests should not be muzzled by the executive power of the state. In the Commonwealth Caribbean this too is a part of the political system that has been transferred from Britain. Churches, trade unions, the mass media, business groupings, farmers, specialist lobbies, and professional associations have all played significant roles in the political life of the various countries of the region. The Commonwealth Caribbean as a whole scores well as a part of the world, particularly the developing world, where the negative freedoms, as they are sometimes called, are firmly enshrined in law and political practice.[39] There can be few in the region (save perhaps some in Grenada and Guyana) who have feared to express critical or dissenting views about those in government in their country. The norm in the region has been a lively, even virulent, taste for lampooning the mighty, as best exemplified in the politics of the calypso. In short, freedom of speech and of association have consistently been taken seriously and have been defended courageously by brave men and women (to the point of martyrdom in Grenada, where Rupert Bishop, Maurice's father, was shot in 1974, and in Guyana, where Walter Rodney was murdered by a bomb in 1980) on the relatively small number of occasions when they have come under sustained attack.

Nevertheless, as is recognized in the literature on pluralist representation, such a system of politics has its drawbacks as well as its strengths. Most marked has been the tendency for elite interests, sustained by wealth, social connection, or education, or all three, to be able to make their voices better heard, and listened to more effectively, than those of popular interests. In particular, given the open market economies that most Commonwealth Caribbean governments have maintained in the postindependence era, private-sector business has been able to exercise considerable and growing political influence. This has been manifested not only in the shaping of public policy but in the ease with which business figures relate to the state, both as clients and as patrons. In many countries too, leading businessmen have been brought into government, personally occupying ministerial office often in portfolios concerned with commerce, tourism, or industry. The concept of business in the contemporary Commonwealth Caribbean also inevitably includes interests that are both local and external, the latter mainly U.S. in origin, and legal and illegal, the latter based mainly on drugs. In fact, the political role of drug money in funding particular parties is an insidious new feature of regional politics and one that has already aroused considerable controversy in Jamaica.[40] In connection with the power of private-sector interests, it is worth noting that most of the major newspapers operating in the Commonwealth Caribbean are run as private businesses, thereby posing great difficulties for governments that want both to bring them under popular control and to maintain traditional freedoms of expression. The Manley government ran into this problem in the 1970s with the *Daily Gleaner* but in the end chose to live with its abuse. The PRG in Grenada and the Burnham government in Guyana were less tolerant and closed newspapers that criticized their policies.

By comparison with the general trend toward accommodation of the private sector and its interests, the articulation of mass viewpoints has been notably less developed. Trade unions, for example, were once in the forefront of radical action, typically socialist in at least some sense in their ideological orientation and aggressive in pursuit of the political and economic rights of their members; of late, they have been drawn more into the nonpartisan tradition of U.S. unionism. As for political parties, they have generally been conceived in the region as tools for mobilizing the vote and winning elections. They have not been built up as mass organizations in the sense of constituting vehicles by which ordinary members can enter the policymaking process. The NJM in Grenada initially talked of movement in this direction but was seduced away by the attractions of vanguardism. The PNP in Jamaica in the 1970s also experimented with ways of involving ordinary members more fully in its affairs and was quite successful for a time, only for the experiment to be rejected in the 1980s as part of the party's move back to the ideological center ground. In fact, some of the many churches in the region have done more in recent years than political parties to give voice to the oppressed, the excluded, and those in a minority.[41]

The considerable gap in the panoply of representation left by this underemphasis of mass or popular participation has given political leaders significant room for maneuver and has provided the context in which a limited authoritarianism has emerged. It can be seen in the role played by "big personalities" in political life, not so much the one or two who became paranoid (Burnham and Gairy) but the fullness of the roll call across all the territories: Alexander Bustamante, Norman and Michael Manley, Eric Williams, Grantley and Tom Adams, Maurice Bishop and Bernard Coard, Vere Bird, Robert Bradshaw, George Price, John Compton, Eugenia Charles, Edward Seaga, and many others too. The trait was first described by Archie Singham in his portrait of the relationship between the "hero" and the "crowd" and was subsequently given classical exposition by Lloyd Best in his conception of "doctor politics."[42] Their argument drew attention to the fact that loyalties have traditionally been given to leaders on a highly deferential, almost messianic, basis and that great works are then expected of them by their adoring followers. It applies to the region still, although it is true that the dominant contemporary style, described in one recent analysis as that of the "managerial doctor," merely offers to handle dependence upon the world system with the most efficiency.[43]

Prospects for the 1990s

The main conclusion to emerge is that a political order has evolved in the Commonwealth Caribbean since the early 1960s that is well suited to the aspirations and characteristics of its peoples. That order can still be labeled a Westminster system. The British colonial inheritance has been adapted in use and over time and can now be said to have been comprehensively "Caribbeanized." The political order of the Commonwealth Caribbean, in other words, is unique—a mixture of First World theory with Third World practice, British form with Caribbean vitality. It is not without its flaws; it may not live up fully to some of the ideals of democracy. Yet it has worked well enough for most of the region's citizens for most of the time over the last quarter-century, and it does appear to have firm roots in popular consciousness. The optimistic scenario for the 1990s is for continued, cautious, conservative adaptation, consistent with the long history of the Commonwealth Caribbean.

By contrast, the pessimistic scenario focuses attention on some of the worrying trends in regional politics. The most threatening, perhaps, is the insidious impact of corruption on public life, precisely because it has the capacity to undermine the efficacy and integrity of every one of the political institutions described in this paper. For the rest, it is, or should be, a matter of concern that revolutionary politics have surfaced in the region, that the military is now talked about more as a potential political activist, that racial divisions remain politically significant, that the taste for messianic leadership still exists, that some national elections attract outside money, and that business interests have come to have almost a veto on the formation of public policy. In the face of these trends, the region has "muddled through" thus far on the bases described. In general, "Westminster adapted" stands up to critical scrutiny surprisingly well. But it cannot guarantee to continue to do so, and the present political order will need conscious defending if it is to survive the remainder of this decade and into the next century.

Finally, it is necessary to be clear about what this chapter has not argued, and that is the case for the autonomy, let alone the primacy, of the politics of any country or group of countries. The political order can be separated analytically from the social and economic orders, and clearly influences them; in turn, it is not immune from their influence: in certain circumstances it can be destroyed by changes in related social and economic matters. On the whole, the contemporary political order of the Commonwealth Caribbean can be said to sit neatly with the prevailing characteristics of both the social and the economic life of the region. The former is marked, above all, by an emphasis on elitism and authoritarianism derivative of the plantation era, and the latter by an adherence to the codes of capitalism born of the realities of the world economy in the 1990s. Politically speaking, Westminster has been adapted in the Commonwealth Caribbean in ways that directly reflect both of these contextual features. For the future, the great risk is that consistent failure on the region's part to find a satisfactory location within the world economy will put pressure on the social structure in ways that gradually but inevitably imperil the political order.

5 | The Future of Democracy in the Caribbean

Evelyne Huber

Conditions Favoring Democracy

Democracy is virtually universally accepted as a desirable form of government in official discourse. Yet, behind the rhetorical consensus, there are considerable differences in interpretation of the "real" nature of democracy. Therefore, it is useful to start with a clarification of the meaning given to the term here. This chapter adopts a formalistic, institutional definition of *democracy;* it treats its substantive dimension, that is, the extent to which power is equally shared and policies result in economic and social equity, as an important related but analytically separate question. Democracy is defined by free and fair elections, at regular intervals, in the context of guaranteed civil and political rights, responsible government (i.e., accountability of the executive, administrative, and coercive arms of the state to elected representatives), and political inclusion (i.e., universal suffrage and nonproscription of parties). Formal democracy has rightly been criticized in many cases for failing to yield greater substantive political and socioeconomic equality. Nevertheless, it is important to understand the conditions that facilitate establishment and consolidation of formal democracy, for two reasons. First, formal democracy has to be regarded as a value in itself insofar as it provides civil and political liberties (or conversely, protection from arbitrary rule and human rights violations). Second, there is an implied assumption that over the longer run democracy is more likely to facilitate peaceful transformation of structures of social and economic domination than authoritarianism, because it offers the many a chance for organization and for achieving a share of power. In fact, some of the very conditions that facilitate establishment and consolidation of formal democracy also promote the realization of its substantive dimension.

In order to assess probable scenarios for the future of democracy in the Caribbean, one needs to start with a brief review of the findings offered by social-science studies on the origins and consolidation of democracy.[1] Since the question of the future of democracy involves developments in the medium and the longer run, the structural type of analysis is more appropriate than the process- and actor-centered approach widely employed in recent studies of redemocratization in Latin America and Southern Europe.[2] Some insights from these process-oriented studies, though, are useful for our question as well, particularly those relating to the role of civil society and the behavior of economically dominant groups.

Democracy is about power sharing. In order for democracy to be installed and consolidated, two kinds of balance of power are required: (1) among different groups within civil society and (2) between civil society and the state apparatus. Within civil society the economic and political power of dominant groups needs to be counterbalanced by the organizational power of groups in the middle and at the bottom of the social ladder. The establishment and consolidation of democracy depend on a delicate balance between pressures from below for political inclusion and threat perception on the part of economic elites. If pressures from below are too strong and radical, that is, if they are accompanied by demands for wide-ranging social and economic changes, dominant groups are likely to use force to keep the lower classes excluded or to reexclude them.

Just as the power of dominant groups needs to be counterbalanced by the organizational power of subordinate groups, the power of the state needs to be counterbalanced by the organizational strength of civil society. On the one hand, the state needs to be strong and autonomous enough to ensure the rule of law and avoid being the captive of particularistic interests of dominant groups, but on the other hand, it must not be so strong and independent of all social forces as to overpower civil society and rule without accountability to organized social forces. Centralized state control over the economy and the presence of a large military and police apparatus are conditions inimical to a favorable power balance between state and civil society.

A strong civil society, then, that is, a strong organizational base of middle and lower classes in unions, professional associations, civic, educational, and cultural associations, religious organizations, and so on, is a necessary though not sufficient condition for the establishment and consolidation of democracy. Both the more traditional, empirical democracy research in the pluralist and functionalist tradition[3] and the newer, process-oriented literature on redemocratization agree with my analysis on this point. The first emphasizes the importance of strong multiple secondary associations for the viability of democracy; the second points out that civil society has to conquer and enlarge the political space provided by the political openings initiated by the authoritarian regimes themselves in order to proceed from liberalization to democratization. A strong civil society can provide a counterbalance to state power and to the economic power of dominant groups. However, external support for the state apparatus, particularly its coercive arm, may enable the state to remain autonomous and to repress even a strong civil society.

Political parties play a special role in the establishment and consolidation of democracy. If linked to strong and autonomous (with regard to the state) organizations in civil society, they can become the prime mobilizers of pressures from middle- and lower-class groups for the installation of democracy and for its maintenance. Where parties themselves and/or organizations of civil society are sponsored and more or less controlled by the state, the autonomous articulation of middle- and/or lower-class interests is eclipsed, and pressures for the installation and maintenance of democracy are weak. At the same time, parties are crucial for protecting the interests of dominant groups under the democratic rules of the game and thus for preventing these groups from attempting to undermine democracy. Where parties fail to perform this function, the perception on the part of economically dominant groups that their vital interests are threatened by the political power of middle- and lower-class groups endangers the survival of democracy.[4]

Cross-national quantitative studies have consistently found strong statistical correlations between the level of social and economic development and the stability of democracy.[5] This has been interpreted in various ways. Certainly the interpretation offered by pluralist and functionalist theories that higher levels of literacy, education, urbanization, and communication make democracy more likely because they create more informed, more interested, more affluent, and consequently less radical citizens is plausible on the surface, but the experiences of breakdowns of democracy at higher levels of development, and the antidemocratic role of the middle classes (i.e., the segments that are most educated, most informed, etc.) in some of these breakdowns in Europe and Latin America, should caution against any uncritical acceptance of this view. An interpretation that emphasizes changes in the social structure and greater dispersion of resources for organization among middle and lower classes resulting from economic development, if linked to an analysis of the power balance in civil society and between the state and civil society, is more useful for explaining both historical cases that conform to the relationship and those that deviate. Despite the disagreements on how to interpret the statistical findings, the point that higher levels of economic development are more favorable for consolidation of democracy is generally accepted.

Another finding of empirical studies of installation, consolidation, and breakdown of democracies is that prolonged and severe economic performance failures endanger the legitimacy of democratic regimes. The fact that the same holds for authoritarian regimes does not make prolonged economic crises any less dangerous for democracies. Particularly where the power balance between dominant groups and middle- and lower-class groups and between state and civil society is not very favorable for democracy to begin with, economic crises tend to strengthen authoritarian tendencies both among the dominant social groups and in the state apparatus.[6] Prolonged economic crises may also make members of the middle and lower classes susceptible to authoritarian appeals or prone to militant, anomic action, particularly where they are not integrated into strong and autonomous organizations of civil society and political parties with a democratic commitment. Finally, prolonged economic crises weaken the state's capacity to extract resources and maintain itself as an effective bureaucratic apparatus.

My emphasis here is on prolonged economic crises. Linz and Stepan argue that democratic legitimacy is somewhat insulated from perceptions of socioeconomic efficacy because (1) claims to legitimacy rest on procedural rather than performance grounds, (2) the possibility of democratic alternation of government and the promise of new policies serve as an insulating factor, and (3) perceptions about past human rights abuses shape a preference for democracy.[7] However, if economic crises are prolonged, lasting a decade or longer, the impact of factors 2 and 3 may be severely weakened. If different democratic governments have proved equally unable to solve the economic crisis or soften its effects for the population, the prospect of alternation ceases to hold much promise. The further the memory of human rights abuses recedes, the less of an asset it becomes for stabilization of democracy. Finally, I do not rest my argument solely on public opinion, but I also argue that prolonged economic crises give rise to structural developments, such as the mushrooming of informal-sector activities, that undermine the capacity of the state to uphold the rule of law.

Political institutions have been found to contribute to the stability of democracy. The role of political parties has already been mentioned but bears reemphasizing. In order for democracy to be consolidated, there need to be at least two strong political parties that command the allegiance of major organized sectors of civil society and thus are able to channel political activity through the formal and legal democratic institutions. Furthermore, either at least one of the parties needs to effectively represent interests of economic elites or none of the parties can be so radical when in government as to close all channels of access to policymaking to economic elites. This is so because de facto exclusion from access to policymaking through democratic institutions induces economic elites to attempt to undermine these institutions and to call for military intervention.[8] Aside from political parties, the structure of executive-legislative relations has an impact on democratic stability. Presidential systems bear a greater danger for political deadlock than parliamentary systems, particularly where electoral systems tend to produce minority presidencies. As Linz and Stepan point out, the United States is the only historically stable purely presidential system in the world.[9] Though parliamentary systems can create political paralysis or instability in the presence of many weak, nonprogrammatic, personalistic, and opportunistic parties unable to form stable coalitions, various constitutional formulas are available to reduce the danger of such occurrences.

The military has certainly played the major role in preventing the installation and consolidation of democracy in Third World countries in the post–Second World War period. Whether the military intervened as an ally of economically dominant groups or acted primarily in its own corporate self-interest or in the personal self-interest of its leaders, large military establishments have constituted a consistent threat to fragile democracies. Though military interventions initially were largely a response to civilian performance failures and civilian calls for military intervention and thus could be regarded as a result rather than a cause of the breakdown of the democratic system of government, military interventionism tended to feed upon itself and to become a cause for the lack of democracy by raising the stakes for the military in the control of the political system to satisfy its corporate interests or its leaders' interests in personal enrichment and immunity from prosecution. Moreover, the absence of a military apparatus strong enough to impose its rule on society in the first place removes the option for civilians to call for military intervention and thus one major threat to democracy. It is worthwhile to keep in mind that the only stable democracy in Central America, Costa Rica, abolished its military after the civil war of 1948. Military governments in most cases also systematically repressed trade unions and political parties and thus critically weakened the democratic potential in their societies.[10] Military domination of politics has been particularly prevalent where external support has encouraged the military to act largely independently of domestic state authority and social forces.

The Establishment and Consolidation of Democracies in the Caribbean

The question why democracies emerged and, with the exception of Guyana and Grenada, have survived in the English-speaking Caribbean can usefully be investigated through a comparative-historical analysis with the Central American countries. In a highly compressed and schematic version of such a comparison one can point out the following: Traditionally, the economies of all these countries were plantation economies, with some industrialization, mining, and tourism added in the post—Second World War period. Thus, the societies were, and to a large extent still are, very hierarchical, and the economies highly dependent on foreign trade and foreign investment. Their level of development, measured in gross domestic product per capita, puts them below the group of upper-middle-income countries in the World Bank classification, where democracy is a relatively frequent occurrence.[11] Nevertheless, there are profound political differences between the two sets of countries, and the English-speaking Caribbean as a group stands out with a democratic record unexpected on the basis of its level of economic development. These political differences are rooted in part in developments in the 1930s.[12]

The depression brought great disruptions to the extremely export-dependent societies in the region. In response to decreasing real wages and increasing unemployment, attempts at labor organization and labor protests emerged in all societies. The reactions of the economically dominant groups to these protests and organizing attempts were universally negative, but the reaction of the state varied widely. British colonialism constituted an alternative, and a less repressive one, to landlord and military control of the state and the use of the coercive forces of the state to repress both the protests and the emerging labor unions and allied political parties. Accordingly, the 1930s marked the beginning of organized political life and opened the way for the subsequent consolidation of civil society in the British Caribbean, whereas in Central America they perpetuated a tradition of repressive oligarchic responses to popular pressures and set the precedent for the primacy of the coercive apparatus of the state and for state control over and repression of the emerging civil society, exercised by either landowner-military coalitions, family dictatorships, or the military alone.[13]

The parties that emerged in alliance with trade unions out of the conjuncture of the 1930s in the British Caribbean became for the most part the driving forces in the nationalist movement, pushing for democratic rule and increased local autonomy.[14] Thus, the demands for decolonization and for democratization became inextricably linked. When independence was finally achieved, the organizational power base of the party-union complexes was firmly established in most countries. The parties enjoyed cross-class support, and mass demands were by and large channeled through the parties into democratic institutions. Economic elites, though initially opposed to democratization, had learned to work with and through the established political parties to protect their interests, using financial contributions and control over print media as major sources of leverage.[15] As a result, they did not actively attempt to undermine the democratic system. The fact that parties and democratic political institutions proved instrumental for all major groups to secure material benefits through what Jorge Domínguez calls the statist bargain (see above, chapter 1) helped consolidate them.

Rapid economic growth and social diversification in the 1960s led to the emergence of new social forces, which were mostly absorbed by existing unions or integrated into the political parties through patronage. Again, this contrasts starkly with the situation in Guatemala, El Salvador, and Nicaragua, where the systematic repression of the organizations of new social forces led to the emergence of broad-based violent revolutionary challenges. Finally, the military apparatuses in the ex-British Caribbean were small upon independence and remained so, with the telling exception of Guyana. In contrast, U.S. military aid supported the aggrandizement and increasing autonomy of already powerful military establishments in Central America, which have become major obstacles to democratization.[16]

Challenges to Established Democracies

The established democracies in the English-speaking Caribbean have several quite strong "democratic assets," that is, conditions that support the functioning of democratic politics. Compared with other Third World countries, their civil society is relatively strong. Unions, professional associations, churches, civic associations, and so on, are firmly established. Also, on the whole, multiclass political parties have strong roots in society, though there is considerable variation in party strength among countries. The parliamentary systems combined with these relatively stable party systems produce governments with control over both the executive and the legislative branches and consequently the capacity to take major political decisions.[17] The state apparatus, while on the weak side, is strong and autonomous enough to perform regulatory and extractive functions with minimally adequate effectiveness. It certainly is not overpowering; in particular, there are no large military establishments. These "assets" give reason for optimism regarding the future of democracy in the Caribbean. Nevertheless, at present and in the foreseeable future, these societies are subject to severe strains and pressures such that the threat to democracy should by no means be taken lightly.

A major challenge faced by the established democracies in the Caribbean is the economic crisis. The crisis assumed its full proportions in the 1980s, but in some cases, notably Jamaica, it had begun even earlier. This enduring crisis has several ramifications that may endanger democracy:

The economic crisis erodes the legitimacy of incumbent governments that are forced to impose austerity measures on their populations and are deprived of any options to demonstrate leadership and innovation in promoting development programs aimed at mass welfare. Democratic politics in the Caribbean from the beginning has been tied to expectations for the delivery of social services, particularly in the areas of education and health. Moreover, political parties have traditionally maintained the loyalty of their supporters in large part through patronage, which has resulted in tangible, albeit limited and sporadic, benefits for the poorer sectors. This statist bargain, to use Domínguez's formulation, also extended to the economically dominant classes, as they received benefits in the form of state protection and contracts. However, resource constraints and external pressures for economic liberalization have made it impossible to sustain this statist bargain. Thus, the inability of incumbents to deliver both universalistic benefits such as health care and particularistic benefits such as public employment and state contracts has weakened the allegiance of voters and economic elites to parties.[18] In the longer run the constraints resulting from the economic crisis tend to erode the legitimacy of politics and politicians and of representative politics per se, because electoral choices make little or no difference, as all governments are under the same constraints. Ultimately, it can erode the legitimacy of the state itself as the state becomes increasingly unable to perform even the most basic social welfare functions.

Loss of legitimacy of democracy as a regime form among mass constituencies does not necessarily bring about its breakdown and replacement by an authoritarian regime, as long as there is no strong support for such an alternative among elite constituencies or sufficient coercive capacity to impose an authoritarian regime. However, as noted, erosion of state legitimacy takes place not only at the mass level but also at the level of the economically dominant classes. These classes lose state protection not only in economic matters but also in other spheres. Loss of legitimacy of democracy and the state itself at the mass level implies loss of respect for the rule of law and thus a reduction in the state's capacity to maintain law and order, to protect its citizens, and to ensure implementation of its decisions. Rising crime rates and outbursts of mass protest threaten economic elites and reveal the state's inability to maintain and legitimize order in the society.[19] A more likely alternative to democracy than a full-fledged authoritarian regime, at least in the short to medium run, is a response to lawlessness and the threat of chaos or anarchy in the form of repressive or preventive measures such as impositions of the state of emergency and the buildup of security forces. In the longer run, habitual reliance on the state of emergency and a strengthening and role expansion of the security forces may well create elite constituencies, most prominently in the security forces themselves, for the imposition of an authoritarian regime. At the very least it will mean serious abridgement of democratic freedoms, and it will also tend to delegitimize political opposition.

The economic crisis has other implications that also point in the direction of erosion of the rule of law. The informal economy has mushroomed as a result of loss of jobs in the formal sector and of the inability of formal channels to provide adequate supplies of goods and services.[20] Whereas the informal economy has undoubtedly had beneficial effects insofar as it helped many people to make ends meet and frequently even smoothed operations in the formal sector, this should not detract attention from the very serious implications of its growth for state authority and capacity. State authority is more or less openly evaded or challenged by informal-sector operators; therefore, the incapacity of the state to enforce the law is made obvious. The extractive capacity of the state is diminished because informal sector activities evade taxation. Moreover, the informal economy augments and spreads corruption in the state apparatus, for example, among customs and traffic police, and thus further erodes the state's capacity to enforce decisions arrived at through democratic institutions.[21]

The economic crisis has also tended to weaken unions. Formal-sector unionized jobs have been lost at a higher rate than revealed by unemployment figures, because they have been replaced partly by informal-sector jobs and partly by jobs in export platforms, where unionization has been prevented. Most of the jobs in the export platforms are filled by unskilled female workers, many of them heads of households, who are highly vulnerable and susceptible to employer intimidation and sanctions against attempts at union organizing. Even where the employment base for unions survived, direct confrontations between unions and governments under International Monetary Fund (IMF) strictures have often ended in defeat for the unions, very dramatically so, for instance, in the case of the electric company workers who participated in the general strike of 1985 in Jamaica. In other cases, union leaderships have correctly perceived that confrontation would be futile and thus have abstained from pressing demands. Again, over the longer run the inability to effectively defend their members' interests cannot but weaken unions. Since unions are one of the forms of lower-class organization that play an essential part in sustaining democracy, such developments are reason for concern. A loss of strength and legitimacy of unions will decrease the capacity of lower classes to resist the curtailment of democratic rights or the imposition of an authoritarian regime, and it will also decrease the probability that social conflict is channeled through democratic institutions.

A further way in which the economic crisis may endanger democracy is by aggravating ethnic and racial tensions. As Selwyn Ryan points out in his chapter, the austerity measures imposed to deal with the crisis are affecting ethnic and racial groups in Trinidad differentially, and very visibly so (see chapter 7). Since economic austerity and adjustment policies affect some sectors of the economy and some occupations more than others, the same holds for other societies where ethnic and racial differences are linked to differences in occupational position and sectoral location. The example of Guyana shows how ethnic tensions manipulated by opportunistic political leaders can undermine democratic processes and institutions.

The problem of drug production and transshipment and of drug money laundering poses another potentially major challenge to the future of democracy in the Caribbean. It endangers the capacity of the democratic states to uphold the rule of law because of its corrupting influence on the state apparatus and because of the widespread resort to violence by those involved in the drug business. Colombia and Bolivia serve as extreme and threatening examples of disintegration of legitimate political authority under the onslaught of drug interests. Such disintegration is likely to have the consequences outlined above for the loss of legitimacy and capacity of the democratic regimes, namely, a drift into lawlessness and a tendency to increasingly authoritarian responses. Since the security forces play the pivotal role in combating the drug trade, the opportunities for corruption among high-ranking members of the security forces are both frequent and extremely lucrative, and consequently the integrity of the security forces and their compliance with directives from democratic governments become particularly problematic.

Fortunately for the survival chances of democracy, the drug cartels have not penetrated the Caribbean countries to nearly the same extent that they have penetrated Colombia and Bolivia. Nevertheless, the corruption scandals in the Bahamas, for instance, are danger signals for the potential influence of the drug trade. Governments of many of the Caribbean countries have expressed concern about the increasing use of their territories for transshipment of drugs from South America.

Jamaica, Belize, and some of the islands of the Eastern Caribbean have a drug problem of their own, namely, the production and export of marijuana. The positive effect of this trade on the economy contrasts sharply with its negative effect on the political system. Though only a fraction of the value of marijuana exports finds its way into the local economy, it still has a significant effect on rural living standards, and it increases the availability of consumer goods. The major negative impact of drug cultivation and export on democracy so far has been the corrupting influence on customs officials and members of the security forces. In addition, the eradication campaigns waged by the governments under U.S. pressure can safely be assumed to have alienated the rural producers from politics and politicians, as they have by no means been offered adequate alternatives as compensation for the loss of their most lucrative crops.

There has been some concern over impoverished leadership and its implications for the future of democracy in the Caribbean. Certainly, the average age of leading politicians and other public officials is rather high and raises the question of succession. Whereas one might argue that the founding generation of independent politics monopolized power for too long and thus drove talented members of younger generations into other pursuits, one has to seek important additional reasons for the problem in the economic crisis of the 1980s. Depressed salaries in the public sector and the lack of options open to political leaders to implement meaningful development policies have motivated ambitious individuals to seek opportunities in the private sector or abroad. For those who have chosen a political career, it certainly is much more difficult to demonstrate innovative and forceful leadership if, for instance, the latitude of action for a government is so heavily reigned in by IMF strictures as to make any departures from austerity and orthodoxy virtually impossible. This constrains not only leaders of incumbent parties but also leaders of the opposition and of popular movements, as they and the public know that alternative designs have extremely little chance of becoming policy-relevant.

The economic crisis has also aggravated the longstanding problem of the brain drain, which in the smaller islands seriously affects not only politics but all areas of social life. If available employment cannot provide an income that ensures a material level of living considered adequate by middle-class standards, emigration becomes an obvious option for highly educated people, particularly those in relatively early stages of their career. Despite such emigration, in the larger islands there remains a significant pool of talented and knowledgeable individuals who are committed to making a contribution to the development of their societies. However, as noted above, it is becoming increasingly difficult to attract these individuals to public service under conditions that so heavily restrict their latitude for creative and effective leadership and keep public-sector salaries far below those of their counterparts in the private sector.

In Jamaica the spread of political violence and the sophistication of the weapons used in its perpetration are reasons for concern. The 1980 election campaign was the high point of such violence and raised the specter of a society drifting toward ungovernability. That the guns remained in use after the election campaign, frequently for criminal activities, and the further inflow of such weapons through the drug trade are disquieting. Nevertheless, the relatively peaceful nature of the campaign for the 1989 election in the wake of a peace agreement between the party leaders suggests that the parties are still powerful organizations and can exercise a crucial moderating influence at least on politically motivated violence. This augurs well for democratic stability, as long as party leaders recognize their responsibility to put the maintenance of democracy above their personal quest for power.

The picture of party strength is entirely different in Trinidad and Tobago, where it gives some reason for concern, particularly because the problem of party politics is tied up with the problem of race. The hope that the victory of the multiracial National Alliance for Reconstruction (NAR) would mean an end to the virtual monopolization of political power by the African-based Peoples National Movement (PNM) and would usher in an era of genuinely competitive party politics and harmonious coexistence of African, Indian, and Creole elements in a multicultural community was not fulfilled.[22] The serious splits in the NAR raise doubts about its capacity to prevent a return to large-scale domination of positions of political power by the PNM. This could lead to severe disaffection among the now better-mobilized Indian community. If one adds to this the already discussed explosive issue of the differential impact of austerity and structural adjustment policies on the African and Indian communities, the potential for a major legitimacy crisis of democratic politics becomes visible.

Prospects for Consolidation of Fragile Democracies

The two cases in the category "fragile democracies" are the Dominican Republic and Grenada. The Dominican Republic lacked a tradition of democracy; the first free election was held in 1962, but within a year the elected president was overthrown.[23] The 1978 elections marked the first truly democratic transfer of power in its history, and even then the results of the election were only respected because of significant pressure from the Carter administration. Grenada has a similarly weak democratic tradition.[24] Democratic politics were first corrupted by Eric Gairy, who was replaced by a coup executed by the New Jewel Movement (NJM), which in turn was ousted by the U.S. invasion in 1983. Thus, both countries have faced and still are facing the problem of consolidating democratic institutions while encountering the same general challenges as the established democracies are encountering, most notably the economic crisis and the drug problem. This combination of challenges makes it all the more difficult to ensure a democratic future.

The main reasons for concern regarding democratic stability in the Dominican Republic in the 1990s are the weakness of the parties and the economic crisis, particularly the interaction between the two. Joaquín Balaguer's and Juan Bosch's parties have always been political machines around their leaders, and the severe factionalization and weakening of the Dominican Revolutionary Party (PRD) in the 1980s set backwards the only party with an organized mass base and a more or less democratic internal structure. This means that at present no party provides effective representation of organized forces in civil society, which severely limits the utility of representative democratic institutions from the point of view of these forces. Given the severity of the economic crisis and the resulting urgency felt by all major groups in society to influence economic policy in order to protect their interests, the danger of decay into a situation where all actors attempt to activate whatever power resources they have inside and outside of democratic institutions is a real one. In other Latin American countries, such situations, well captured in the concept of praetorianism, have frequently given rise to military intervention in politics.

The controversial reelection of Balaguer in 1990 and his inability to deal with an economic situation that rapidly went from bad to worse did nothing to strengthen either his party or other democratic institutions. In the face of widespread power cuts, virtually idled industry, and severe disruptions in food supplies, a collective of popular organizations along with unions called several strikes and protest actions. However, the organizational and thus disruptive power of the lower classes is still at a lower level in the Dominican Republic than it was, say, in Argentina, Uruguay, or in the urban areas in Brazil when democracy in these countries broke down into praetorianism and then military rule. Furthermore, the international context is less supportive of military authoritarianism than it was in the 1960s and early 1970s. Therefore, while the formal trappings of democracy may well survive in the Dominican Republic, they may come to hide distinctively nondemocratic practices of repression and aggrandizement of executive power.

Nor are conditions in Grenada particularly favorable for consolidation of democracy, because the lack of a democratic tradition also means a lack of an infrastructure of consolidated parties and affiliated organizations. In particular, there is no strong union movement linked to one or more democratic political parties. Unlike in the other islands, the main labor organizer and leader, Gairy, did not join a prodemocratic nationalist movement; instead, he corrupted democracy, using his office for personal gain and ultimately moving toward the rigging of elections and selective repression of opposition. Thus, the democratic thrust of organized labor was eclipsed, rather as it was by Juan Perón in Argentina. There was some increase in popular organization under the New Jewel government, but the organizations that were formed were sponsored by the state and greatly weakened by the trauma of the self-destruction of the NJM and of the U.S. invasion. Heavy U.S. and Caribbean maneuvering in the reconstruction of political parties and the first elections after the invasion did not help to build the strength, autonomy, and legitimacy of parties and organizations in civil society needed for stable democracy. The split in the New National Party, the maneuvering preceding the 1990 elections, the uncertainties surrounding the coalition negotiations after the elections, and the collapse of the coalition in early 1991 are indicators of continued fragility of democratic institutions. On the side of prodemocratic factors, the efforts to achieve greater political integration with the other members of the Organization of Eastern Caribbean States are contributing to the consolidation of democratic institutions, as the other members are all democracies.

Prospects for Democratization of Authoritarian Regimes

In the course of the work on this volume, Haiti switched back and forth between this section and the preceding section. In early 1991 it had entered the preceding section, but for the reasons to be outlined presently, the prognosis in the last draft of this chapter was that "prospects for democracy in Haiti appear far from bright." Accordingly, it did not come as a surprise that Haiti was back in the present section by late 1991. The country has no democratic tradition whatsoever. It held the first democratic elections in its history in December 1990, and before the president-elect could even take power, a prominent member of the deposed Duvalier dictatorship staged a coup attempt.

The reasons for the failure of democracy to be consolidated in Haiti are many.[25] A still relatively weak civil society and party system confront a military apparatus with sufficient coercive capacity to terrorize the society but with insufficient institutionalization and professionalization to constitute a reliable partner in negotiations about democratic consolidation. Unlike military regimes where splits between hard- and soft-liners provided room for maneuver to civilian political actors and the possibility of concluding pacts for greatly reducing the political role of the military institution, the Haitian military regime is severely factionalized around personal aspirations for power. There is little tradition of professionalism and discipline, and agreements protecting the corporate interests of the military institution under a democratic regime were not likely to satisfy and elicit compliance of various aspiring leaders and their supporters.

Civil society and the party system are kept weak by the low level of development of the society and by the long history of repression. The building of real political organizations only became possible after Duvalier had been ousted. This means that such organizations would still be weak under any conditions. In addition, in Haiti the low level of industrialization makes unionization very difficult, and resource scarcity also greatly impedes the buildup of party organizations. The weaknesses of parties and of democratic institutions mutually reinforce each other. Under the semipresidential system of Haiti, careful coalition building or at least principled accommodation would be essential, but the absence of strong parties makes such coalition building difficult. If one adds to all this the fact that the first presidential election was won by a radical priest who caused alarm among domestic elites and considerable concern in the Bush administration, the danger signals for the first democratic regime in Haiti were conspicuous.[26] Given the unfavorable structural conditions for democratization, even strong international pressures in the short run may at best create a facade of democracy, and a fragile one at that.

Of the two other non-Hispanic Caribbean countries that remain clearly nondemocratic—Guyana and Suriname—Guyana seems to offer the more realistic prospects for progress toward democratization. It has a strong tradition of popular organization and party politics. The racial composition of the society and the tradition of racial mobilization by political leaders are important obstacles to democratization in Guyana. Yet, the comparison to Trinidad, for instance, shows that racial divisions do not make democracy necessarily unviable; rather, their effect depends on their particular articulation with class and with the state. In the Guyanese case, the class structure, with clear occupational and geographical segregation of the ethnic groups and with an initially weak middle class; the radical orientation of the initially multiracial Peoples Progressive Party (PPP) as the main representative of the organized lower classes; the fact that the African minority ethnic group was firmly lodged in the administrative and coercive arms of the state apparatus; and the intervention of external forces on the side of the dominant classes allied with the African-based Peoples National Congress (PNC) all worked together to cause a breakdown of democracy.[27] Some of these same factors still are operative and obstruct redemocratization, despite the toll the economic disaster has taken on the PNC's support. What is most important, Burnham greatly expanded the state apparatus, strengthened its repressive arm, and solidified PNC control over it all. Furthermore, the radical left (the PPP and the Working Peoples Alliance [WPA]) is still the main force in the opposition, and there are deep divisions in the opposition. Two parties did not join the Patriotic Coalition for Democracy (PCD), the umbrella opposition coalition, and even the member parties of the PCD could not agree on a joint list of candidates for the elections due in 1991.

Given the total control of the PNC over the state apparatus and the high risks for the PNC associated with free elections, external pressures were indispensable for moving Guyana toward honest elections. The U.S. government had taken the official position that free elections were essential if significant amounts of financial support were to be made available. CARICOM leaders, working through the Council of Freely-Elected Heads of Government, which is chaired by ex-President Carter, also added their weight to demands for free elections.[28] At the invitation of President Hoyte and leaders of the opposition parties, Carter visited Guyana in October 1990 and was able to forge an agreement on electoral reform that included the drawing up of new voter lists and the counting of ballots at the polling sites. Subsequently, the government claimed that the process of voter registration was very time-consuming and necessitated the postponing of the elections that would have been due by March 31, 1991. Only sustained economic and political, external and internal pressures combined proved capable of pushing Hoyte to hold the promised elections he lost. However, the elections of October 1992 were marred by mob rioting, which did not bode well for resolving PNC domination of the military and the state apparatus and consolidating democracy.

Though Suriname was formally democratic between January 1988 and December 1990, de facto it remained an authoritarian regime because Desi Bouterse, the former military ruler, remained the real power behind the scenes, and the civilian government did not control the military.[29] In December 1990 longstanding tensions between the government and the military led to a military coup that ousted the formally democratic government. Some of the key obstructions to real democratization were the insurgencies among the Bush Negroes and the Tucayana Indians, the involvement of the military in the drug trade, and the weakness of civil society and political parties.

The insurgencies kept the military in a very prominent role. Peace talks between the civilian government and the insurgents led by Ronnie Brunswijk were first opposed and later taken over by Bouterse. Rather than accepting the agreement negotiated by the civilian government or seeking another solution through negotiation, the military has pursued the path of armed struggle, fomenting divisions and violence among different groups of insurgents. The military clearly has no intention whatsoever of subordinating itself to any constitutional form of rule. On the contrary, it has been actively undermining the rule of law, physically assaulting police forces, which are independent of the military. Police officers involved in investigating human rights violations by the military and military involvement in drug trafficking have been murdered, and police facilities have become targets of military attacks.[30]

On the side of the civilian political forces there are serious problems as well. In December 1982 political murders perpetrated by the Bouterse regime wiped out the leadership of the traditional ethnically based parties. These parties dominated the National Assembly again during the second democratic period, but the new leadership faced legitimacy problems among the traditional party supporters and also opposition from newer and more radical groups, which attacked the older parties for having collaborated with Bouterse's government and which denied legitimacy to the newly established democratic institutions. Also, civil society remains weak, and there is no close connection between parties and other organizations through which demands could be channeled into democratic institutions. Accordingly, these institutions did not command strong mass allegiance, and the bloodless coup met with only weak internal opposition. Internationally, the coup was strongly condemned by the Organization of American States as well as by several CARICOM leaders, who recommended that Suriname be denied observer status because of the coup.

However, as in Haiti, as long as internal conditions remain so unfavorable for democracy, external pressures are very unlikely to lead to genuine democratization.

Policy Implications for the U.S. and Caribbean Governments

The first point to keep in mind with regard to U.S. policy is that attempts at outright imposition of a political system, and particularly a democratic system, from the outside through diplomatic ultimatums or military intervention are extremely hazardous and doomed to failure unless internal conditions are conducive to democratization. Thus, policies have to be aimed at creating and sustaining the internal conditions that make democracy stable and, conversely, at transforming the conditions that sustain authoritarian forces and regimes. By this I do not mean to imply that there cannot arise situations at critical junctures where direct diplomatic pressures may be effective, such as in the case of the Dominican Republic in 1978, or where international mediation or observation of elections may be effective, such as in Haiti in 1990. However, such situations are the exception rather than the rule, and free elections are only a first step toward consolidation of democratic rule. In general, long-term, consistent incentives and direct support for democratic procedures and forces, as well as disincentives and lack of support for authoritarian procedures and forces, are the only potentially effective means for promoting democracy.

Given the importance of the economic crisis both as a challenge to established democracies and as an obstacle to the consolidation of fragile democracies, finding a solution to the debt crisis that lightens the debt-service burden of Caribbean countries and gives them room for action to restimulate growth and restore social services is a central part of any policy aimed at strengthening democracy in the region. Political action in this area is in fact quite feasible, as a large portion of the debt of many Caribbean countries is bilateral and multilateral, not commercial.[31] Concrete proposals for dealing with the debt problem are discussed by Robert Pastor and Richard Fletcher in chapter 14 of this volume. What is important from the point of view of consolidation of democracy is that the U.S. government and the IMF refrain from indiscriminately imposing liberalization, privatization, and orthodox austerity measures and instead accept a variety of policy approaches, including more state-interventionist ones. In contexts of initially high levels of economic inequality such as those prevailing in the Caribbean, markets have highly inegalitarian distributional consequences that can only be attenuated by state intervention. Since theorists of democracy as well as the empirical quantitative literature agree that high degrees of resource concentration are not favorable for democratic consolidation, this means that state intervention in the area of redistribution is an essential contribution to democracy.[32]

Essential complementary policies to negotiating an alleviation of the debt burden are measures to stimulate trade, in particular access for Caribbean exports to the U.S. market and a search for markets for Caribbean goods in other countries of the region. In both debt renegotiation and trade stimulation, regional collaboration and progress toward integration are crucial. Individualistic strategies have had disappointing results, even in cases such as Jamaica under Edward Seaga, where the Reagan administration was most favorably disposed toward special concessions.[33] Collaborative efforts have a higher potential for success, and to the extent that they are successful in promoting economic development, they promote conditions favorable for democratic consolidation in the Caribbean. For the U.S. administration this means abandoning its preference for bilateral agreements and dealing instead with Caribbean nations as a group. For Caribbean governments this means intensifying efforts at regional economic integration and political collaboration.

Regional collaboration is also important in efforts to promote policies aimed more directly at strengthening prodemocratic forces and democratic institutions. Such policies can take the form of collective incentives and support for democratic forces as well as collective pressures on antidemocratic forces and governments. In order to strengthen democracy, Caribbean governments should support political parties and organizations in civil society, particularly unions and middle-class professional organizations, on a nondiscriminatory basis (i.e., organizations opposing incumbents should have the same rights to such support as those supporting them, provided, of course, that they are committed to the democratic process). Various formulas are available for the provision of public funding; for example, funding may be based on the number of votes received, or on the number of members paying dues. U.S. funds could be made available through multilateral institutions such as CARICOM to governments for public funding on such nondiscriminatory bases. By the same token, governments that corrupt the electoral process and harass or repress political parties, unions, or other organizations in civil society should be pressured to abandon such policies by other Caribbean governments and the U.S. collectively. Where governments persist in their repressive policies and prodemocratic organizations are clearly identifiable, support could be channeled directly to those organizations through multilateral institutions.

The question of the use of economic sanctions—e.g., withdrawal of aid, credits, and other concessions by the United States or exclusion from regional economic cooperation by other Caribbean countries—to pressure governments in a democratic direction is a difficult one. In general, promotion of economic development is the best way to strengthen prodemocratic forces in the long run, and therefore the use of economic sanctions is sometimes counterproductive. Also, regional economic groupings, particularly a strengthened and enlarged CARICOM, may provide a forum for the collective articulation of criticism and the exercise of pressures on member governments to respect democratic procedures. Expelling authoritarian governments from such organizations may cause this option to lose effectiveness.[34] On the other hand, economic sanctions may be called for in the short run to make a strong political statement and support diplomatic pressures, particularly if human rights abuses are involved or when a regime is shaky and economic sanctions can further weaken it and at the same time encourage the domestic opposition. Even under such conditions, however, humanitarian aid in kind, such as medical supplies and basic foodstuffs, should continue. Also, if politically feasible, providing aid to political parties and organizations in civil society directly and on a nondiscriminatory basis through multilateral institutions should be considered.

Just as different approaches of governments in the area of economic development should be tolerated by the United States, so should different approaches in the area of redistribution and social mobilization. Reducing very high social inequality directly contributes to the stabilization of democracy. Moreover, redistributionist policies aimed at human resource development improve the capacity of lower classes to organize and thus indirectly contribute to democracy by strengthening the democratic infrastructure. Policies aimed directly at raising the level of organization and participation of lower classes, such as policies that encourage unionization and provide opportunities for involvement in decision making in community affairs and at the workplace, can further strengthen this infrastructure. Since the state necessarily plays a crucial role in redistributionist and social mobilization policies, U.S. acceptance of such policies means abstaining from enforcing the strong antistatist bias that has guided U.S. actions toward developing countries.

Since the complex issues of the drug trade and national security are dealt with by Ron Sanders and Neville Linton (in chapters 12 and 13, respectively), a few brief remarks will suffice here. Any attempts to deal with production and shipment of drugs will have to be accompanied by attempts to deal with the demand side. This implies more than stepped-up law enforcement efforts in the United States, namely, long-range drug re-

habilitation programs and, what is most important, economic development programs for urban poor communities. In efforts to curb production,
the economic situation of peasant cultivators has to occupy center stage.
Simple destruction of crops unaccompanied by offers of economic alternatives is bound to be countered by new intensified efforts at production
of these crops. Therefore, general economic development policies should
contain specific measures to promote agricultural production in areas
where drug crops are prevalent. An approach to the problem that emphasizes these elements rather than simple reliance on coercive force reduces
the pressures for the buildup of a strong security apparatus, with its potential negative consequences for democratic rule.

Both Sanders and Linton agree that it is neither feasible for each of the
Caribbean nations to build up an adequate security apparatus on its own
nor desirable that scarce resources be so allocated. Rather, the nations of
the region need to work together to find ways to police Caribbean waters
effectively and assist the individual states in defending themselves against
drug traffickers and other threats to democracy, such as coup attempts.[35] A
collective approach to security as suggested by Linton would comprise
provisions for the peaceful settlement of conflicts and for the use of non-
military sanctions, as well as for the deployment of regional forces. One
could add to his suggestions the observation that a truly multilateral force,
to be deployed in crisis situations by a multilateral command on the request of democratic governments, would be much less likely to become
involved in domestic politics than national security forces and would lack
the coercive capacity to impose an authoritarian regime.

The security issue brings us back to the importance of regional collaboration. Democracy has traditionally been regarded as a domestic affair, installed and maintained by an appropriate balance of power among domestic social forces. Though this is a crucial condition that makes democracy
viable, the need for a power balance between the state and civil society
brings international influences into focus. The state is not only a domestic
actor but also an actor in the international system of states and the international economy, and as such exposed to external pressures. For small
states to protect their autonomy and their ability to sustain the provision
of essential public goods such as health, education, and security expected
from democratic governments, international cooperation is rapidly becoming indispensable.

The capacity of states to provide basic social services is not only important for the maintenance of formal democracy but crucial for any movement toward substantive democracy, that is, toward a society where the
many hold a real share of power and can use that power to improve the

material conditions of life for those in the lower ranks of the social order. In the beginning of this essay I justified the exclusive focus on formal democracy on the grounds that democracies protect the human rights of their citizens and the rights of out-groups to organize and gain a share of power. If, however, the levers of power, i.e., the state apparatus, access to which is to be shared, become ineffective because of economic constraints, then these promises of formal democracy become elusive. Since a significant source of these economic constraints lies in the international system, represented most dramatically by the pervasive role of the IMF, and since individual action of small developing nations vis-à-vis this system is largely futile, international collaboration among such nations is essential to protect formal democracy and even more so to realize the promise of substantive democracy.

In an increasingly interdependent world, where large and economically strong nations are moving toward greater economic and political cooperation, small and economically dependent nations can hope to protect their room for maneuver only by following suit. In the case of the Caribbean, prospects for success of economic and social development initiatives could be greatly enhanced by regional cooperation. Attempts at regional collaboration and integration have a long and troubled history. Nevertheless, Caribbean leaders never lost sight of this goal; the establishment of the West Indian Commission headed by Sir Shridath Ramphal in November 1989 signifies one more instance of the recognition of its importance. Caribbean leaders will ignore the need for substantive progress in regional economic and political cooperation at their own peril and at that of the democratic aspirations of their people.

2 | CASES

6

The Eastern Caribbean States: Fledgling Sovereignties in the Global Environment

Vaughan A. Lewis

When, in 1983, the government of the Eastern Caribbean territory of St. Kitts and Nevis chose to exercise the option of full sovereign statehood, this choice by such a small entity could no longer be a surprise to the other sovereign members of the international community. In a sense the real surprise might well have been that the country was choosing to exercise this option at such a late stage.

The accession to independence of St. Kitts and Nevis in fact left only a very few of the smallest Anglophone territories of the eastern sector of the Caribbean archipelago, together with the very small territories under Dutch and French jurisdiction, in situations of constitutional dependency. For a variety of reasons, however, it seems unlikely that these entities will be tempted into the status of sovereign statehood in the near future.

The dissolution of the West Indies Federation in 1962 and the rapid accession of the larger states of the archipelago (Jamaica, Trinidad and Tobago) to independence, left the smaller British colonies of the Eastern Caribbean in a state of anomie—bewilderment as to how to proceed as far as their constitutional evolution was concerned. This sense of anomie was heightened when Barbados, with whom attempts were being made to form a smaller independent federation, decided in 1966 to proceed on its own to sovereign statehood and somewhat later to end its membership in the common monetary and currency arrangement that encompassed the

Eastern Caribbean states (the Eastern Caribbean Currency Authority) and to establish a monetary system and currency of its own.

It was in fact twelve years after the independence of Jamaica and Trinidad and Tobago that the first of the other Eastern Caribbean states, Grenada, decided that it should proceed to independence—a decision that gave rise to much domestic commotion as some sectors of the population sought to assert their opposition to the exercise of this option. Thereafter, and periodically between 1974 and 1983, other Eastern Caribbean states proceeded to independence, the leadership of each country inevitably arguing that while some form of political integration among these countries would have been preferable, there seemed to be no immediate option left except single-island statehood, given the urgent necessity to be able to take full advantage of opportunities for assistance for their economic development available from the international system.

The situation in the Anglophone Caribbean by the beginning of the 1980s, then, was one of political fragmentation, in the sense of being the opposite of the political integration of the region that was expected to be the case when active discussions on self-determination and self-government commenced in the period after the end of the Second World War. But the single-island-independence option was always felt by the political class of these countries to be somewhat unsatisfactory as a base for optimal economic development, given their perceptions of the constraints to development of small size, constraints widely advertised in the economic and sociological literature of the time.[1]

As a consequence, in the 1960s the leadership of the Caribbean countries adopted the main academic and policy recommendations proposed as an antidote to small-size constraints—the mechanism of regional economic integration. It was accepted that a process of regional economic integration could be established and pursued irrespective of the constitutional statuses of the participating countries. And in fact, the process was initiated in 1965 by three countries that, while well advanced in colonial constitutional status, were not independent—Barbados, Guyana, and Antigua. The proposal was intended to encompass the then independent states of Jamaica and Trinidad and Tobago; and by the time the Caribbean Free Trade Area (CARIFTA) agreement came fully into effect in 1968 these two latter countries had been joined in sovereign statehood by Barbados and Guyana.

The main operational distinction made within the CARIFTA agreement was in fact an economic rather than a constitutional one: the distinction being between the More Developed Countries (MDCs) and the Less Developed Countries (LDCs). On the other hand, the distinction did correspond with the two categories of the then independent and nonindependent countries, this in a sense reflecting the old British principle that fitness for self-government was to be demonstrated by indicating a capacity for economic viability.

As is well known, CARIFTA subsequently evolved into the Caribbean Community and Common Market, or CARICOM, indicating the desire of the member states for creation of an effective common market, along with strong institutions for cooperation in a number of functional spheres, and cohesion in the making and execution of foreign policy, particularly foreign economic policy.

While the Eastern Caribbean states assumed full membership first in CARIFTA and then CARICOM, as well as in the establishment of the Caribbean Development Bank, designed largely as a compensating mechanism for the LDCs in the integration process, it became apparent that their sense of anomie was not completely assuaged by such membership. In the 1960s the perception was still strong among these countries that autonomous activity even within the CARIFTA framework was an insufficient basis for economic and political viability and security. The territories of the Eastern Caribbean therefore set about establishing what could well be deemed a parallel set of cooperation and integration institutions specific to themselves. These institutions were intended to establish a general framework for managing existing areas of joint activity (judicial and monetary cooperation), for ensuring specific institutional arrangements for economic integration and development, and for providing a certain visibility and potential for unified activity in the limited spheres of foreign relations permitted by the U.K. government.

Thus were established in the second half of the 1960s the West Indies Associated States Council of Ministers (WISA) and the Eastern Caribbean Common Market, along with the Eastern Caribbean Commissions in London and Ottawa, quasi-diplomatic joint foreign representation institutions. The Eastern Caribbean Currency Authority (shorn of Barbados's participation) and the Eastern Caribbean Supreme Court remained in existence. And to these were added the Directorate of Civil Aviation for the Eastern Caribbean States, designed to assume responsibilities relating to air navigation, safety, and security previously undertaken by a broader British Caribbean institution; and the Eastern Caribbean Tourism Association (ECTA), concerned with providing visibility and capacity in tourism promotion and marketing.

This was a fairly wide array of associated institutions for a group of "non-self-governing" territories, even though some of the institutions did derive from the colonial orientation toward federal-type arrangements for small entities in geographical proximity. In some degree the grouping of institutions constituted a wider network of integration than that which came to characterize the CARICOM arena. And it did in some measure indicate the stronger sense of the constraints of small size operating in the minds of the Eastern Caribbean political leadership as against those of the leaders of the larger independent countries.

The onset of independence for the majority of Eastern Caribbean states between the mid-1970s and the mid-1980s brought in its train the decision to upgrade WISA, to consolidate most of the other cooperation institutions under the umbrella of the upgraded institution, and to give that institution full international legal personality. Thus was established, in 1981, through the Treaty of Basseterre, the Organization of Eastern Caribbean States (OECS), sitting, as it were, on a historical framework of progressive and successful institutionalized cooperation.

Almost contemporaneously the decision was taken by the same grouping of (OECS) countries to upgrade the Eastern Caribbean Currency Authority into a full-fledged Eastern Caribbean Central Bank (ECCB). The existence of the OECS and allied institutions such as the central bank can be seen as indicating the use of integration and cooperation institutions by these individual, very small entities in their search for economic development and for economic and political security.

The International Context of Caribbean Independence

The period of time between the assumption of independence by the large Caribbean states (in the early 1960s) and that of the smallest Eastern Caribbean states was characterized by substantial change in the nature of the international environment. The Caribbean states that came to independence in the 1960s were at least able to begin their sovereign existence in a period of relative global stability. The disorder subsequently engendered in world politics and within the United States by the Vietnam War was not yet evident. Though the Soviet Union was intent on active competition with the United States, within the hemisphere itself there could be little doubt as to American dominance. The United States was in 1962 (the year of Jamaican and Trinidadian independence) in a triumphant mood engendered by its "victory" in the Cuban missile crisis. And by 1965 (a year before the independence of Barbados and Guyana) the U.S. leadership reinforced its sense of dominance by quelling the uprising in the Dominican Republic. With the elaboration of the Alliance for Progress, the U.S. government exuded confidence in its capacity to assure hemispheric order and economic development. The newly independent Caribbean states easily accepted this order as potentially beneficial to themselves.

By the end of the 1970s, both the global economic and political climates had changed. Trends that had only been barely perceptible before were now clearly evident. In the arena of international economic relations the following began to impress themselves:

1. The old preferential systems that had managed and dominated international trade whether in agricultural or mineral commodities had gradually diminished in significance. For the Caribbean this gradual diminution was marked by a persistent shift in its trading and investment patterns away from the United Kingdom and toward the United States; and also by the decision of the United Kingdom to reapply for entry into the European Common Market, making clear that there would have to be a change in the Commonwealth preferential trading system that underpinned trade between herself and her Caribbean colonies and former colonies. In the wider world the rise of OPEC signaled the rising tide of economic nationalism, which itself brought in train negative and protective responses from the multinational corporations. Jamaica and Guyana took a leading role in forming an OPEC-type International Bauxite Association and in seeking to share in the assets the multinationals held in their countries and the profits they derived from them.

2. Weaknesses in the economic policy of the United States led to the end of the era of fixed exchange rates and a certain instability in the world monetary order.

3. The revolution in the technology of communications, associated with the development of the microchip and computerization, was effecting major changes in the possibilities for physical mobility (transportation) and for verbal and visual communication. Changes in transportation methods brought new possibilities for tourism expansion; changes in means of verbal and visual communication brought information and knowledge with new directness and speed, affecting cultural patterns and bringing to bear new ideological influences on populations.

4. Finally, demand for and prices of major mineral and agricultural commodities—the so-called export staples, which were the dominant sources of foreign exchange for most developing countries—were continuously unstable. In Jamaica, Trinidad and Tobago, and Guyana, the normal pace of economic activity substantially changed from the middle of the 1970s onwards for better, and then for worse, as a result of these movements in commodity demand and prices. The smaller Eastern Caribbean countries began to feel the effects of changes in world currency values on

the price of their main agricultural commodity—bananas—and on tourism arrivals patterns. In addition, the effects on the larger Caribbean countries of the decline in commodity prices and in the demand for some Caribbean commodities (e.g., bauxite) led to a decline in the availability of foreign exchange and a consequent decline in demand by those larger countries for the incipient industrial and agroindustrial products of the Eastern Caribbean traded within the context of CARICOM.

In one sense, the transformation in 1973 of CARIFTA into CARICOM (through the Treaty of Chaguaramas) was an indication of Caribbean governments' awareness of the implications of the environmental trends described above and of the need for some effective institutional response. CARICOM, grouping both independent and nonindependent Caribbean states, was in part intended to provide the independent countries with a greater diplomatic weight, and the nonindependent (Eastern Caribbean) countries with a diplomatic umbrella, for coping with these perceived and felt trends.

It was in fact under this umbrella that the governments of the largely nonindependent Eastern Caribbean countries (Grenada had become independent in 1974) were able to respond to the United Kingdom's reorganization of its relations with Europe, in the recognition that their institutional status as U.K. colonies would not entitle them to substantially different treatment from that accorded to independent states as a consequence of the negotiations between the United Kingdom and European Economic Community (EEC). These negotiations led the Caribbean countries into a new economic-cum-diplomatic framework, established in 1975 by the First Lome Convention. This meant the creation of the four-party network—Europe and Africa, the Pacific states, and the Caribbean states (the ACP bloc)—for participation in which the Caribbean recognized that it had to become, as a diplomatic unit, more institutionally cohesive if it was to be able to exercise influence and derive benefits. The deliberations leading to the First Lome Convention in fact began to induce into the thinking of the smaller nonindependent states considerations as to the significance of, and necessity for, sovereign statehood.

A further response on the part of the Caribbean states to the changing environment was indicated in what appeared to be an inclination toward a more active relationship with the United States.[2] The cooperative though largely passive relationship of the 1960s began to change, as a governmental response to the local economic nationalism thrust, the influence of the superpowers' ideological competition and the black power cultural-political influences emanating from the United States and penetrating the Caribbean cultural-political milieu. An upsurge of "left" and "populist" thinking in both the independent and the nonindependent states had its effect on the political leadership: in countries such as Jamaica and Guyana it led to a more critical stance, widely interpreted as anti-American, toward the United States. In Grenada by the end of the 1970s, it led to the establishment of the Peoples Revolutionary Government (PRG).

These trends foreshadowed the muted diplomatic division that came to characterize the Caribbean states in their response to both the post-Vietnam atmosphere of superpower competition and a rising Third World nonalignment thrust. In diplomatic terms, the Caribbean governments were seeking by the end of the 1970s to "cover" this division by agreeing to accept the need for "ideological pluralism." But by this time Dominica, St. Lucia, and St. Vincent and the Grenadines had become fully independent and were beginning to express reservations about the utility of the diplomatic orientation which Grenada had joined some of the larger colleagues in adopting. (A change of government in St. Lucia in 1979, however, led to a close alliance between St. Lucia and Grenada.) In this they were largely joined by the government of Barbados, while the government of Trinidad and Tobago preferred to adopt a muted stance of "nonintervention," asserting the view that small countries should not be operationally active (for or against) in disputes involving the superpowers.

Also in the second half of the 1970s, the Caribbean states became more aware of the significance of the geographical proximity to themselves of the states of South and Central America and of the need to establish some form of diplomatic relationship with them, in particular with those whose boundaries washed the Caribbean Sea. Within the framework of CARICOM, the Venezuela-Guyana territorial controversy had alerted them to the possible implications of what they saw as the predatory thrust of a country much larger than themselves. In relation to South and Central America, therefore, the prevalent attitude of the CARICOM governments, with their belief (strongly asserted by Trinidad and Tobago in particular) in the integrity and autonomy of a Caribbean defined largely in archipelagic and cultural terms, was that CARICOM should be both a protective shield and an instrument for dealing with their "Latin" neighbors.

But during this period Venezuela made a major diplomatic and aid thrust into the Eastern Caribbean states even though many still were not independent, a thrust to which the governments of these Associated States (of the United Kingdom), as they were called, were not unhappy to respond positively. In this way, along with their activities within the CARICOM framework, they were able to demonstrate the limited competence in foreign affairs the British government had granted them.

By the end of the 1970s, however, the largely passive attitude toward

South and Central America was changing as the new revolutionary government of Grenada sought to establish an alliance in diplomatic orientation with Sandinista Nicaragua. This of course reflected the changing nature of the Caribbean's geopolitical and ideological environment and added to the muted diplomatic division in the Caribbean Community, in which the newly emerging sovereignties of the Eastern Caribbean found themselves largely on the conservative side.

The international context of these states' new independence was, then, largely a context of turbulence. To this was added a growing regional (CARICOM and Caribbean Basin) economic and diplomatic instability. This was very different from the context of the early to mid-1960s, when Alexander Bustamante, the leader of the newly independent Jamaica, could (in 1962) confidently declare, "We are with the West"—a sentiment in which he was largely joined by the leaders from Trinidad and Tobago, Barbados, and Guyana as they took their countries into independence.

The OECS States in the Regional and International Context of the 1980s

By the beginning of the 1980s the small Eastern Caribbean countries were substantially independent states. Antigua and Barbuda attained sovereignty in 1981, and St. Kitts and Nevis, as indicated earlier, by 1983. Only Montserrat, the British Virgin Islands, and Anguilla remained constitutionally dependent on the United Kingdom. The decision of the independent entities plus Montserrat to form the Organization of Eastern Caribbean States reflected now a joint decision to maximize the possibilities for cooperation in order to take advantage of the economic and political situation with which they were faced both within CARICOM and within the wider international context.

This decision also reflected an acute sense of what they believed to be the disadvantages of small physical population and economic size, and the limited scale of operations in economic organization deriving from these. The political leadership was acutely conscious of the now widely emphasized propositions that small size inhibited the development of appropriate economies of scale necessary for the growth of cost-efficient industries, limited the size of the market that could become available as a domestic base for such industries, and therefore necessitated linkage of their separate markets and of their physical assets if a viable basis was to be provided for economic development.

The Caribbean Common Market Agreement (as part of the Treaty of Chaguaramas establishing the Caribbean Community) had also recognized the particular size disabilities of these Eastern Caribbean states. Thus the agreement granted the states described as LDCs special concessions, derogations, and incentives that amounted to special advantages vis-à-vis the MDCs, particularly in the area of industrial development. These special advantages were seen by the MDCs as compensatory measures designed to induce the LDCs to join in creating the wider market of CARICOM, which by international standards of comparison was itself still a small one.

The hope of the OECS countries was now to use their consolidated strength through the Eastern Caribbean Common Market, the compensatory measures, and the concessionary assistance provided by the Caribbean Development Bank as a basis for the organization of a variety of export-directed industries that would establish themselves in MDC markets as the MDCs themselves, with their infrastructural and historical advantages, moved on to more sophisticated levels of industrialization.

In some measure this objective began to be achieved. A number of what were referred to as "light" industries—manufacture of agro-based products such as coconut-based soaps and other detergents, textile goods based on imported raw materials, and leather goods, for example—were developed in this regard. But the LDCs soon found the economic climate beginning to turn against them as the MDCs, in particular Jamaica and Guyana, began to run into economic difficulty as a result of crises in foreign-exchange availability by the first half of the 1980s. During the course of the second half of the decade, the oil boom that had created a substantially widened market in Trinidad and Tobago itself began to peter out, and that country too became afflicted by a foreign-exchange crisis.

The response to economic crisis by the MDCs was the imposition of licenses and other nontariff barriers to trade on imports from CARICOM (as well as imports from the wider world), with direct effects on LDC exports. The prevailing situation in the CARICOM region has been well described by DeLisle Worrell:

> Caribbean countries' economic fortunes diverged markedly during this period. The Trinidad and Tobago economy grew because of new oil finds and high product prices, but at the expense of ongoing inflation. The Bahamas, Barbados, Belize and some of the Lesser Antilles [OECS states] were able to take advantage of revived demand for tourism and some agricultural products. Jamaica and Guyana were unable to cure their external imbalances, stimulate investment and increase supplies. They suffered continuous income loss, chronic balance of payments deficits and rising unemployment. . . . The next two years, 1980–81, saw a new round of inflation in the industrial world,

grimly attacked and defeated at the cost of severe recession. The new crisis plunged all Caribbean countries into difficulty. Inflation surged, real incomes fell, jobs were lost and external imbalances worsened. . . . The period since 1982 has been one of great uncertainty in international markets. . . . Jamaica and Guyana remain deep in the crisis of adjustment. Devaluation, trade controls and demand management have so far failed to cure the external imbalance and to establish a base for renewed growth.[3]

Thus the prospect of utilizing the CARICOM market as one channel for the pursuit of economic growth and export-led development began to fail to materialize as far as the OECS states were concerned. The MDCs of CARICOM themselves felt it necessary to undertake a series of unilateral economic policy measures that had beggar-my-neighbor effects in terms of CARICOM trade as a whole.

This situation led to a certain loss of confidence by the OECS countries in the CARICOM environment as a base for giving them a "jump-start" into export-led development. It induced consideration of a stronger emphasis on tourism development and agricultural diversification directed toward the wider extraregional economic environment as the basis for economic growth. In time this led the OECS governments to create a number of what might be called "joint infrastructural institutions" directed at providing them with platforms for action at the collective level to make up for their incapacity to organize these at a local (national) level. Thus at the end of the 1980s the Eastern Caribbean Investment Promotion Service, the Eastern Caribbean Export Development Agency, and the Eastern Caribbean Agricultural Diversification Coordination Unit were created. At the level of national economic policy, the creation of these institutions has been accompanied in many of the OECS states by measures of structural adjustment designed to diminish levels of public expenditure and provide some incentives for private sector–led growth.

In summary, then, the inability of the major countries in the CARICOM system to successfully carry through their domestic economic adjustments meant that the flanks of the regional economic system became weakened in terms of their capacity to undertake their attributed role of maintaining the coherence of the system. This left the smaller (mainly OECS) countries exposed and weakened the capacity of all countries in the region to sustain regional agreements in general.[4]

At the same time, the difficulties of the regional environment came, and persisted, at a period when the smaller entities felt the necessity to undertake three tasks simultaneously: (1) domestic economic adjustment involving a shift of resources from the government to the private sector; (2) the modernization of agriculture in the face of insecure long-term prospects for existing staples exports, particularly exports of bananas to the European Economic Community; and (3) finding concessionary resources for infrastructural investment to provide an adequate basis for expected foreign investment, which was seen as being the major propeller of economic growth and employment creation.

At the level of the international economic environment, by the end of the 1980s the governments of the OECS countries were becoming aware, too, of a variety of circumstances that would pose challenges to their traditional modus operandi. First, the framework of their relations with Europe was beginning to change. The creation of the European Single Market by the end of 1992 now posed the possibility of the end of preferential arrangements for their agricultural commodities—sugar and in particular bananas, whose production and export dominated the total exports of at least three of the countries (Dominica, St. Lucia, and St. Vincent and the Grenadines). The OECS governments had sought to ensure during their negotiations with the EEC (within the EEC-ACP framework) on the establishment of the Third Lome Convention that whatever changes occurred within the European Common Market would leave the protected status of their agricultural exports in a no less disadvantageous situation than currently existed.

The problem, however, was that with the insistence by a large number of EEC states that their common market should be *generally* liberalized and deregulated, a question arose about the capacity of the United Kingdom (with whom preferential arrangements had originally been agreed) to sustain the islands' position. This problem was, and is, exacerbated by the weak institutional (diplomatic) presence and representational capacity of the OECS countries in the countries of the European continent. Their limited constitutional capacity for foreign relations prior to independence had left them with a diplomatic presence only in Britain. Their ability to negotiate and lobby for their own case and interest has therefore been restricted in a situation made worse by their limited human and financial resources to sustain such activity.

Additionally now, the recently completed EEC-ACP negotiations toward the conclusion of a Fourth Lome Convention have seen a European acceptance of a widening of the Caribbean element of the ACP grouping to include the non-Anglophone Dominican Republic and Haiti. This has increased the number of countries required to share the concessionary-assistance component of the Convention, while the actual quantum of such assistance has not been substantially increased. The OECS and other

CARICOM countries view this development from the perspective that the Dominican Republic and Haiti now add a population of about 11 million to the Caribbean grouping, while those countries have per capita incomes below those characteristic of the majority of CARICOM countries. (This development has brought into relief a longstanding muted discussion within CARICOM on the "deepening versus widening" of the Caribbean Community, cognizant as the CARICOM countries have been of the fact that in terms of population they constitute a relatively small part of the Caribbean archipelago as a whole.)

A second aspect of the relevant international economic environment was the gathering insistence of the international financial community that the OECS countries, small and limited in resources as they might be, now had per capita incomes that took them out of the category of eligibility for fully concessionary financial assistance. The initiative from the World Bank in the second half of the 1980s that these countries were ready for "graduation" from eligibility for such assistance came as a shock to a grouping of states that hitherto had considered themselves to be LDCs within the restricted arena of the Caribbean Community.

In the face of this challenge, the OECS countries, with the help of other regional and extraregional governments, mounted a diplomatic initiative opposing the perspective of the World Bank. This was partially successful in that it achieved a temporary withdrawal of the World Bank decision. The OECS governments were aware, however, that the problem would still loom on the horizon and posed a severe impediment to their plans for further infrastructural development based on concessionary assistance channeled mainly through the Caribbean Development Bank. They continued, therefore, to insist that the peculiar disadvantages deriving from their status as very small island entities were deserving of special consideration by the international aid institutions.[5]

A third aspect of the countries' international economic environment in the 1980s concerned their relationship in terms of aid and trade with the United States. Following the U.S. intervention in Grenada in 1983 (to which I shall refer below), there developed a heightened interest on the part of U.S. officials in ensuring that increased flows of aid for infrastructural and private sector–led development were directed toward the OECS countries. In addition, these countries, along with the other CARICOM states, were encouraged to adhere to the Caribbean Basin Initiative (CBI) as a means of increasing the possibilities for trade and investment in the area.

As the geopolitical interest of the United States shifted to other areas of the globe, the OECS governments found that the aid levels began to decline, while the possibilities for trade through the CBI mechanism were limited by the exclusion of some areas in which the Caribbean might have been said to have a comparative advantage and by what they deemed exclusionary regulations (relating particularly to the areas of plant disease and veterinary medicine) that had the effect of inhibiting their agricultural exports.

The OECS governments tended, therefore, to argue that the CBI is incomplete as a measure for inducing trade or investment and that aid levels are too inconsistent to ensure the continuous development of institutions that would ensure the advancement of their potential for inducing development. Consequently, they began at the beginning of the 1990s to propound the view that what was required from the United States was a more holistic approach to trade, aid, and investment, an approach akin to that developed between themselves, as part of the ACP group, and the EEC under the Lome Conventions.

The Regional and International Political Environment

While the regional and international economic environment exhibited a certain instability during the course of the 1980s, in that period as well OECS governments began to develop concerns about the geopolitical environment. As the superpowers came increasingly into contention in the course of the 1970s, so too did the CARICOM countries. The situation by the end of the 1970s is instructive. Differences in ideological orientation and in strategies of development separated Jamaica and Guyana from most other countries of the region. In addition to pursuing what they asserted to be socialist strategies of economic development, those two states sought to forge diplomatic, economic, political, and cultural relationships with Cuba at precisely the time when political relations between the United States and the Soviet Union had begun to harden, Cuban international activity being one of the sources of this hardening.

By 1979 the United States was being influenced in its view of the Caribbean by two new circumstances. First was the overthrow of the government of Grenada led by Eric Gairy and its replacement by the PRG, which soon showed its determination to adopt a stance in foreign relations of anti-imperialism, nonalignment, and close relations with other hemispheric radical governments, including Cuba and Nicaragua. Second, and related to this, was the prospect of the creation of a nexus of states across the Caribbean Basin hostile to the United States—Nicaragua, Jamaica, Grenada, Guyana, Suriname. It should be recalled that in 1975 the United States had reacted with some nervousness to the use by Cuba of airports in the English-speaking Caribbean (including that of Barbados in the Eastern Caribbean) for the transport of troops and equipment to Angola. The United States would in that context see the development of new Cuban "allies" in the region as relating not simply to her defined security interest in the Caribbean Basin but, more important, to her wider global interests.

What is noteworthy here is that by the beginning of the 1980s a coincidence of concern had developed between some of the Caribbean states and the U.S. government and other governments in the hemisphere. First, the governments of the majority of the OECS countries that had reacted with some degree of fear at the nature of the removal of the Gairy government in Grenada and at the character of the regime that replaced it had their fears exacerbated by the radical (referred to as pro-Cuban) foreign policy of the PRG. Second, Brazil began to take a more severe view of the developing foreign-policy orientation of the new military regime in Suriname, and Venezuela developed a concern related to both Suriname and Grenada.

At this point the OECS governments began to consider a more institutionalized approach to regional security in the Eastern Caribbean and the means and appropriate diplomatic relationships required to develop this. In this consideration they were joined by Barbados. It should be noted that at this point only the government of Barbados had a standing army (defense force). Later the other governments were to develop within their police forces special security units capable of cooperating with the Barbados Defense Force in cases of emergencies within the subregion. The two hemispheric middle powers—Brazil and Venezuela—took the approach in the first instance of using diplomatic and material enticements in an effort to restrain the two radical regimes in their immediate environment from "excessive" foreign-policy radicalism.

Almost a year after the establishment of the RSS, in October 1983, Grenada's PRG, led by Prime Minister Maurice Bishop, was overthrown, the Prime Minister assassinated, and the regime replaced by one that the governments of the other OECS states assumed would likely be more radical than the one led by Bishop. As is well known, an alliance led by the United States and encompassing defense and security forces from Jamaica (now led by a conservative regime) and the members of the RSS intervened in Grenada and overthrew the military regime established there. I have elsewhere described in some detail my own view of the rationale for the approach taken by the OECS states to this intervention; however, some observations are in order.[6]

First, it had been apparent for some time that the discussions that had been ongoing over a period at the level of the CARICOM forum on the need for what was called "mutual security" were leading to no practical conclusion. Geographical distances, in addition to the differences deriving from the "ideological pluralism" characterizing the region, inhibited this. There was, therefore, prior to the establishment of the RSS, a certain institutional vacuum in the region as far as security arrangements were concerned. The limited military facilities of the OECS countries compared with the relatively extensive security apparatus (armies, coast guards, navies) of the larger CARICOM states obviously had left the OECS states with a sense of insecurity not felt by the larger countries. Up to October 1983, it appeared to the OECS governments that a collective consensus was lacking as to whether there was a regional environment requiring protection, as distinct from individual states with their own separate and particular security interests in need of protection. In the Eastern Caribbean the OECS governments had substantially taken the "regional environment" approach.

Second, certain kinds of questions merited consideration if operational plans for mutual security were to be put in place. At the narrower technical level:

a. What level of security capabilities could be derived from within the Caribbean?
b. What level of capabilities needed to be sought from outside the region if this was deemed to be necessary?
c. If recourse to extraregional sources for technical assistance was deemed necessary, how was this to be undertaken so as to maintain both the reality and the appearance of individual and collective sovereignty?
d. In the actual geopolitical situation of the Caribbean, what extent of diversity of foreign assistance was possible?

At a broader level:

a. What kinds of political crises could and should be met with indigenous sources of regional assistance?
b. What political circumstances would require recourse to extraregional assistance?

Within the CARICOM system, the approaches taken to some of these questions in the actual context of the Grenada intervention reflected differing senses of security and insecurity among the member states. Certainly the opposition to the intervention by Trinidad and Tobago and Guyana in particular reflected their greater sense of security and their possession of what they believed to be appropriate security and diplomatic capabilities for resolving the crisis in Grenada in a nonconflictual manner, and in a manner that would not require extraregional military assistance. As I have argued elsewhere, no consideration was given by them to the stronger sense of insecurity felt by the smaller Eastern Caribbean states and "to the perception of the RSS countries that such micro-states in close geographical proximity constituted in some measure a geopolitical community with a need for security arrangements based on mutuality and reciprocity of obligations."[7]

The Grenada intervention led to a furor in the United Nations and at the biennial meeting of the Commonwealth held in November 1983. Both meetings were characterized by a certain level of condemnation of the intervention, though the nature of the deliberations of the Commonwealth led to some degree of understanding of the position of the small Eastern Caribbean states, as well as to a consensus that the problem of small-state vulnerability was one of substantial significance to a large number of states in the international community, both small and large. A perceptive analysis of the problem was done by an independent team established by the Commonwealth Secretariat, and its findings, including practical recommendations, were subsequently published.[8] On the basis of these findings, the Commonwealth Heads of Government later recommended particular steps that could be taken by small states and forms of assistance that could be rendered by larger nations.

In the aftermath of the 1983 crisis, the U.S. government increased its security assistance to the OECS countries both on a bilateral basis and on a multilateral basis through the RSS. This gave rise in academic and journalistic circles to claims of undue "militarization" of the Eastern Caribbean. (In my view, the passage of time has shown that there was no objective basis for such claims.) What was more important was that by 1990 other states in the region seemed to have come to accept the view of the existing membership of the RSS that the system as it stood was incomplete and should include other CARICOM countries. This view was reinforced by the attempted coup d'etat in Trinidad and Tobago in June 1990, an event that extended into the period when a meeting of CARICOM Heads of Government was being held in Jamaica.

At the conclusion of that meeting a statement was issued, parts of which are worth quoting at some length:

> Having taken account of the increasing vulnerability of small states, including the small states of the Caribbean Community, to a range of external and destabilizing forces and in particular the recent crisis in Trinidad and Tobago, [Heads of Government] Adopted the following Resolution:

... *Recalling* ... that previous Meetings of Heads of Government and Meetings of the Standing Committee of Ministers responsible for Foreign Affairs of the Community had discussed various proposals in respect of arrangements for mutual security assistance but that no system had been put in place encompassing the Caribbean Community as a whole;

Noting however, that with the establishment of the Regional Security System in October 1982, arrangements covering some Member States of the Caribbean Community had been brought into existence and that such a system is also the basis for cooperative arrangements with other countries concerned with the maintenance of peace and security in the Region; ...

Agree on the necessity to review existing arrangements in support of regional security in order to provide a basis for assistance to all members of the Caribbean Community; and

Resolve that to this end, a Committee of Member States to be convened in Barbados should be established to give further consideration to this matter and report to the Chairman of Conference of Heads of Government before the next Meeting of the Conference, taking into account the experiences of the Regional Security System.[9]

This decision represented in effect a vindication of the approach taken by the OECS governments and Barbados in 1982 in establishing the RSS, an approach that was greeted at that time in many quarters as representing an inducement to foreign intervention and militarization, and in contradiction to the view that the Caribbean should be what was described as a "zone of peace."

Further Institutionalization within the OECS

Over the 1980s the countries of the OECS proceeded to undertake a process of harmonization of policies and laws and joint activities of a functional cooperation nature in a number of areas: creation of a single fisheries zone to take advantage of the two-hundred-mile exclusive economic zones through cooperative monitoring and surveillance and common procedures with regard to access to their fisheries resources; harmonization of civil aviation legislation and procedures through the Directorate of Civil Aviation; efforts at common promotion and marketing of tourism; and liberalization of the Eastern Caribbean Common Market, including the abolition of tariffs for most goods produced within the subregion and having an appropriate local raw material content.

Further, the challenges posed to these small states by the necessity to undertake negotiations to advance or protect their interests as a result of the European Community's approach to a Single Market; the governments' perception that a renegotiation of the Caribbean Basin Initiative and of a similar Canadian initiative, CARIBCAN, are necessary; and developments and experiences in other spheres, such as international aviation, have gradually led many of the Eastern Caribbean governments to the view that a greater centralization of the OECS decision-making process may be necessary, including more joint or collective representation in various international forums. In some countries (particularly among the governments of Dominica, Grenada, St. Vincent and the Grenadines, and St. Lucia) this has led to an expressed desire for some form of political unification.

The general inclination to create institutional and political harmonization does however appear to arise from the following: [10]

1. That there is the need to demonstrate to both aid donors and investors that a spatial framework for development projects of significant scale does exist and that there is a planning and implementation capacity of a certain degree of coherence to complement it. The experience of some of the countries with the banana industry in recent years indicated that if there is a framework for aggregation of productive capacity and a decision-making system to match it, then these small islands can meet the scale of production and scale economies necessary to sustain reasonable foreign demand requirements.

2. That the financial systems of the countries need to be aggregated and harmonized in such a manner as to indicate credible arrangements for sustained repayment of loans and for raising counterpart funds for projects large enough to make an impact on employment.

3. That these small countries need to aggregate their human resources to provide credible presences in international negotiating forums and in the international trading and investment marketplaces and that in this connection scarce and specialist intellectual talent requires a sufficient base for mobility and remuneration if it is to be retained in the subregion.

4. That while in the realm of tourism specific countries may have specific and differentiated attractions, the need to provide visibility in the metropolitan markets for tourism requires joint efforts at promotion and marketing and the aggregation of financial resources to support such efforts and that, further, to match the diversified attractions of geographically larger tourism destinations, a framework of multidestination tourism among the islands of the subregion is necessary and can only be coher-

ently achieved on the basis of joint planning and decision making to ensure, among other things, equitable distribution of benefits.

5. That multidestination tourism arrangements, the development of a capacity to meet the response to joint promotion efforts, and the current changes in international air transportation arrangements in particular all require a concerted approach to aviation arrangements for the subregion.

6. That developments deriving from the new Law of the Sea Convention require a coherent, joint approach to maritime delimitation matters, to foreign access to exclusive economic zones particularly in respect of fisheries, and to protection of the marine environment if the region's tourism industries are to have a sustained existence.

7. That for small island states sharing the semienclosed Caribbean Sea, a joint approach to maritime surveillance and mutual security arrangements is necessary; this requirement has been reinforced in the minds of decisionmakers in light of the dangers that the illegal movement of narcotic drugs now poses.

It is clearer now to many OECS leaders than it may have been some years ago that the arrangements for collective approaches to many of these areas of economic and functional cooperation require more secure and more centralized political decision-making machinery than now exists. Arrangements are being made for discussions concerning appropriate forms of such machinery and the appropriate timing for their implementation, though these will be subject to positive results from the popular referenda that are to be held.

It will easily be recognized that some of these requirements for relating to the international environment for the purpose of furthering development apply to the larger CARICOM system. Further, it would appear that in certain areas the OECS subregion itself does not constitute an optimally discrete geographical or functional zone and that the arrangements for political coordination that might be prescribed for that subregion could, for effectiveness, be more appropriately extended to a wider set of states within the Eastern Caribbean: one thinks immediately of the areas of tourism, aviation, education, and international representation in particular forums, in addition to the area of security, discussed above.

Some Conclusions from the Past and Issues for the Future

The Eastern Caribbean states, while in large measure not inclined to follow the economic and foreign-relations policy orientations pursued by some of the larger countries in the 1970s, would still have drawn from the latter's experiences the negative consequences of binding domestic and foreign policy within ideologically rigid confines. External circumstances, too, did in some degree force a certain caution with regard to the conduct of policy in the OECS subregion. As discussed earlier, the fact that the world economy was forced into a period of instability and recession as a consequence of successive oil price increases precisely at the time when the small countries were acceding to independence did serve to remind them of the difficulties of dependence on largely single-commodity sources of foreign-exchange revenue and the consequent problems of successful economic adjustment.

The majority of the OECS economies, therefore, managed to sustain some stability in this unstable regional and international context, the Eastern Caribbean Common Market becoming, toward the end of the 1980s, the single largest market for goods produced and traded within CARICOM. Nonetheless, it would be fair to say that all governments and policy analysts within the region had their sense of the smallness, fragility, and dependence of the countries' economies, and of the regional economy as a whole, reinforced as they saw both trade and growth decline in the area for much of the time.

The governments of the small Eastern Caribbean countries, unlike their larger counterparts, all remained within the single Eastern Caribbean Central Bank and so restricted their capacities to individually increase the money supply, which assisted in the maintenance over the period of their financial and economic stability. This approach to monetary arrangements might well have seemed to other Caribbean and developing countries as involving a compromise of their ability to exercise their newly won sovereignty. In fact, it can well be said to have helped to sustain such sovereignty as small countries can have in the modern financial and economic environment.

Many of the larger CARICOM states, in contrast, involved themselves in an overemphasis on the use of certain policy instruments deemed to be associated with the exercise of sovereignty: central banks as manipulators of the money supply, virtually nonconvertible currencies in terms of their use in regional trade, licenses of various kinds as nontariff barriers to trade in times of economic difficulty, and restrictions on capital flowing within the Common Market. All these were seen as instruments for reducing dependence and protecting the viability of the states' economies. In reality, they reduced cooperation among countries in the region, reduced the capacity of the trading regime to flourish, and in the medium term increased dependence.

This particular approach to the question of (economic) sovereignty reflected an orientation in the wider developing world prevalent in much of the socioeconomic literature concerning the concept of dependence. Caribbean policymakers and analysts have always had a strong sense of the smallness, fragility, and dependence of the states' open economies and of the regional economy, as well as of the sensitivity of the economies to shifts in international trading patterns or in the economies of their major trading partners. But the tendency has been to view these structural attributes as negatives to be diminished or removed, rather than to accept them as givens of the countries' international existence. There has also been a tendency to seek to use policy instruments to control the international environment rather than as means of selective adaptation to that environment. Perhaps because of the minute size of their economies and their extreme dependency, the smaller Eastern Caribbean states have been more prone up to now to accept dependency as given, to recognize the need for adaptation, and to use the available instruments provided by sovereignty as means for regional cooperation.

It would seem appropriate at this juncture in Caribbean economic development to recognize that as many small countries as large ones in the global economy have attained viable economic existences and much wealth—historically small countries such as Switzerland and Luxembourg; in the contemporary period the "dragons" in Asia, including Singapore, whose landmass is almost exactly the size of St. Lucia's. These countries all recognize or have recognized that policy flexibility and structural adaptation are the name of the game, combined with a persistent political stability and training and retraining of human resources so that flexibility in the use of the labor forces can be made to respond to policy flexibility and the need for structural adaptation as external markets change their demands.

Policymakers in these countries have recognized, too, that a proper integration into surrounding larger, viable economies and even into economic systems dominated by multinational corporations is a requirement for their own viable economic growth. They recognize that such integration imposes constraints at some levels of policy making, constraints on "sovereignty" in economic, financial, and monetary policy making. The Benelux countries' currencies follow and are constrained by the behavior of the German mark, but those countries recognize that the link gives their economies a certain stability.

There are, then, enough successful small-economy countries in our present world to remove from the minds of policymakers undue pessimism about the possibilities for viable growth of the small Caribbean economies. The Eastern Caribbean area, for example, defined to encompass the OECS countries, Barbados, and Trinidad and Tobago, has a population about equal to that of Singapore, and many more "natural endowments" either for industrial and agricultural production or for tourism than exist in that country. The CARICOM area also has, however, a series of man-made impediments to effective aggregation of the commodities available for production, to the effective flow of capital and human resources, and to the effective promotion of and investment in the endowments available for tourism development. And it is these, rather than the CARICOM countries' dependence on the major economic powers of the world, that create weakness.

The challenge for the Eastern Caribbean countries, as well as, it might be said, for the larger states, would appear to be to find a form of institutional management for their integration process that enhances the possibilities for further integration even where the instruments of such management seem in the short run to constrain "sovereignty." A major deficiency of Caribbean as well as other Third World integration systems has been their inability to sustain the implementation of policy measures—either because there appear to be short-term losses or because sectoral interests having some influence in these democratic and populist systems can impede measures deemed to be disadvantageous to them. Current difficulties being experienced in the Caribbean Common Market in the course of the implementation of a common external tariff are illustrative of this problem. It remains to be seen whether the currently ongoing discussions for widening further coherence of the OECS integration, either through further centralization of the integration control and implementation measures or through some form of political unification, will lead to conclusions that meet the challenge as it has been described here.

Finally, a challenge exists in the future capacity of these small states to advantageously adapt to external initiatives that have the effect of redefining the geopolitical configuration of the region, and of its immediate environment, in ways that governments may not have anticipated. Two examples of this process might be given. First, as the Caribbean countries have responded to Europe's redefinition of its own regional economic environment and of its aid and trade relationship with the Third World through the mechanism of the Lome Convention, the Anglophone Caribbean countries have been forced, as I have hinted above, to consider the redefinition of the CARICOM region as defined by themselves. This is the "deepening versus widening" issue, involving the question whether countries such as Haiti and the Dominican Republic, and even subsequently Cuba, should have a place in the Caribbean Community and Common Market. This would appear to correspond with external indications of what might be desirable, as the EEC, for example, seeks to deal and negotiate with the totality of these countries as, in some sense, a single bloc. This has given rise to fears in the Anglophone countries that their small size might lead to a situation in which they could be "swamped" by countries with larger populations and lower per capita incomes.

The establishment by the CARICOM Heads of Government, at their meeting in Grenada in 1989, of a West Indian Commission (under the Chairmanship of Sir Shridath Ramphal, the former Commonwealth secretary-general) to examine the process of Caribbean integration as it has developed so far and to look at the implications of establishing institutionalized relationships with other Caribbean states indicates at least a recognition of the problem and the challenge.

A second example inheres in the decision of the major hemispheric powers—the United States, Canada, and Mexico—to negotiate a free trade area and to subsequently offer some form of participation to other hemispheric countries. Again, this has given rise to fears in the Anglophone Caribbean that any potential benefits from even a renegotiated Caribbean Basin Initiative would be reduced and that the CARICOM states, with limited financial resources, small labor forces, and small markets, might be unable to sustain themselves in the competitive economic process that the greater free trade area implies.

In fact, seen from the perspective of this global level, the North American free trade area initiative would seek to reduce the distinction maintained in the CARICOM area between small and large countries and economies, placing them all on the same plane. And it raises for all governments in CARICOM the question whether their Common Market is seen, from the international perspective, as an economic space capable of effective organization and coherence for development and maintenance of a "Caribbean" identity.

For the Anglophone Caribbean countries, and for the smaller entities of the Eastern Caribbean in particular, the learning process in international relations has had to be swift. And these fledgling sovereignties are now faced with little time to develop capabilities or strategies for dealing with their changing global environment.[11]

7 | Structural Adjustment and the Ethnic Factor in Caribbean Societies

Selwyn Ryan

Many Caribbean societies are currently undergoing what have been euphemistically described as structural adjustment policies. The policies involve, among other things, the downsizing of the public sector, the privatization of resources previously owned and managed by the state or parastatal bodies, and the transfer of resources from the urban to the rural areas in the interest of stimulating food production and trade reforms, the aim of which is to provide positive signals to would-be exporters and to reduce or eliminate the protection previously given the local manufacturing sector. The structural adjustment policies also involve the introduction of "realistic" foreign exchange rates, the switching of expenditure from consumption to production, economic pricing of goods and services, especially for utilities, health and educational services, and the progressive attenuation of welfare subsidies of one kind or another.

Some Caribbean territories now have in place formal arrangements with the World Bank (IBRD) and the International Monetary Fund (IMF) that tie these policies to phased inflows of funding from international agencies or commercial banks. This formal link exists with respect to Jamaica, Guyana, Barbados, and Trinidad and Tobago. Other territories, while not formally strapped to the IMF or the IBRD, have begun to pursue similar policies in an attempt to forestall the need to enter into forced relationships with them.

In most cases, analysts, including those attached to the IBRD and the IMF, have focused on the implications of structural adjustment policies for the economic and social well-being of the society as a whole as well as for selected underprivileged groups at the pedestrian levels of the society, such as workers in overmanned public- and private-sector companies and women, who are said to suffer more than their male counterparts when such policies are put in place. The focus has been primarily on the class and gender implications of the new economic policies.

This chapter seeks to focus on the impact that structural adjustment policies have had and are likely to have not only on the poor but also on the future relationships between ethnic groups in Trinidad and Tobago and Guyana. The argument is that structural adjustment policies could well erode whatever gains have so far been made in terms of creating a less race-conscious society and could in fact lead to an intensification of ethnic rivalries. The chapter also argues that new "power-sharing" arrangements have to be worked out and put in place if political and social collapse in the face of increased competition for dwindling economic resources is to be avoided.

The Case of Trinidad and Tobago

Trinidad and Tobago is a society in which two "racial" groups are evenly balanced in numerical terms. According to the 1980 census, the two groups—one African, the other East Indian—each account for roughly 42 percent of the population. Fourteen percent of the population is of mixed "racial" ancestry, primarily European and African and African and Indian, with the remainder being of European, Chinese, or Syrian ancestry. Between 1956 and 1986 the twin-island state was governed by the Peoples National Movement (PNM), support for which came primarily from the African and mixed population. Despite many challenges to its hegemony over the thirty-year period, the PNM survived because of a combination of factors. Of primary importance was the leadership of Eric Williams. Williams captured the imagination of many Trinidadians and Tobagonians in 1955–56, and many of these and their children continued to remain loyal to him up until his death in March 1981.

The PNM also survived because, for most of the period, the economy showed positive growth, and the government was able to expand levels of employment; increase wages; extend infrastructural facilities; and provide more, and to a degree better, facilities in the areas of health, education, and social services. Given the availability of financial resources, especially after 1974, when the price of oil was increased because of the activities of the Organization of Petroleum Exporting Countries (OPEC), patronage was also disbursed to a large number of persons who were grateful to the party and remained dependent on it. These included project workers, low-income homeowners, and renters who were placed in the housing developments built by the state and offered low-mortgage interest rates or low rents.

Many Afro-Trinidadians did not agree with allegations that they were the prime beneficiaries of state patronage under the PNM regime. In their view, they received the "crumbs," while businessmen belonging to the Indian, European, Chinese, and Syrian communities received most of the lucrative contracts that were available over the period, particularly in the boom years. They were also not unequivocal in their view that they were dominant in the public sector, as is widely asserted, especially by Indo-Trinidadians. In a survey conducted by the author in 1984, 46 percent of the Afro-Trinidadians in the sample were of the view that Indo-Trinidadians had preferred access to jobs and promotional opportunities in the public sector, while only 12 percent felt that Afro-Trinidadians had preferred access. By comparison, 55 percent of the Indo-Trinidadians felt that Afro-Trinidadians were more favored in this regard.

Many citizens of African and mixed descent were of the view that the continuation of whatever access they enjoyed to resources (or hoped to enjoy) was dependent upon the preservation of PNM rule. They were demonstrably unwilling to share public resources and symbolic space with other ethnic groups, not only because they regarded these as scarce but because they deemed them to be their legitimate and prescriptive right by reason of their earlier historical presence in the territory and the greater proximity of their culture and patterns of behavior to the superordinate colonial culture by which public norms are referenced.

Despite the enormous advantages the PNM enjoyed as a party in terms of the structure of Trinidad and Tobago society, the party was overwhelmingly defeated in December 1986 by the National Alliance for Reconstruction (NAR), a coalition of opposition parties, dissident PNM elements, and new voters. The NAR received 67.3 percent of the popular vote and obtained thirty-three of the thirty-six seats in the legislature. The PNM, which was supported by 31.24 percent of the electorate, won the remaining three seats. With the collapse in the price of petroleum from twenty-six dollars per barrel in the early eighties to nine dollars per barrel in 1986, there was little money available to "bribe" the underclass electorate in Trinidad's politically critical East-West Corridor. The cutbacks in petroleum-driven public-sector expenditure also affected employment in the private sector, which depended heavily on the pump-priming activities of the state sector.

Many noneconomic factors, however, contributed to the NAR victory. The victory of the NAR was the culmination of almost a half-century of effort to unite the sectionally and ideologically fragmented opposition parties. The concept of a united front was first adumbrated in 1946 and underwent many transformations before becoming a reality in 1985–86. In the 1985–86 version, all the opposition parties and political outgroups, the National Joint Action Committee (NJAC) excepted, came together to present a unified alternative to the PNM under a leader who was sociologically acceptable to all. That the NAR also had in its ranks many former PNM stalwarts also helped to neutralize the race factor. Some of the candidates and visible members were also members of the PNM. Blacks therefore now felt safe in carrying through with the disposition to change that had long been indicated in the opinion polls.

While it is true that Indians and minority elements voted in substantially larger numbers for the NAR and against the PNM, this had invariably been the case in elections between 1956 and 1981. That the NAR won the election thus had less to do with the fact that Indians and minority groups financed and voted overwhelmingly for it (in the Indian-dominated constituencies the NAR invariably won 80–85 percent of the popular vote) than with the fact that about 45 percent of the black electorate voted for the NAR, with larger proportions as one went up the social class scale. The middle- and upper-middle-class mixed and black elements supported the NAR, while the bulk of the black underclass stayed with the PNM.

The split in the black electorate allowed the NAR to win key seats along the Corridor. If one were to look clinically at the electoral returns in areas where people of African or mixed ancestry predominated, one would find that the PNM did much better than the global figures suggested. Whereas the party received 31 percent of the popular vote nationally, it won 41 percent of the vote along the urbanized East-West Corridor, where it had always been dominant. In certain constituencies along the Corridor, the PNM was only defeated because of the overwhelming support the NAR received from voters of Indian, white, and mixed ancestry.

Events following the election revealed just how fragile the coalition was. Indeed, the coalition began to crumble within its first year in office. The triumph of the NAR in December 1986 had generated a wave of optimism that the country had at last found a political vehicle to give expression to its hopes for creating a genuine multiracial and multicultural community. Instead of neutralizing the race factor, however, the election result served to activate group consciousness and struggle over the spoils of office. Compounding the problems facing the coalition were the dire economic circumstances that faced the country because of the excess of expenditure over revenue and because of the bunching of its short-term external debts and the shortages of foreign exchange, with all that this meant for the country's ability to import plant, raw material for industry, food, and other basic necessities.

In December 1988 the prime minister and the minister of finance noted that whereas in 1984 external debt servicing was 18 percent of total merchandise exports, by 1988 it had doubled to 36 percent and was expected to rise to 42 percent by 1990 if no rescheduling agreement was put in place. After at first resisting advice that it should go to the IMF as a condition of getting both its debt to commercial banks rescheduled and badly needed foreign exchange support, in 1988 the NAR decided that there was no other alternative but to do so. Prime Minister Robinson noted that given the conditionalities attached to the IMF loan, going to the Fund was not a decision that was lightly taken:

> Given the falling price of oil in 1988 and the squeeze being imposed by the commercial banks, a failure to go to the IMF would have resulted in a curtailment of the population's consumption and welfare that would have been intolerable. The entire society would have ground to a halt. One could have sought to reschedule the foreign debt, but that was impossible without the cooperation of the IMF. The implications of not going to the fund were therefore serious.
>
> The resources available to the Government in 1989 would have been TT $1,213 million less. This is more than half the 1987 wages and salaries bill. In other words, without a Fund agreement, it would have been necessary to cut our wages and salaries bill by some 50 percent or alternatively, make similar draconian cuts in our welfare appropriations, capital programme and goods and services. However hard people think things are now, please be assured that they would be far harder if we did not obtain the inflows of foreign resources we have now managed to obtain.[1]

The prime minister indicated that the policies being put in place had not been forced upon him by the IMF. They were his policies, designed to restructure Trinidad and Tobago for independence, an extremely serious and difficult task. In his view, "Trinidad and Tobago had come to the end of one era when the state was seen as a tireless mother and now stood at the threshold of another."

For a long time, certain unhealthy and dangerous notions have been propagated in our society. They included the notion that the state could somehow be a tireless mother, forever providing, a guarantor of welfare, and a haven of security, while making no demands of effort and energy on our part. There was also the propaganda that hard work bore no necessary relation to our survival and success. Now all of this must change . . . when we talk about restructuring in Trinidad and Tobago, we are talking about restructuring for the 21st century. The country has to be prepared for the 21st century. Some heads may be knocked together. Some people may be shaken. All that is part of it.[2]

Ethnic Politics and the Rationalization of the Sugar Industry

Compounding the resource reallocation process was the government's decision to push ahead with plans to rationalize the country's state-owned sugar industry, Caroni Ltd., which has been a major drain on the treasury. Between 1975 and 1990 the company accumulated TT $2.2 billion in deficits and an annual deficit of TT $180 million largely because the cost of producing sugar was well below the price at which it sells on the international and domestic markets. In 1987–88 it cost Caroni TT $5,000 to produce one ton of sugar; with the rationalization measures introduced by the company, the cost was reduced to TT $3,600, but the break-even price was about TT $2,600. According to one calculation, it cost taxpayers TT $235,000 per worker over and above wages and benefits between 1975 and 1988 to keep Caroni in operation. In the view of some, including the IBRD, the industry was not viable.

The government's plan was to cut sugar production to seventy-five thousand tons by 1993, and to produce this entirely for the domestic market. This involved closing down one of the two major sugar refineries. It also meant leaving the growing of canes entirely to peasant farmers, leasing some of the lands released from sugar to farmers to produce agreed crops, and including the remainder of the land in a national program of land distribution for the production of crops other than sugar cane. The policy also involved the retrenchment of some seventy-five hundred workers over a five-year period and the creation of a new joint-venture commercially oriented company that would be responsible for the development and marketing of products produced by Caroni under its diversification thrust.

The NAR's decision to come to grips with the Caroni issue gave rise to an intense debate as to what should be done with the industry and those whose livelihood and social relations were defined by sugar. One view was that the cultural context of the industry should be the defining concern. It was argued that in the wake of emancipation and the introduction of indentureship, two cultures emerged in Trinidad—the creole culture, which was identified with the urban areas, and the Indian culture, which was associated with the rural population. Indian culture and the sugar industry came together in practice and worked as a total system. The plantation was not only an economic system but a social system as well, in that it looked after many of the welfare, recreational, and religious needs (festivals, etc.) of the sugar worker. It underpinned the sugar worker's entire existence, including that of his relationship with his extended family. To quote John La Guerre, senior lecturer and head of the Department of Government of the University of the West Indies, St. Augustine, Trinidad:

> There are now about 10,000 workers on the payroll of CARONI Ltd.
> In most cases they are the major providers for their respective families.
> To remove this source of livelihood is to strike at the very basis of the
> family. Retraining at this stage of their lives is not easy. Having been
> socialised for generations into what was described as "the discipline of
> the plantation," it would not be easy to make the transition from one
> way of life to another. One immediate consequence would be the ero-
> sion in the status of the head of the household and ensuing instability
> in the family unit.[3]

The sugar industry must thus be viewed differently from those other state enterprises that were being rationalized, La Guerre argued. "It must be regarded as a special case and its proposed restructuring must be handled with care and understanding." La Guerre agreed, however, that it was just as important to take into account social and cultural factors in the restructuring of the public service and the security services, which are "largely dominated by the African descended community."

It was argued further that reducing the amount of sugar produced and the consequent displacement of seventy-five hundred workers would destroy the economic viability of the Indian community. It would affect not only the sugar worker and the cane farmer but also many firms that supplied services needed by the industry and firms that supplied the basic and other needs of those who lived and worked in areas linked to the industry. The surrounding community would die economically, according to La Guerre, who also noted that those workers who had been displaced over the years had received so little by way of compensation that they were able to do little with it. "The displaced workers are now making greater use of the pawn shops," he complained. The social consequences would be equally traumatic: "Instead of groups, one would have atomized individuals. The community would have disintegrated. One of the first casualties would be religion. Without the support of other institutions, the displaced workers and their families would be easily tempted to find salvation in one fundamentalist sect or another. A disintegrated community also provides a fertile ground for the emergence of extremist leaders and radical social movements."[4]

La Guerre's views were challenged by others who argued that it was a fallacy to say that Indian culture could not survive without sugar or land or that the economic future of Indians in Trinidad and Guyana was somehow tied to sugar, when there was evidence to the contrary. The dominant view in the Indian community, however, was that articulated by Dr. La Guerre.

Given the inability of the state to find the cash to compensate workers adequately, Caroni's governing board recommended that workers be compensated partly in cash and partly in land. The board proposed that 5,535 acres be distributed in 1988, and 7,880 acres each in 1989 and 1990. This proposal, however, sparked a great deal of controversy. It was welcomed by most workers (though not by all of them: some wanted only cash) but was generally rejected by the non-Indian community. Supporters of the board's plan argued that if the sugar industry was to be wound up, the assets should go to those who had worked in it for the last 150 years and who had saved it from destruction after the plantations were abandoned following emancipation. Moreover, as La Guerre argued, "if the objective is to establish cane production on the lands so distributed, one expects that the criteria for award would ensure that only those with the necessary experience and skills would receive lands for cane farming."

Several arguments were adduced by those opposed to the policy of "land to the Indians" in the sugar industry as compensation. One view held that the descendants of the African slaves also had some residual claim to that land. They were entitled to their "grandfather's backpay." Others claimed that several thousand black urban workers had lost their jobs over the last five years and many have received little or no compensation, either in cash or in kind, from the assets of companies that had gone into receivership or out of business. Why should Indian workers be treated differently? In their view, equity demanded that the lands the state held in trust for the nation should be made available to *all* nationals who wished to cultivate land as a means of earning a livelihood. And indeed, one of the reasons why Indians have suffered less deprivation as a result of growing unemployment is that many either had family land or squatted on nearby state lands, on which they planted crops for sale or home consumption. Any policy that failed to recognize that a desire for land on which to grow food was not limited to the Indians but was also becoming an Afro-Trinidadian preoccupation would be robustly opposed by the African community.

Given the controversy and the hostility of the Indian community to the proposals, the issue was shelved, at least for the time being, and when and how the matter would be resolved in the future remains unknown. All that can be said is that the Africans will resist any plan to hand Caroni lands over to the Indians, and the Indians, who feel that Caroni is their *Janma Bhoomi* (motherland) in a sociological sense, will insist that the state treat them with the same solicitude that they claim was shown to Africans in the public service, the utilities, and the state enterprises.

IMF Success Story or Classic Failure?

Throughout 1989 and 1990 a number of sharply conflicting views were expressed about the economic and political viability of Trinidad and Tobago and its ability to regain the levels of development achieved in the mid-seventies and early eighties. Some analysts were optimistic, while others were very pessimistic. Government spokesmen affected to believe that a turnaround in the economy was imminent. In his 1990 Budget Speech, the minister of finance, Selby Wilson, told the country that the major indicators suggest that "there is considerable room for optimism." The minister also told Parliament that a mood of optimism pervaded the country:

> There is a new feeling of hope, a new confidence, a realisation that
> our sacrifices have not been in vain and that there is now in place
> an economic framework which is conducive to the expansion of the
> economy, and to the participation of all sections of the community
> in productive economic activity. In terms of the production perfor-
> mance, the available indicators suggest that the long period of eco-
> nomic stagnation is bottoming out and that the economy is poised for
> a slow but steady upward advance. The preliminary data suggest that
> real GDP in 1989 may have declined by 3.7 per cent. This, it must be
> stressed, compares with a decline in real GDP of 4.3 percent in 1988,
> 6.7 percent in 1987 and a cumulative decline of over 20 percent be-
> tween 1983–1986.[5]

The Central Bank's 1990 *Annual Survey* revealed that real gross domestic product (GDP) in fact fell by 2.4 percent in 1989, compared with 4.7 percent in 1988. The overall balance of payments deficit in 1989 fell to

3.5 percent of GDP, compared with 3.7 percent in 1988. The current account deficit, however, widened from 2.4 percent of GDP to 2.8 percent owing to higher interest payments, which caused a deterioration of the investment income account.

Some businessmen and business spokesmen, while being realistic, also saw the light at the end of the tunnel, however long that tunnel might be. They claimed that many businesses were becoming leaner (a euphemism for saying they have fired excess staff), more cost-conscious, and more resilient and that they were poised to take advantage of the "takeoff" when it occurs. They noted too that there has been some upward movement in share prices and renewed activity in the construction industry, particularly in the area of housing.

Some outside observers were also optimistic. Courtney Blackman, former governor of the Central Bank of Barbados, expressed the view that Trinidad and Tobago might well be the success story for which the IMF was searching: "To outsiders looking in, Trinidad and Tobago provides a fascinating case study of the structural adjustment process, complete with currency devaluation, IMF Standby Agreement, fiscal reform, privatisation and incomes policy—the whole works. So far the country has passed all its performance tests. It could well become the success story which the Fund sorely needs after numerous failures in the debt-distressed Third World."[6]

Ironically, after announcing in the 1991 Budget Speech that it would not draw down the second tranche of its loan entitlement from the IMF because of the rise in oil prices that followed in the wake of the Gulf War, the government was forced to introduce a mini-budget in April 1991 when oil prices in fact fell. It estimated that there would be a budgetary shortfall of TT $228 and that the drawdown from the IMF would have to be made after all.

Academic critics of the government claim that official talk about turn-around, whether "incipient," "imminent," "impending or prospective," was hopelessly naive. In the view of Dennis Pantin, an economist at the University of the West Indies, Trinidad and Tobago was headed straight for the "Valley of Debt." Pantin made comparisons with the Jamaican experience to show that Trinidad was likely to experience a fate similar to that of its CARICOM partner:

> Heedless of all of the evidence about the negative impact of IMF/World Bank policy, the Trinidad and Tobago Government has been negotiating a World Bank SAL. The proposed loan is for US$ 40 million, disbursed over two years. There is the expectation of an equivalent

sum from the Japanese Export-Import Bank, subject to acceptance of
the World Bank loan. At best, therefore, we can expect US$ 40 mil-
lion from both sources in the first year. The conditions attached to
the World Bank loan will, however, convert our undoubtedly difficult, but still manageable, economic problems into a full-blown economic crisis. We justified the IMF Agreement on the basis of finding
an "orderly solution" to our debt bunching problem. In next to no
time, we will be rationalizing further IMF agreements on the basis
that "we have no choice," because we have no foreign exchange to
repay all of these additional foreign loans.

We do have a choice. We can refuse the World Bank loan. We can
also reduce our foreign borrowing to the absolute minimum. Unless
good sense prevails or the pressure of public opinion wins out, this
country will unwittingly blunder its way into the Valley of Debt.[7]

Another economist, Lloyd Best, regarded the talk about turnaround as
the by-product of the monumental ignorance or innocence of the intellectual class in Trinidad and Tobago.

It is a confusion sown by a failure to grasp that there is no chance of
restoring the old equilibrium to the economy—barring an act of God
which, by its nature, can bring only a temporary respite. We could
conceivably enjoy new hydro-carbon rents for a while but after they
are done, we would be back to square one, or worse, if realism is
postponed in the interim, as it would be, if a long season of austerity
did not result in a change in our preferences, our tastes, our habits
and above all, in the experience we would have had in facing up to
adversity. In the context, the first task of a competent management is
not to moot the restoration of the old equilibrium and therefore to
imply that a turnaround is somehow an automatic or at any rate a
comparatively simple process. No, the first task of a competent management is to acknowledge that the economy has been and still is
tending ineluctably towards a new equilibrium which is not at all
to be confused with the old one for at least one explosive social and
political reason. The reason is that, measured in terms of income
and employment, the new equilibrium cannot but be reached at an
immensely lower level of activity than the one we enjoyed at the
height of the boom.[8]

Trinidad's problem, in Best's view, was not the gnomes and dragons of the
World Bank or the IMF. The problem was that the politicians, with their
short-term political preoccupations, were not leveling with the people and

not telling them "what is to be done" to stop the rot. Lamented Best, "The worst is yet to come!"

The IBRD and the Economic Commission for Latin America and the Caribbean (ECLAC) agreed that the economic problems facing the country were deep-seated and likely to become worse at least in the short run. According to ECLAC, the per capita product fell by 41 percent in Trinidad and Tobago between 1980 and 1989. The IBRD also noted that the forms and conditions attached to the structural adjustment loan imposed additional strains on the country's population in the short run. Unemployment is seen to be the most critical issue. While the labor force grew by almost 43,000 by 1989 (from 445,000 in 1982), the economy lost 23,000 jobs over the same period. Average unemployment, which stood at around 15 percent of the labor force in the mid-1970s, had fallen by 1982, the end of the boom, to about 10 percent. By the first quarter of 1988 it had increased to almost 23 percent (or 111,000), and it was concentrated in the young, with more than 40 percent of the unemployed in the 15–24 age category. The IBRD expected unemployment to rise in the coming months as the public sector was downsized.

The IBRD also noted that wages in the private and public sectors, both nominal and real, had declined. In the public sector the wages and salaries bill was reduced by over 60 percent in real terms over the period 1982–88, although the number of public servants remained relatively stable. Cuts in public-sector spending also eroded living standards. To quote the IBRD's report:

> Standards of Living have been affected by the sharp decline in the level of Government investment and services. Since 1982, annual investment has been cut by more than 90 percent in real terms; and recurrent expenditure by more than 50 percent. In real terms, the overall spending on health and education has been cut by about two-thirds. The welfare programs, predominantly old age pensions, social assistance and food subsidies, and the school feeding program, have remained at about five percent of total recurrent expenditure, representing a halving in real terms. The same broad sectoral pattern of expenditures, has been maintained over the period, implying mostly a strategy of cuts across-the-board rather than rigorous priority setting. The necessity to sharply reduce transfers to public utilities and to increase tariffs exacerbates the potential for declines in living standards.[9]

The bank also admitted that "poverty appears to be on the increase, though it may not have reached crisis proportions."

Data collected in 1989 by Ralph Henry, an economist at the University of the West Indies, indicates that 264,000 people, or 22 percent of the population, live below the poverty line. That line was drawn at TT $288.47 per month (U.S. $68) for a single person.[10] The poor include not only the "old poor" but the "new poor," who had been employed during the boom years but are now on the bread line. According to the secretary of a Catholic charity, "The new poor used to be domestics, temporary project workers, store clerks, linesmen, construction workers or people who ran small businesses. They were retrenched or can't get work anymore. They can't pay their rents or mortgages. If they are forced to pay their mortgage so that they do not lose their house, they can't pay for anything else. They can't even buy food."[11]

Up to the end of 1989, workers and the unemployed behaved with a great deal of maturity and restraint in the face of the economic crisis. They grumbled and protested in various ways, including a one-day show of resistance that effectively shut down much of the public sector. But they did not follow their counterparts in Caracas, Santo Domingo, Egypt, and other parts of the Third World by taking part in violent street protests and vandalism in commercial centers. There was always the question, however, whether they would continue to act with such restraint or whether some unplanned incident might occur that would trigger social convulsion, as was the case in 1970.

In the early months of 1990, trade unions threatened to bring the country to a halt after the Carnival celebrations ended. Errol McLeod, president of the Oilfield Workers Trade Union, told workers on February 16, 1990, to "gird themselves for an intensification of struggle against the government adjustment policies."

> After the masquerading on Monday and Tuesday, the mass mobilisation of people will start and we will see the biggest assembly of poor people, bigger than anything that we may have seen in the 1970s. We are going to fill up Woodford Square and we are not just going to go around any Parliament. We are going to occupy the whole of Port of Spain and nothing is going to run in the Trinidad and Tobago Electricity Commission (T&TEC) or in the oil industry. Not a bus is going to move, not a teacher will go to work. It will be like the day the earth stood still.[12]

McLeod was at the time addressing a rally called by trade unions and other political, social, and religious organizations that had grouped themselves into a new coalition (the Summit of Peoples Organizations). The coalition called upon the government to break off dialogue with the IBRD and the IMF and reverse the policies that had been put in place to downsize the public sector in general and the public utilities in particular. It also called for a restoration of the wages and benefits that had been hypothecated by the government. The government made gestures in the direction of an accommodation with the protest groups, but its commitments to the IMF and the IBRD made it difficult to go very far in that direction. Its genuflection to an accommodation was ritualistic. To many observers, confrontation seemed imminent.

In 1970, Carnival was followed by a dramatic outbreak of social protest that later mushroomed into the closest thing to a social revolution the country had witnessed so far. There were thus fears that "history" would repeat itself in 1990 if the lessons of 1970 were not learned by the society, since the underlying social conditions were certainly there. In a risk analysis report written for a potential investor in February 1990, the author expressed the view (somewhat prophetically) that "one cannot rule out the possibility that a political incendiary might succeed in igniting the combustible material which is strewn throughout the society." Indeed, the perception of crisis in early 1990 was more pervasive than in 1970, since unlike in 1970, the disillusioned element now included not only the have-nots, who had been led to expect that once the political kingdom (independence) was won, "all else would be added," but also those who thought they had escaped the social traps of their history but who now feared that they had lost what they had managed to achieve in the sixties and seventies for themselves and their children. The latter included persons who lost (or feared they would soon lose) their jobs, their homes (because of an inability to service mortgage commitments), their savings (because of the collapse of near banks), their insurance protection (because of the collapse of a few general insurance companies or because of their inability to pay premiums), educational opportunities for their children (because of steep increases in the cost of higher education), and retirement income, to name but a few of the concerns that generated anxiety and anomie.

The Muslimeen Insurrection of July 27

The debate about the condition of the Trinidad and Tobago economy and how the losses and gains were being allocated between and among the ethnic communities and various class strata was dramatically interrupted by the Muslimeen insurrection of July 27. That insurrection involved the invasion of the country's Parliament and lone television station by armed members of the Jamaat-Al-Muslimeen ("Grouping of Muslims") community. The leader of the Jamaat, Abu Bakr, told a stunned nation that the government had been overthrown and the prime minister and his cabinet were under arrest. The attempted coup collapsed after six days of negotiation between the rebels and the protective services, but the damage done to the society in terms of lives lost, injuries, psychological trauma, destruction of property by arson, and looting in the capital city and environs was substantial. As the society sought to analyze the roots of the crisis and allocate blame, it became apparent that while a great deal of attention had been focused on the problem of the Indian community and its claims for fuller incorporation in the political and social mainstream of the society, the immediate threat to the stability of the system was the marginalized young black male in the urban areas. Individuals and organizations that had been working with these elements, whether in the schools, churches, or other cause groups, had been warning the society for some time that this particular problem was critical and that while the country must of necessity pay attention to budget deficits and the conditionalities required by the IMF, there was a critical human problem that needed to be urgently addressed. The society was being told, in so many words, that if it failed to provide bread, butter, books, and emotional support, it would have to pay the equivalent in guns and prisons. The prison population had in fact increased by 300 percent since 1983.

Available statistics had indicated that the dropout rate for young males in the school system was higher than that of any other group. Norma Abdulah, of the Institute of Social and Economic Research, University of the West Indies at St. Augustine, consulted the 1980 census and reported the following:

> About 53 percent of young persons aged 15–24 have acquired secondary education, with a much larger proportion of females than of males having reached that level of attainment. In addition, young women also had a fairly high proportion who had completed 6 or more years of primary education relative to their counterparts. By contrast, the proportion of males who had less than a complete primary education was, in 1980, nearly twice as high as the comparable proportion of females.[13]

Other analysts in the university's Faculty of Education, using survey data, also reported that the problem had become worse in recent years, especially as it related to young black males. Annette Wiltshire, an ex-teacher from one of the city schools that cater to this element, also warned about the existence of "deep-rooted problems with certain of our youth, problems which have been long in gestation." She noted that over the years these youngsters accumulated a "deficit" in the social and educational system that they never managed to "pay off." Wiltshire noted that many of these youths display an apparent dichotomy in the behavior of this group. "They show respect, honesty and kindness on the one hand, and aggression and violence on the other." Wiltshire saw the link between violence and religion in the ability of some of the "new" religious leaders operating in the country to offer those who feel marginalized something to believe in, something the traditional churches, the family, and the school have not been able to do.

> The psychology of the devotees of Imam Abu Bakr capitalise on a thorough understanding of the "cumulative deficit" of individuals faced with serious problems. They replace family and present a new society. They even fill a spiritual vacuum, hence the dichotomy identified. The Jamaat-Al-Muslimeen substituted family and society for these youths. It addressed their powerlessness and unmanageability in the face of repeated failures and disappointments—that sense of hopelessness in the face of a life which has spun out of control. Organisations such as the Jamaat fill the void. They provide the experiences which contribute to the development of self-esteem. They assist them in gaining competence in activities which they then come to value—one of which is some kind of power, some capacity to control one thing or the other including self. This time around, for some of them it happened to be an M14 or AK-47 looking down the noses of respectable citizens and persons in authority, denuded of respect as they had perceived themselves to have become. With pride they personalised their weapons and this made the power emanating from them an extension of their own selves.[14]

Father Clyde Harvey, an Anglican parish priest, brought a similar perspective to bear on the Abu Bakr phenomenon. Father Harvey noted that Bakr had many silent and not so silent supporters in his parish and wondered "why many of our people, especially black males, feel alienated in this society." These youngsters, he notes, are not "immoral" but "amoral." "Many of them just do not know basic moral values" or at least had an alternative set of values. Harvey located the problem, at least in part, in the failure of the established churches and their male members in particular to provide role models for the marginalized black youth.

> The Christian churches, with their majority female attendance, need to think long and hard about all this. Those Christian gentlemen who call upon the church to do more for our youth must note that the work of the church among young men will be constantly negated

if adult males are not seen to be actively engaged in the life of the
church. A society which says that grown men don't go to church
regularly seriously undermines the influence of the church in the
lives of young men.[15]

Many of these young blacks spent their time "liming" or playing either
basketball on street corners (basketball is essentially a lower-class sport in
Trinidad and Tobago) or soccer. Many were offspring of families that had
been broken as a result of divorce, migration, or absenteeism on the part
of one parent, usually the male. Many did not know their fathers. Many
were also recent, or relatively recent, immigrants from neighboring islands." Many "hated" the system blindly and saw nothing wrong in "rip-
ping it off" to feed themselves and their families or just for "kicks." Many
sought refuge in mind-expanding drugs. Many ended up in trouble with
the law.

The problem of the marginalized black male is of course not unique
to Trinidad. The problem is endemic in the wider Caribbean, the United
States, and Great Britain. Tim Hector, publisher of *Outlet* in Antigua, in
fact warned that the "Abu Bakr phenomenon could manifest itself anywhere in the region." "In every Caribbean island I have been in, I have
seen Abu Bakr in various guises. They are tired of words. They want action. All they need is the guns to bury the old oppressive order. They have
no theory of society, nor any viable vision of the future. It could happen
by either the bullet or the ballot box."[16]

The Agony of Guyana

Guyana today stands poised on the brink of a political disaster of enormous magnitude. Whether that disaster occurs depends very much on the
outcome and consequences of the 1992 general election, which all agree
is the most critical in the country's history. Given the plural nature of Guyanese society, every election has in a sense been a critical election. This is
so because elections in Guyana are not merely about which party, which
program, or which ideology prevails. More fundamentally, elections determine which racial group enjoys hegemony, which one is "on top." The
race issue has always dominated Guyana's politics, but more so since 1953,
when Guyana's first election under universal suffrage was held. The sa-
lience of the race factor has continued to give to politics in Guyana its
peculiar quality of violence and ethnic confrontation. The demographic
pattern has also helped to aggravate Guyana's political predicament (see
table 7.1). The Indian majority, concentrated as it is in the plantation sec-

TABLE 7.1. Ethnic Distribution of the Population of Guyana, 1960–1980

Race	1960 No.	%	1970 No.	%	1980 No.	%
Negro/black	183,950	32.8	218,401	31.2	231,330	30.5
East Indian	267,797	47.8	362,736	51.8	389,760	51.4
Chinese	4,074	0.7	3,402	0.5	1,842	0.2
Amerindian	25,453	4.3	34,302	4.9	39,867	5.3
White	3,217	0.6	2,186	0.3	770	0.1
Mixed race	67,191	12.0	72,317	10.3	83,763	11.0
Others	8,415	1.5	5,998	0.9	3,266	0.4
Not stated	233	0.0	502	0.1	8,021	1.1
Total	560,330	100	699,844	100	758,619	100

Sources: British Guiana Population Census of 1960 (Central Statistical, Port-of-Spain, 1968); *1970 Population Census of the Commonwealth Caribbean* (Kingston: Census Research Programme, University of the West Indies, 1976); *1980–81 Population Census of the Commonwealth Caribbean* (Published for the Caricom Secretariat, by the Statistical Institute of Jamaica, Kingston, 1984).

tor (rice and sugar), is essentially a rural population, while the African, European, mixed, and Oriental elements are concentrated in the villages and the two urban centers of Georgetown and New Amsterdam.

The rural-urban dichotomy has helped to intensify the intransigence of party politics in Guyana. It meant that any government dominated by Indians would be rurally based and would have to seek to maintain its power in the "jaws" of the African heartland, so to speak. The fact that the latter group, for historical reasons, was dominant in the public service and the protective services also meant that any government that had its power base in the Indo-Guyanese community was likely to encounter resistance, if not outright sabotage, from Afro-Guyanese, especially if they were of the view that resources were not being allocated fairly. Such a government would in all likelihood be considered illegitimate, even if legal. A similar difficulty emerged when the Peoples National Congress (PNC), a party that had its center of gravity in the Afro-Guyanese, came to power in 1964. Such a party could expect and did encounter resistance from the farming community, which produces a considerable proportion of Guyana's agricultural income and provides a large portion of its commercial services.

Both ethnic communities are thus in a position to inflict a great deal of damage on the national community, making effective governance difficult. One expression of this problem is the frequency with which strikes take place in Guyana. Indeed, some sort of strike activity is a daily feature of life in Guyana. Some of these strikes are genuine industrial disputes and in some cases benign. Others have clearly been politically motivated and have involved considerable loss of life and economic productivity. In the 1963–64 period, in particular, the strikes assumed the proportion of a civil war. Between January and June 1964, 136 persons were killed and 779 were injured.

Desmond Hoyte, PNC leader and head of government, complains that the opposition objected to everything the government did, its aim being to delegitimize and prevent it from performing creditably. The temptation on the part of a government that believes it is being deliberately harassed is to use force and authoritarian measures to cow the opposition. This strategy is, however, counterproductive in that it merely gives rise to a new round of strikes and extralegal boycotts. As one commentator noted, "State repression by one and demonstrations by the other were the means of managing conflict. The political institutions lacked cross communal legitimacy however effectively they governed or even handedly they formulated politics and administered the government."[17]

The political culture of Guyana is thus fundamentally different from that which obtains in the rest of the Anglophone Caribbean, even though the Guyanese share many of the common cultural characteristics found in the insular Caribbean. Like the islands in the Caribbean, Guyana inherited the English common law and the traditions of Westminster. (While there is a Dutch cultural increment, this does not appear to be of much significance politically.)

While the plural nature of the society and the areal distribution of the population explains a great deal about the character of contemporary politics in Guyana, it does not tell all. Of equal importance is the quality of the political leadership that emerged during the postwar era of Guyanese politics. In a sense, Guyana was unfortunate in that its leaders, after initial efforts to build a biracial coalition in 1952–53, sought to establish and ensure the dominance of one racial group over the other. The decision on the part of Forbes Burnham, president of Guyana and political leader of the PNC, to declare the ruling party paramount in its relationship to the state was a particularly unfortunate development in Guyana's political history and goes a long way toward explaining Guyana's contemporary political dilemma. Whatever the ideological justification for such a redefinition of the role of the ruling party, the consequence was the establishment of a racially based dictatorship (the token representation of Indians in the government notwithstanding) with membership of and loyalty to the PNC becoming the passport to office and to economic and social resources.

As the scope of state ownership or control of the economy expanded—

80 percent of the salaried positions in the society are said to be controlled by the state—Guyanese of all ethnicities, social classes, and professional callings came to realize that any activity that openly challenged or appeared to challenge the PNC would be suppressed, with the result that most Guyanese, including Afro-Guyanese, have been cowed into submission. The feeling that they are "imprisoned" in their own country is, however, particularly acute among Guyanese of Indian ancestry, who feel that the doctrine of paramountcy and the constitutional and electoral arrangements introduced in 1968 were mechanisms used to disenfranchise them and neutralize the fact that they constituted the majority group in Guyanese society. They see themselves as a "vanquished community."

The silent war between Guyana's two dominant communities has been fought on many fronts. The main areas of controversy have been the allocation of resources to various sectors of the economy, the allocation of jobs in the public sector, the ranking given to the various religious communities, the manner in which the various ethnic groups are hierarchized in the social system, and in the manner in which the electoral system is organized. The collapse of Guyana's economic system has served to sharpen the debate between the two major ethnic groups concerning who the principal gainers and losers in the struggle for resource shares are as Guyana seeks to reconstruct its economy under the tutelage of the IMF, the IBRD, and other multilateral and bilateral funding agencies.

Guyana's Economic Recovery Plan (ERP), its equivalent to the structural adjustment program in place elsewhere, has caused severe dislocations in an already ailing economy. Massive devaluations have caused dramatic price increases for food, utilities, transportation, and all services. It is estimated that while the real value of wages increased by 28 percent between 1960 and 1979, it decreased by 52 percent between 1980 and 1989. While in 1960 the real minimum wage was G $42.88, in 1989 it was G $2.11. The decline was accelerated even more dramatically in 1990 as a result of further crawling devaluations. To what extent has the ERP impacted more severely on the two major ethnic communities? The matter was recently raised by the Commonwealth Advisory Group, chaired by Alister McIntyre, which reported in August 1989. According to that report,

Another myth that has to be dispelled concerns the unequal distribution of the benefits of growth among particular ethnic groups. The opinion is still held in some quarters that agricultural development is likely to benefit disproportionately the East Indian members of the population, because of the alleged distaste of Afro-Guyanese for agricultural employment and for rural life. This perception runs counter to both local and regional experience. There is no reliable evidence of the existence of this phenomenon in Guyana, and there is substantial involvement by people of African descent in the agricultural sector of most Caribbean countries. We suggest that the policies regarding investment in agriculture be reviewed and that special measures be adopted to ensure that no individual or group is left at a disadvantage in terms of the availability of land, credit and extension services.

One of the benefits of economic growth is that it widens the options for the exercise of occupational preferences. There is in principle nothing disadvantageous about finding a high concentration of East Indians or any other racial group in a particular sector, if it is the case that other groups have freely elected to work and run businesses in other sectors deemed to be more profitable and more consonant with their lifestyles. Restricting the participation of particular racial groups in certain sectors is a recipe for economic stagnation and decline which in turn would negatively affect the opportunities for the participation by other groups in business activity and employment in the rest of the economy.

Those who voice concern about racial predominance in certain lines of activity do not fully understand the interrelationships which develop routinely in an economy between individuals, groups and sectors. Indeed, one of the benefits of a society comprised of individuals with different ethnic backgrounds and historical endowments of skills, is the advantage it provides in meeting the cosmopolitan requirements of an increasingly interdependent world. Multiracialism is a great asset to Guyana; negative thinking must not be allowed to turn it into a liability. The government of Guyana is deeply committed to equality of opportunity irrespective of race, colour, and sex, especially as it impinges on human resources development. In perception as well as in reality, Guyanese need in the years to come to draw upon their different ethnic and cultural backgrounds to ensure that no avenue for economic development is left unexplored.[18]

Contradictory points of view were expressed by way of response to the McIntyre Report's formulation of the problem. Henry Jeffers, dean of the Faculty of Social Sciences of the University of Guyana, responded:

The framers have such faith in the free market that it clouded their vision in the important area of race relations. The Report claimed that there are distinct advantages in having a multiethnic society. . . . "Political feasibility" [however] prevented the Report . . . from facing the issues. . . . The belief in the free market prevents the designers of the report from recognising that the central point about racism is that it is subversive of the objectivity which is the hallmark of a true market situation. The natural flow of employment, investments and profits between races, classes and groups which the report seems to visualise is curtailed where racial discrimination exists. The history of Black America, indeed our own history, is replete with examples where racial considerations prevented (and some would say continue to prevent) persons from being employed in jobs for which they are qualified or having access to various resources. Institutional racism exists and, even if we believe in the free market, we must be sufficiently sensitive to recognise that national policies will have to be put in place to prevent its negative impact.[19]

Leslie Melville, executive secretary of the Federation of Independent Trade Unions of Guyana (FITUG), was of the view that the Afro-Guyanese have suffered more as a result of the crisis.

The secular poverty has more ravaged the urban poor as witnessed by the evergrowing pavement dwellers. The extended family and the assistance it afforded is being slowly destroyed. And of concern, is that the urban poor are mainly from one ethnic group. The McIntyre Report . . . speaks of the unemployed female heads of households as one of the vulnerable groups. However, the plight of that group can be extended to all low income heads of households, both male and female. It is recognised, however, that the female is more affected, as they so often fall prey to the exploitative efforts of the new rich, devoid of a conscience. Here again, the group more affected is from one ethnic group although it is recognised that the cancerous evil is spreading to other ethnic groups.

Melville further argued that

the entire Programme is premised on wage restraint and the determination of prices by the market forces. It follows therefore, that it is the Afro-Guyanese that will be making most of the sacrifices and receiving the least of the gains. It is here where I disagree with the Report, for the unequal distribution of the benefits that is sure to follow is no myth but a grim reality, and is of serious concern to the Federation for which I speak.[20]

Other spokesmen for the Afro-Guyanese community agree that the community has suffered more as a result of the crisis than have the Indo-Guyanese. It is claimed that the Indians have several strings to their bow, so to speak. They are better unionized and thus better paid. Those in the informal sector also pay less tax. It is also said that the Indo-Guyanese rely more on the collective income of their extended family system than do the Afro-Guyanese, whose family system is more nucleated. Being primarily a rural people, the Indo-Guyanese can also fall back on subsistence or commercial farming of the produce they sell at market prices. They are thus less affected by the official policy of wage restraint that is the hallmark of the ERP. Wages and salaries were in fact frozen in 1979.

Indo-Guyanese spokesmen do not agree with these views. They note that while it is true that a few Indian businessmen have done very well economically, the bulk of the Indo-Guyanese community suffer as much as their African counterparts. They constitute the rural poor. Those in rice cultivation are unable to find the wherewithal to buy jute bags, twine, fuel, and fertilizers, and many have had to abandon rice cultivation. The problem was said to have been made more acute because of the fact that the Rice Marketing Board does not pay rice farmers a fair price for their produce, nor are farmers paid promptly for their deliveries. There is thus no incentive or profit in growing rice. In 1989 Guyana produced 81 percent of what was produced in 1975. Reports are that many farmers sell their product across the border rather than through official channels.

The same demotivation applies to sugar cultivation, and this also expressed itself in declining tonnages produced by the industry. In 1989 Guyana produced a mere 56 percent of what it produced in 1975. In response to the assertion that wage rates are higher in sugar than in bauxite, it was argued that bauxite workers receive bonuses and perquisites to which sugar workers are not entitled.

Many Indo-Guyanese have reacted to the crisis by migrating to Trinidad and Tobago, Canada, and the United States; fifty thousand are said to have crossed the border into Suriname or Venezuela. Many have migrated to the urban centers of Georgetown and New Amsterdam, and some have turned to drug trafficking, prostitution, and huckstering. The family has also come under pressure as both females and males have left spouses and children behind in search of the wherewithal to survive.

It is evident that both groups are being battered by Guyana's economic crisis, and it is difficult to say which group is suffering more economically. It can, however, be argued that Indians are worse off in the sense that in status and symbolic terms, they feel a greater sense of alienation and marginalization. They know that they are in the majority and believe that electoral fraud and the coercive activities of the state apparatus have contrived to relegate them to the cellar position in Guyanese society. Many feel intimidated and choose to be deferential in order to avoid violence to their person and property or discrimination in the allocation of resources or services dispensed by officialdom. Indo-Guyanese are of the view that they are the main victims of the "vampire culture" that has grown up in the public service, that is, the system that now requires citizens needing state services to make under-the-counter payments for services that should be free (e.g., application forms) or available at nominal cost. Those who speak on behalf of the Indo-Guyanese are quite convinced that unless steps are taken to ensure that they are brought fully into the mainstream of Guyanese society and permitted to function as political equals in a democratic Guyana, overt and covert resistance to the system will increase. This would have deleterious effects on the economy, and Guyanese of all ethnic affiliations would suffer. In their view, the ERP is certain to fail unless the democratic imperative is understood and addressed. All observers agree that a settlement of the political crisis is the sine qua non for achieving success with the ERP. As the McIntyre Report phrased it, "We emphasize the need . . . for a political system which encourages the participation of all Guyanese in the recovery program and a restoration of confidence in the ability of the government to manage the economy and share its benefits widely."

Conclusion

What, then, needs to be done? The state in the Caribbean in general and those countries that have "plural" social systems in particular have to be more creative in managing the problems of resource allocation. Market solutions have to be supplemented by other kinds of balancing mechanisms if social peace is to be maintained. Whatever might be the appropriate role of the state in the affluent societies of the North Atlantic, the state in the Caribbean cannot be a mere "night watchman." The Latin American and Caribbean Institute for Economic and Social Developing Planning warned regional governments in 1989 that the state in the Caribbean needed a "new approach."

> The principal functions which the State must assume in the region are those of compensation. The compensatory function of the State, as a fundamental principle of social policy, requires "positive discrimination," in favour of the poorer groups. This requires, *inter alia,* the selective provision of social services, that is to say the directing of scarce resources to the neediest groups within the population, if any real impact is to be made and establishing a protective network for the weakest groups in the population affected by the crisis.[21]

The IBRD's *Development Report, 1990* also recommends that in addressing the problem of structural adjustment, governments should:

— encourage the development of market incentives, social and political institutions, infrastructure, and technology that provide the poor with income-earning opportunities.
— increase access to social services, especially primary health care, family planning, and education.
— provide income transfers and . . . protect the poor from economic shocks.

The authors of the Report observe further that "adopting the recommended strategy is not simple." "The main obstacle is the unwillingness of national leaders to commit themselves fully to reducing poverty. Doing so can redistribute income from other, often politically vocal, citizens. The key trade off of the strategy is not between growth and poverty, but between the interest of the poor and the non-poor." The Report recommends that in countries in which poverty reduction programs have not been put in place, aid, if given at all, "should be targeted to children, women, the aged, and other highly vulnerable people."[22]

As this analysis shows, however, the problem with affirmative action programs in plural societies such as Trinidad and Tobago and Guyana is that any attempt to focus on the plight of one segment by allocating to it what others might consider to be excessive budgetary or symbolic allocations invites reactions from other segments who feel that they too are marginalized and likewise in need of social compensation of one kind or another. There is little question, for example, that in Trinidad and Tobago, as in Guyana and Suriname, there are substantial numbers of Indians who live below the poverty line and who are clustered in areas that are inadequately serviced with proper roads, running water, electricity, and schools, to say nothing of other social amenities that some of their counterparts in the urban areas take for granted. The rural Indian who plants or reaps sugar cane, watermelons, and other agricultural products or who is a small animal husbandman can quite legitimately complain about his suffering and plight. His urban counterparts in the retail sector, as well as the Syrians, can also claim to have a plight of their own in that they are frequently the objects of robberies, looting, and other kinds of predatory behavior that impact negatively on business success and generate anxieties about the security and safety of their investment and their physical well-being. Other groups claim to be socially if not economically marginalized in that their contributions to the society are not recognized or promoted as being valid. All of these elements will argue at one time or another that any attempt to focus on the plight of one group must of necessity be at their expense given the scarcity of resources. They see the game as being of a zero-sum variety and not one that can reward all players equitably.

The prime minister of Trinidad and Tobago has complained that it was impossible to propose any structural social change in Trinidad society without raising questions relating to ethnicity. It was a factor that seriously complicated policy making. As he noted in his 1989 Budget Speech:

> The major complicating factor in this country in devising proper plans and programmes and politics—is the element of ethnicity, and we must not get away from that. It has been virtually institutionalized in our history. The public sector is largely populated or manned by persons of African descent and the sugar areas and part of the commercial sector largely populated by French Creoles and people of East Indian descent. So if you touch the public sector, there are some mischievous people in the society who go around and say you are hurting people of African descent. How do you change a situation like that? While you are thinking of the public sector in economic terms, others are thinking of the public sector in ethnic terms. So you encounter all sorts of unforeseen difficulties. There are movements and currents under the surface which are not brought to light. It is time that those currents are brought to the surface and a deliberate attempt be made by the government to address them—late in the day it is true, but better late than never.[23]

How, then, can the legitimate concerns of all these competing groups be addressed without the society's destroying itself in the process? In the context of Trinidad and Tobago, there are three major political parties, all of which claim to be confident of victory when the next general elections are held. But few genuinely believe that any of them has the leadership and other supporting resources to cope successfully with the existing problems of the society as well as those already visible on the horizon. As the events of July 27, 1990, revealed, there are also a number of out elites who are totally disenchanted with the conventional political system and who want to smash it politically and militarily and replace it with something else. The latter have not been very clear about what the alternatives are except to say that they must be more people-oriented and that the people must be empowered.

It used to be fashionable to argue that the problems of resource allocation in ethnically divided societies could best be solved by adopting a socialist ideological system. The experiences of the Soviet Union and Eastern Europe have, however, given the lie to the argument that one can "solve" the "nationalities question" by lubricating the clashing gears of communal interest with the ideological oils of the Marxist or socialist formula. The Westminster alternative, in which "the winner takes all," has also proven to be inadequate to the problems faced by these societies, as have the one-party systems that proliferated in the Third World in the sixties and seventies. Both formulas have exacerbated the problem. Nor have formal coalitional arrangements succeeded in cooling the fires under the ethnic cauldron, as the case of Trinidad and Tobago well exemplifies. Coalitional arrangements are difficult to sustain over time.

One suggestion worth consideration is that Caribbean states such as Guyana, Suriname, and Trinidad and Tobago put in place some sort of power-sharing formula that falls short of a formal coalition or a national government. The formula should be attempted even if one party wins sufficient seats to form a government on its own. One thinks here of changes in the mechanisms of policy making and not in the formal or constitutional framework. We are now fully aware that winning electoral coalitions produced by high-tech public relations campaigns, with their emphasis on the negative features of rival parties or candidates, do not necessarily produce effective governments. These campaigns not only stigmatize the parties but also delegitimize the political system. The experience of the NAR between 1986 and 1990 confirms that there is a fundamental difference between electoral "stagecraft" and "statecraft." What Hedrick Smith observes about American politics is equally true of plural societies in the Caribbean and elsewhere:

Governing demands people skills: the less flashy crafts of persuasion, judgement, management, and negotiation. Campaign success often turns on exploiting temporary advantage; governing success needs patient year-in, year-out consistency and pursuit of policies. It is outside politics versus inside politics.

The contrast between the whirling, emotional world of the campaign and the unyielding, sometimes boring reality of government lies in the difference between word and deed, between the quick hit and quiet discourse; the quick hit pitched to impress a mass audience versus the quiet discourse that engages support from political peers. It is rhetoric versus reflection, polished policy recipes and clever evasions versus hard-headed ordering of priorities and uncomfortable decisions. The campaign is a fairy tale, long on promises and short on the "how" of getting there and "with whom." The campaign thrives on polarizing issues with personalities, on projecting the romantic illusion that one leader can make all the difference. It is factional sometimes go-it-alone politics. But again, no single leader has that much power—governing cannot succeed without teamwork and compromise . . . compromise is the lifeblood of workable government.[24]

The leaders of all political parties, major trade unions, business organizations, and other associations of significance in the country need to get together "across the aisles" at a summit that would meet at certain fixed periods under a chairperson unconnected to any of the political parties. The summit would identify and prioritize the critical policy issues facing the country and seek all party endorsement and support for their implementation over a sustained period as resources permit while seeking to ensure that no one group "wins" everything or "loses" everything in the process. Tradeoffs will have to be made in such a concourse between and among contending groups in what would in a sense be a third house of Parliament. The party, or parties, in power will of course continue to "govern" and be responsible for policy implementation in the normal way. Those in power will also make the routine decisions that are a necessary part of governing, since not every issue will be pivotal and salient enough to require mediation in this forum. The idea might well be dismissed by many as a harebrained scheme. But Caribbean states have experienced a great deal since achieving independence, and it may be that some effort should be made to channel some of that social learning into institutions that might be more relevant to their peculiar political circumstances.

8 | The Dominican Republic: Contemporary Problems and Challenges

Jonathan Hartlyn

The Dominican Republic has had a troubled history. In the nineteenth century, this included foreign occupation, regional uprisings, and caudillo rule; in the twentieth century, military occupation by the United States (1916–24) was followed by the thirty-one-year reign of Rafael Trujillo (1930–61). It has now been some thirty years since the fateful day in 1961 when assassins' bullets put an end to Trujillo's life, ushering the Dominican Republic into a new era. To understand the country's current problems and challenges, it is necessary to have a sense of the nature of past legacies and of the seemingly vertiginous changes within the country over the past three decades. In addition, it is important to understand how recent dramatic shifts in the global economy have affected the island republic.

The Dominican Republic's history of authoritarian rule and of extensive U.S. involvement in its internal affairs has left a legacy of cynical, distrustful, and conspiratorial politics. Yet, since at least 1978 the country has had regular competitive elections. No other Hispanic Central American or Caribbean country with a similar authoritarian legacy has had the extent of democratic success that the Dominican Republic has achieved. However, the country's democratic politics remains fragile and uninstitutionalized. One central indicator of this is the fact that the country has not yet undergone a critical, and overdue, generational change in leadership.

To a remarkable extent, politics in the country remains dominated by the presence of two venerable octogenarian leaders, Joaquín Balaguer and Juan Bosch. Balaguer served in many high-level posts under the Trujillo government and was his puppet president in 1961; in addition, he was president in the period 1966–78 and was reelected in both 1986 and 1990. Bosch, a major Trujillo opponent from exile, was elected president in 1962, though he was overthrown after only seven months in office, and only narrowly lost the 1990 elections. The dominance of these two figures reflects in part the failures of younger political leaders, particularly in the period 1978–86.[1] That failure was generated by a tragic confluence of political hubris, negative international economic circumstances, private-sector opposition, and government policy errors.

The country's economic challenges as it enters the 1990s and the next century also result from the interaction of historical legacies, policy choices, and dramatic international changes. Before discussing the country's multiple economic challenges, though, it is crucial to underline just how much the country has been transformed economically, socially, and culturally over the past thirty years. An isolated, mostly rural country of 3 million when Trujillo was killed, the Dominican Republic today is a vibrant, internationally connected, mostly urban country of some 7 million. Although serious poverty remains, and has been getting worse in the recent past, the population is better educated and better off materially than around 1960.

Yet the Dominican Republic today confronts serious economic problems, similar to those of its neighbors: low growth, high inflation, balance of payments problems, massive public-sector deficits, a bloated, inefficient state, and deteriorating services to the country's most needy. The history of the country's descent into its current problems bears a strong resemblance to that of many of its neighbors, though it also has its peculiarities. Over the 1960s and 1970s the country was largely dependent upon sugar and other traditional exports (and for a period in the late 1960s on U.S. foreign aid) for foreign exchange. Over the past decade, however, the country has been forced to undergo a painful, delayed, and so far only partial restructuring of its economy, due particularly to the collapse of world sugar markets. It has sought, though only in fits and starts, to expand into export assembly manufacturing, new agroexports, and tourism, while confronting an onerous debt burden accumulated particularly in the late seventies and early eighties.

Many of its problems come from earlier periods. From the Trujillo era, the country has been saddled by a massive but irrationally constituted public sector, as all of Trujillo's holdings were nationalized. Fiscal short-falls, patronage politics, inefficiency, and corruption have all made the problems of the state sector worse. Parts of its business sector appear more comfortable operating by calculating the political risks of functioning in a patrimonial system than by determining market-driven economic risks. At the same time, rationalization of the country's tax structure has been suc-cessfully resisted. All these factors together have had a negative impact on the population's living standards over the past decade, with the worst con-sequences appearing to fall disproportionately on the poor. While there is large-scale migration from Haiti into the country, 7–10 percent of the Do-minican population now lives overseas, mostly in the United States. Re-mittances from overseas Dominicans represent a critical source of foreign exchange for the country, yet a tragic "brain drain" has also been robbing the country of some of its best talent.

This chapter is divided into two main parts. In the first part, I explore the country's web of inherited and current problems, from the legacies of the nineteenth century into the present. I first examine the nineteenth and early twentieth centuries, the Trujillo era, and its immediate after-math. Then I look at the impact of more recent political and economic circumstances and choices, addressing Balaguer's first twelve-year period (1966–78), the two administrations of the opposition Dominican Revo-lutionary Party (PRD) (1978–86), and Balaguer's most recent govern-ments (1986 to the present). In the second part of the chapter I examine the importance of political-institutional, societal, and economic factors in determining future possible scenarios into the next century. I argue that both the most optimistic scenario—democratic consolidation with eco-nomic growth and social reform—and the most pessimistic one—severe political fragmentation with economic stagnation, dramatic social turmoil, and at the limit military intervention—are unlikely. Most likely, at least for the short term, is democratic survival, with little growth and increased social turmoil.

Historical Legacies, International Vulnerability, and Policy Choices

Foreign Occupation and National Insecurity

The Dominican Republic's nineteenth-century struggle for indepen-dence and for formal sovereignty was difficult and generated a strong sense of national insecurity. The country remains marked by an ambivalent per-ceived need to rely on the protection of stronger neighbors counterbal-anced by a nationalist resentment of their seemingly overwhelming and at times arrogant presence. Initial independence from Spain, declared in 1821, lasted only a few months in the face of a takeover by neighboring Haiti. In 1844 independence (or secession) was declared anew. The country successfully withstood some fifteen years of attempts by Haitian governments to reincorporate Dominican territory. Fear of Haiti—which evolved into a strong racist sentiment—led Dominicans to seek protection from powerful third countries, chiefly France, Spain, and the United States. Complex interactions among Dominican governing groups, opposition movements, Haitian authorities, and representatives of these powers ensued.[2] Government revolved largely around a small number of caudillo strongmen and their intrigues involving foreign powers. Spain was persuaded to reannex the country in 1861 (when the United States could do little, as it was preoccupied with its own civil war), but internal opposition finally helped restore independence in 1865. An effort to convince the Grant administration to take over the country failed when the U.S. Senate rejected it. Gradually, however, Dominican dependence on its northern neighbor grew.

Financial obligations, political instability, and U.S. involvement in Dominican affairs expanded from the late nineteenth century and served as the backdrop for the U.S. military intervention in 1916. The assassination of Ulises Heureaux ("Lilís") in 1899, ending a seventeen-year reign, led to a period of tremendous upheaval, aggravating the country's serious debt problems.[3] By 1905, Dominican customs was headed by a U.S. appointee, a relationship that became formalized in a 1907 treaty that also paid off all previous loans with a new one making the United States the country's only foreign creditor. U.S. troops finally landed in 1916 to "protect the life and interests" of the American legation and other foreigners.[4] Dominicans expected a brief U.S. military presence that would depart following elections, and even U.S. officials had not planned for a lengthy occupation, though it ultimately lasted until 1924. In the end, the most significant measure of the U.S. occupation forces was the establishment of a new Dominican constabulary force in tandem with the withdrawal of U.S. forces. In the Dominican Republic as elsewhere in Central America and the Caribbean, U.S. officials hoped that the establishment of new constabulary forces initially under U.S. tutelage would permanently depoliticize the armed forces in these countries, serving to bolster stable, constitutional government.

The United States helped establish a relatively effective national military institution in a country where previously there had been none and where traditional powerholders were weak. As Abraham Lowenthal notes: "From the time of independence until the U.S. occupation of 1916 ended the period of *caudillo* politics . . . the Dominican Republic was not characterized by a powerful triad of oligarchy, church and military, but rather by exactly the reverse: an insecure grouping of elite families, a weak and dependent church, and no national military institution."[5] Then, largely unintentional but somewhat predictable consequences of the occupation in combination with shifts in U.S. policy toward noninterventionism provided an opportunity for the head of the country's newly established military force, Rafael Trujillo, to take power.

The Trujillo Period and Its Immediate Aftermath, 1930–1966

Trujillo built a state and established a nation, though his methods were brutal and his discourse racist. His massive economic holdings and his use of tax incentives to foster initial import-substituting industrialization evolved into major economic liabilities for the country. And his political style had a profound negative impact on the country's political culture. Fears of the spread of communism after the Cuban Revolution, once again led the United States to become extensively involved in Dominican affairs in the years prior to and after Trujillo's death. But initial hopes for democratization, raised by Trujillo's assassination and the 1962 democratic election, were dashed by a military coup that followed in 1963 and then by a brief civil war that led to a U.S. invasion in 1965. In 1966 Trujillo's puppet president at the time of his assassination, Joaquín Balaguer, was elected and assumed the presidency.

Trujillo's rise to power and initial consolidation built upon historical patterns of caudillo rule within the country, on structural changes that were a consequence of the U.S. occupation, including the establishment of a more professional armed forces and improved transportation and communication services in the country, and on the U.S. shift to a policy of noninterventionism. Improved communications and infrastructure in a country that was still relatively poor, unintegrated, and isolated meant that Trujillo had the means to put down potential regional rebellions without necessarily having to incorporate and control effectively the country's entire population.

Upon assuming office, Trujillo quickly began a process of personal concentration of power, state building, and national consolidation, while gradually enunciating a discourse of nationalism, work, order, and progress. Gradually, he became the uncontested leader of the Dominican Republic. How was Trujillo able to maintain near total control over the country for as long as he did? Among the many factors, we may include structural ones of geographical isolation, weak traditional powerholders, and a more effective repressive apparatus, ideological ones revolving around a national "project" that Trujillo was able to articulate and then employ in justifying his vast financial empire, political ones having to do with Trujillo's use of repression, cooptation, wealth, and corruption, and international ones relating to complex relations with the United States.

Trujillo's initial schemes to enrich himself revolved around the creation of state or commercial monopolies. He then gradually moved into industry, forcing owners to allow him to buy up shares, while also enjoying healthy commissions on all public works contracts. After the Second World War, Trujillo expanded into industrial production. His most massive investments, however, were made in sugar, which was largely foreign-owned. The planning and implementation of Trujillo's sugar operations, however, were so poor that if they had not received numerous state subsidies, they would have lost money.

Trujillo's economic holdings at the time of his death were incredibly extensive. Around 80 percent of the country's industrial production was in his hands. Almost 60 percent of the country's labor force depended directly or indirectly on him, 45 percent employed in his firms and another 15 percent working for the state.[6] And all of these industries, landholdings, sugar mills, banks, and other enterprises became "state patrimony."

By the late 1950s, Trujillo was facing growing domestic opposition, exile activism, and international pressure, particularly from Latin American governments, several of which had historical enmities with Trujillo. The question, however, was how Trujillo was to be removed from office and who would replace him. The answer further reflects Dominican vulnerability and says nearly as much about the nature of U.S. foreign policy as it does about Dominican politics. A shift in attitude on the part of the United States played an important role in Trujillo's ouster and the inability of his family to remain in power, and this shift was a reaction to the Cuban Revolution. From 1959 to 1961 the United States engaged in "its most massive intervention in the internal affairs of a Latin American state since the inauguration of the Good Neighbor Policy."[7] This extensive involvement continued following the death of Trujillo, culminating with the 1965 intervention and its aftermath. A summary of U.S. policy intentions during this period is provided in President John Kennedy's often-cited dictum that in descending order of preferences the United States would prefer a democratic regime, continuation of a Trujillo regime, or a Castro regime and that it should aim for the first but not renounce the second until it was sure the third could be avoided.[8]

Covert and overt pressure, including cutting off the U.S. sugar quota and Organization of American States (OAS) sanctions, were applied on the

Trujillo regime. Finally, conspirators who had largely been former supporters of the regime successfully assassinated Trujillo on May 30, 1961. Following Trujillo's death, attention immediately focused on what kind of regime would replace him. It took additional threats of U.S. military intervention, which were forthcoming due to national security concerns, to force Trujillo's relatives from the island.

Nevertheless, democracy was not to come to the Dominican Republic at this time. The country had been dramatically changed by the Trujillo era, and the state was now an even more significant prize, as Trujillo's holdings became state property. There were, however, no functioning political institutions, and there was a legacy of conspiratorial, manipulative politics. Eventually, Balaguer, who had been serving as president when Trujillo was assassinated and retained his post, was forced into exile, and a council of state did oversee democratic elections, held in December 1962. But the winner of those elections, Juan Bosch, was overthrown by a coup only seven months after being inaugurated in February 1963. The Dominican military had never been purged of its Trujillista elements, and Bosch had strong opposition from business groups and the Church.

This coup was to lead eventually to another U.S. intervention. On April 25, 1965, the Dominican government attempted to put down a civil-military conspiracy that sought to return Bosch to power. This provoked a series of events leading to the "constitutionalist" uprising in support of Bosch and then resulted in the U.S. intervention three days later as the "loyalist" Dominican military was unable to control the growing civil-military rebellion. That intervention was the result of an exaggerated fear on the part of the United States regarding a potential "second Cuba."[9]

Ultimately, negotiations over 1965–66 to arrange a peaceful surrender of the constitutionalist forces surrounded by foreign troops in downtown Santo Domingo, to prevent a new outbreak of hostilities, and to provide for elections were successful. Bosch and Balaguer were the two main candidates. Bosch, understandably, felt betrayed by the United States, which had blocked his possible return to power and turned on his militant supporters. Balaguer, in turn, ran a skillful and energetic campaign, promising peace and stability. Balaguer was clearly the candidate favored by most conservative business interests and by the officer corps that retained control of the armed forces. Furthermore, many Dominicans were convinced that Balaguer was also the candidate strongly favored by the United States. Although the civil war had been largely contained to urban areas, it left some three thousand dead and the country polarized. Balaguer's electoral victory was viewed as tainted by many in the country, and his administration was viewed as lacking in moral legitimacy. Legacies of intermittent

U.S. intervention and of authoritarian conspiratorial politics will need to be overcome if Dominican democracy is to be consolidated.[10]

Balaguer's Authoritarian Period, 1966–1978: Midwife to Democracy?

In his patrimonial style, his predilection for grandiose public construction projects, and his emphasis on the country's Hispanic essence, Balaguer resembled Trujillo in many respects. However, in his treatment of economic, military, and political power Balaguer differed in several critical ways from the strongman under whom he had served, in part due to changes in Dominican society and in international circumstances. With regard to the economy, a business sector developed during this period that was linked to the state but still somewhat autonomous from it. With regard to the military, Balaguer was unmistakably a civilian figure, if still an authoritarian one, who controlled the military by awkward, "divide and conquer" strategies. And in the realm of politics, opposition parties were never totally banned or eclipsed. All these factors played a central role in explaining how a democratic transition could occur in the country in 1978. In that year, a more moderate PRD, without the presence of Bosch, who had left to found a new party in 1973, won the elections and assumed power.

The Balaguer period 1966–78 was one of high economic growth, averaging a 7.6 percent increase in real gross domestic product over the whole period and 11 percent in the years 1968–74. Growth was based upon increased export earnings, import substitution in consumer goods promoted by generous tax incentives, and public investment projects. It was facilitated by the U.S. sugar quota and generous economic assistance, particularly in the early Balaguer years. Balaguer ruled in a patrimonial fashion, as he sought to maintain a predominant political role by ensuring that he was the central axis around which all other major political and economic forces revolved. At the same time, he eventually undermined his position by promoting the development of business groups separate from, even if dependent upon, the state. In this, his government contrasted sharply with that of Trujillo. However, organized labor remained extremely weak, a combination of repression, cooptation, and extremely restrictive labor legislation (Trujillo's 1951 Labor Code was never updated).[11]

Relations between business and Balaguer were complicated by the growing incursions of the armed forces into business and into politics. Balaguer had a commanding presence within the military as a result of his ties to the Trujillo period, his anticommunism, his statesmanlike caudillo figure, and his acceptance of military repression as well as large-scale corruption. However, he clearly was not a military figure, as Trujillo had been. He sought to manage the military by playing off the ambitions of the leading generals and shifting their assigned posts. Yet he occasionally confronted serious challenges, such as a coup effort in 1971, which he successfully dismantled.

The initial Balaguer years were a period of relative polarization, with repression from government and sporadic terrorist activities by opposition groups. Some two thousand additional Dominicans were killed in a six-year period after the 1965 occupation. Following his electoral victory in 1966, Balaguer ran again and won in elections in 1970 and 1974. In these elections, however, the military placed strong pressure on members of the opposition, most of whom ultimately withdrew prior to election day. However, Balaguer also assiduously practiced a policy of cooptation. PRD and other party figures were brought into his government or offered diplomatic posts. Similarly, several radical opponents were given posts at the public university and granted a degree of autonomy to act within that sphere. The extent and nature of repression, particularly after 1976, was considerably less than in the Trujillo years.

By the 1978 elections, Balaguer had alienated a number of his former supporters due to his drive for power, his reelectionist aspirations, and his policy decisions. An economic downturn finally affected the country around 1976, when the sugar boom that had offset oil price increases faded. In addition, the country's substantial growth, industrialization, and urbanization had expanded middle-sector and professional groups disgruntled by Balaguer's patrimonial politics, which appeared to discriminate against newer and regional groups. In the absence of any "threat" from below, some were supportive of democratization, and a few, of the PRD directly.

Changes within the PRD between 1974 and 1978, including its efforts to strengthen its international contacts, particularly with the U.S. government and the Socialist International, and the firm position of the Carter administration in the tense days after the elections were also significant factors in ensuring the democratic transition. These changes in the PRD were facilitated by the surprising decision of Bosch in 1973 to abandon his party and establish another, more radical and cadre-oriented one, the Party of Dominican Liberation (PLD).

The postelection, preinauguration period was tense, and electoral results were "adjusted" to provide Balaguer with some "guarantees," namely, a majority in the senate (which appoints judges). Yet the succession went through. Fulfillment of the country's many democratic aspirations, however, were not to be fully realized.

Democratic Hopes and Economic Realities: The PRD and Balaguer Again, 1978 to the Present

The Dominican Republic since 1978 can be considered a political democracy. However, in the 1980s the country was forced to begin a difficult economic restructuring even as historical legacies and other political and institutional factors also encouraged regime fragility. Although fears of direct military intervention in politics have receded, democratic practices have not yet become consolidated.

In a number of key respects, not all of them of their own making, the Guzmán administration and the subsequent presidency of PRD leader Salvador Jorge Blanco (1982–86) turned out to be acute disappointments. In particular, initial hopes that the Jorge Blanco administration could be an important example of a less personalistic, more institutional, reformist presidency fell short under the impact of the country's economic crisis, executive-congressional deadlock, and the reassertion of customs of patronage and executive largesse. By the end of Jorge Blanco's term, the PRD was a factionalized organization that had been forced to oversee a brutal economic adjustment and that confronted widespread accusations of corruption and mismanagement. Although civil liberties had generally been respected during the PRD years, there were no significant advances in democratic institutionalization or participation nor reforms of a social or economic nature. Rather than leaving a legacy of lasting political and economic changes implemented by a social-democratic party, the period of PRD rule was one of populist expansion followed by a complex up-and-down process of wrenching economic stabilization involving extensive negotiations with the International Monetary Fund (IMF) and other international creditors. Bitter party wrangling and eventually division of the PRD resulted.

The country's economic crisis of this period was a result of a complex web of international and domestic constraints compounded by policy errors. Negative international circumstances included the sharp increase in oil prices following the second OPEC oil shock, the dramatic increase in international interest rates and declines in export volumes, sugar prices that fell in 1977–79 to rebound in 1980 and then fall sharply again even as the U.S. sugar quota was being reduced, and declines in the prices of other Dominican exports. Yet policy moves by the Guzmán administration, including expansionist fiscal policies, large-scale increases in public-sector jobs, exchange rate policy, and the structuring and financing of public enterprises all came under heavy criticism. Similarly, Jorge Blanco's management of negotiations with the IMF, particularly their protracted nature, and his turn to a clientelistic style of governing were harshly criticized; this was compounded by charges of corruption. At the same time, business groups were able to thwart fiscal measures and shift the burden of adjustment onto other groups in society even as the struggle for state spoils further fueled political fragmentation.

Nevertheless, significant steps toward economic stabilization were taken under the Jorge Blanco administration. An initial accord formalized with the IMF in January 1983 was suspended in the late fall of that year because of the continued growth in public expenditures. Then, in April 1984 the government imposed price increases on fuel, food, and other items as part of a package of measures taken in order to reach a new accord with the IMF and renew international credit flows. Protests led to a full-scale "IMF riot," which was tragically mismanaged by the armed forces unleashed by the administration, leading to scores of deaths. Talks with the IMF were suspended, but finally in January 1985 the administration took the painful step of unifying the country's exchange rate for all transactions at the higher free rate. Over 1985 and 1986 the government successfully complied with an IMF standby program. However, the program of devaluation, a tight monetary policy, and control of public-sector expenditures induced a sharp recession in the country; the country's gross domestic product declined in 1985 (estimates range from 1.2 percent to 5 percent) for the first time since the 1965 civil war and U.S. intervention. Inflation in 1985, at an annual rate of 37.5 percent, also reached what had been a record (until it was superseded in subsequent years).

In the months prior to stepping down from office, however, Jorge Blanco lowered fuel prices by more than the drop in international prices, increased public employment and food subsidies, and granted massive numbers of tax exemptions for the importation of automobiles and other industrial and commercial goods. Dominican observers surmised that these efforts were intended to position the president for a potential electoral comeback in 1990, while enriching his close associates (whether for personal or future political use).

Economic decline and divisions within the PRD paved the way for the remarkable presidential comeback of Joaquín Balaguer in 1986, who won a narrow plurality victory over the PRD. At the same time, Juan Bosch and his PLD received 18 percent of the vote, doubling the percentage received in the past election. To the surprise of many, Balaguer began his term in office by denouncing mistakes and irregularities carried out by his predecessors, leading ultimately to the arrest of former president Jorge Blanco on corruption charges. Yet the administration did nothing to remove factors that foster corruption. In the end, Balaguer's campaign of moralization appeared to have had primarily a political impact, helping to further discredit the PRD and adding fuel to preexisting bitter internal disputes, while not appearing to have had much impact on levels of corruption within the country. At the same time, the fact that the trial of Jorge Blanco dragged on into Balaguer's subsequent term helped demonstrate the poor state of Dominican judicial structures.

Structural conditions and past behavior patterns have strongly favored corruption in the country, as has the expropriation by the state of Trujillo's massive holdings. During Balaguer's twelve-year presidency, large-scale public investments were contracted out without competitive bidding, and "commissions" on state purchases continued to be standard practice. Top military officers also operated with considerable autonomy and enriched themselves considerably. Under Guzmán, public-sector employment for PRD faithful grew considerably (by 72 percent between 1978 and 1982). Serious claims of corruption were made against members of Guzmán's family, particularly following his tragic suicide just weeks prior to the inauguration of the new president. No evidence has been presented to support the many extravagant charges, and Guzmán's despondency may also have been linked to the fact that Jorge Blanco, his bitter opponent within the PRD, had gained the party nomination and won the election over Guzmán's opposition. Guzmán felt abandoned by previous collaborators and feared harassment by Jorge Blanco. At the same time, the country has never seriously implemented civil-service legislation, and public-sector salaries have been kept at extremely low levels. Thus, many middle- and lower-level public officials depend on "speed payments" as well as second jobs to augment their pay. This tends to be even more true when inflation has eroded the value of already low wages, which has been the case for much of this recent period.[12]

In an additional effort to boost his popularity, Balaguer also sought to revive the economy quickly, principally by carrying out a number of large-scale public investment projects. He pursued a policy of vigorous monetary expansion, fueling inflationary pressures and eventually forcing the government to move toward a system of exchange controls. Inflation, brought down to around 10 percent in 1986, climbed to 58 percent in 1988 and 41 percent in 1989, reaching a new peak of around 100 percent in 1990, a year in which the economy also went into a severe recession. Until late 1990 the government sought to control inflation primarily by focusing on the exchange rate and on black-market operations rather than on underlying economic forces, including government policies. Through a patch-work of policies, the administration was able to limp through the May 1990 elections without a formal stabilization plan. But in the second half of 1990 the administration began to implement stabilization measures in spite of national strikes in August and November. An agreement with the IMF was finally reached in July 1991, leading to another two-day national strike.

In spite of the country's serious socioeconomic problems, Balaguer was able to win a narrow plurality victory in the 1990 elections. In elections marred by irregularities and marked by charges of fraud, the eighty-three-year-old incumbent edged out his eighty-year-old opponent, Juan Bosch, by a mere twenty-five thousand votes. José Francisco Peña Gómez, the PRD candidate, emerged as a surprisingly strong third candidate. By 1990 the PRD was irreparably split along lines that had formed during the bitter struggle for the 1986 presidential nomination. Peña Gómez had stepped aside for Jacobo Majluta then, but he vowed not to do so again. Peña Gómez had primarily concerned himself with developing the PRD's insti-tutional base and its international links with the Socialist International. The failure of numerous efforts since 1986 to settle the dispute, as well as extensive legal and political wrangling, eventually left Peña Gómez in con-trol of the PRD apparatus. Majluta, a more conservative, "machine-style" politician, hinted that he would be interested in serving as Balaguer's run-ning mate. In the end, he ran at the head of a new party that he had established and came in a distant fourth.

In 1990 the Dominican Republic experienced its fourth consecutive democratic, but also incident-prone, elections. They demonstrated both the fragility and the resilience of the country's political process. One of the tasks for the Dominican Republic in the 1990s will be to accomplish a necessary generational change of political leadership while seeking to pre-clude greater political fragmentation. This will need to be accomplished even as the country seeks to strengthen its state institutions and addresses its multiple social and economic challenges.

The Dominican Republic Faces the Twenty-first Century

As the Dominican Republic moves into the twenty-first century, what is the best one might hope for it, and what is the worst one could fear? Aspirations are for progress toward democratic consolidation combined with economic growth and social reform. Fears are that instead the coun-try might face severe political fragmentation with economic stagnation, heightened social turmoil, and perhaps at the limit, military intervention. A middle scenario would foresee democratic survival, stagnant or little growth, and increased social turmoil.

Factors determining which of these three possible scenarios might be realized relate in broad terms to the polity, to the civil society, and to the economy. Regarding the first, central issues relate to the state, democratic governance, and the nature and evolution of the political party system. With regard to the second, questions revolve around the strength of organizations in society and the challenges and potential benefits that processes such as migration might represent. The third refers to the ability of the country to rectify past policy errors and respond correctly to current opportunities and constraints. With regard to each of these, the country faces multiple challenges. However, there is increased consciousness regarding these issues within the country; in combination with certain international circumstances, the middle scenario sketched above may represent the country's most likely future.

Governance and Political Institutions

One factor essential both for democratic consolidation and for stable economic growth is related to governance. Critical issues include the development of strong and effective state institutions and of vigorous and representative political parties, as well as effective civilian control over the armed forces. Over the medium to long term, the Dominican Republic needs to reduce stifling presidentialism and centralism and build greater institutional capacity. A useful constitutional reform would be the prohibition of immediate presidential reelection. In the absence of civil-service regulations and as a result of extremely low pay and often difficult working conditions, there is next to no tradition of public service in the country. Even institutions that have been able to maintain higher standards and pay scales and are nominally independent, such as the Central Bank, are deeply affected by extensive presidential powers, which inhibit the development of professionalized norms and the building of state capacity.

A paradox of the country's large state apparatus, begun by the expropriation of Trujillo's holdings and then gradually added on to over the years, is that the state is omnipresent but extremely weak. Over recent years, economic crises and high inflation have had additional negative consequences with regard to the state's abilities to provide services, regulate, and produce. The provision of education and health by the state has been deeply eroded by a lack of resources, by low morale among employees, by deteriorating infrastructure and lack of supplies. State regulatory capacity has been capricious and uneven. In recent years, businessmen have complained bitterly of the long delays and unpredictability of customs charges on imports, even as overall levels have appeared to increase in an effort to garner greater state resources. At the same time, effective enforcement of environmental or labor regulations has been weak. Finally, the state as producer has deteriorated greatly. State enterprises have suffered from lack of renovation of their equipment and production processes, from employment practices based on political and partisan criteria rather than on efficiency or market criteria, and from numerous other problems.

One of the most problematic enterprises is the state electrical company. Historically, it has had to sustain millions of pesos in unpaid bills from other state agencies. Manipulation of meters, delays in payments, and "agreements" with company officials have compounded problems for the company, which also suffers from an excess of personnel and tremendous losses due to poor maintenance. Tariff rates are among the highest in the region, even as consumers are subjected to such frequent outages that many firms, as well as wealthier individuals, have invested in their own generating equipment. In effect, this has represented a grossly inefficient de facto privatization of electricity generation. In recent years, the government has acceded to permit some private sale of electricity and has begun an effort to refurbish the state generating capacity.

Economic deterioration and high inflation have also had devastating consequences on the country's human resources. Haitian migration into the Dominican Republic has continued, as has often brutal exploitation of Haitian labor in agriculture, particularly cane cutting. At the same time, many educated, middle-class Dominicans have sought to migrate to the United States, while others have been forced to leave poorly paid salaried jobs in the public sector to seek revenue in other ways or else work in more than one job. For some analysts, the lack of civil-service legislation and low pay are seen as breeding grounds for corruption. For a president, as long as overall levels can be kept within limits, the fact that some government personnel feel obliged to supplement their revenue in this fashion can be viewed as a form of "control" over them: under certain circumstances they could be forced out for "illegal" acts. It also provides privileged access to certain elements of the private sector.[13] Many in the private sector are opposed to higher public-sector wages on the grounds that higher salaries would mean more taxes, while corruption might still continue. Currently, much entrepreneurial talent is devoted to scheming to get around state regulations, take advantage of weak state capacity, and make large profits in business relationships with state enterprises and, in general, to calculating "political" as opposed to market risks.

For more effective democratic control and governance, other state institutions also require strengthening, particularly the legislature, the courts, and the Central Electoral Board (JCE), responsible for managing and overseeing elections. The congress lacks appropriate administrative, technical, and physical facilities. Under the two PRD administrations (1978–86), the congress often served an obstructionist role, fed by internecine PRD struggles. Under Balaguer, the congress has been maintained in a relatively subservient position, facilitated by the fact that his party has retained a majority in the senate, which fills judicial posts as well as names the judges to the JCE.

The ambiguous status of the JCE has contributed significantly to the recurring irregularities, charges of fraud, and reliance on ad hoc commissions of notables or international observers that have affected recent Dominican elections. The JCE's president and members are elected by the senate for a four-year term concurrent with that of the president of the republic. The president controls disbursement of the JCE's budget. In addition, the JCE shares responsibility with the executive branch for managing the offices that provide the personal identification cards that citizens must present, along with electoral carnets disbursed by the JCE, in order to vote. All of this becomes particularly problematic when an incumbent president is seeking reelection. Opposition candidates fear that the electoral registry and other electoral procedures may be manipulated to favor the governing party. These problems were all particularly acute in the 1990 elections.

Many reforms intended to assure greater independence and autonomy of the JCE have been prepared, but congress has never enacted them. The encouraging sign is the number of independent studies that have been realized by different Dominican academic and professional groups calling for administrative improvements and the fact there is some overlap in their recommendations. At the appropriate political moment, they could be at least partially implemented.

One area of continuing tension in many Latin American and some Caribbean countries revolves around civil-military relations; however, in the Dominican Republic this appears to be an issue of less and less concern. During Balaguer's twelve-year period (1966–78), the military played an openly partisan role in support of his administration and gradually grew in power and influence. Balaguer placed one general involved in coup plotting in exile in 1971 (he subsequently returned and has become a Balaguer supporter). However, President Guzmán took advantage of the presence of many foreign dignitaries and a high-level U.S. delegation at his inauguration in August 1978 to force the retirement of several of the most prominent activist generals. Under the subsequent administration of President Jorge Blanco, numerous other officers were forced to resign (several were subsequently brought back by President Balaguer). The general who served as Jorge Blanco's minister of defense was also tried on corruption charges under Balaguer. But the net effect of the series of successful elections and transfers of power from one party to another, combined with these changes in the military, has been to reduce considerably fears of a military intervention. There is little conviction among business and professional groups that the military would be more effective governors or economic managers and real concern that the violence and bloodshed that could be generated by a coup attempt would hurt the country's economic prospects, affect tourism, and impact on relations with the United States and other industrial democracies.

However, for the country to move toward deepening and consolidating its still fragile democracy, it is not enough simply to hold elections and be free of threats of potential overthrows. An active, participatory citizenry is also important, and one factor facilitating this would be a vibrant, representative party system. From the 1978 elections to the present, the country has gradually moved to greater political fragmentation. In the 1978 elections there were only two major parties, Balaguer's Reformist Party and the PRD. However, over time, Bosch's PLD increased in electoral strength, and the PRD became factionalized and eventually divided. Although Balaguer's and Bosch's relationships to their parties are very different, with Balaguer's power being more directly personalistic, the two leaders have both resisted to date naming successors or facilitating a smooth succession of party leadership.

What shape the country's party system will take once these two leaders are no longer active on the political scene remains an open question. Successfully managing this succession in leadership will be a critical test for Dominican democracy. However, it is encouraging that all major party figures will now have had some direct experience in democratic politics, either in power or as part of the opposition in the congress. Although the PLD has been very bitter about the results of the 1990 elections and continues to claim that fraud assured Balaguer's victory over Bosch, the active role of many PLD leaders in legislative and municipal affairs bodes well for their continued participation in electoral politics.

Social Structure and Societal Organizations

Democratic politics and a vigorous economy will also depend upon an active and engaged citizenry and a dense web of organizations and groups in society. Unfortunately, the combination of economic decline and public policies focused on public works rather than basic needs over the recent past has led to a deterioration in basic services to the majority of the population in terms of health, education, and nutrition.

Economic decline and political factionalism has also led to further fragmentation of the country's labor movement. A smaller percentage of the country's economically active population is now organized in a larger number of federations divided by personal and political loyalties. During the 1990 electoral campaign, the political fragmentation ran so deep that the labor movement decided simply not to hold a rally to celebrate Labor Day on May 1.

However, business, professional, and other middle-class organizations and a fragile but still important network of neighborhood associations has gradually grown in the country. Various industrial groups that emerged as industrialization surged under Balaguer in the 1966–78 period strengthened the nearly moribund National Businessmen's Council (CNHE) in 1978, partially out of fear of the new PRD government. From a very antagonistic relationship with government, they gradually evolved toward a more institutionalized series of exchanges with the PRD administrations. Under Balaguer, however, they have tended to revert to more personalistic and patrimonial exchanges with the government.

At the same time, a number of middle-class organizations have emerged expressing dissatisfaction with the continuing personalistic nature of government, seeking state reforms and more regularized patterns of behavior between the state and groups in society. The number and quality of documents analyzing the country's major political, social, and economic problems that appeared during the 1990 campaign and the thoughtfulness of their proposed solutions was extremely impressive. The country also has a remarkably active press, with a large number of newspapers carrying a wide variety of opinion pieces and analyses.

Yet, an increasing number of middle-class Dominicans appear to be "voting with their feet," opting to migrate out of the country. The loss of many professional and technical personnel as a consequence of low salaries and poor working conditions in the country is especially tragic and complicates efforts toward economic restructuring. A combination of macroeconomic stability and selected policies targeted to encourage return migration together might induce some of these individuals to come back to the island. In the face of sharply declining public services, particularly water, electricity, and transportation, and of escalating food prices, neighborhood associations have emerged throughout Santo Domingo and other urban centers to carry out major protest actions. Their level of coordination has tended to be low, and their links to opposition political parties have been tenuous.

At different times, such as in moments of political crisis, Church leaders have sought to serve as intermediaries between the government, business groups, and labor groups (who have occasionally served as proxies for the neighborhood organizations as well). Not surprisingly, however, given the power disparities among the actors, accords have not been reached. At the same time, the government has clearly been concerned that full-scale implementation of stabilization measures would lead to powerful reaction from society. The Balaguer administration has wished to avoid a repetition of the 1984 protests and deaths at all costs. This has led to the zigzagging patchwork of economic policies as the government has sought to "muddle through" its economic problems.

The Economy and Economic Policies

The country has been in the midst of a painful but overdue economic transition. At the end of 1990 it faced an onerous debt burden of some $4.2 billion (excluding late interest on arrears) to multilateral agencies (24 percent); bilateral lenders (36 percent to the OECD Paris Club and 14 percent to others); private commercial banks (24 percent); and others (2 percent). World sugar markets have gradually, if unevenly, collapsed; thus, the sugar quota actually increased slightly in the late 1980s. However, the country has finally closed some of the most inefficient state mills and has sought to diversify its economy principally by expanding export assembly manufacturing in free trade zones, new agroexports, mining, and tourism. The Dominican Republic now has the largest number of hotel rooms in the Caribbean, and tourism represents the single largest earner of foreign exchange for the country. The Balaguer administration is hoping that 1992, celebrating the five-hundredth anniversary of Christopher Columbus's landing on the island, will be a banner year for tourism; the Pope is expected to participate in the Latin American Bishops Conference, to take place on the island in that year.

In an effort to reactivate the economy, and reflecting his own personal style, Balaguer also embarked upon an extremely ambitious series of public construction projects that fueled monetary expansion, inflation, and public deficits. Some of these, such as the massive Columbus lighthouse, are associated with tourism and the 1992 celebrations. However, the administration was forced to impose a patchwork of new taxes; in an effort to restrain inflation it reimposed exchange controls and then through coercive methods sought to force delivery of dollars to the Central Bank. The government gained some breathing room by the unexpectedly high level of remittances of dollars from overseas Dominicans, some it is suspected by individuals involved in the retail drug trade in New York. It also suspended payment on its private and bilateral debt.

However, eventually the foreign exchange constraint became too great, since international creditors were unwilling to grant new funds in the face of growing arrears. Balaguer moved to implement stabilization measures, including tariff reforms, exchange liberalization, relaxation of price controls, reductions in public-sector deficits, and promises of privatization. These steps facilitated an agreement with the IMF in July 1991 and could open the door for renegotiation of official bilateral and commercial debt over 1991 and 1992, leading to increased infusion of loans and economic recovery.

In 1990 the Dominican Republic faced one of its most difficult years in recent history. President Balaguer was forced to negotiate an economic adjustment with international creditors from a weak political position. His government lacked a degree of moral legitimacy because of the narrow mandate he received in the 1990 elections and the charges of fraud made by the opposition parties. In addition, he retained only a razor-thin majority in the senate and was almost two dozen votes short of a majority in the chamber of deputies. Balaguer's principal advantages were the considerable powers the constitution grants the president and the fact that most powerful groups in society, no matter how unhappy they may have been with particular policies of his government, saw no other viable alternative as preferable. In addition, neither of the two opposition parties, the PLD and the PRD, appeared interested in provoking widespread bloodshed. The possibilities for an effective coalition between the two parties was limited due to personal factors, giving Balaguer some additional room to maneuver.

Notwithstanding the government's reluctance to move toward more market-oriented policies with regard to the exchange rate, to monetary growth, and to regularizing its debt situation, the porousness of the state and the absence of certain kinds of policies helped foster an entrepreneurial dynamic. This dynamic was somewhat unplanned and chaotic but has helped generate some growth and employment, though without as much social benefit as might otherwise have been the case.

This has been particularly evident in the dramatic growth of the country's free trade zones. Foreign investment in these zones need not be recorded with the government, which also grants generous concessions.

There has been a veritable explosion in the number of free trade zones operating in the country and in total employment levels, which increased over the 1988–90 period by some 40 percent to around 120,000 workers.

At the same time, problems with the provision of electricity could limit further expansion. The country is also beginning to reach its ceilings on textile exports to the United States. There has also been increased pressure on the U.S. government from human rights groups and organized labor in the United States to cancel Dominican trade privileges under the Generalized System of Preferences (GSP) due to constraints on labor organizing in the free trade zones and to gross mistreatment of migrant Haitian cane cutters. Modest changes by the Balaguer administration allowed the U.S. government to rule in favor of the Dominican Republic in early 1991, but these issues will almost certainly continue to be relevant.

Over the next several years, though, the country will confront more significant international pressures for market-oriented policies and will need to consider how to mitigate their potential impact regarding social equality (the quality, as opposed to the stability, of democracy). The country will need to consider how to begin to create more kinds of jobs in tourism and in the free trade zones, jobs that pay higher wages and provide more possibilities for technical advancement or that can provide more extensive linkages to the local economy. It also should try to place state revenues on a more stable basis by enactment of fiscal reforms. In addition, more concerted programs to improve health and education and improvements in the provision of basic services are also essential.

The country must also think much more seriously about its changing international environment, seeking opportunities where it may primarily recognize potential dangers. One of these feared changes lies in the potential impact on foreign investment flows into the Dominican Republic if a North American free trade agreement between Canada, Mexico, and the United States is successfully negotiated. This would force the country to consider the issues of Caribbean integration and of more rapid movement toward a free trade regimen much more seriously. Another change is a possible political thawing and economic opening of Cuba, which is currently viewed with preoccupation in the Dominican Republic, since Cuba could then become a much greater competitor for both investment flows and tourist dollars. A third continues to be the need for stable relations with its politically unstable neighbor, Haiti, and the search for a solution to the issue of Haitian migrant labor.

Effective management of any of these areas, however, is difficult to imagine without improvements in the institutional capabilities of the state, understanding from economically powerful domestic private groups, and a sufficient political consensus among the currently fragmented major political actors.

Conclusion

As we have seen, the Dominican Republic's contemporary problems build upon historical legacies, past policy choices, and the international environment. Legacies include conspiratorial politics, patrimonial rule, and intermittent engagement on the part of the United States. Other challenges focus on past development patterns and policy choices, including the difficulties engendered by the appropriation of Trujillo's holdings and then of certain subsequent economic policies, the country's unwieldy but porous state apparatus, the penchant for expansive projects, and a business sector accustomed more to measuring domestic political risks than to aggressively pursuing new export markets. Finally, the collapse of world sugar markets and new patterns of global investment place constraints on the country's development options. The viability of more purely national development strategies, particularly for smaller nations, appears to be sharply declining.

In this context, one can think of three sets of major challenges the country faces: political-institutional, societal, and economic ones. The significant problems analyzed in each of these areas suggest that the most hopeful scenario—of consolidated democracy, stable growth, and social reform—is very unlikely to be realized. At the same time, there are sufficient elements of change and of innovation in each area to suggest that the most pessimistic outcome is not inevitable. Over the next years, democracy will almost certainly survive, though it may not fully flourish, in the country. As difficult economic adjustments continue, the country may experience only low rates of growth and increased social conflict.

In the broader Latin American context of hyperinflation, violence associated with guerrilla, terrorist, and drug-trafficking activity, near collapse of judicial and other state institutions, and incredible electoral volatility, the Dominican Republic may not appear to be doing so badly. Nevertheless, the country's problems with poverty, migration, economic restructuring, and fragile state and political institutions demand attention and in some cases urgent reform.

Although in this chapter I have noted the vulnerability of the Dominican Republic to broader international market forces and to influence by major powers, particularly the United States, my emphasis has been on domestic processes and constraints. This reflects a perspective that even given significant international limitations, decisions made within the country will have a major impact regarding the nature and quality of its democracy, the welfare of its people, the strength of its institutions, and its overall degree of maneuverability in the international system. Nevertheless, in conclusion, it is important to reiterate the substantial impact that policies taken by the United States, other industrialized countries, and international financial institutions have on the Dominican Republic. An innovative combination of policies from international actors with an appropriate mix of policies and reforms within the Dominican Republic could help move the country successfully into the twenty-first century.

9 | The Role of the Puerto Rican People in the Caribbean

Juan Manuel García-Passalacqua

Will Puerto Rico play a leading role in the Caribbean in the coming century? Intellectuals in Puerto Rico have argued in recent years for and against a role for the island in the Caribbean. José Luis González, an exiled writer living in Mexico, made a determined call in 1980 for the "Caribbeanization" of the island. Edgardo Rodríguez Juliá, an essayist of a younger generation, questioned that proposition, arguing that it was too late to redirect the island's world-view toward its neighboring geographical region, since islanders had already opted for the "American way of life" and had no real kinship for the sister islands.[1] In this, he echoed Trinidadian Eric Williams's dictum that Puerto Rico was inevitably directed toward becoming a state of the United States, turning its back on the Caribbean.[2]

Under present conditions, however, it will not be Puerto Ricans alone who decide what role, if any, they will play in the Caribbean region. In testimony before the U.S. Congress in 1986, Department of State official Michael Kozak stated that "the efficacy of international relations to the United States depends upon the foreign activities of the territories and commonwealths, as well as those of the States fitting within the framework of an overall U.S. foreign policy."[3] As long as it remains a territory of the United States, Puerto Rico's role in the Caribbean will ultimately be decided in Washington. The island's status as a U.S. territory has long been an unresolved issue, and for the past several years it has been the subject of pending legislation in the U.S. Congress. As long as the Congress fails to make key decisions about Puerto Rico's status, the island's future role in the Caribbean will continue to be clouded in uncertainty. The future of Puerto Rico's role in the Caribbean depends on a final definition of its political relationship with the United States.[4] To put the matter more starkly, the role of Puerto Rico in the region (and what is most important, its neighbors' perception of that role) would be completely different if the island were a state of the union. It is one thing to be a state of the United States in the Caribbean; it is another thing to be a Caribbean state.

To answer the question of what Puerto Rico's relationship to the United States should be, one must decide whether Puerto Rico should be conceived of merely as a geopolitical territorial entity or whether the Puerto Ricans are conceived of as *a people*. I have argued elsewhere that Puerto Ricans must be seen as a people, that is, as a nation-in-formation.[5] In this chapter, I argue that the immediate interests of the United States and the long-term interests of the Puerto Rican people coincide in affording the island and its people an active role in the Caribbean.

The Point of Departure

There is a Caribbean world-view, although as J. H. Parry, Phillip Sherlock, and Anthony Maingot have stated, the isolation that still exists in the West Indian consciousness will continue until the national history of each of the islands is set in the context of Caribbean history. The history of the whole, they add, "illumines the history of each."[6] Puerto Rican majorities, distracted by a historical mirage of possible membership as a state of the union in the United States of America, have not yet seen themselves within the context of a larger Caribbean history.[7] Rather, they have been accustomed to thinking of themselves as part of Spanish, then U.S., then insularist history. Until now, Puerto Ricans have not had a clear self-consciousness as a Caribbean people.

It is my view that the status question is finally on the road to being resolved in a manner that will allow that self-consciousness to emerge. The debate in the U.S. Congress in 1990 on a bill that would lead to a plebiscite in Puerto Rico to decide between commonwealth status, statehood, and independence revealed significant resistance in the congressional committees to making Puerto Rico a state of the union.[8] It is entirely possible that once the issue is joined, the United States will give Puerto Rico an unequivocal no. It would be a mistake to suppose, however, that if that is indeed what happens, self-definition as a Caribbean people will be automatic. For that, Puerto Ricans will have to acquire a new understanding of their own history, principally through a revision of that history as taught in the island's schools; only a future generation will be fully prepared to assume a role in the region.

This new self-consciousness has to be developed in the people more than in the elite. It will have to be developed by an understanding that Puerto Rico's history, like those of the other peoples of the Caribbean, is one of a struggle against colonialism.[9] In order to explain that struggle and the current environment in the Caribbean, I present a historical overview, including a discussion of the cold war's effects on the region. This is followed by a brief discussion of the rise and fall of the Puerto Rican politico-economic model, which at one time was touted as the vehicle by which the island would influence the rest of the region. Then I assess past policies and scenarios for the future, ending with a proposal for a future Caribbean role for the people of Puerto Rico.

The Historical Effects of Colonialism

Colonialism and the sugar plantation defined the history of the Caribbean islands. Their concomitant, slavery, gave Caribbean societies their most important social trait. Dependence on the external world for survival was the end result of this history. Fear has been the mechanism of control for centuries.[10] It is against these two historical determinants that Puerto Ricans must struggle if they are to create a new agenda for themselves in the region.

One crucial element would be the acceptance by Puerto Ricans themselves of the common trait of *negritude,* a trait they share with the rest of the Caribbean. The expression of the African soul has survived in the region.[11] Yet in Puerto Rico the elite has lived for centuries under the delusion that it belongs to the "European," or white, world, preferring to identify itself with Spanish royalty rather than with Puerto Rico's Afro-American roots. The distinction between elite and masses in Puerto Rico, promoting two different world-views, is a second major obstacle regarding Puerto Ricans' own nature that must be surmounted before a consensus can be built regarding their role in the Caribbean.[12]

These two problems regarding the future do not imply a lack of consensus regarding other values. The American, French, and Haitian revolutions had a lasting impact on the island's historical consciousness. Puerto Rico inherited from the late years of Spanish rule, from the United States, and from other related events a strong democratic tradition that has produced twenty-four successive elections in this century. Moreover, the island's political life was born out of the antislavery fight within imperial Spain. Abolition permitted the emergence of the Caribbean peoples, even if social structures remained intact. Liberty was achieved for many, but without a national identity.[13] This is the crucial deficiency in the shaping of any regional role for Puerto Rico. Unless and until that national identity becomes clear to the Puerto Rican people and, what is most important, to their neighbors, nothing can be done to prepare Puerto Rico for a positive role in the Caribbean.

The history of the Caribbean region reached a turning point when the plantation economy was replaced by the sugar *central* after 1890. Moreno Fraginals points out that economic concentration promoted the emergence of latifundia, peonage, seasonal unemployment, internal and external migration, and modernization (trains, telegraph, electricity, steel foundations, etc.). This development led to the economic hegemony of the United States, mostly as the buyer of sugar, in the region.[14]

After 1871 the United States approved legislation that had the effect of bringing Cuba, Puerto Rico, and the Dominican Republic under U.S. economic control, and by 1880 the three islands' sales of sugar were mostly to the United States. Economic annexation was the precedent for active military intervention and control. In 1900 the three islands produced 4 percent of world sugar; by 1920 they produced 23 percent. A modern sugar industry thrust Puerto Rico and the rest of the Caribbean into the world economy.

From 1898 to 1930, U.S. power in the region grew. The United States repeatedly intervened militarily (in Cuba in 1898–1902 and 1906–9; in Santo Domingo in 1905 and 1916–24; in Puerto Rico from 1898 to the present). After the construction of the Panama Canal, the influence of European powers declined and the strategic importance of the region increased.[15] The First World War and the fear of a German naval attack in the Caribbean led to an increased U.S. military presence and other measures designed to strengthen U.S. defenses: the invasion of Haiti in 1915, the invasion of Santo Domingo in 1916, the purchase of the Virgin Islands from Denmark in 1917, and the concession of American citizenship to the Puerto Ricans in 1917.[16]

An important difference must be noted. While Cuba produced native investment and a criollo oligarchy that opted for independence, Puerto Rico was controlled exclusively by absentee capital, did not develop a criollo ruling class, and thus was not inclined toward independence.

The world depression that began in 1929 and the drop in the role of sugar in the world market created a crisis that in turn prompted militant nationalism to develop in the region in the 1930s. The United States

moved to crush nationalist sentiment in Puerto Rico (an effort that continued uninterrupted until the early 1980s).[17]

With the advent of Franklin Delano Roosevelt's Good Neighbor Policy
in 1933, the United States reduced its military presence in the region,
withdrawing its troops from the Dominican Republic and Haiti. However,
those who came to power in most of the islands were political pawns subservient to U.S. policies, such as Rafael Leónidas Trujillo in the Dominican
Republic, Fulgencio Batista in Cuba, Anastasio Somoza in Nicaragua, and,
one might argue, perhaps Luis Muñoz Marín in Puerto Rico. It was this
"stable" era of U.S. political pawns that so dramatically ended in the region between 1960 and 1990.

The United States and the Caribbean in the Cold War

In the mid-twentieth century colonialism took a new shape in the Caribbean.[18] World War II, the Atlantic Charter, and the foundation of the
United Nations spurred the new paradigm of "self-determination" for the
region. Decolonization followed promptly; the British, the French, and
the Dutch designed new formulas in an attempt to accommodate their
presence in the region to the new winds of ideological change.

The French possessions were assimilated as departments of France, the
Dutch possessions were given local autonomy, while Britain disposed of
its possessions by granting them independence. The United States, however, instead of recognizing the aspirations of independence in the island's
leadership, made clear to the government of Luis Muñoz Marín in 1947
that such an option was impossible.[19] The United States limited itself, in
1952, to granting Puerto Ricans the right to draft and live under a constitution. In the rest of the region, independence opened the gates for a Caribbean consciousness, for ethnicity, negritude, nationalism, and a new
appreciation of a rich artistic culture.[20] In all these respects, Puerto Rico
has lagged behind.

Since 1898 the premises of American policy in the Caribbean have
been strategic.[21] U.S. policy has passed through several stages in the region:
naval predominance, direct interventions, and prolonged occupations before the First World War; partial withdrawals between the Great Depression and the Second World War; military expansion and subordination
during World War II; counterinsurgency and containment during the cold
war; and an agonizing reappraisal after the Vietnam War.

After 1947, the cold war and the policy of containment of communism
conditioned all developments in the Caribbean. Universal suffrage, granted
in all jurisdictions, led to the slow development of autochthonous political

systems in which local elites served as intermediaries between multinational capital and the local populace. In 1959 these arrangements were shaken by the Cuban Revolution. That revolution defined the U.S. agenda for the region and, consequently, that of the region itself. For three decades cold war tensions prevented any consideration by the United States of changes in Puerto Rico's colonial status.[22]

Ivonne Acosta has demonstrated that U.S. policies after World War II conceived of Puerto Rico as a key element to contain "communism and subversion" in the region.[23] Moreover, during the cold war years, Puerto Rico became an ideological alternative to Cuba.[24] The military and propaganda roles given to the island by the United States left unattended other, much more important aspects of its potential role in the Caribbean. U.S. policy was dominated by attempts to thwart the Cuban Revolution and to prevent "another Cuba" in the region. Puerto Rico has played a key role in what Pierre Charles has called the U.S. policy of "preventive counterrevolution."[25]

A few examples suffice. More than twenty U.S. military installations dot the island. Roosevelt Roads Naval Base in Ceiba, in the easternmost part of Puerto Rico, is a recognized station for submarines carrying nuclear weapons.[26] Allen Dulles supervised the Bay of Pigs invasion of Cuba from San Juan. The naval base at Ceiba was a key factor in the invasion of the Dominican Republic. The invasion of Grenada was rehearsed in and supported by the bases in Puerto Rico. Puerto Rico was and is, in effect, a major U.S. strategic base in the Western Hemisphere. The role assigned to Puerto Rico was essentially a negative one, that of a defensive platform. Puerto Rico in this period remained a prototype of the "modernization of colonialism," recognized by President George Bush recently as "decades of unwise policies."[27]

In the late 1980s the failure of the Cuban Revolution and of the whole Soviet system created a window of opportunity to design a new U.S. policy for the region. For the first time, there is a possibility for the Puerto Rican people to go beyond their traditional role as the inhabitants of a Malta or a Gibraltar. The United States can end the colonial era, and Puerto Ricans can move toward a much more positive role in the Caribbean.

The Rise and Fall of the Puerto Rican "Model"

In the late 1940s Caribbean economist Arthur Lewis designed a proposal for industrialization-by-invitation for the islands in the region. After considerable pressure by the United States on the government of Luis

Muñoz Marín, Puerto Rico enthusiastically adopted an industrialization policy of attracting U.S. investment with tax exemptions for U.S. corporations and low wages.[28] As James Dietz has pointed out, the redirection of the Puerto Rican economy had the net result of moving it closer to the United States.[29] In effect, the island's leadership decided to operate under the constraints of colonialism. In 1946 the hope for independence was killed within the governing Popular Democratic Party (PDP), and an ever-increasing dependence was adopted as an ideological tenet.

The Puerto Rican "model" led to years of growth but also misdevelopment. Its costs were the ruin of agriculture, great gains for foreign capital, and a dependence on absentee multinational corporations, which were using the island as a tax haven. Moreover, there were limits to dependent growth.[30] No effort whatsoever was made to promote indigenous development or even to define a role for local entrepreneurship. Standards of living improved mostly due to handouts from U.S. taxpayers, not as a result of a successful economic design. Growth did not become development in the sense of an internally generated economic dynamic. Instead, the island became increasingly dependent on the United States not only for investment but for social welfare and other public funds.[31] This, in turn, caused an enormous increase in the support for full assimilation as a state of the United States, a process begun in the elections of 1956. In 1968 the first island-born pro-statehood governor came to power in Puerto Rico.

After the defeat of the statehooders in 1972, the "model" went into crisis. The application of U.S. minimum wage laws (promoted by annexationist groups) had destroyed the basis for profits and the usefulness of tax exemption. Industries began to leave the island for Taiwan or Korea. Attempts at replacing the role of light industry with a petrochemical complex, begun in 1963, failed with the OPEC decision to raise the price of oil. After 1976 the island entered into a period of outright dependence on federal welfare handouts to survive without a major social upheaval, coupled with a new emphasis on federal tax exemption as an incentive for new industries to locate on the island (this time, mostly pharmaceutical multinationals).

Economic experts have concluded that the model failed because of the total absorption of the economy into that of the United States. Without its former low-wage structure and with many other developing countries offering tax and other incentives, the island lost its competitive position in the world. Reflecting the weakening economy, in the last quarter-century a veritable political stalemate has developed, with the exponents of the old commonwealth "model" winning three elections but losing the other three to the proponents of outright statehood. A majority of the Puerto Rican electorate endorsed statehood for the first time in a September 1989 poll and later in the 1992 elections.[32]

The Caribbean Role: Problems and Prospects

Between 1948 and 1968 the PDP, hegemonic in local politics, made several feeble attempts to define a role for the island in the region. From its inception the Caribbean Commission, the postwar coordinating organ for the metropolitan powers in the region, met in San Juan. In 1961 the government of Puerto Rico assumed the administrative role for the Caribbean Commission, "the doubtful honor of a moribund colonial enterprise."[33] By 1964 Puerto Rico had withdrawn from the commission, and it was left to die.

In 1965, with a new vision of its regional role, the government of Roberto Sánchez Vilella organized the Corporación para el Desarrollo del Caribe (CODECA) and initiated procedures to gain admission to the Caribbean Development Bank, initiatives that were promptly dismantled with the first electoral victory of statehood forces in 1968. When the commonwealth party returned to power in 1973–76, it again attempted to revive a Caribbean role for Puerto Rico, but these efforts were dashed with the return of the statehooders to power in 1977. Furthermore, other Caribbean states refused to admit the island governed by annexationists, fearing it would be an extension of the power of the United States in the region.

In January 1985, upon its return to power once more, the PDP announced a determination to "Caribbeanize" Puerto Rico.[34] It was a policy announcement without precedent in Puerto Rican history but one that produced few successes in the late 1980s. The reason was precisely the ambiguity of the island's political status.[35] The project of the government of Rafael Hernández Colón was to use the funds that U.S. corporations were required to deposit in Puerto Rican banks because of the tax exemption afforded by Section 936 of the U.S. Internal Revenue Code as a means to promote bank loans for development projects in the Caribbean.[36] (This tax exemption is provided by a 1921 law that applies to U.S. territories and possessions and that was originally directed to help the Philippines.) These loans would be provided to projects that established "twin plants" in nearby islands but had Puerto Rico as the final point in the production chain, thus affording the tax exemption for the companies undertaking manufacture in the region.[37]

In 1990 Puerto Rico's government gave great emphasis to this project for the Caribbean. It prompted the investment of $646.8 million in eighty specific projects in eleven countries in the region. The investments have created 19,726 jobs in those countries, plus 4,000 in Puerto Rico. Projects are now under way in Dominica ($2 million), the Virgin Islands ($9 million), Barbados ($13 million), the Dominican Republic ($21 million), Jamaica ($80 million) and Trinidad ($147 million). Furthermore, the Puerto Rico–U.S.A. Foundation (financed by Section 936 corporations) announced a multimillion-dollar fund to finance small- and medium-sized projects in the region.[38]

Under the Caribbean Basin Initiative (CBI), the U.S. government pledged a good-faith effort to provide at least $100 million in financing and direct investment in Caribbean Basin countries annually. After several years, it was clear that the use elsewhere in the region of funds provided under Section 936 had been held back by a lack of credit guarantees. On January 24, 1990, the administration of Governor Rafael Hernández Colón announced the creation of the Caribbean Basin Projects Financing Authority. This new agency was designed to strengthen the program by providing guarantees and thus facilitating loans for projects in Caribbean nations authorized to receive funds under Section 936. It was hoped that this move would help Puerto Rico "fulfill its commitments to Washington."[39] It was also explained that the new effort was undertaken in order to prevent the revocation of the Internal Revenue Code exemption, then under review in Congress.

The inducements for foreign investment under the provisions of the CBI have until now had only modest success. The recent surge in investments in the region through the Section 936 mechanism, however, offers some hope that this part of the CBI could become a dynamic force in the future. But this depends on what happens to Section 936 corporations in Puerto Rico, and that in turn depends on what happens regarding the island's juridical status vis-à-vis the United States. If statehood were granted to Puerto Rico, the uniformity clause of the U.S. Constitution would, of course, prohibit continuation of such a tax exemption. Under independence, it could operate as a foreign tax credit coupled with local subsidies for job creation.[40] Under the present status, neither the other nations nor the multinationals have any assurance that the exemption will not be revoked by the next U.S. Congress.

Finally, the question whether Puerto Rico has any future role in the Caribbean has been raised formally with the other islands in the region. A Caribbean Community (CARICOM) summit was held in 1990, with 13 heads of government and more than 150 delegates attending. It dealt with "planning a strategy to meet future challenges of the world economy with regional responses."[41] Puerto Rican Under Secretary of State for External Relations Amadeo Francis requested that the island be granted observer status in CARICOM. Francis was advised that if Puerto Rico becomes a state of the American union, it cannot belong to CARICOM in any capacity. On March 26, 1990, Francis met with CARICOM Secretary-General Roderick Rainford in Guyana and subsequently told the press about CARICOM's "blunt" objections to Puerto Rico's being granted observer status if it became a state of the union.[42] At the beginning of the 1990s, the uncertainty about Puerto Rico's political status continued to hinder any significant progress toward Puerto Rico's assumption of an effective role in the region.

Toward a New Policy for Puerto Rico and the Caribbean

As the Puerto Rican electorate moves toward asking for full membership in the American body politic, the Caribbean peoples move toward nationalism and regional cooperation. The CBI is primarily an effort by the United States to protect its hegemony in the region and to promote "development." Yet the policy is woefully insufficient to rearticulate a system of relationships between the region and the United States.[43]

A relationship between the Caribbean and the United States that meets the needs of both sides must be based on the changed realities of the world at the end of the twentieth century:

— The Caribbean should no longer be viewed by the United States simply as a strategic asset, especially now that the global confrontation of the superpowers has ceased to exist. The Caribbean must now be seen as a near neighbor of the United States whose political, economic, and social health directly affects the well-being of U.S. society.

— The Caribbean needs a new development model that relies on building on the region's great advantages in *human capital;* this will emphasize public investment in education, health, technology, and the pursuit of efficiency through policies that promote competitiveness, indigenous entrepreneurship, and a reasonable degree of agricultural self-sufficiency.

— A policy of attracting multinational investment should be based on the region's real, as opposed to artificial, comparative advantage. An investment policy based on bank deposits and tax exemption subject to the whim of the U.S. Congress increases, rather than solves, the uncertainty in the region; moreover, the twin-plant *(maquiladora)* model is by itself totally insufficient to address the problems of the region.

— Extraregional powers should be invited to cooperate in the development of the region.
— Regional cooperation should be encouraged by emphasizing multilateral, rather than bilateral, approaches to the region's problems.

Puerto Rico could play a leading role in implementing these new policies for the Caribbean Basin. Puerto Rico holds a central position in the region as its transportation, communications, financial, and economic hub. That reality, dictated by geographical and historical considerations, should be recognized and permitted to operate in building a new and prosperous Caribbean.

A Time to Choose

The world's foremost Caribbeanist, Gordon K. Lewis, saw the situation clearly thirty years ago.[44] He said then that the Caribbean's historical project had to be a federal alliance that would look toward its own interests. This would be accompanied by a joint nationality created by the forces of democracy and nationalism. A third element of his view of the future would be a system of collective security. None of these goals would be possible, he said then, if Puerto Rico were not given its *soberanía* (sovereignty). A sovereign Puerto Rico would no longer be seen as a U.S. pawn in the region and would be afforded the respect it deserves as a crossroads for North and South America. Cured of the malaise of domination, the Puerto Rican people could assume the role of an "honest broker" between the Americas. The formulation of a world-view by the Puerto Rican masses had been "obstructed," Lewis said, by an "insularist" and "isolationist" tendency. The absence of a militant negritude in the island had prevented its Caribbeanization, and an overdose of pragmatism had prevented the vision of a Caribbean destiny for the island. In a converging world, he concluded, when former colonies begin to contribute to the world, Puerto Rico will define and achieve its unique role.

As we enter the 1990s the picture is much clearer. Ana Lydia Vega, a young writer, has argued that Puerto Rico's collective subconscious has integrated its African past only recently. After what she terms "a defensive nationalism," islanders have begun "an Afroantillian vindication," abandoning their "galloping hispanophilia," which had been the initial response to the threat of cultural dissolution posed by Americanization. *Mulataje* (Creole pride) has only very recently been discussed as a positive value. Puerto Rico is no longer alienated from its geopolitical neighborhood.[45] The Eastern Caribbean islanders can now relate to Puerto Ricans because Puerto Ricans have finally come to recognize (even in the very difficult realm of race) their common origin and their common destiny. However, even at this point the elite in Puerto Rico call this new disposition (in the disastrous words of Governor Rafael Hernández Colón) a mere "rhetorical ascription." Puerto Ricans have not yet arrived, concludes Ana Lydia Vega, at the definitive expression of their essence as a people, but "all seems to indicate that the hour of our Caribbeanization has arrived a century after Hostos, Betances and Ruiz Belvis [the founding fathers of Puerto Rican nationhood] preached the need to unite, over all impediments, to achieve a common salvation." In other words, Puerto Rico is ready to design and embark on its own national historical project, one that has deep roots in its intellectual history. The United States should act unequivocally to promote it.

I have attempted to show in this chapter how sharply the role of Puerto Rico in the Caribbean is circumscribed by its ambiguous and uncertain relationship to the United States. What then, are the prospects of a change in the status quo? I offer four scenarios leading to a resolution of that question.

As a *commonwealth*, under the U.S. flag, with the dollar as currency, with property rights under the U.S. Constitution, with wages and industrial exemptions regulated by the U.S. Congress, and with Puerto Ricans being U.S. citizens, Puerto Rico differs so profoundly from all other Caribbean entities that not much can be done to promote a role for the island in the region. Even if the rest of the Caribbean becomes more like Puerto Rico, if the islands become part of the North American Free Trade Area (NAFTA), their political condition will certainly differ from Puerto Rico's present commonwealth status. It is obvious that the old Puerto Rican political "model" is not applicable or exportable to the rest of the Caribbean.

As a *state* of the United States, Puerto Rico will have no reason to play any role in the region. Former Senator Barry Goldwater did propose recently the creation of an "archipelago state," in which all small nations in the region would become municipalities of Puerto Rico, in the model of the Hawaiian Islands. That, of course, is an absurdity. Other than that, the island could become what Dade County in Florida has become for Latin America, but that would be a role of *entrepôt*, devoid of any unique role for the people of Puerto Rico.

As a *sovereign* people, be it under free association or under independence, Puerto Ricans could continue and expand the present program of financial and industrial promotion for the region, with the additional advantages pointed out by the Congressional Budget Office.[46] A clear, consistent policy could be devised for a role for Puerto Rico in the region.

There is, of course, a worst-case scenario. Smaller or less developed islands may be "scared" (Anthony Maingot's word) of Puerto Rico. Or Cuba may turn capitalist and claim for itself a leadership role in the region that would transform it into Dade County II. Or the Puerto Rican masses may end up not wanting any identification with the Caribbean. Or the United States may decide to postpone any decision regarding Puerto Rico, leaving the island in the limbo in which it has lived for half a century. All these events may be possible but are not desirable.

The fact is that sometime in the 1990s the United States may face a request from Puerto Rico for admission as a state of the union. Statehood can garner around 50 percent of the vote in a plebiscite. Politically, that percentage of endorsement is certainly not enough for admission. As one U.S. senator remarked: "It isn't that we don't love you; it's that you don't love us enough." Moreover, sentiment in the United States on statehood is similarly divided. What should the United States do? Speak unequivocally and say no.[47] The statehood issue is not one of self-determination but one of "mutual determination," since it is the sovereign that must decide whether to admit the island or not.[48] Evasion due to the fear of seeming undemocratic will only prolong indecision and crisis. The true feelings of the United States must be made known to the people of Puerto Rico. Then Puerto Ricans would be free to organize themselves as a nation.

This chapter recommends a single key policy: The United States should take the bold step of disposing of the territory and transferring sovereign power from the U.S. Congress to the people of Puerto Rico, with a nexus of "free association" with the United States in matters of defense and security. The United States should speak clearly, refusing statehood and offering the status of a true Free Associated State to Puerto Rico.

While commonwealth is a form of territorial status under the sovereignty of Congress, free association is a political relationship based on the sovereignty of the associated state: it is a compact between equals. They are two completely different political options. A political status as a true Free Associated State instead of the present Commonwealth, would liberate Puerto Rican energies for playing a leading role in the region.

Why and how could Puerto Rico lead? Its extensive democratic and electoral tradition, its developed infrastructure, and the advantages in economic growth it enjoys when compared with other islands in the region would make a Free Associated State of Puerto Rico a pole of attraction for its neighbors.[49] A new generation of leaders could then move the Puerto Rican people from the sidelines to the center of the Caribbean.

One problem persists. The United States does not recognize that it has a colony in the Caribbean. This lack of *autoconciencia* (self-recognition) does not permit a definitive dialogue to begin. That contradiction between U.S. colonialism and a new Puerto Rican historical project has to be solved immediately. Puerto Ricans can then begin to shape their own history.

3 | POLICY

10 | The Economies of the English-speaking Caribbean since 1960

R. DeLisle Worrell

In 1991 most economies of the English-speaking Caribbean were plagued by slow growth or stagnation, high unemployment, foreign exchange deficits, and living standards that were either declining or under threat. In addition, a few countries had high inflation, deteriorating social services, crumbling roads, unreliable utilities, and depreciating capital equipment. The exceptions were mostly to be found among the smaller territories, which boasted robust growth, improving living standards, enhanced social services, and improved infrastructure. The larger countries, and those with greatest promise in 1960, had done least well, while the smaller and less well endowed had prospered.

Throughout the region, some segments of the Caribbean population enjoyed considerably better living standards than in 1960, even in countries that experienced economic difficulty. The quality of life for the middle classes had improved in all countries, though in some cases they were not as well off as in 1980. Working-class lifestyles, however, did not improve so significantly. Health services were generally better, but housing, sanitation, education, and nutrition were still not at acceptable levels for the majority of the working class. There was wide variation in working-class living standards between countries and within larger territories. Education levels were high except in rural Jamaica. Housing and sanitation were often good except in selected urban communities, and malnutrition was a problem in some rural communities.

The economic performance of the Caribbean over the last thirty years was a surprise and a disappointment. From the perspective of 1960 most Caribbean leaders and intellectuals might have foreseen more vibrant economies with adequate living standards for all and a modern infrastructure. The 1950s and the early 1960s saw the first flowering of economic thought on the Caribbean by native thinkers. The major influences were Arthur Lewis's paper on industrialization in the Caribbean, the establishment of the Institute of Social and Economic Research, and the grouping of young intellectuals under the New World banner. They all agreed on the need to exploit the Caribbean's human and physical resources to eliminate poverty, unemployment, and want and to enhance material prosperity. Everyone agreed that elements of the strategy to achieve these goals should include improved educational opportunities, a wider range of export products from the region, and measures to obtain the maximum retained value from each dollar of exports. The dominant view also held that there was a vital requirement for foreign investment to provide technology transfer, marketing expertise, and finance. There should be a fiscal regime to induce investment, with provisions more or less equivalent to those offered by today's free trade zones. There was an influential minority view that argued for deliberate policies to maximize gains from import substitution. Foreign investment was to be nationalized so as to improve financial retentions and enhance the quality of local expertise. This minority view turned out to have been seriously in error, while the dominant view was very seriously flawed in its conception and implementation. In a world economy as benign as that witnessed in the 1960s these deficiencies may not have proved fatal, but the world of the 1970s and 1980s turned out to be much more hostile to the Caribbean than could have been anticipated.

The Caribbean in 1991

The Caribbean, with a population of about 5 million persons, stretches in an arc from Belize on the Central American mainland to Guyana on the north coast of South America. Belize and Guyana may be considered islands in a vast uninhabited hinterland—most of their populations are settled on the coast—and all the rest are islands. They are relatively rich in natural resources for their small size. Their agricultural resources have provided the basis for prosperity (interspersed with depression) over three hundred years of history in which they produced sugar, bananas, and other food products. The region produces bauxite, oil, and some precious metals. There are unexploited resources of timber and hydroelectricity. The fine weather, good beaches, and scenic variation make for strong tourism potential. The region's cultural diversity and creative talent have attracted worldwide attention in music, street festivals, art, and sport. Education is of an international standard.

On the basis of composite development indicators the Caribbean stands in the middle ranks of world economies. A few countries—the Bahamas, Barbados, and Trinidad and Tobago—have per capita incomes in the region of U.S. $5,000, a literacy rate above 90 percent, a life expectancy at birth of over seventy years, extensive rural electrification, and infant mortality rates below twenty per thousand. This is an overall profile that compares favorably with those of the lower ranks of the industrialized countries and betters those of some of the newly industrializing countries of Asia. At the other extreme are countries such as Guyana, with per capita incomes in the region of U.S. $500 and with decrepit electricity services, but with over 90 percent literacy and a life expectancy of over seventy years. This puts them well above countries with a similar per capita income in terms of the quality of life. With the exception of Jamaica, where educational standards are marred by a 40 percent illiteracy rate, the social indicators for the Caribbean are all better than for countries with comparable per capita incomes.

Caribbean economies are driven by the expansion of exports of goods and services. The diversity of human needs is such that self-sufficiency is not possible for anything beyond a primitive subsistence level of living. The region does not satisfy the minimum market size for even 10 percent of the expenditures that households require to satisfy basic needs.

Most Caribbean countries still lean disproportionately on a single export good or service. In the case of the Bahamas, Barbados, and Antigua, it is tourism; in the case of Dominica and St. Vincent, bananas; oil in the case of Trinidad and Tobago; and sugar in the case of Belize and St. Kitts. The exceptions are Jamaica, which has substantial receipts from bauxite as well as from tourism, export agriculture, and assembly in the free trade zone area; Guyana, which has bauxite, export agriculture, and some gold; and St. Lucia, which has diversified from banana exports to tourism and the export of light manufacturing.

On the basis of current economic performances countries may be placed in four categories. In the first are countries with reasonable growth and an external payments balance or surplus. They include the Bahamas, Belize, and some members of the Organization of East Caribbean States (Antigua and Barbuda, Dominica, Grenada, Montserrat, St. Kitts and Nevis, St. Lucia, and St. Vincent). Then there are countries with unbalanced growth (i.e., growth with a secular external payments deficit) or countries that are stagnating even though they have an external balance; Barbados, Trinidad and Tobago, and some OECS countries would be in this category. The third category includes countries with unbalanced growth and stagnation together with a serious debt problem; Jamaica is the conspicuous example. Finally, there are countries with such a severe crisis of confidence and with such dilapidated social services, public utilities, and communications that their prospects are extremely dim. In what follows, I try to explain the divergences of performance that have produced this spectrum of circumstances.

Economic Changes at Independence

The single change of major economic importance at independence was the establishment of central banks with responsibilities for maintaining a sound currency. Previously currency had been issued by four boards, one each for the East Caribbean, Jamaica, Belize, and the Bahamas. The currencies were backed by sterling reserves. Other economic changes and policies antedated independence, which was a very gradual process. Caribbean countries had all achieved self-determination with universal adult suffrage in the 1940s and 1950s. Trade and industrial policies were autonomous from that time onward, development plans were formulated, fiscal incentives introduced, and institutions established to provide finance and investment promotion. Formal independence was largely a ceremonial affair. Countries assumed responsibilities for foreign affairs and defense and changed the title of their head of government from premier to prime minister and that of the head of state from governor to governor general or president.

Even the establishment of central banks was not a result of independence. They might have been set up earlier but for the intention to form a regional central bank for the short-lived West Indies Federation. After the failure of the federation in 1962, governments made the transition to independence over the 1960s and 1970s, setting up central banks some time afterwards (jointly in the case of the OECS).

Central banks were a potential source of economic instability from their inception. The strongest motive for their establishment was the desire to have an additional source of finance for government. Under the currency board arrangement, governments were limited in their ability to borrow against the currency. The boards could accept only a small proportion of IOUs from banks or government; for the most part, banks had to present foreign exchange in order to obtain currency. This restriction was eased significantly in the later days of the currency boards, when up to 40 percent of their assets could be in the form of advances and securities. The central banks went one step further, effectively abolishing legal and conventional limits on the issue of local debt.

Central banks may give a useful degree of flexibility in the economic response to shocks, but they may be extremely destabilizing if they provide the fuel for excessive spending. The most direct and most damaging method of inflating national spending power is for the government to borrow from the central bank to finance its expenditures. The incomes paid to civil servants, the transfers to households, and the payments to government contractors are all made with currency that was not generated by production nor supplied by any equivalent foreign exchange. In the closed economy this "helicopter money" causes inflation directly. In the open economy it results in excessive foreign spending, depleting foreign reserves, depreciating the exchange rate either on formal or informal markets and producing inflation as a result of the depreciating currency.

The 1960s

The decade of the 1960s was a period of expansion thanks to favorable supply and marketing for primary products both new and traditional. There were advances in health services, public utilities, transport, and housing. At the end of the decade, however, a large proportion of the labor force remained unemployed. The infrastructure in many countries was still deficient, and there were large areas of poverty in cities and in the countryside. The economic progress in the 1960s was deemed inadequate because investment was insufficient, there was insufficient local value retained from exports, the export base was too narrow, the degree of labor absorption was too low relative to the growth of output, and the economic benefits seemed too concentrated.

The Commonwealth Sugar Agreement (CSA) provided a period of relative prosperity for sugar production in the Caribbean in the 1960s. Record sugar production levels were achieved in Barbados, Guyana, and Jamaica at the middle of the decade. Virtually the entire production was sold to the United Kingdom at prices that improved steadily over time. The CSA price was averaged across all the Commonwealth suppliers. Caribbean costs tended to be above the median, but Caribbean producing countries apparently enjoyed a sufficient margin to encourage high levels of output. The price seems to have been just sufficiently competitive to spur technical change and a search for higher levels of productivity.

The 1960s saw the maturing of bauxite mining in Jamaica. Operations began in the 1950s, and by the end of the 1960s the phase of rapid expansion was complete. Rapid growth to maturity after a slow initial period of groundbreaking activity is typical of the production cycle. It was inevitable that the 1960s growth in Jamaica's bauxite would not be repeated.

Guyana's bauxite production dated from much earlier and was well established by the 1960s. Guyana benefited from expanding North American demand for alumina. The Caribbean was well placed to be North America's most accessible source of supply, and the producing companies in the Caribbean owned their own smelting plants for alumina in North America. Guyana also produced a special grade of bauxite used in lining steel furnaces; this grade was only available in China apart from Guyana.

The Bahamas, Barbados, and Jamaica were borne on a rising tide of tourism during the 1960s. The introduction of fast, efficient jet aircraft created a new and immense market for Caribbean tourism. Previously only the wealthy and those with ample leisure time could afford to holiday so far away from home. The 1960s witnessed rapid growth in tourism in the more accessible islands.

There were also some light manufacturing, assembly operations, and food processing, attracted mainly by the Caribbean's low labor costs relative to those in the United States. The importance of tax incentives for investment in manufacturing remains a bone of contention. It is unlikely to have been a prime factor. Manufacturing proved disappointing as a source of foreign exchange, but it had a better capacity to absorb labor than any other sector, and it made a disproportionate contribution to the alleviation of unemployment.

Very little of the Caribbean economic growth of the 1960s may be attributed to these countries' own initiative. The CSA was preserved by the efforts of the British sugar refining interests, who also had interests in sugar production in the Caribbean. Tourism was the result of external technical change and the Caribbean's fortunate location, and bauxite was mined at the initiatives of North American companies. This implied a lack of economic autonomy that many thought to be necessary for effective independence. It put economic growth on a fragile base with no safety net in case foreign institutions lost interest in Caribbean growth. There was also a suspicion that Caribbean earnings were disproportionately low, and it was observed that export growth was heightening economic inequality in some countries.

These perceptions colored some economic policy in the next decade. One government embarked on a program of nationalization in a misguided attempt to chart its own economic course. All governments gave some support to import substitution, although it was patently obvious that the market potential was small and would be quickly exhausted. Deliberate attempts were made to effect income redistribution via government tax and spending policies. Efforts to promote additional exports continued, and some new institutions and fiscal provisions were introduced toward this end.

The Economic Crisis of 1971–1975

Popular methodology dates an "oil shock" in 1972–73, but in fact the prices of imports to the Caribbean started to accelerate noticeably in 1971. The oil price increase worsened dramatically what were already deteriorating terms of trade. The crisis was heightened by the coincidence of inflation and economic stagnation in the Western world, the phenomenon of "stagflation." The demand for Caribbean tourism fell because of the rise in transportation costs and the fall in real incomes in tourists' countries of origin. The cost of producing aluminum rose substantially because of its high energy usage, and demand for the product declined.

There was some compensation for the Caribbean in the extraordinary rise of commodity prices in 1974 and 1975, which brought a large windfall to sugar producers. Alas, it was too fleeting to redress the loss in international spending power that the Caribbean had suffered over five years of relentless import inflation. Trinidad and Tobago, the region's only oil exporter, was the sole country to benefit. Barbados, which produced a little oil for domestic use, was able to soften its external losses.

Initially Caribbean responses to the crisis were uniform across the region. They included mild credit restrictions, selected import controls, modest external financing, and a conservative fiscal policy that kept deficits below 3 percent of the gross domestic product (GDP). There were some exceptions—for example, the fiscal deficit in Barbados was 7.5 percent of GDP in 1973—but they were quickly corrected. This left a significant burden of adjustment to be borne by the population. It was absorbed with no marked decline in the quality of life, in the standard of infrastructure, or in the delivery of social services. However, it did mean that aspirations and targets set at the beginning of the decade had to be postponed. Impatience to get on with the national economic agenda may have been at the root of subsequent policy errors in Jamaica and Guyana.

In 1974, after a protracted and inconclusive negotiation with bauxite companies for a new tax formula to increase Jamaica's share of earnings, the government unilaterally imposed a levy on the industry. It immediately increased government revenues by one-third. In the same year Barbados, Guyana, St. Kitts, and Jamaica received the first of two years' sugar windfall receipts.

The Jamaican government immediately assigned the increased revenue to reduce unemployment via a massive, hastily contrived and enormously wasteful capital development fund for roads and other infrastructure. Naively, it did not prepare for retaliation by the bauxite companies. They slashed production, which they were able to do quite painlessly because of the softening of the alumina markets. The government's receipts from the bauxite levy were dramatically reduced, and Jamaica was left with a large and growing deficit. The least costly policy would have been to curtail the "make work" program and restore the budget deficit to manageable proportions. That must have seemed suicidal to the government, with elections due in under two years. Instead, the government used newly minted Bank of Jamaica currency to finance the unexpected deficit. The inevitable result was to exhaust foreign exchange reserves and to precipitate a balance of payments crisis.

The government of Guyana used windfall receipts from sugar to purchase the assets of virtually every foreign enterprise of any importance remaining in the country. Nationalizations had begun on a large scale a few years earlier with the purchase of a large mining operation at the turn of the decade. The sugar windfall was squandered to complete the process in a single year, with nothing allocated for investment that might boost production. At the beginning of 1976 Guyana's foreign exchange reserves were ample; by the end of that year they were down to zero.

The Barbados government sequestered much of the sugar windfall by a special tax and fund set aside for housing. The large fiscal deficit of 1973 was trimmed by new tax measures. There was only modest borrowing from the newly established Central Bank. Growth faltered in 1975 only, and foreign exchange reserves levels were sustained.

There was no active policy response in the OECS countries, Belize and the Bahamas. Expenditure adjusted to the adverse shocks immediately. The windfalls were small, but they were immediately available for spending. The pain of adjustment fell directly on the working classes, and rural populations were forced back on their own resources. Progress with the development of essential feeder roads and the enhancement of public utilities, social services, and amenities was halted.

The Aftermath of the First Crisis, 1976–1979

The second half of the 1970s was an era of high prosperity for oil-rich Trinidad and Tobago. Its booming demand for imports stimulated the exports of its neighbors, notably Barbados. The demand for tourism and growing exports of agriculture revived the economies of countries that had avoided adventurous expenditure policies in the early 1970s. Output in the Bahamas, Barbados, the OECS countries, and Belize expanded. Domestic inflation in these countries subsided as the increases in import prices eased. Unemployment rates slowly began to fall. Foreign borrowing was undertaken for improving airports and upgrading health and education facilities. Domestic and foreign investment appeared in hotels, in the assembly of light manufactures, in food processing. Foreign exchange reserves rose.

There was stark contrast in the experiences of Jamaica and Guyana. Excess spending in Jamaica led to a balance of payments crisis, aggravated by a vocal government ideology that eroded the confidence of both Jamaican and foreign investors. Foreigners and Jamaicans disinvested in tourism, agriculture, and other sectors, and there followed a speculative capital outflow. The government of Jamaica reacted with futile attempts to ration the insufficient supply of foreign exchange. Draconian measures for allocating foreign exchange and controlling imports were put in place. They did not curb import spending, and their major effect was to stimulate a large unofficial foreign exchange market, on which the Jamaica dollar was effectively devalued.

The chaotic rationing system depressed production, and the government devalued the currency under pressure from the International Monetary Fund (IMF). However, it failed to bring the fiscal deficit under control. Overspending continued, foreign exchange shortages were endemic, economic output declined, and inflation could not be tamed. Political and social tensions heightened, and a climate of fear enveloped the capital city. The mobile middle and upper classes migrated out of the country in growing numbers. The Michael Manley administration, its socialist dreams shattered and its leaders devoid of new ideas for tackling economic problems, seemed relieved to surrender the reins of office to the Jamaica Labor Party in 1980.

The Guyanese government made valiant attempts to bring its fiscal accounts into balance, but it was frustrated by declining output and incomes. The wholesale replacement of management in nationalized firms overstretched available management capability, and performance declined, especially in export sectors. Corporations that were intended to yield net revenues required government subventions to meet expenses. Moreover, the Guyanese government instituted a fierce regime of trade restrictions, with quotas and bans on a long list of consumer goods. It was accompanied by formidable exchange controls and strict rationing of foreign exchange. In spite of increasing evidence of unofficial trade in goods and foreign exchange and a decline of recorded output, the government remain wedded to the strategy of self-sufficiency to the end of the decade.

The Crisis of 1979–1981 and Performance in the 1980s

In 1979 oil prices rose sharply to levels few could have anticipated, only to fall even more dramatically in the following years. At the same time, North American and European economies contracted, depressing the demand for tourism and minerals. Oil price fluctuations created a major adjustment problem for Trinidad and Tobago. The whole decade of the 1980s was absorbed in efforts to accommodate to it. Jamaica remained in disequilibrium, and Guyana was driven further into crisis. Barbados once again adjusted, but its economic progress brought new challenges to increase productivity, in the face of which the economy faltered. The OECS, the Bahamas, and Belize bore the brunt of adjustment directly and resumed growth in the aftermath of the crisis.

The government of Trinidad and Tobago spent most of the 1980s in a reluctant and protracted effort to adjust to diminished economic circumstances. Up to the mid-1970s, national expenditures had remained relatively restrained, and a substantial proportion of the oil windfall was accumulated for investment designed to diversify exports away from oil. These investments were large, with long gestation periods, in steel, fertilizer, and derivatives of petroleum. Most have only become operational in the mid-1980s. They may yet prove to represent a sensible and far-sighted government investment strategy. Although these products operate in competitive markets, their plants are of a size that can make a significant contribution to export diversification. Export transformation of this magnitude could not have been obtained without deliberate government choice.

As time went by, however, and oil prices remained high during the 1970s, the expectations of the population escalated, and it became more and more difficult to contain expenditure. Rising incomes in the oil sector drove up prices and costs in other sectors, effectively destroying what was left of export agriculture and manufacturing exports, as firms priced themselves out of markets.

The oil price collapse abruptly removed the foundation for the high level of national expenditure, but it was several years before the government and people of Trinidad and Tobago were prepared to accept the consequences. Retroactive wage increases of over 50 percent for public servants and state corporation workers were still being implemented in 1982, and no serious fiscal curbs were contemplated until 1985. Meanwhile, the country ran through a very large stock of foreign exchange reserves that had been accumulated during the oil boom. Adjustment measures began in earnest around the middle of the decade with the tightening of import and exchange controls and a devaluation in 1985. Controls stimulated informal market transactions and a depreciating exchange rate, as might be expected, but they did depress real imports. However, they proved insufficient to achieve a sustainable balance of payments. The missing element was measures to curb excess spending. A bloated civil service, rapid increases in wages, and a drop in oil royalties and taxes had converted the large fiscal surpluses of the 1970s into fearsome deficits. The National Alliance for Reconstruction administration, elected in 1987, was prepared to grasp the nettle with wage cuts, reduction in civil service rolls, the introduction of a value-added tax, and other draconian adjustment measures. These measures were supported by a further small exchange rate depreciation. Adjustment was not complete by the end of the decade, but a slight recovery in the price of oil eased the burden, and the investments of the 1970s came on stream, making a significant contribution to foreign exchange earnings.

Of the non-oil exporters, the smaller, less developed ones performed better economically in the 1980s. This was less through their own efforts than because of their relative underdevelopment and the potential for exploitation of untapped resources. St. Lucia, St. Vincent, and St. Kitts benefited from the discovery of unexploited tourism potential. Resurgent tourism demand in North America and Europe especially benefited Barbados, the Bahamas, and Jamaica. A weak U.S. dollar in some years provided a windfall in sugar and bananas, and Belize benefited from its unexploited agricultural potential. Government investment in roads, ports, public utilities, education, and law and order facilitated the new investment, but other government policies had no effect. Tax reforms in Grenada and Dominica were a rationalization of chaotic systems rather than an attempt to change the directions of incentives or the burden of taxation.

Antigua entered a phase of rapid expansion experienced by most maturing tourist resorts. The economic performance of the Bahamas faithfully mirrored North American tourism trends: it was depressed during the 1980–83 recession and improved during the second half of the 1980s. Belize's external accounts were affected by transborder transactions with Mexico, stimulated by flight from a depreciating peso. Growth and external stability in the late 1980s was based on agricultural expansion and the exploitation of new lands. In Dominica a few food processing operations were established for export to the Caribbean market, but bananas remained the economy's mainstay. The Grenada economy was depressed by political instability, while Montserrat showed steady growth on the basis of tourism. The economy of St. Kitts stagnated in the early 1980s, but with the beginning of tourist expansion late in the decade the rate of growth picked up. In St. Lucia rapid growth in the tourism sector provided a supplement to an export economy based on bananas. There was a little growth in St. Vincent based on banana output, but the country remained among the poorest of the OECS countries.

Barbados faced a unique challenge among the English-speaking Caribbean states, having sustained economic progress over more than two decades. Living standards and real wages had risen to the point where Barbados was no longer competitive in basic low-quality goods and services. If the country was not to regress, investment had to be directed toward improving quality and productivity. It was necessary to establish product differentiation in existing markets and to invest in discriminating markets and in products that could command high prices. Regrettably, Barbados has thus far not made that transition. Export growth has slowed, while national aspirations for continuing gains in the standard of living have become embedded in the society. Overspending has been fueled by excessive fiscal deficits and supported by foreign borrowing. This left Barbados with a severe external disequilibrium at the end of the decade, with excess foreign exchange spending, a rising debt-service ratio, unpromising export prospects, and insufficient investment in the export sector.

The Jamaican government received a very large infusion of foreign loans to cushion the shock of inflation and recession and to complete the unfinished task of adjustment inherited from the 1970s. There was an extraordinary amount of foreign financing, especially from multilateral institutions, because Jamaica was seen as a test case of orthodox adjustment policy. This created special difficulties for Jamaica later, because the program did not succeed in restoring a balance of external payments, and the country was left with a large number of relatively short-term debts that could not be rescheduled because of the operating rules of the international institutions.

The main features of the Jamaican adjustment program, which were in effect in various guises throughout the 1980s, were (1) repeated attempts to contain the fiscal deficit by means of expenditure cuts, tax reform, and the sale of public assets; (2) liberalization of trade and reduction of tariffs, accompanied by a much more cautious liberalization of exchange controls; (3) flexible management of the nominal exchange rate by a variety of devices, including a managed auction; (4) liberalization of interest rate management; (5) reform of public institutions; (6) privatization of development institutions; and (7) privatization of export promotion agencies.

The measures did serve to restore confidence in economic management, and the government was able to improve public utility services, roads, and essential infrastructure, but overall they failed to stabilize the balance of payments and to restore growth trends. Moreover, there were signs of deterioration in health, education, and social services. The failure to balance external payments was due largely to external circumstances, particularly a very soft market for bauxite and alumina. But for that circumstance, fiscal and exchange rate measures might have secured a balance of external payments.

The deterioration of social services may be blamed largely on the inadequacy of IMF and World Bank orthodoxy in the early 1980s. By the end of the decade the Washington institutions had come around to accepting the need for special attention to social services in adjustment programs, but such concerns were totally absent from the programs agreed upon with Jamaica and with other countries in the early 1980s.

The liberalization of the trade regime was sensible. The restrictions were expensive to operate and worthless in terms of rationing foreign exchange; however, the liberalization of the financial sector had the perverse effect of raising the real interest rate to such high levels over extended periods of time that it discouraged long-term investment and heightened expectations of inflation. Still, there was significant if inadequate investment in tourism and free trade zones. The combination of a weak export market, old-style IMF conditionality, inappropriate financial liberalization, and overborrowing left Jamaica with average real incomes not much above the 1980 level, and with external payments arrears, a depreciated currency, insufficient investment, and an unsupportable debt-service ratio.

The new international recession of the early 1980s found the Guyanese economy in the throes of severe fiscal adjustment, the most recent in a series of efforts to restore external balance after the 1976 policy errors. This shock completely derailed the adjustment effort, and the fiscal deficit quickly went completely out of control. All foreign credit dried up as external arrears mounted. Essential imports of both producer and consumer goods were unobtainable. Export supply was severely curtailed, especially in the mining sector. Extensive controls on foreign exchange, imports, and prices became increasingly irrelevant as informal traders took over the task of providing basic goods and services and not a few luxuries. The government endured a period of policy inertia that lasted well into the 1980s, while roads, public utilities, educational facilities, health facilities, and sea defenses went into decay and disrepair. A large proportion of skilled and professional workers emigrated, notwithstanding the draconian penalties imposed on emigrants.

By the time the Guyanese government addressed itself to the task of economic management in the late 1980s, external arrears exceeded the value of GDP by more than 50 percent, income per capita had declined to among the lowest in the hemisphere, electricity and telephone services were in a state of dilapidation, fuels, drugs, and essential supplies were often interrupted because of lack of foreign exchange, public buildings were in disrepair, and sea defenses were in a parlous state. Desperate attempts are being made at a complete about-face in economic policy, abandoning state control and autonomy, inviting foreign investment, depreciating the exchange rate, and raising interest rates; as yet no progress can be reported.

Assessment of Performance and Future Prospects

The reasons for the disappointing overall Caribbean performance were adverse external circumstances, policy errors, and omissions and weaknesses in policy design. The adverse external circumstances included unstable prices (e.g., the effects of oil prices on the Trinidad and Tobago economy), adverse terms of trade (e.g., the fluctuations in the prices of primary products other than oil), the recession in many export markets (e.g., bauxite), and rising foreign interest rates, which increased debt burdens.

The policy errors included restrictive trade and foreign exchange regimes in Guyana, Jamaica, and Trinidad and Tobago; nationalization in Guyana and to a lesser extent in Jamaica in the 1970s; excessive fiscal expansion in Guyana, Jamaica, and most recently, Barbados; and interest rate liberalization in Jamaica and recently in Guyana. The omissions and weaknesses in policy design include the lack of an adequate strategy for export promotion and poor design of fiscal policy. Priorities were not assigned for the delivery of government services in the execution of fiscal strategy.

There has been almost a total failure to diversify the sources of export revenues. The Bahamas and Barbados are "one-crop," tourist economies, Belize depends entirely on agriculture, and the OECS countries depend on either bananas or tourism. Trinidad and Tobago stands the best chance of meaningful diversification, thanks to government investment in large export enterprise; even there the diversification is not assured success. Jamaica's foreign trade zones are of minor importance and have ceased to expand. The failure to mount a deliberate, adequately staffed and financed medium-term export promotion drive centered on selected industries and products is the major lacuna in economic policy in the Caribbean. The elements of such a policy would include the provision of venture capital;

market development grants; market research grants; product development grants; quality control grants; and training grants. It would include relief from tax on inputs and profits in the export sector. It would include special tax incentives for investment in exports. The nation would institute export achievement awards. Government finance could be provided for export marketing companies run by the private sector; these incentives would be provided only to selected priority items of nontraditional exports.

The major flaw in the design of fiscal policy was the capricious and cavalier approach to fiscal cuts. Expenditures were not matched to the delivery of services and deliberate choices made according to assigned priorities. Expenditures were cut on the basis of the line of least resistance. As a result, capital expenditure was cut most heavily. Voluntary retirement schemes were made generally eligible, so that retirees were drawn indiscriminately from among the most and the least essential of government services. Expenditure was also cut by neglecting maintenance and providing insufficient supplies for efficient delivery of government services. The result has been the erosion of services and infrastructure that may be essential for the resumption of economic growth.

Policy Prescriptions

The countries in which there currently is growth with no balance of payments problem but in which there are signs of stagnation on the horizon need to institute successful programs for export diversification. Those countries that are already experiencing economic stagnation or have a balance of payments problem need demand management policies in addition to policies for export diversification and human resource development. Countries with an unmanageable debt-service burden, specifically Jamaica and Guyana, need to reduce that burden to a level that does not squeeze investment and essential consumption.

Export Diversification

Export diversification programs need not involve entirely new products, though there ought to be some of these. There is considerable room for diversification around existing exports, for example, specialized tourism markets, product differentiation, geographically concentrated marketing in high-income areas, jealously guarded quality of products and service, cost-effective marketing, first-class expertise in selected areas, and production of special sugars and syrups, rums and rum drinks, molasses for selected markets, and sucrose alcohols. Other possibilities include selective clothing markets, production of specialized marine products (with special emphasis on environmentally benign methods), and high-quality exports of fruit and vegetables.

The Caribbean's progress in export diversification has been disappointing because of deficiencies in export marketing expertise, the deflection of human resources from exports to the nontradable sector, and the absence of a national sense of urgency about the export challenge. In addition, there is a lack of understanding of the need for and the sources of productivity increases to maintain export competitiveness.

EXPORT MARKETING. The export marketing strategy should be characterized by selectivity, a case-by-case approach, a medium-term horizon, and official policies to seek out and reward successful export marketers. The export marketing thrust should be selective because human resources are scarce and export marketing is a demanding exercise. Governments and firms that are sufficiently large to address the export market must choose a few items with which to spearhead new exports. A carefully planned and researched medium-term strategy is required. It is unlikely that success will be assured within the first three to five years. Firms must command sufficient financial resources and be assured of support from government to sustain the export effort for that period of time. There must be systems to monitor and assess progress and to make corrections as necessary. Successful exporters should be given public recognition, tax relief, and additional financial resources if needed.

DEFLECTING RESOURCES FROM THE NONTRADABLE SECTOR. Most profitable companies in the Caribbean invest in real estate, and the region's best marketers devote their energies to domestic insurance and retailing. Even a small proportion of the funds spent on shopping centers and office buildings in the last decade would have served to finance considerable investment in exports. Teams of the most aggressive agents and retail sales persons could begin to make inroads for quality products in North America and elsewhere. The greatest mileage is to be made by seducing finance and marketing skills away from nontradable activity into exports. Policies to ensure this might include a strong bias toward exports in the tax system as well as in the structure of salaries; tangible rewards to successful export pioneers; and a welcoming environment for export marketing, that is, a market characterized by a lack of red tape, recognition of the importance of exporters' contribution to the economy, hotlines to circumvent administrative hurdles, and so on.

A NATIONAL CAMPAIGN TO UNDERSCORE THE URGENCY OF THE EXPORT CHALLENGE. It will eventually dawn on Caribbean insurance companies, financial institutions, and trading companies that real estate and nontradables have rather uncertain prospects in these open economies. Unless economic expansion is based on foreign exchange earnings, it precipitates a foreign exchange crisis, which leads to drastic contraction in nontradable activity. In contrast, a firm engaged in the export of goods and services is proof against domestic recession and is insulated from the consequences of overambitious fiscal policy. However, domestic firms may not acknowledge this reality until the country experiences a dire balance of payments crisis and exchange rate uncertainty, when investor confidence is badly shaken, investment horizons have become very short, and foreign exchange seed money has become scarce. Governments and leaders in the private sector have a responsibility to advance the consciousness of the direction of future growth by emphasizing an export orientation.

INCREASING PRODUCTIVITY TO MAINTAIN EXPORT COMPETITIVENESS. In a growing economy, increases in real wages lead to increases in the cost of production of exports (with given technologies and labor intensities) and a tendency toward reduced export competitiveness. Unless productivity is increased, exports will stagnate and nontradable activity will contract because of the deficit in net foreign exchange earnings. Productivity can be increased by investment in new products, new processes, and improved quality. It requires increased job flexibility and enlightened labor practices that promote self-motivation.

Stabilization Policies

All Caribbean countries need policies for active export diversification. In addition, many need firm policies to stabilize their balance of payments. Balance of payments crises in Caribbean economies are the result of persistent national expenditure in excess of national output and income. Typically, over 50 percent of expenditure goes for imports, while only one-third of income is earned in foreign exchange. If expenditure grows faster than income over several years, the country uses up all loan proceeds and exhausts foreign exchange reserves. Currency devaluation is inevitable, usually after a desperate and futile attempt to "conserve" foreign exchange via exchange controls.

The only effective way to restore balance of payments equilibrium is to reduce national expenditure to levels that may be financed out of national income. The principal instruments are restriction of money creation to finance the government, a tax policy to control private spending, and controls on government expenditure. Ancillary means include interest rates set to discourage capital flight and to switch funds between the government and the private sector and an active policy to stabilize the exchange rate at a level that eliminates any excess demand for foreign exchange.

Stabilization policies must be accompanied by policies for export diversification, human resource development, and the improvement of infrastructure. The shape of the government's expenditure budget will be influenced by these latter requirements.

MONEY CREATION. The principal cause of exchange rate instability in the Caribbean is the printing of money to finance government deficits. To stop money creation, governments must reduce or eliminate deficits on their own accounts and on those of state corporations. Except for the East Caribbean Central Bank, no Caribbean central bank has the independence of government that would allow it to limit credit to the government at its own discretion. Statutory limits can be and have been changed at will; therefore, the only way to avoid money creation is to ensure a deficit that is so small as not to require any. How small that deficit must be depends on the depth of the balance of payments crisis and the extent of overspending in the private sector. The larger the balance of payments deficit, the smaller the allowable fiscal deficit. If the private sector runs a large deficit, the government cannot run a deficit as well.

TAXATION. The instrument for adjusting private expenditure is taxation. If private expenditure is too high, the government must increase tax rates to absorb a greater proportion of incomes. A reduction in disposable income is the only measure that will arrest imports, except in the short run of a few months.

Arguments have been advanced that changes in the tax structure might be engineered so as to switch expenditure from imports to domestic goods or to switch income from consumption to investment. However, both in theory and in practice there is little to support these arguments. No matter how high the import tariff, Caribbean countries must import flour, medicines, animal feed, oil (except Trinidad and Tobago), rice (except Guyana), textiles, footwear, toiletries, transportation equipment, generators, metals, and so on. The availability of foreign exchange is exhausted long before we come to the end of the list of essentials. Price alone will not reduce levels of importation; only the ability to purchase will. For much the same reason, forgiving taxes on saving is unlikely to lead to an increase in investment. What is much more important for countries with a balance of payments problem, the kind of investment that has attracted the largest share of finance in the Caribbean is just as harmful as consumption. Most investment, and an increasing percentage of incremental investment, is in real estate; very little is for exports of goods and services. Strong tax incentives are needed for a switch from investment in nontradables to investment in exports, together with taxes on nontradable activity to provide funds for the export drive.

GOVERNMENT EXPENDITURE. The target for government expenditure (including expenditure on state corporations) is determined by the allowable deficit, that is, the deficit that does not require money creation, and by decisions about tax policy. Policymakers must juggle between combinations of more tax, more expenditure and less tax, less expenditure in pursuit of a collection of social and economic goals: income distribution, export promotion, employment, maintenance and development of human resources and infrastructure. The objectives are many, but so are the options: changing priorities and allocation of expenditure, different mixes of public and private provision of services, means tests, marginal cost pricing for government services, direct grants versus tax relief and tax adjustment for income redistribution, and so on. The objective should be to attain the most ample provision of services most efficiently and within the constraints of the available financial resources.

INTEREST RATES. Countries that institute suitable fiscal correction will wish to supplement it by policies to keep interest rates a little above comparable international interest rates as a disincentive to capital flight. This policy only works after the exchange rate has stabilized and fear of depreciation has dissipated. It is quite futile to try to counter that fear by interest rate policies. To do so results in astronomical interest rates, which are a formidable barrier to any long-term investment.

Interest rate policy may also be used to shift finance at the margin between the private and public sectors to give the government a little more room to maneuver. By bidding up the rate on government paper, the central bank may make credit to the government more attractive to banks than credit to the private sector. But this policy must be applied with a gentle hand; if the central bank pushes too far, interest costs will swell the budget deficit.

While it is counterproductive for the central bank to structure a whole range of interest rates, interest rate policy cannot be left to "market forces." A small number of dominant financial institutions can be expected to exploit their oligopoly to earn rents. Central banks have not been able to do much about such rents; "controlled" interest rate spreads are just as wide as the uncontrolled. But central banks may at least ensure that interest rate trends respect the fundamentals, such as the trend in foreign interest rates and government borrowing requirements.

EXCHANGE RATES. In the open economies of the Caribbean the exchange rate will settle at whatever rate balances the supply and demand for foreign exchange. If the central bank tries to maintain some other rate, unofficial foreign exchange transactions become increasingly common. It becomes more and more difficult to obtain foreign exchange at the official rate, disparities between the official and unofficial rates increase, and in the end the central bank is forced into steep devaluation. If the central bank creates money to finance excessive spending by the government or the private sector, the gap between the supply and demand for foreign exchange may not close, and the value of the currency keeps on falling. Devaluation is highly inflationary, and continuous exchange rate deprecia-tion sets up very strong expectations of inflation. Formal and informal indexation becomes commonplace, reinforcing the inflationary pressure. The solution is to impose sufficiently tight fiscal policies to eliminate money creation. Caribbean governments may choose to fix exchange rates, but they may not do so directly. To fix the exchange rate, governments must choose a fiscal policy that brings national expenditure in line with national output (and foreign investment inflows).

It is something of a misapprehension to think of exchange rate adjust-ment as a tool of policy. The only central banks that may set exchange rates at will are those with large stocks of foreign exchange reserves, but banks with plentiful foreign exchange reserves hardly find any reason to tamper with the exchange rate. Exchange rate policy is more properly re-garded as an outcome of other economic policies and economic circum-stances. The only responsibility the central banks exercise is to identify a path toward the equilibrating exchange rate. Even that target is beyond their grasp unless fiscal policy is brought to bear to balance expenditure and output.

TRADE POLICY. The considerable debate over trade policy in the Ca-ribbean is something of a diversion. It is based on the false premise that import-substituting industry diverts money and skills from export indus-try. Industries producing for CARICOM are small by international stan-dards. They absorb a trivial amount of the available finance for investment, and they use relatively few of the marketing and other skills available to the Caribbean. Most of the money and skills needed for exports are de-voted to real estate, distribution, and nontradable services. The issue is not exports versus import substitution but exports versus nontradables. The reduction in antiexport bias is irrelevant; what is needed is an anti-non-tradables bias. The elimination of quantitative restrictions is desirable, not because of any stimulus for exports, but to broaden the scope of consumer choice, increase competitive pressures on domestic producers, and elimi-nate opportunities for influence peddling and corruption.

Debt Servicing

Only two CARICOM countries, Jamaica and Guyana, have an intrac-table debt-service problem. All others can find policies that permit them to meet their obligations, stabilize external payments, and resume economic growth. Jamaica and Guyana are condemned to stagnation unless their debt-service burden is reduced. It is on that basis that the Caribbean should negotiate for debt restructuring. Presumably no one has an interest in the long-term impoverishment of the borrowers, not even the lenders. The pressing need is to restructure debt owed to multilateral financial institutions. Creative practical schemes must be devised and supported. Other kinds of debt relief, such as unilateral debt forgiveness, Paris Club restructurings, the Brady Plan, and so on, may provide some debt relief but will not make for a feasible growth path for Jamaica and Guyana.

Regional Monetary Arrangements

The most fertile environment for an export promotion strategy in the Caribbean is within a regional framework. The prospect of a stable money for the region, guaranteed by a regional central bank, would serve to curb inflation, eliminate exchange rate fluctuations within the region, facilitate regional joint production in goods and services, and allow regional financial flows to make for a more practical size of capital market. In the area of human resources, firms are constantly frustrated by an inability to find suitable talent within national boundaries. The provision for making up that deficiency from within the region is inefficient, lengthy, and inadequate. In theory, skills may be brought in, but in practice the conditions attached (such as uncertain tenure, no provision for spouses, restricted access to mortgage finance, and long administrative delays in processing work permit applications) are an effective barrier.

Regional monetary integration can be effected by stabilizing the balance of payments of each CARICOM member country. Once there is no longer an excess demand for foreign exchange, the rationale for exchange control disappears, and so does the incentive for capital flight. Intraregional capital flows would no longer be a threat to the economic stability of any member country. Monetary integration requires compatible fiscal policies, not necessarily fiscal policies that are identical. Fiscal policies are compatible when they contain demand within the foreign exchange earning capacity of the state served by each government.

There are two possible paths to such policies. One proceeds by setting criteria for qualification of any country that wishes to join the monetary union. The criteria would include adequate foreign exchange reserves maintained over a sufficient time period, plus currency stability over a sufficient period to ensure confidence in the national currency. Any country that qualified on these criteria would be eligible to join the monetary union. The coordinated monetary policies of this unit would be managed by a joint monetary council with powers to control money creation along the lines of the East Caribbean Central Bank's Monetary Council.

The alternative would be to establish a "hard" Caribbean dollar to circulate alongside existing currencies. It would be backed by foreign exchange and would be legal tender everywhere. There would be no exchange controls on accounts in hard Caribbean dollars. The hard Caribbean dollar would also be administered by a supranational constitution, which would enable it to resist national demands to create money. As people shifted out of the existing national currencies of dubious provenance into a new currency that maintained its real purchasing power, governments would lose the capability to print money. They could continue to print money in national currencies, but less and less economic activity would be covered by transactions in national currencies.

Conclusion

The economic prospects depend on how close Caribbean countries may come to good economic policy. The ideal is a conservative fiscal deficit, a government tax bias toward exports, and an expenditure list that, within the constraint of the fiscal deficit, accords with priorities set out for the delivery of government services. The exchange rate should be fixed and supported by ample foreign exchange reserves. Governments should squeeze national spending by tighter fiscal policies if necessary in order to stabilize external payments. Administrative controls on prices, imports, and foreign exchange should be avoided. Nominal interest rates should be held in line with foreign interest rates in a low-inflation regime. Low inflation may be secured by a constant nominal exchange rate. If the external balance is so extreme that it may not be immediately corrected, managed exchange rate movements may be necessary, and it may be necessary to tolerate high levels of inflation until one comes within sight of a restoration of external balance. In these circumstances it may be necessary to attempt to tie the real interest rate to the real rate prevailing on international markets. This is an extremely tricky and uncertain operation and should be regarded as a temporary expedient in an attempt to achieve the ideal of a fixed exchange rate and stable prices. Countries need to institute a national commitment to a clearly articulated, well-funded export promotion strategy.

Prospects depend on the prices and markets for traditional exports, which will continue to provide surpluses for the sustenance of the economies during the period of transition to a more diversified export strategy. There are no promising growth prospects for Guyana and Jamaica in the

1990s because of the extent of their external indebtedness. For growth to be possible in Jamaica, considerable debt forgiveness will have to be secured. Guyana's problem is so large that it appears quite unmanageable. No other country has an intractable problem, although debt-service ratios in Barbados and Trinidad and Tobago are now uncomfortably high. Guyana is also the only country where there is an acute problem of policy credibility, as was seen in the hostile reaction to the implementation of stabilization policies in 1989 and 1990.

The private sector in the Caribbean must share a genuine conviction of the central importance of the export-dominated growth strategy. They must be seduced in part by the demonstration effects of conspicuous export successes. Part of the inducement must be by way of incentives through the fiscal system. There must also be penalties for investment that is diverted away from exports and toward nontraded activities and real estate. The export thrust must be supported with an education policy that includes provisions for specific skills in priority areas and with economic education about the nature of the foreign exchange constraint to growth in small open economies.

No Caribbean country presently has good medium-term prospects. The countries that grew in the late 1980s have no means of assuring their continued expansion. They depend mainly on one major product, which is likely to come to maturity and then level off. No country has a credible strategy in place for export diversification. Nonetheless, the countries that have been expanding do have the potential for self-sustained growth provided they maintain existing fiscal policies and introduce the appropriate export promotion policies.

Some countries need to tighten fiscal policy, reorder their fiscal priorities, and stabilize their balance of payments. Included in this group are Barbados, Jamaica, and Trinidad and Tobago. These policies must be combined simultaneously with the required export promotion strategy. With the best that it may do, Jamaica is unlikely to be able to raise its standard of living because of its debt-service commitments. In Guyana the political and social preconditions for a resurgence of investment do not yet exist.

11 | The International Economy and the Caribbean: The 1990s and Beyond

Stephen A. Quick

The decade of the 1990s promises to be a difficult period in the economic life of the Caribbean. Sweeping changes in finance, technology, politics, and trade are likely to alter the pattern of global production in ways that will pose new challenges to the small island states of the region. Lacking the population to become major centers of final demand, and in competition with other low-wage producers in Africa, Asia, and Latin America, Caribbean nations will find that many of their past economic development strategies are no longer effective. In this new world, all of the states in the region will need to undertake a rigorous reassessment of both their resources and their development strategies. They must define a role within the evolving world economy that produces adequate employment growth and rising living standards for their populations. This, in turn, will require a systematic reorientation of economic policy toward exports and international competitiveness, a reorientation that is already under way in most countries, where it is starting to pose severe challenges to the domestic political system.

Trends in the World Economy

During the 1980s, three global trends converged to bring about a major change in the world economy. First, the capacity of the global *communica-*

tions system expanded enormously, with such innovations as broadcast satellites, fiber optics, and global computer networks. The communications revolution transformed the marketing of products from a national enterprise to an international one, where firms sought to organize consumer tastes and preferences everywhere on the planet. The communications revolution also transformed the process of controlling production. In the digital era, it became possible for a single headquarters staff to control effectively the production of goods in a dispersed network of factories worldwide.

Second, the 1980s witnessed an enormous increase in the pace of *technological innovation*. Innovation produced a wave of new products and dramatically shortened the useful life of many existing products. Innovation also sharply altered the raw materials requirements of many production processes in ways that reduced the market power of producers of primary products.[1] The significance of labor costs in the production process was also reduced by technological innovation, since profitability was influenced far more by the ability of the firm to respond quickly to customer needs, to have access to good transportation and communications networks, and to mobilize the investment needed to stay at the cutting edge of technology.

Third, the 1980s were characterized by unprecedented *liberalization of financial markets*. In virtually all industrialized countries, money was allowed to flow across national borders with unprecedented ease. In such an environment, firms doing business in one country no longer needed to rely solely on the savings of that country to provide finance for their new investment. Conversely, savers in a given country no longer were restricted to domestic investments as an outlet for their savings. If investment demand and therefore interest rates were higher in one country, savings flowed easily across borders to capture the higher returns.

These three major trends helped create an integrated "world economy" whose central dynamic is the process of new capital investment. Rapid technological change meant that the successful firm had to step up its rate of investment, both to develop new products and to match the cost-cutting innovations of global rivals.[2] Recovering the costs of such investment within the shortest possible time meant that firms needed to tap the broadest possible market for their products, which put them under enormous pressure to develop marketing networks worldwide. The revolution in communications made it technically possible to organize both production and marketing on a global basis, and financial liberalization provided a mechanism of ready finance for investment virtually anywhere on earth.

Corporations and the State: New Limits on Economic Policy

This new international environment has profound implications for economic policy. The less integrated, less competitive international economy of the past permitted countries broad latitude in shaping domestic economic activity through fiscal, monetary, and trade policies. In the emerging world economy, however, the ability of governments to pursue independent economic policies has been sharply constrained. Governments previously made extensive use of monetary, fiscal, regulatory, and trade policies to influence the character of economic activity within their borders. National firms were often favored at the expense of multinational ones, and an expansionary bias was built into many macroeconomic policies. In response to rapid market growth and preferences for national firms, multinational enterprises stepped up the pace of cross-border investment, in effect establishing a "national" presence in many countries at once. During the 1980s, direct foreign investment grew nearly four times as fast as GNP in the industrialized world.[3]

Once established in foreign markets, however, multinational enterprises often lobbied for a reduction in trade barriers and regulatory incentives, confident of their ability to compete both domestically and internationally. Much of the movement toward regional "free trade" agreements in Europe, North America, and Asia has been actively supported by the multinational business firms operating in these regions.

The changing realities of the international economy have substantially increased the leverage of global corporations. With capital and technology mobile, countries find it increasingly difficult to follow policies that differ from those pursued elsewhere in the world economy. Rapid money growth or expanding government deficits, for example, can quickly lead to capital flight, which destabilizes a nation's currency. The result of these trends was noted in the following terms in a recent article in the *Economist:* "Foreign direct investment has already reduced the freedom of governments to determine their own economic policy. If a government tries to push tax rates up, for example, it is increasingly easy for businesses to shift production overseas. Equally, if governments fail to invest in roads, education and so on, domestic entrepreneurs are likely to migrate. In short, foreign investment is forcing governments, as well as companies, to compete."[4]

The New International Economy and the Problem of "Development"

This new need for governments to "compete" has helped transform the debate about development strategy. In the decades after the Second World

War, most large developing countries sought growth by exporting primary products and developing domestic substitutes for imported goods behind high external tariff walls. The strategy often worked because the industrial world needed raw materials, domestic entrepreneurs were willing to invest on the strength of protection, and multinational firms were sufficiently attracted by large markets that they were willing to accept the regulations and restraints that were part of this development strategy. The oil crises of the 1970s reinforced this strategy. Oil import bills rose dramatically, but so did the prices of other primary commodities. Most large developing countries borrowed to finance huge internal deficits during the 1970s and 1980s rather than take the painful steps needed to bring consumption into line with income.

This entire approach was brought to an abrupt halt by the global recession of the 1980s, which coupled rising interest rates on external debt with falling prices for primary products.[5] The subsequent "debt crisis" also cut off access to external debt capital for most developing countries. At the same time, changes in communications technology were turning firms with multiple national subsidiaries into truly *global* production entities, which now chafed under the regulatory restraints associated with import substitution. Rapid technological innovation also rendered obsolete (and therefore unmarketable) many of the manufactured goods produced behind protective walls in the developing world.

This new international environment was much more supportive of an alternative development strategy, the "export-led growth" model of the Newly Industrializing Countries (NICs) of Asia—Taiwan, Korea, Singapore, and Hong Kong. Initially, the NICs also protected domestic industry, but it was a protection designed to encourage investment and exports. The NICs also actively encouraged multinational firms to establish factories in their countries, viewing such competition as healthy for the growth of domestic manufacturing industry.

The NICs provided the rest of the developing world not only an alternative development model but also intense *competition* for capital investment. The attractiveness of the NIC approach to internationally mobile capital quickly became apparent, and this approach to policy became what economist John Williamson called the "Washington Consensus" on "macroeconomic prudence, outward orientation and domestic liberalization."[6] In practice, the Washington Consensus translated into cutting both public deficits and domestic demand, dismantling trade protection, enacting policies to encourage international private investment, and devaluing the currency to produce a competitive exchange rate—in short, emulating the NICs.

The Caribbean and the World Economy

The pattern of economic growth in the small island states of the Caribbean has been shaped by the global trends noted above. All of the Caribbean islands formed their initial links to the international economy as exporters of agricultural commodities, particularly sugar and bananas. Later, some countries developed significant exports of bauxite (Jamaica, Guyana) and oil (Trinidad and Tobago). More recently, tourism has become a major export sector on a number of islands, while manufacturing has become significant in Puerto Rico, Jamaica, Trinidad and Tobago, and the Dominican Republic. Despite considerable sectoral diversification within the region, the exports of most islands remain dominated by a single product.

An important part of the explanation for one-product dominance of island exports is the phenomenon known as "Dutch Disease." When a very small country finds a ready world market for one product, the export boom in that product pulls local resources away from other industries and undermines their competitiveness.

In the first few decades after the Second World War, international markets and trading arrangements encouraged excessive specialization in tropical agriculture. The Commonwealth Sugar Agreement provided a ready U.K. market for the region's principal export during the 1960s, at a time when the U.S. market was also relatively open. Many Caribbean countries were granted preferential access for agricultural products in the European market through both multilateral agreements (the Treaty of Rome Association, the Yaounde Conventions, and most recently, the Lome Convention) and bilateral concessions (particularly the U.K. export subsidy on Caribbean bananas).

The inflation of the early 1970s contributed to this pattern, raising sugar prices and providing a spur to the development of mineral resources such as bauxite and oil. This inflation also, however, provided the first sign of trouble, since the prices of imports to the islands started rising faster than export prices, leading to deterioration in the terms of trade for many islands. This deterioration in the terms of trade accelerated sharply with the first "oil shock" for all of the islands except Trinidad and Tobago, an oil producer, and the oil refiners of the Bahamas and the Netherlands Antilles.

In company with much of the developing world, the nations of the Caribbean sought to cushion the blow of the oil crisis through external finance rather than domestic austerity. Current account deficits swelled enormously, hitting a high of 31 percent of GNP for Guyana in 1976, with Jamaica, Barbados, and Haiti posting deficits in excess of 10 percent of

GNP. These deficits were financed with surprising ease through a combination of direct foreign investment (particularly in tourism) and both grants and loans from official creditors. Unlike the larger debtor countries, however, most Caribbean islands received only scant financial assistance from commercial banks during this period.[7]

Statistics on international direct investment in the Caribbean are difficult to obtain, but recent reports suggest a decline in these flows during the 1980s.[8] Equity investment in the extractive industries was hit by declining commodity prices and by conflicts between governments and multinational corporations, particularly in Jamaica and Guyana. Such conflicts throughout the developing world in the 1970s caused a number of multinational firms to shift their focus toward expanding resource extraction in more "stable" countries.[9] Tourism attracted some foreign investment, but the aggregate financial impact was not large, due to the preference of international hotel and resort companies to finance construction locally while retaining a management contract to operate the facility.

Prospects for financial flows to the Caribbean do not appear to be particularly bright, and a recent review by the World Bank concluded that "all but a few of the countries are likely to confront a scarcity of external financing."[10] During 1990 the United States cut aid allocations for the Caribbean substantially, as priorities shifted toward fighting the drug war in the Andean countries, rebuilding Panama and Nicaragua, and supporting the liberalization of Eastern Europe.

Recent developments in debt policy are more encouraging, particularly for those countries with heavy debt burdens to official governments. Canada in 1990 announced a cancellation of debts owed by many Caribbean countries, and the Bush administration's Enterprise for the Americas initiative supported the concept of debt forgiveness on official bilateral debt. Despite these changes, most Caribbean islands remain in need of substantial external financing if they are to grow fast enough to absorb population increases and manage even a modest rise in per capita consumption levels. Such financing will need to come from private sources, since the recent World Bank survey of the region cited above found that only 40 percent of the needed funds were presently available from official sources.

External Trade in the 1980s

The marked deterioration in the region's access to external finance during the 1980s provoked a major shift in emphasis in development strategy: from seeking finance for imports to seeking markets for exports. Caribbean countries had previously sought and won preferential access to the European market through the U.K. banana subsidy and some of the provisions of the Lome Accord, but exports to the United States became the focal point for regional trade policy with the announcement early in President Reagan's first term that the United States would launch a major "initiative" for the Caribbean Basin.

In its original conception, the Caribbean Basin Initiative (CBI) was to offer both free access to the U.S. market for the region's exports and substantial new investment funds to take advantage of the new market opportunities. As the proposal made its way through Congress, however, the planned investment funds were deleted, and restrictions were added that limited access to the U.S. market for certain key products. When finally passed in 1983, the CBI explicitly excluded textiles, footwear, sugar, oil, leather, luggage, and beef.

These exclusions sharply diminished the potential trade benefits to the region from the CBI. Since many of the region's exports already enjoyed duty-free access prior to the CBI, and many others were limited by non-tariff barriers untouched by the initiative, only a small minority of the region's exports derived any benefit from the CBI.[11] In fact, total U.S. imports from the Caribbean actually fell substantially following passage of the CBI, as sharp cuts in the region's sugar quota and declining oil imports overwhelmed the expansion in such nontraditional exports as vegetables and fruits, tobacco, industrial chemicals, fish and shellfish, and electronic components and parts.[12] Nontraditional exports from the Caribbean did grow substantially during the 1980s, but a large fraction of the growth owed little to the benefits of the CBI. Exports from the Caribbean under the reassembly provisions of the U.S. Tariff Code (Sections 806 and 807), for example, regularly exceeded the value of imports under preferences granted by the CBI.

Investment also showed no significant change with the CBI. A recent report by the U.S. International Trade Commission concluded that "overall, levels of new investment in beneficiary countries in the region remain disappointingly low."[13] There were several reasons for the disappointing investment response. First, obviously, was the elimination of public funds to support investment from the original CBI proposal. Of greater significance, however, was the fact that the CBI promised duty-free access to the U.S. market for a period of only twelve years, a period too short to convince private investors to take the risks of Caribbean production. Finally, the exclusion of textiles and apparel from the CBI removed the sector of greatest potential interest to investors.

Prospects for expanded trade and investment under the provisions of the CBI remain uncertain. In 1986 the rules governing financial deposits of Puerto Rican tax-exempt (Section 936) firms were liberalized to permit such funds to be invested elsewhere in the Caribbean. In 1990 the trade provisions of the CBI were made permanent (albeit with largely the same product exemptions as the earlier law). Together, these changes could create both a larger pool of investable funds and a greater desire on the part of entrepreneurs to take the risks of Caribbean production.

Despite these positive developments, the overall trend in global trade policy does not appear to be particularly supportive of Caribbean trade. Heavy European subsidies continue to depress the world sugar price, and a recent General Agreement on Tariffs and Trade (GATT) decision criticizing the U.S. sugar quota system has met with stiff resistance from the U.S. Congress, which passed a 1990 Farm Bill that continued the old sugar quota system. Changes in global trade policy are also likely to eliminate preferences formerly enjoyed by Caribbean producers. The EC delegation to the Uruguay Round recently tabled a proposal for an elimination of all barriers on most tropical agricultural products. This proposal would open up European markets generally but would also eliminate the advantages granted to Caribbean producers under the Lome Accord.[14] Caribbean banana producers are likely to lose their preferred access to the U.K. market when the single European market is completed in 1992.[15] The U.S. Enterprise for the Americas initiative is also likely to grant to other nations in Latin America the benefits previously granted only to the Caribbean.

Taken as a whole, these changes mean that Caribbean producers are likely to see a reduction in preferential market access agreements, possibly coupled with a general lowering of external barriers in all major markets. These changes could potentially improve growth prospects for Caribbean exports, but only to the extent that Caribbean producers are low-cost suppliers by world standards. And it remains to be seen whether Caribbean producers can be the world's low-cost suppliers of even the most basic goods.[16]

Development Strategies for the 1990s

In the 1990s the island nations of the Caribbean must craft new development strategies in the context of a much more competitive international environment. Loans and grants from official sources will not be adequate to meet the region's growth needs; they will need to be supplemented by private capital flows if growth is to be maintained at an adequate level. Private capital will, however, have other markets equally eager to attract it, and the diminished value of Caribbean trade preferences will reduce the attractiveness of the islands if local costs are significantly above those prevailing in other developing countries.

This tough international environment will require difficult policy choices in the islands, where the task of government has always been to achieve a delicate balance between employment growth, consumption growth, and social stability. New employment is needed to accommodate the rapid growth in the labor force associated with young populations and relatively high birth rates. Consumption growth is needed not only to meet the basic needs of those at the lower end of the income distribution but also to retain the more mobile professional and middle classes. Social stability is particularly important for the plural societies of the Caribbean, where racial, class, and cultural divisions pose special threats to stability.

The old formula for reconciling these objectives relied on primary-product exports to support what Jonathan Hartlyn elsewhere in this volume calls a "massive but irrationally constituted" state apparatus. This apparatus protected an inefficient private sector from international competition while simultaneously using both subsidies and government jobs to distribute income and employment broadly through the society. The importance of the state to the economy tended to push all social conflicts into the government arena, where public spending and subsidies became the easiest solution to every problem. Raising adequate tax revenue to fund the subsidies almost always proved politically impossible, and large public-sector deficits became the inevitable consequence. Similar political pressures also led to a persistent overvaluation of the exchange rate, encouraging consumption and imports at the expense of exports.[17]

For a period of time, this formula worked tolerably well, but in a world of falling commodity prices, the model could be sustained only through external financial flows, and such flows are clearly no longer available at previous levels. Thus far, few countries have coped effectively with the new financial environment, with most simply cutting public spending along the lines of least resistance rather than refocusing public spending on a new strategy of growth. (See DeLisle Worrell, chapter 10 of this volume.)

The new external environment has also not brought about any major change in trade policy. Despite the strong moves toward trade liberalization in Mexico and elsewhere in the hemisphere, most Caribbean governments continue to protect the private sector behind both tariff and non-tariff barriers. Even though CARICOM has proposed a relatively high common external tariff (CET), individual countries continue to maintain high and variable local barriers to imports. Duty-free zones established on various islands to avoid the restrictions imposed by protection have been only partially successful.[18]

As a result of excessive protection and ill-considered fiscal retrenchment, few islands have either a public sector or a private sector that is prepared for what appears to be an increasingly competitive struggle for access to world export markets. If the islands are to prosper in the 1990s, this will have to change. Since they can no longer count on external finance on a large scale, the islands will have to expand exports rapidly in order to pay for the imports they are clearly not prepared to forgo.

Around the world, in industrialized and developing countries alike, there is a growing recognition that maintaining access to world markets will require a substantial commitment to *investment* broadly conceived. Manufacturing firms need to invest to keep up with new technologies, while service firms need investment to maximize productivity growth. Governments need to make new investments in infrastructure and "human capital" to facilitate private-sector activity.

The investment imperative is no less for the Caribbean. Unlike their larger competitors, however, small islands do not have the luxury of diversifying investments broadly across sectors. As the smaller Asian NICs have realized, small economies must make strategic choices among investment alternatives and hope their choices are correct.[19] For the Caribbean, this means, first, deciding in which sectors to concentrate investment, and then, deciding which groups in society should make the needed investments.

Investment in Which Sectors?

The choice of sectoral strategies differs markedly among the islands, due to differences in natural and human resource endowments, but several broad generalizations seem to stand out from the available literature. *Primary products* appear to have little fundamental appeal to new investors. The 1990 *World Development Report* projects growth in primary-product prices of only 0.2 percent per year through the 1990s, and this after what it calls "a dip in the short run."[20] Such projections reflect the increased use of synthetics and recycling in the industrialized countries, as well as the reduction in raw material needs as output in the developed world shifts from goods to services.

Agriculture would appear to be a more promising area for many Caribbean islands, as a means to both reduce imports and absorb a share of the growing labor force. Yet despite the economic advantages of diversified agricultural production, few islands have been successful in promoting broad growth in this sector. Some have managed to develop "export enclaves" in the agricultural sector to export high-value products such as melons, shrimp, and winter vegetables to the U.S. market, but these successes have not translated into improved agricultural self-sufficiency.

There appear to be several reasons for this failure. Generally, Caribbean islands are high-cost producers of many staple agricultural products and are unable to compete against the subsidized agricultural output of the industrialized world. Broad-based agricultural development therefore would require maintaining domestic food prices well above world levels, a practice that few governments with large urban food consumers have been prepared to embrace. Without such protection, the principal opportunities in agriculture appear to lie in the high-value "niche" markets, which might benefit from the reasonably efficient air transport system linking the islands to U.S. markets.

Manufacturing was the key to the success of the Asian NICs, and many hold out hope of a similar future for the Caribbean economies. Puerto Rico has already become the world's first industrialized tropical island, and the manufacturing sectors in Barbados, Jamaica, Trinidad and Tobago, and the Dominican Republic have expanded significantly in recent years. Yet a close look at the manufacturing sector in the Caribbean reveals some critical differences with the Asian NICs. Most islands have two quite distinct manufacturing sectors. The first produces goods for local and regional markets on the strength of external protection, goods that cannot meet the tests of cost or quality in world markets.[21] The second consists of labor-intensive assembly operations, producing products destined for the U.S. market, often under the duty-free provisions of Sections 806 and 807 of the U.S. Tariff Code. While such firms generate exports and jobs, they generally pay low wages, have limited linkages with the rest of the economy, and produce little value added or foreign exchange for the rest of the island economy.

For most of the islands, therefore, manufacturing means low-paid assembly work, an industry in which the islands are in competition with producers offering even lower wages. This is a strategy that holds greater promise for the poorer nations, such as Haiti and the Dominican Republic, which can compete with China or Bangladesh on the basis of low wages. Other islands are caught in a kind of limbo, with wage rates too high to compete as low-wage assemblers but without the technological infrastructure to follow the lead of the Asian NICs and shift toward high-value-added integrated manufacturers.[22]

Services would appear to be a more promising growth area for the islands. The income elasticity of demand for services in the industrialized world is high, and a recent OECD report suggests that service promotion may be an effective growth strategy for the developing world.[23] Tourism is, of course, already the largest industry in the islands, and it is an industry that is projected to grow rapidly as long as there is no recession in the United States. Tourism is a "rent-based" service industry, and the plentiful beaches and attractive scenery of the islands give the Caribbean a comparative advantage in earning rents from the U.S. market. Tourism is not without its problems. Critics point to its high capital intensity and heavy import demands, its weak linkages to the rest of the economy, its seasonality, and its sensitivity to business-cycle fluctuations in the industrialized world.[24] Tourism also imposes environmental burdens, which may set limits to the rate at which this sector can grow. Despite these objections, most observers conclude that tourism offers the most appealing growth prospects of any major industry.[25]

Other service industries also have shown considerable growth potential on several islands. The improvement in regional communications, including the establishment of digital "teleports" such as the one in Montego Bay, Jamaica, make it possible for island firms to compete in the growing international market for data-processing services. International banking and insurance operations have grown rapidly in Puerto Rico, the Cayman Islands, the Bahamas, and the Netherlands Antilles.

In considering sectoral investment options, island governments need to be mindful of the "Dutch Disease" problem endemic to small economies. The successful development of one sector may push up island costs to the point where other industries are rendered uncompetitive. A decision to push ahead with tourist development, for example, could undermine the chances of success in data processing or manufacturing.

Investment by Whom?

The local private sector in the islands thus far has not demonstrated a great enthusiasm for international competition. Most local businesses are focused entirely on the protected domestic market, and much of their business activity is concentrated in real estate, construction, and retail distribution. In Puerto Rico, for example, of the two hundred largest island-owned businesses, only three are significant exporters to nonisland markets.[26] This reality has generated considerable concern about the ability of the local business class to take the entrepreneurial risks associated with penetrating new export markets.[27] Of particular concern is the willingness of the local "big business" sector to take such risks.[28]

Risk aversion by local entrepreneurs has led many islands to look to international corporations as the lead investors in their export promotion strategy, particularly in tourism and manufacturing. In comparison with other developing countries in the hemisphere, however, Caribbean islands have had more difficulty in attracting global corporate investment. One major reason is that the domestic market is so small that foreign firms must plan to export virtually all of the output, and empirical studies of foreign investment behavior have found a distinct preference for larger domestic markets.[29]

Traditionally, Caribbean nations have pursued both U.S. and European corporations, with attention turning more recently toward Japanese firms. Since such firms tend to be very large and concerned about the scale problem in small islands, Caribbean governments might wish to consider pursuing foreign investors accustomed to operating on a smaller scale. Korea and Taiwan both have firms accustomed to global exports from small facilities, and the decision taken in 1989 by the Taiwanese government to finance an industrial park in Costa Rica may indicate growing interest in the Caribbean region.[30]

The state has been called upon to play an entrepreneurial role in many of the Caribbean islands, but the results have been generally disappointing. Public enterprise was the cornerstone of the early development strategy in Puerto Rico, but losses in these enterprises quickly shifted the focus to attracting industry rather than public entrepreneurship. Elsewhere, public enterprises often picked up the "lemons" discarded by the private sector in an attempt to salvage jobs (sugar refining) or ran prestige projects (airlines) that the local market could not support. As a result, there are almost no success stories of public enterprise in the Caribbean, and little current inclination to expand public entrepreneurship in the face of a worldwide trend toward privatization.

Implications for Policy

If the state cannot be expected to play a role as direct investor, it must find one as facilitator of the new strategy of enhanced export competitiveness. In the words of one Caribbean commentator, "The state must be the jockey, not the horse." Being an effective jockey means creating a climate conducive to rapid expansion of export-oriented investment by both the domestic private sector and international corporations. While this formulation sounds innocuous enough, it amounts to nothing less than a revolution in economic policy in the Caribbean. Moreover, this revolution can potentially undermine the carefully crafted social compromise that underlies the stability and democratic character of most of the islands.

It is helpful to approach the issue of investment climate from the perspective of international investors, who must be attracted to a given location and therefore define the lengths to which the state must go in making a country hospitable to investment. For such investors, the sine qua non for local attractiveness is macroeconomic stability. Wild swings in inflation and interest rates, along with abrupt movements in the exchange rate, damage the ability of an international investor to realize and repatriate profits.

Macroeconomic stability in turn requires stability of policy direction in the economy. One recent student of international investment noted that the "fear of policy inconsistency" is now the premier concern of foreign investors. Allaying these fears "requires going beyond the advertising of a good investment climate in the present, to finding a way for host authorities to bind their own hands (and the hands of their successors) as far as six to eight years in the future."[31]

With some notable exceptions, the past history of the Caribbean contains little of this sort of macroeconomic stability or policy consistency.[32] Instead, governments have regularly monetized deficits to maintain expansions, only to face sharp contractions and currency devaluations when the prior strategy proved unsustainable. Such strategies purchased a measure of social peace, but at the price of a deterioration in the islands' investment climate.

This history suggests three basic observations about the future of economic policy in the Caribbean:

1. *Monetary autonomy is a major threat to macroeconomic stability.* DeLisle Worrell notes in chapter 10 of this volume that "central banks were a potential source of economic instability from their inception," largely because they gave governments the opportunity to cover fiscal deficits with money creation. These potential disadvantages were counterbalanced in the past by the ability to use monetary policy to cushion an island economy against shocks, but given the recent trends toward integration of global capital markets, it is appropriate to ask whether these advantages are still worth the potential instability associated with independent national central banks, particularly in light of recent movements elsewhere toward restricting national monetary autonomy.[33]

If it were decided that limiting autonomy made sense for the small nations of the Caribbean, there are two routes the region could pursue. The first would involve following the lead of Puerto Rico and Panama and adopting the U.S. dollar as the national currency. The second would be to follow the lead of the Eastern Caribbean states, which have established a multi-island central bank with strict limits on its ability to finance fiscal deficits in member states. The international stability of the EC dollar throughout the 1980s puts it in sharp contrast to the national currencies of other, much larger islands in the region.

2. *Fiscal policy must also be reshaped to improve the climate for export-oriented investment.* Internationally mobile capital is notoriously averse to taxation, and the locational disadvantages of developing countries strengthen the argument for low taxation of capital income as a device for attracting investment.[34] Yet in the Caribbean, few islands have a fiscal system capable of extracting adequate revenue to fund public services without taxing capital. Individuals either have too little income, are too hard to monitor, or derive too much of their income from the "informal economy" to provide an adequate tax base. Governments have therefore generally struck a deal with local investors to tax capital income directly (in return for import protection) or to tax it indirectly (in the form of duties on imports). Both arrangements serve to entrench external protection and force external investors to seek refuge in duty-free export-processing zones.

Yet changing the tax climate to be more favorable to investors holds enormous potential for social conflict, since such changes require either an overall shrinkage in the activities of the state or a redistribution of the tax burden onto noninvestors. Both of these trends can be seen in the recent tax reform in Trinidad and Tobago, where a new value-added tax, combined with a cutback in government services and subsidies, fanned the popular resentment that gave rise to the looting that followed the recent hostage taking.

Improving the investment climate while avoiding a regressive shift in taxing and spending is possible, but only if a government is prepared to confront the power of domestic elites in its search for a more competitive strategy. Most local wealth in the islands is held in the form of real estate, which largely escapes effective taxation. Unlike machinery, real estate is an "immobile" factor of production, whose taxation would not diminish an island's international competitiveness. Yet even the very broad-based "tax reform" effort recently undertaken in Puerto Rico completely avoided any reform of the property tax system.

3. *Public spending to promote investment must expand significantly, possibly at the expense of more traditional governmental functions.* One of the paradoxes of the contemporary world is that investors demand services from the state but are unwilling to pay for them through taxes on property

income. In the Caribbean, exporters are demanding better roads, ports, electricity, and telecommunications facilities as a precondition for new investment, as well as expanded police protection to lower the costs to exporters associated with the region's drug trade.[35]

At the same time, attracting international investment capital requires a substantial increase in public-spending education, training, and other "human capital investments." This means not only improvements in basic literacy, which is already high on many islands, but also substantial improvements in secondary and technical education. The lack of managerial and technical expertise in particular appears to be a concern to international firms evaluating Caribbean locations.[36] With island education budgets already strained by efforts to attain universal primary enrollments, it may prove difficult to accommodate these additional demands.

In addition to spending more on infrastructure, most islands need to invest substantial resources in the promotion of local exports in global markets. Ideally, this is a task that could be accomplished on a regionwide scale, through the creation of a Caribbean-based export trading company, since the costs of marketing in global markets are high. Such investments are particularly necessary if the strategic goal is the expansion of exports by locally owned firms that lack established international marketing networks. In addition to spending on such investment "incentives," governments also find themselves called upon to bear increased fiscal burdens as a result of *successful* attraction of foreign investment. Manufacturing and tourism both create heavy environmental burdens, and remediation of these burdens falls on the public sector.

Conclusion

The policies needed to reshape the investment climate in the islands involve fundamental tampering with the social and political contract that has produced social stability and political democracy for most of the postwar period. The state will find fewer resources at its disposal to manage social conflict and may find itself called upon to repress dissent arising from its "development" policies. To the extent that the "Washington Consensus" urges the islands to follow the development model of the Asian NICs, it is important to recall that serious repression of labor demands in pursuit of international competitiveness has been a fundamental part of that strategy.[37]

As Franklin Knight and Evelyne Huber have pointed out elsewhere in this volume (chapters 2 and 5, respectively), an ability to craft ingenious social compromises has been an essential part of the Caribbean political structure for decades. The best hope for the economic future of the islands is that this capacity will enable them to meet the challenges of a more competitive international environment without sacrificing the open character of their societies.

12 | The Drug Problem: Policy Options for Caribbean Countries

Ron Sanders

The Drug Problem in the Caribbean

The transshipment of illegal drugs through the Caribbean en route to destinations in North America and Europe has resulted in several major problems for the Caribbean: (1) corruption of officials; (2) drug abuse and a rise in crime; (3) diversion of scarce foreign exchange resources from the process of development to combating drug trafficking and drug abuse; and (4) threats to the sovereign authority of Caribbean states by the involvement of the United States of America in policing the waters of the Caribbean and establishing organizations within Caribbean countries for dealing with the drug problem. This chapter describes the drug problem in the twelve independent countries of the Commonwealth Caribbean (those territories that were former colonies of the United Kingdom) and considers measures these countries might take to address the problem.

Corruption and a Threat to Democratic Institutions

The world trade in illicit narcotics is said to be in the vicinity of $500 billion per annum, and the efforts by governments of both large and small nations to stem this trade have been small by comparison. For instance, the United States, which is in the forefront of the effort to combat drug trafficking, is now spending a total of only $6 billion a year in all areas, including drug education at home and interdiction abroad. Caribbean countries are spending far less and are unable to compete with the large sums of drug money that are readily available. As an example, in the fiscal year 1989–90 Antigua and Barbuda budgeted to spend only $2 million on combating drug trafficking; in reality much less was spent.

These huge differences in financial resources lie at the root of the drug barons' power to corrupt. The commissioner of police in Antigua and Barbuda—one of the better-off small island states—earns no more than $2,000 per month, and a senior customs official makes $483 per month. By comparison, pilots flying light aircraft on behalf of the Colombian drug barons are reported to earn $5,000 per kilogram, and their planes carry an average of 300 kilograms; this translates to $1.5 million per shipment. If we take the pilots on the one hand and the police and customs officials on the other as the representatives of the front line in the battle of drug trafficking, it becomes clear that small countries cannot win. Police and customs officials are simply not compensated sufficiently to resist bribes.[1] Bribery and corruption do not stop at customs officials; the 1984 *Report of the Commission of Inquiry* in the Bahamas concluded that at least one minister, a member of Parliament, and an assistant commissioner of police "corruptly accepted funds from known drug smugglers."[2] Further, in March 1985 the head of government of the Turks and Caicos Islands, Norman Saunders, and two of his ministers were arrested in Miami for facilitating the transshipment of drugs to the United States.

In 1990 a commission of inquiry was conducted in Antigua and Barbuda into the circumstances surrounding the transshipment in Antigua in 1989 of a consignment of guns and ammunition from Israel to the late José Gonzalo Rodriguez Gacha, a notorious Colombian drug baron. The commission concluded that Vere Bird, Jr., a minister of the government and son of the prime minister, provided an end-user certificate to the government of Israel, without the knowledge or authority of his government, for a quantity of arms and ammunition ostensibly for the Antigua Defense Force but actually for supply to Rodriguez Gacha. The commissioner noted in his report: "I entertain no doubt that Mr. Vere Bird Jr., was paid by, or at least with, money emanating from Senor Rodriguez Gacha, for the services rendered to the arms shipment."[3] The inquiry also established the complicity of the head of the Antiguan army and customs officials in the affair.[4]

Drug Abuse and a Rise in Crime

Accurate statistics are not available in the Caribbean on the numbers of people involved in drug abuse or the numbers of crimes that are drug-related. There are several reasons for this. Among them is that the police record crimes for what they are, for example, "break and entry." No mention is made of the reason for the crime, which may well be to secure cash for purchasing drugs. But it is known that between 1984 and 1986 trafficking in narcotic substances increased in the region by 8,265 percent and the amounts increased from 8,250 kilograms to 712,778 kilograms.[5] Also, the majority of drug users in Caribbean countries do not register with rehabilitation centers. In 1989 the minister of health in Barbados lamented that while the number of drug addicts seeking help at the hospital had increased from 7 in 1986 to 115 in 1988, he had "reason to believe" that not all who should were seeking help.[6] Although official figures do not fully reflect the number of users, they do reveal a rising spiral. In Trinidad and Tobago, for instance, the number of admissions to hospitals for treatment related to cocaine and marijuana addiction rose from 376 in 1983 to 1,041 in 1989, and arrests for cocaine possession or trafficking rose from 5 in 1980 to 625 in 1989.[7]

The incidence of crime has increased throughout the Caribbean, and a significant number of new convicted criminals have a drug problem. The official brochure of the West Indian Commission, an independent commission established by Caribbean heads of government to help prepare the region for the future, states that "the number of West Indians abusing drugs and addicted to them is escalating with dangers for the productive capacity of the country and the control of crime."[8]

Diversion of Scarce Foreign Exchange Resources

In an article entitled, "The Colombian Nightmare: Drugs and Structural Adjustment in the Caribbean," Dennis Pantin argues that combating drug trafficking severely taxes the foreign exchange resources of Caribbean countries.[9] All of these countries face significant balance of trade deficits, and the three largest in population terms—Guyana, Jamaica, and Trinidad and Tobago—also have overwhelming debt problems. Indeed, the International Monetary Fund currently runs economic recovery programs in all three states. But foreign exchange is vital in all of the Caribbean countries for the maintenance of their productive sectors, which still fail to offer jobs to half the young people seeking employment. Combating drug trafficking is therefore a further demand on already scarce foreign exchange. And while precious foreign exchange in ailing economies is being diverted to coping with drug trafficking, it has been observed that the presence of drug-related resources "enables some of our countries to better resist the economic crisis as they generate employment, inject foreign exchange into dollar-starved economies and enable investment to be made in other productive areas; in short, temporarily to cushion the crisis."[10]

Threats to the Sovereign Authority of Caribbean States

The Governments of Caribbean states are concerned about threats to their sovereign authority posed by the manner in which the U.S. government has sought to deal with the interdiction of drug traffickers and money laundering in the region. This was most strongly expressed in July 1988, when the Ninth Conference of Caribbean Community Heads of Government wrote, through its chairman, V. C. Bird, the prime minister of Antigua and Barbuda, to U.S. President Ronald Reagan "on a matter which threatens to create discord and division between the friendly nations of the region on the one hand and the United States on the other." The letter stated that among the concerns of Caribbean governments were the "attempts to extend domestic United States authority into the neighboring countries of the region without regard for the sovereignty and independent legal systems of those countries."[11] Among those attempts were the pursuit of suspected drug traffickers into Caribbean waters and their arrest by U.S. authorities within the jurisdiction of the Caribbean.

Caribbean governments have been subject to more than a little coercion by U.S. agencies to allow them to select the local personnel for drug enforcement units and to participate in planning, if not in directing, their operations.[12] The regional governments have faced similar demands from U.S. agencies for the establishment of national drug councils to review the situation with respect to drugs and take appropriate action. The Caribbean countries have not responded uniformly. Some have cooperated fully. The government of the Bahamas, which obviously believes that it has to go the extra mile to clear the country's name after earlier accusations of facilitating drug trafficking, was the first government to allow joint hot pursuit of suspected drug traffickers in its national territory by U.S. law enforcement agencies. Other governments have set up drug councils but limited their powers.

The acquiescence by some governments to U.S. pressure has not gone unnoted, nor has it been welcomed, by significant groups in the region. For instance, a conference of bishops and pastors held in June 1990 concluded that Caribbean governments' policies on drug interdiction and banking secrecy "are not derived from a Latin American and Caribbean diagnosis of the problem but from the United States approach to the topic." The conference concluded further: "We are once again faced with the imposition of unilateral policies and ideas whereby one country determines what the others should do without taking into account their problems and real needs."[13]

Measures That Might Be Taken

Caribbean governments have not reached a uniform or even a coordinated policy on the drug problem in the region. Indeed, while some governments appear to have a policy for dealing with the problem at a national level, others seem to have no policy at all. The countries that have instituted concrete measures for addressing the drug problem are the Bahamas, Jamaica, and Trinidad and Tobago. Other territories, with fewer resources, have implemented some measures largely at the behest of the United States. These include the creation of small, undermanned and underequipped drug enforcement units and cooperation with the U.S. Coast Guard in stopping and searching vessels in Caribbean territorial waters. But as one Jamaican minister has pointed out, the measures taken by all the Caribbean countries individually "fall short of a regional response which will be necessary in the development of a sustained Caribbean initiative. The Caribbean countries do not possess either the facilities or the resources to achieve this most important objective."[14]

A Sustained Initiative

A sustained Caribbean initiative to deal with the drug problem would seem to require several important components, including:

1. The ability to police Caribbean waters effectively and particularly to pursue and arrest vessels carrying illicit drugs
2. The capacity to police ports and airports to guard against the transit of illicit drugs
3. Well-manned, well-financed, and well-equipped narcotics units
4. Stringent and common legislation allowing not only for heavy fines and long terms of imprisonment but also for confiscation of property and other assets of those convicted of drug offenses
5. The capacity for sharing intelligence within the Caribbean and with extraregional territories
6. The maintenance of the sovereign authority of Caribbean states
7. Bilateral extradition treaties with non-Caribbean states for the extradition of citizens and noncitizens from and to each other's jurisdiction
8. The continuous education of the entire population—through the mass media, the education system, and interpersonal communications—about the dangers of drug use

9. A vigorous diplomatic process designed to mobilize the United States, Canada, European countries and international agencies into providing additional resources to Caribbean countries dedicated to helping them to more forcefully interdict drug traffickers, to provide acceptable alternatives to the financial benefits of the drug trade, and to mount effective antidrug education programs throughout their communities

It is obvious that apart from adopting stringent and common legislation for dealing with drug traffickers, Caribbean countries individually do not have the capacity to successfully implement the measures mentioned above. They simply lack the financial resources. Even at the diplomatic level, while the government of Jamaica enjoyed some success in getting the United Nations General Assembly to accept a Resolution on a Global Program of Action against Illicit Narcotic Drugs in January 1990, it fell short of Prime Minister Michael Manley's original intentions. The prime minister had proposed the establishment of a "multilateral force, under the aegis of the United Nations, which would provide assistance in particular situations requiring intelligence and interdiction capabilities beyond the resources of the individual states." The General Assembly agreed to consider "the feasibility" of such a United Nations facility.[15]

While individual Caribbean states have the capacity to adopt common and stringent legislation to deal with drug traffickers, only the Bahamas, Barbados, Guyana, and Jamaica have passed such legislation. An attempt by the government of Trinidad and Tobago to introduce a law met with widespread hostility on the basis that it could be used for political victimization.[16] The six independent smaller islands of the region have had the legislation under consideration for more than two years. Yet, common legislation is imperative to a successful Caribbean initiative against drug trafficking, for traffickers will simply focus their operations on those territories where the penalties are lightest.

The Need for a Regional Authority

The countries of the Caribbean could more effectively formulate and implement a narcotics policy containing the elements outlined above if they did so collectively and in a cohesive fashion. But this would require a regional authority with supranational powers capable of establishing the bodies required; managing the policy, including supervising the drug enforcement units; drafting the necessary antinarcotics legislation; negotiating equal bilateral extradition treaties with other states; executing an education program against drugs; and mounting a diplomatic *démarche* on behalf of all the Caribbean states.

The acceptance and implementation of this concept, or something similar to it, is probably now more possible than before. There is an undisputed acknowledgment throughout the region that individual states cannot cope with the drug problem. Similarly, there is an increasing recognition that acquiescence to U.S. demands is not an acceptable remedy for the lack of capacity to deal with the problem. For, while close cooperation with the United States is evidently required, simply caving in to U.S. demands seriously threatens the autonomy of Caribbean governments.

A majority of Caribbean countries are displaying a greater readiness to deepen their integration arrangements under the umbrella of the Caribbean Community and Common Market (CARICOM). Caribbean governments might consider the establishment by treaty of a commission made up of a governing body of, say, Caribbean foreign ministers and a small, high-quality secretariat to formulate and implement a narcotics policy for the region as a whole. Decisions of the governing body would have to be legally binding on every government and would best be made by a majority vote of two-thirds of the membership.

While this concept would surely place the Caribbean countries in a more advantageous position to deal with the drug problem, it would require considerable support from the international community. For even though the implementation of such a concept would undoubtedly improve the region's capacity for decision making and action, as well as for bargaining, the area would still lack the financial resources to man, equip, and maintain the necessary program of interdiction, education, and rehabilitation. However, the commission conceived above, closely focused as it would have to be, would be more able to attract both program and project financing for its work from major donor states and international agencies. Certainly, it would be able to forge cooperation agreements not only with the United States but also with Canada and the residual metropolitan powers in the Caribbean, namely, France, Britain, and the Netherlands. These cooperation agreements could include exchange of intelligence among drug enforcement units, supply of equipment and funds to the Caribbean, and joint policing of the Caribbean waters.

Possibilities in the Existing Situation

The commission proposed here is one policy option that Caribbean governments might consider and that the U.S. administration and other governments and international agencies might find easier to deal with than twelve governments. However, in the existing situation there *are* twelve governments. What could each of them do to combat the drug problem more effectively than they do at the moment?

First, each could protect itself from being more attractive to drug traffickers than others by adopting similar legislation to that which exists in the Bahamas, Barbados, Guyana, and Jamaica restraining the assets of those accused of drug trafficking before they are convicted and confiscating their property if they are convicted.

Second, they could enter into an agreement among themselves, not only for the exchange of intelligence but also to enable the police force and coast guard of each country to carry out arrests in the others' jurisdictions. At the moment, the coast guard of one Caribbean country cannot pursue suspected drug traffickers and make arrests in the territorial waters of another, even though these countries enjoy a very close and interdependent economic and political relationship under CARICOM.

Third, they could collectively enter into treaties with the United States and other countries for the extradition of citizens and others. If these treaties are uniform and equal, they could prove to be an effective deterrent to traffickers. It is significant that the measure that most threatened the Colombia drug barons was the agreement by the Colombian government to extradite them to the United States. Such a measure is unlikely to be popular in some Caribbean states, but it has a greater likelihood of acceptance if all Caribbean governments institute it.

Fourth, each government should consider entering into a bilateral agreement with the United States allowing U.S. agencies hot pursuit and right of arrest within the jurisdiction of the Caribbean state. Some countries now informally permit the United States to carry out hot pursuit in their territorial waters, and they blind their eyes to arrests made there. This is an acknowledgment that they do not have the means to police the waters themselves, and by pretending that they are unaware of arrests, they preserve the right of sovereignty. But if this practice is to continue, it should be placed on a legal basis, with some mechanisms for monitoring and review by Caribbean states themselves.

The Urgent Need for International Support

Given the lack of financial resources and the dire conditions of most of their economies, it is difficult to see what else Caribbean governments could do at the individual level to combat the drug problem. Even the urgent task of antinarcotics education and rehabilitation of drug addicts is beyond the financial capability of many of these states. There is, therefore, a pressing need for international support. In this context, the U.N. Resolution on a Global Program of Action Against Illicit Narcotic Drugs, which began with Michael Manley's proposal for a multilateral force, among other things, is very useful. But the United Nations has committed itself only to considering the feasibility of such a force, and it has stressed that account has to be taken "of its ability to perform its increasing tasks in the light of existing mandates."[17] It is well known that the United Nations is short of money, and it is unlikely that its financial status will greatly improve in the near future. Thus, despite the resolution, it may be some time before the United Nations is able to help the Caribbean states to deal with the drug problem that confronts them.

Against this background the United States, as the major purchaser of the illicit narcotics that transit the Caribbean, should take a lead role in mobilizing international support to help ease the economic burdens of Caribbean countries. Such support would place individual Caribbean states in a better position to deal with drug trafficking. Among the measures that major donor countries and international agencies could implement are debt forgiveness, guaranteed markets and duty-free access for major Caribbean commodities, and increased aid for the development of infrastructure. The United States could also play a lead role in mobilizing funds for the United Nations to quickly execute the Resolution on a Global Program of Action against Illicit Narcotic Drugs. Indeed, if the program were to get off the ground, it could prove to be an effective mechanism for the United States to deliver help to Caribbean countries and other states without facing the charge of violating sovereignty.

Unless such assistance is forthcoming, Caribbean governments will be able to do little more than scratch the surface of the drug problem in the region. Their inability to act will pose great dangers to their fragile democracies, dangers that may ultimately render the region unstable. At the same time, the United States, Canada, and Western Europe will continue to confront the reality of a Caribbean gateway to their countries for hundreds of tons of narcotics, with all the adverse effects for their populations that flow from it.

13 | The Future of Regional Security in the Caribbean

Neville Linton

Security concerns in this chapter are political rather than economic and are limited to the Commonwealth Caribbean, as these territories have a common history, are linked by CARICOM, and traditionally, with respect to security issues, have been associated both of their own will and in the eyes of outside powers. In these territories security has always been limited to passive defense, since none was large enough to project its will beyond its shores (unlike Cuba and, with respect to each other, Haiti and the Dominican Republic), and defense has been either against an extraregional foe or for the purpose of maintaining domestic order.

In colonial days and in the century before independence, peace at the international level was clearly the responsibility of the colonial power save for the period when that power was at war. In the Second World War the alliance of the imperial powers with the United States meant that Washington established a network of military and communications bases in the region, some of which remain today. In the same century, social and political discontent often raised its head at the domestic level and could usually be contained by the local police, occasionally with the help of the local military. Rarely was there need for a show of direct force from the metropole, as happened, for example, in the case of Guyana in 1953 when the Cheddi Jagan government was ousted and the constitution suspended.

Having inherited an external peaceful environment, most Caribbean states after independence decided on a low profile with respect to military establishments. Most were content to keep to the pattern of a police force and volunteer militia. Initially, only the three largest territories—Jamaica, Trinidad and Tobago, and Guyana—decided to have armies; and only the latter, with its long borders with Venezuela, Suriname, and Brazil, and facing territorial claims from the first two, could have claimed to need a military establishment for conventional external security purposes. Later, when the other land-based CARICOM country, Belize, gained its independence, its unresolved boundary problem led to the British government's keeping a military presence there since independence. Initially the emphasis in all cases was on a security force related to domestic order and to controlling smuggling across borders, sea, and land. The fundamental reality is that save for Guyana and Belize, CARICOM states started their independence phase with no sense of threat to their national security and territorial integrity. Therefore each state felt that it could deal adequately with national security, and there was no thought of treating security as a priority in the regional integration movement. When some sense of threat did develop, as at the domestic level in terms of dissident political movements and secessionist attempts and at the international level in terms of fear of ideological subversion from, say, Cuba or challenges from drug or arms smugglers and associated mercenaries, it was still felt, especially at the level of the More Developed Countries (MDCs), that individual states could cope through the police, customs, and intelligence services, and given a certain amount of intraregional cooperation.

Even Guyana and Belize, which had major territorial challenges to deal with, handled these problems independently, although they did rely heavily on, and did benefit from, coordinated regional diplomatic support. It should be noted that Guyana reached out widely in the international community for support using the channels of both the United Nations and the Non-Aligned Movement very effectively, apart from leaning heavily on neighboring Brazil, while Belize depended upon British military assistance apart from the diplomatic support it gained from neighboring Mexico. It is instructive that in both these cases a neighboring state was ready to appreciably assist a small state threatened by another neighbor—experiences indicative of elements that could be used for a regime of collective security cooperation in the Caribbean Basin.

The region's casual approach to security issues changed significantly in the 1970s under pressures both domestic and international. At the domestic level, the desire for regional cooperation surfaced in the late 1970s when the small Eastern Caribbean states faced a series of political challenges. There was a series of insurrection attempts in Dominica and St. Vincent and a claim of a coup plot in Antigua.[1] After a coup threat in Dominica early in 1979 and an aborted mercenary "invasion" plot against Barbados, the government of Prime Minister Tom Adams in Barbados took the forefront in advocating regional cooperation by calling for joint coast guard patrols with Antigua, St. Lucia, and St. Vincent and, later, by sending troops to assist St. Vincent during an uprising—a first in regional military initiatives; in 1981 Barbados sent military advisers to Dominica in a parallel situation. It is noteworthy that Barbados, having made a new assessment of its security needs, abandoned its policy of not having a military establishment and developed a Defense Force in 1979, while Dominica terminated its Defense Force in 1981 in reaction to the frequency with which soldiers had been involved in political initiatives over the preceding decade.

Nineteen seventy-nine was a key year in the development of regional attitudes toward security. The Grenada revolution of Maurice Bishop's New Jewel Movement (NJM) occurred in March, and in October the U.S. government both announced a new policy toward the Caribbean and assumed a new militancy toward Cuba, involving the establishment of a new Caribbean Joint Task Force. The U.S. government also initiated action for a program of security assistance to selected Eastern Caribbean countries. Within the region itself Tom Adams, on his first official visit to neighboring Port-of-Spain, signed a Memorandum of Understanding (MOU) with Prime Minister Eric Williams of Trinidad and Tobago in which they noted the growing complexity of the security problems of the Caribbean; it was significant that the problems highlighted did not include any ideological references but focused instead on terrorism, piracy, and the use of mercenaries. As yet there was no major concern about drugs.

Following its agreement with other regional governments on joint coast guard patrols, Barbados sought to upgrade its military establishment, and Britain agreed to provide coast guard training and assistance. The trend toward a properly institutionalized regional security system came to a head in October 1982 when the Eastern Caribbean Regional Security System (RSS) was established by an MOU signed in Roseau on October 30; the member states were Antigua and Barbuda, Barbados, Dominica, St. Lucia, and St. Vincent and the Grenadines. The agreement was for cooperation to provide for "mutual assistance on request" in "national emergencies, prevention of smuggling, search and rescue, immigration control, maritime policing policies, protection of offshore installations, pollution control, natural and other disasters and threats to national security."[2] After independence in September 1983, St. Kitts and Nevis joined, and finally Grenada on January 1, 1985. Thus at present the RSS consists of seven island states.

The RSS came just one year after the establishment by the smaller Eastern Caribbean states of the Organization of Eastern Caribbean States (OECS) in June 1981. In Article 8 of its charter, provision had been made for a Defense and Security Committee whose responsibilities suggest the awakening security concerns, especially with respect to mercenary threats, of these newly independent small states and perhaps their heightened awareness of vulnerability in a region where both the United States and Cuba had recently become more politically vigorous and where the Peoples Revolutionary Government of Grenada was asserting novel foreign policy positions that aligned it more with the Soviet bloc than with traditional CARICOM postures. Thus the Defense and Security Committee had responsibility "to advise the Authority on matters relating to external defence and on arrangements for collective security against external aggression, including mercenary aggression, with or without the support of internal elements, for coordinating the efforts of Member States for collective defence and the preservation of peace and security against external aggression and for the development of close ties among the Member States of the Organization in matters of external defence and security, including measures to combat the activities of mercenaries, operating with or without the support of the internal or national elements, in the exercise of the inherent right of individual or collective self-defence recognized by Article 51 of the Charter of the United Nations."

Given that the OECS had just been formed, it appears that initially there was not a clear idea as to the type of mechanism that would be set in train to operationalize Article 8, and it would seem that it was the impetus of Barbados, and specifically of Prime Minister Tom Adams, that led to the emergence of the RSS as a practical instrument in this respect. Barbados was outside of the OECS but had similar concerns and imperatives as the OECS states. It was the only MDC that had been the subject of a couple of quite ineffectual attempts at mercenary invasion and also the MDC most openly concerned about political developments in Grenada, which it felt could have spillover political effects in neighboring islands. This group of states therefore was responding to imperatives for collective security out of a commonly felt need that was not shared, at the time, by Jamaica, Trinidad and Tobago, Guyana, Belize, and the Bahamas. These latter states had made little headway in the wider grouping of CARICOM in terms of collective security arrangements, because the subject was not a priority and also because they felt that their defense needs could be handled by national mechanisms and by ad hoc regional diplomatic cooperation.[3]

With the shattering events of Grenada in October 1983, the arrangements provided for under the OECS treaty and the MOU were brought into play in crisis circumstances that could not have been predicted and that probably were more demanding than the framers of these two instruments might have anticipated.[4] The RSS members acted decisively and commissioned an intervention, with the U.S. government forces playing a leading role. This was the first such collective security exercise in the region's history, and the intervention, especially the U.S. factor, led to serious divisions in the Caribbean community.[5]

It might be logical to expect that this led to serious, systematic, and urgent attention both to the question of mechanisms for regional collective security and to the conditions, sources, and nature of external bilateral or multilateral assistance. However, once the dust had settled, the wider CARICOM region relaxed and settled back into its regular pattern, with its concomitant focus on regional economic issues. This would seem to suggest that the Grenada case was seen as an aberration and that the fundamentals of the region's security situation had not changed. For the RSS states, however, the Grenada intervention was a stimulant; and thereafter the RSS, which in 1983 had only been in existence for a year, has become a more established institution, with units that are well-equipped and under continuous training for cooperative action.[6] The RSS forces did not participate in the actual fighting in Grenada but were part of the subsequent occupying force. A senior RSS officer commented, "Without the RSS it would have been difficult, if not impossible, for police, Special Service Units (SSUs) and soldiers from six member states to be landing on the island on D Day, 25 October 1983. In this case, as in all likely scenarios speed of action was critical. This quick reaction would have been impossible without the mutual cooperation and understanding between governments and commanders that the MOU had generated."[7]

In the aftermath of Grenada, Prime Minister Tom Adams sought energetically to strengthen the regional defense system by upgrading the RSS into a standing regional force. Various estimates about size and cost mentioned at the time ranged from about 1,000 to 1,800 strong at establishment costs from U.S. $10 million to U.S. $100 million. The proposal was actually discussed with Secretary of State George Shultz during his visit to the Eastern Caribbean in February 1984, but nothing came of the proposal; the United Kingdom was also lukewarm to it. What is more important, there were doubts even within the RSS states (e.g., St. Vincent and

St. Kitts and Nevis) about the need for such a force and the cost of maintaining it.[8] In addition, important political sensitivities underlay the reluctance to deepen the relationship, principally a fear in some quarters that in the case of questionable claims of coup attempts the RSS might be deliberately used to crush left-leaning political movements.

The RSS remained in its original form, but in the years immediately after 1983 its military equipment was improved significantly, and regular training from U.S., U.K., and Canadian sources was institutionalized. The equipment and training of the regular forces of the member states were also upgraded, especially those of the Barbados Defense Force. When Caribbean leaders met with Canada in Jamaica in March 1985, Prime Minister Adams anticipated that the postconference communiqué would reflect an agreement that members had negotiated with one voice on issues of security assistance from external powers. This did not materialize, and security has not been a major issue on the CARICOM summit agenda since then.

While the Grenada events led to the firming up of the RSS, the exercise underlined the inadequacy of the RSS and the limited role it could play. It is particularly clear that in any major operation there would be need for logistical and communications support from outside powers. Indeed, quite apart from crisis situations, the basic routine surveillance work of the region—of seas, territorial waters, and air space—cannot be adequately done by the present coast guard and air arm services. The fact is that no single Caribbean country has the assets by itself to deal with major pollution-control problems, fisheries protection, search and rescue operations, and natural disasters. In such a situation, collective security does seem to be a minimum option, and it has the advantage of providing a basis around which outside assistance can be organized.

After 1983 Jamaica continued the pattern of cooperation that had begun with its participation in the Grenada intervention by joining the annual war games exercises of the RSS. Thus, it was Trinidad and Tobago that was the outstanding outsider, outstanding because of the strategic importance of its location, its resources as a major CARICOM country, and the size of its military establishment. Over the years Trinidad and Tobago has only been an observer at the war games, but it has indicated that it would join fully in the training process, including the games, from 1992. Such an eventuality would mean that all major regional defense establishments would be in the habit of regularly cooperating in defense training exercises and that even in the absence of an actual CARICOM-wide collective security treaty, there was a developing concept of practical cooperation at levels where it mattered. The Grenada crisis clearly showed that regional nonmembers of the RSS and OECS would be ready to be a part of an OECS-RSS exercise.

But what the Grenada crisis pointed up even more was the gulf in getting agreement on collective security action, whether or not such action involved assistance from outside powers. The specific arguments of the Grenada intervention case that arose at the meeting of the CARICOM Heads of Government have been discussed elsewhere and need not detain us here.[9] However, the case does demonstrate what are perceived to be the problems in establishing a collective security system. A positive aspect was the universal assumption that a government established by violent and unconstitutional means was unacceptable, but disagreement was really over whether there should be a negotiated solution or a military one, particularly given the frank recognition that a military solution required extraregional military assistance.

It was quite traumatic for regional elites that such assistance came from the United States, as the region had always looked somewhat askance at the historic role of power in U.S. relations with its Latin American and Caribbean neighbors. There was an acute awareness of the implications of getting further into the U.S. zone of influence and of developing armies trained to American ways of thinking and acting, armies that might begin to see themselves politically as guardians of the society. In fact, in the ensuing years it would seem that the command of the RSS has deliberately sought to balance the U.S. influence by keeping up the traditional reliance on British linkages.

Grenada was seen as an aberration in a region that has always prided itself on its democratic tradition and stable societies; thus, after that crisis there was no serious impetus to follow through toward instituting adequate machinery for political crisis management. Yet in July 1990 there was an attempted coup against the Trinidad and Tobago government, another aberrant case undoubtedly, but it did happen, and it demonstrated the inherent vulnerability of these small states.[10]

Potential Threats to Caribbean States

The threat scenario in which collective security could be helpful is much the same in the Caribbean as with other small states. The following discussion covers both external and domestic threats.

External Threats

Save during periods of global Great Power conflict, the small Caribbean states have not in practice been vulnerable to external threat. A fundamental contemporary reason is that the United States has been a natural "guardian" of the whole region as a by-product of Washington's guarding its own Atlantic sea lanes. There is also the increasing possibility that both Mexico and Venezuela might also see themselves in guardian roles vis-à-vis small Caribbean states.[11] Certainly the fact that arms transshipped through Antigua eventually made their way to the drug network in Colombia must be a matter of concern to Latin American neighbors.

The Caribbean situation is such that intraregional conflict is unlikely (save for the only land-border case, between the Dominican Republic and Haiti) as long as the Belize and Guyana cases continue on their patient, sedate trend toward settlement. At the hemispheric level, so far only the United States has been seen as a likely invader. Given the decline of the cold war, situations for direct U.S. invasion are not easily conceivable; but the substantial military presence of the United States in the Caribbean remains, including military installations in the Commonwealth Caribbean. However, situations of extreme civil war or of takeover controlled by drug- and arms-related mercenaries could possibly lead to interventions by Venezuela or Mexico, the regional powers whose surrogate security role in the region could increase in a non–cold war environment.

In other island regions piracy has reemerged as a serious problem, and it must be considered a possibility that arms and drug smugglers might prove to be a serious threat to governments whose territories often consist of a number of small islands over which their physical control is slight. A heightened Caribbean consciousness about the seriousness of the drug problem as a security threat was reflected in recent initiatives, especially by Jamaica and Trinidad and Tobago, in international forums, including the United Nations, to get a multilateral force to assist states in intelligence and interdiction and to establish commissions of inquiry and an international criminal court for offenses related to drug trafficking. In the case of Dominica in 1981, it seems that if the mercenaries had been successful, a puppet government might have been set up to do their bidding. The same, incidentally, was said to be the game plan in the Indian Ocean case of Maldives in 1988.

Increasingly, the control over maritime resources is being recognized as a problem area.[12] The region lacks the resources for adequate fisheries zone protection and for routine surveillance flights. Control over other natural resources could also be a problem at times, for example, illegal trading in precious minerals, which leapfrog over borders through the sophisticated networking, communications, and transport equipment of international operators. This, of course, has already happened, particularly with mari-

juana in Jamaica and Belize. The simple reality is that narcotics and terrorist activities are threats that by their nature require international cooperation to meet them.

Domestic Threats

The range of potential domestic threats is wide: military coups, succession struggles, riots, civil unrest, seizing of hostages, natural disaster, and
threats to the environment. It has been at the domestic level that security
threats have usually arisen, and these threats might be to a regime or to a
domestic order, whereas external threats might also be threats to sovereignty. There is a clear credo in CARICOM, which was averred most recently during the attempted coup in Trinidad and Tobago, that governments in the region would only recognize regimes that came to power by
legitimate means. In addition, a variety of linkages add up to the CARI-
COM states' comprising a true region. If these states hitherto have balked
at the concept of intervention, it has been largely because it did not seem
necessary. However, the Trinidad and Tobago case in 1990, coming relatively soon after the 1983 Grenada crisis, should underline the necessity.
The CARICOM states were quick to confer at the level of heads of government and to offer direct military help through the RSS, although this was
not used by Trinidad and Tobago during the actual confrontation.[13] Since
the RSS has had training specifically for dealing with domestic challenges,[14] its use, however limited, earlier in the process would have provided an excellent opportunity to promote regional cooperation and further the idea of regional collective security. A more integral involvement
might well have speeded up settlement, as it would have sent a message to
the coup leader that his crime was against the region; moreover, it would
have been a salutary warning to others in the region who might have
such illegitimate ambitions. But here the traditional insular approach triumphed, as both the Trinidad Defense authorities and the government
wished to show that they could handle the problem without outside help.
It should be stressed that the participation of outside forces does not necessarily have to be in a combat situation; the very fact of their presence
makes a contribution, both politically and operationally. Moreover, the
affair had an international dimension that was of importance to the whole
region; it seems beyond doubt that the substantial arms hoard of the in-
surrectionists, the Jamaat-Al-Muslimeen, came from Arab sources, probably Libya. Given the earlier evidence of Libyan political activity in the
Eastern Caribbean, the need for a regional approach to terrorism is surely
underlined.

Occurring even more often than political threats, however, are threats from natural disasters. The Caribbean is a hurricane zone whose security is threatened annually in the most fundamental way. A fair amount of regional cooperation exists with respect to disaster relief, and the commitment toward this was heightened in the wake of the devastation of hurricane Hugo in 1989. Immediately thereafter a process was initiated to set up a permanent joint CARICOM disaster relief task force based on the region's military and with special training and equipment to this end.

External Assistance

Bilateral Assistance

The 1990 crisis in Trinidad and Tobago did not involve as challenger a charismatic political figure or an established, well-organized group as in the case of the NJM coup in Grenada and crisis there in 1983. Yet it did raise the question of the possibility of extraregional assistance, since the flushing out of dissidents, if it came to a pure military confrontation, would best be done by troops trained in counterinsurgency methods. The question of inviting the British Special Air Services (SAS) was mooted at the time in some quarters both in Trinidad and in the region.[15]

There is a natural reluctance to call upon bilateral assistance from the former colonial power, the hemispheric hegemonical power, or others. If, however, there were an understanding in CARICOM that such requests be made only after consultation with the other CARICOM powers, that would be an improvement, although it could still make for strong interregional discontent, as in the case of the 1983 Grenada crisis. On that occasion Trinidad and Tobago would have been equally upset if Grenada had, for instance, invited the Venezuelans to deal with the anti-Bishop forces or if a rump of the Bishop government had asked the Cubans to quell and mediate the situation. Clearly, inviting foreign armed activity into the region can be said to affect the interests of other states, and CARICOM states need to come to terms with this issue. Admittedly, a situation wherein regional concurrence becomes necessary for such invitations, bilateral or multilateral, would in effect be a surrender of some sovereignty, but the realities of the security situation would suggest that the time is ripe for these larger security issues to be handled at the regional level.

As an interrelated and interdependent world enters the twenty-first century, it is time that the small states of the Caribbean were realistic about some of the outmoded "rights" of the concept of sovereignty, which were fashioned for other times and quite different places and situations.

Multilateral Assistance

If requests for assistance could be made to a multilateral agency rather than bilaterally to another state, the proposition of seeking outside assistance would be much more acceptable to CARICOM member states. Even so, such assistance would usually be for cases of external aggression rather than for domestic coups. The obvious options are the Organization of American States (OAS), the United Nations, and beyond these, although not as clear-cut an option, the Commonwealth. A fundamental consideration, however, is that multilateral agencies cannot respond as quickly and suitably as could another state.

The OAS machinery as it exists could theoretically be used to mobilize hemispheric military assistance, but it has no track record in this respect. However, given the weight in numbers of the CARICOM states, it might be worth exploring whether a special regime of assistance for small member states can be agreed upon. Like the United Nations, the OAS has an advantage in that there is a standing agency in Washington, so quick decisions are theoretically possible. However, the problems involved in activating the machinery at the military end, plus the problems of Latin American troops operating in the significantly culturally different CARICOM area, loom as major drawbacks. Nevertheless, it would be useful to have such a regime in place even if the military machinery were hardly used, since many situations are measurably affected by economic sanctions, political leverage, and moral pressure plus the threat of military action. Now that the OAS includes both the United States and Canada, all four of these can be meaningfully used. There is reason to assume that Canada is likely to advocate stronger measures by the organization to support small member states, given its long and close association with the CARICOM regime.[16]

The United Nations seriously addressed the problem of the security of small states only recently, when the Maldives, after its 1988 coup attempt, took the lead in the General Assembly in getting passed a resolution to explore mechanisms for the protection of small states.[17] This led to a report by the U.N. secretary-general to the General Assembly on his findings in 1991; however, the General Assembly requested further study and a report by 1994. It is to be hoped that the ultimate outcome will be more action-oriented than the U.N. 1985 comprehensive study on concepts of security.[18] The possibilities could include both the already existing watchdog facility in the secretary-general's office, which monitors potentially explosive situations, and a version of the Palme Commission proposal of 1982, which could be tailored to suit small states rather than the wider ambit of non−cold war issues among Third World small states therein originally suggested. The need is for mechanisms that could mobilize appropriate diplomatic and military assistance at short notice; the United Nations can provide the former within its present setup and with imaginative use of the secretary-general's powers, but the latter could require arrangements allowing forces with the relevant equipment and training to be deployed quickly.[19] Even within the U.N. process, therefore, giving priority to the use of regional arrangements has an obvious advantage, as the U.N. Charter recognizes. But regional politics can itself be on occasion a hurdle, and a small state may not wish intervention led by the regional hegemon. And since coups in small states can occur and be entrenched very quickly, it is worth considering whether a regime vis-à-vis small states should not have procedures by which the Security Council could rapidly either utilize or bypass regional mechanisms.

Given the end of traditional East-West confrontation and signs of increasing relevance for the United Nations, a security regime relating to small states and involving their specific acceptance would seem to be, both politically and militarily, a manageable area in which the organization can vigorously flutter its security wings. The CARICOM states should be in the forefront in ensuring a positive and creative outcome to the secretary-general's exercise.

In the wake of its special report on the security of small states, *Vulnerability: Small States in the Global Society*, the Commonwealth has not taken any concrete collective measures with respect to its own recommendations vis-à-vis political security, although there has been increased intra-Commonwealth bilateral cooperation. Both Australia and New Zealand have close ties with nearby Pacific states, while India demonstrated its willingness to act supportively to the Maldives in 1988. Canada is the closest Commonwealth power to the Caribbean but is not a neighbor; thus, while after 1983 it did increase its security-related technical assistance, it is unlikely to play the more committed role that close regional proximity fosters elsewhere.

While Commonwealth powers are ready to give bilateral assistance, they are clearly shy of any multilateral commitments. A basic reason is that the larger states do not perceive the Commonwealth as a security community, and in terms of security, most states are obviously more comfortable operating at a regional level than across the wide range the Commonwealth covers. Some would argue that once the arena gets beyond the region, it should be a concern of the global community, that is, the U.N. system. Of course, since the Second World War nonregional security alliances such as NATO have come into being, but such alliances are linked by a sense of common threat. Since contemporary economic, trade, cultural, and communications linkages make for a global village, our concepts of security arenas need not hold to the traditional patterns, particularly when the common purpose would be the security of a set of states admittedly incapable of defense against both significant external attack and bold domestic coups.

The Commonwealth, in which the membership of small states is a dominant and proud feature and which, in commissioning its vulnerability study in 1983, stated that the international community had a moral obligation to provide effectively for the territorial integrity of such states, should be challenged to do more in the area of physical security.[20] A Commonwealth commitment that implied a willingness where necessary to mobilize immediate moral and material support for small states whose security is threatened could be a valuable buttress for the regional efforts of such states.

It should be noted that in the *Vulnerability* report there were no specific recommendations on the subject of pan-Commonwealth action; the Expert Group urged that "Commonwealth governments should consider with sympathy requests for ad hoc forces to assist members facing acute security problems" (Rec. 76), but it emphasized that the secretary-general "might consider it advisable" to take initiatives "to determine whether there is a wish for pan-Commonwealth action" (Rec. 61). This recommendation has not been taken any further and could be firmed up and given an imprimatur of specific acceptance by the Commonwealth Heads of Government. The CARICOM region, as the most integrally linked small-state region in the Commonwealth, is well suited to take the initiative in advocating such a Commonwealth commitment; the reality is that no concrete proposal to implement its recommendations at the multilateral level has been put to Commonwealth circles since the *Vulnerability* report.

Conclusion

CARICOM states undoubtedly would like to maintain the image of a region with no chronic instability and thus no need for a major security perspective. On the other hand, in recent years a school of thought has emerged that has been raising a specter of militarization in the region. Much of this analysis assumes an innocent Caribbean and a scheming United States and certainly stretches the meaning of *militarization*. [21] The reality, however, is that in today's global village the vulnerability of these islands has increased, especially because their fragile regimes cannot easily cope with the economic and social problems that beset them. Obviously, continuing strengthening of democratic and egalitarian practices should be the pattern of regional development. But they also require both time and domestic order if they are to achieve social justice and "develop" adequately, and in order to do so, they need to take more deliberate steps to defend and preserve the polity. The region has a strong democratic tenet and does not deal harshly with political rebels; thus yesterday's revolutionaries, after causing considerable economic and social upheaval, loss of development momentum, and even loss of life, usually end up either living quite respectably in the society or, consistent with the traditional regional pattern, migrating to a middle-class life in greener pastures.

The time is ripe for concrete regional action to deal with what no longer can be considered a marginal problem or problems that arise largely because of psychotic or hegemonical policies. Indeed, there is even a possibility that the United States could retreat into a navel-gazing phase in which "minor" problems could be left to stew in their own juice, since Washington would have no sense of an ideological threat and clearly has never had a sense of being responsible for nurturing the progress of the CARICOM area. Regional security will have an economic cost, but prevention often runs cheaper than cure, and the suggested emphasis is on a system rather than on creating a substantial military establishment. There may well be advantageous impacts on foreign policy, since the region will be seen from the outside world as being one security arena, which should be of some significance for relations with the United States, Venezuela, and Brazil. In some domestic circles the development of a regional security agreement might be looked on as both premature and dangerous, since it would be coming before regional political unity. Such objections should not be a hindrance, as the security system would not be such as to increase "militarization," and its presence and functioning is likely to deepen the integration process. Moreover, a security arrangement of limited scope will be for defensive purposes and need not commit any member state with respect to extraregional issues; however, its existence could have the added advantage of encouraging prudence in the foreign policy of individual member states.

What is required then is a commitment to a collective approach to security. A regime to that end would involve:

1. A mechanism for peaceful settlement of disputes through good offices, mediation, and conciliation. According to the circumstances, this could be collectively organized through the CARICOM Secretariat or be bilateral.

2. Agreement on what constitutes threats to security involving regional consultation and, in certain cases, action. The sticky points here would be the political cases, as regional consensus should be easily achieved vis-à-vis the regime of the seas, drugs and arms trafficking, and disaster cooperation. Guidelines would need to be developed with regard to the type of situations in which intervention is acceptable. Equally necessary would be agreements and machinery to ensure that immediately after a successful intervention there would be steps to arrange for a genuine democratic assessment of the wishes of the populace.

3. A mechanism for calling rapid meetings of a relevant agency to deal with a "threat" scenario. In the July 1990 case of Trinidad and Tobago, for instance, the meeting of the heads of government was ad hoc and fortuitous (as a meeting was already scheduled). The rules of operation of such an agency would be crucial and would cover questions on whether a request for a meeting and for "action" could come from any government or only from the beleaguered government, the vote necessary for "action" (e.g., consensus or majority), and the authority for requesting extraregional security assistance. In the 1983 Grenada situation, for instance, it was argued in some quarters that invitation of an *outside* power should only proceed on a consensus vote.

4. Research into the types of sanctions, other than military force, that could be effectively applied in the case of a crisis. In the Grenada crisis (1983) regional governments clearly lacked any experience with such alternatives. Moreover, if a sanctions regime had already been in place, it might have served as a constraint on the radical faction.

5. Agreements on the size, nature, and training of regional forces and their possible roles. It is true, for instance, that Port-of-Spain's reluctance in July 1990 to accept the RSS was conditioned by the lack of an agreed formula for inviting such troops and of understandings as to their role. The routine priority use of regional force units would be in combating narcotics and terrorism and to help with civil assistance operations. There is no suggestion here that such forces need be any larger than present establishments, though they would need better training and equipment. The training should also be oriented to heighten their regional consciousness, civic sensibilities, and democratic values. In the July 1990 Trinidad and Tobago case there were some signs of an uneasy balance between the military command and the "rump" govern-

ment that was in charge during the crisis. There was an unfortunate impression of a "strong" military command clear about what it wished to do, capable of doing it, and thus in command of the situation, in contrast to a "weak" regime that could not really command respect and did not solve either the political-economic problems of the state or the immediate crisis. A government in such a crisis negotiating only with its own military could be at a disadvantage, and the public's confidence in the government might waver; however, if there were a regional force, this psychological aspect should not arise.

6. Significant upgrading of the regional communications information and intelligence system and networking.[22] The need here cannot be overstressed; a comprehensive outline is to be found in the *Vulnerability* report, which also stresses the need for linking into and support from metropolitan networks.[23] An adequate regional intelligence network could have alerted CARICOM both to the developing tensions in Grenada in 1983 and to the arms supplies in advance of the Trinidad 1990 crisis. Domestic regimes also demonstrate major weaknesses in terms of the use of information, and the Port-of-Spain authorities were constrained by this factor in handling the crisis.[24]

7. An understanding that collective action could be undertaken by appropriate subgroups, such as the OECS, or there could be an ad hoc arrangement.

8. Diplomatic initiatives aimed at achieving an implicit understanding in friendly metropolitan centers and through the United Nations and the OAS that security in small states requires continuing financial and logistical support from those sources. Equally important is the need for postcrisis financial and economic support, as the early restoration of confidence is a vital aspect in achieving a stable society.

The foregoing regime requires both urgent research and discussion.

At the same time that an agreement on collective security is achieved, it would be necessary to establish agencies underpinning the maintenance of democratic practices in the territories so that normal and valid protest would not be frustrated. Such arrangements would include, at the formal level, a CARICOM commission on human rights and a CARICOM court of appeal, and at the informal level, a regional undertaking that no government would hinder the invitation by private bodies of outside unofficial observers to national elections.

Regional governments should signal that in the future they would not feel restrained in condemning a regional government for internal repression, as such matters impact on regional security and welfare.

254 I NEVILLE LINTON

CARICOM member states should be aware of the necessity for continuous confidence-building efforts vis-à-vis the United States so as to avoid major misunderstandings, given the strategic location, for the United States, of the Caribbean region, and given the know-how and information available in that country.[25] More attention should be paid to lobbying in the United States with relevant interest groups and both government and nongovernment agencies. Similar activity is also needed with regard to the key Latin American neighbors—Brazil, Mexico, and Venezuela—and the United Kingdom.

At the CARICOM summit meeting in July 1990 the heads of government in their final communiqué agreed "on the necessity to review existing arrangements in support of regional security and decided to establish a Committee of Members States to look into the matter and report before the Twelfth Meeting of Conference." This is not a particularly indicative mandate, but the opportunity certainly exists for taking concrete steps to move the region forward in this important sector.

14

Twenty-first Century Challenges for the Caribbean and the United States: Toward a New Horizon

Robert A. Pastor and Richard D. Fletcher

The Caribbean approaches the end of the century with a wide array of experiences that contain valuable lessons. The issue is whether the region is ready to learn from its past failures and successes and chart new directions. In 1960 there were only three independent countries in the Caribbean—the Dominican Republic, Haiti, and Cuba—and all three were trying to rid themselves of dictatorship. Only the Dominican Republic succeeded. Haiti conducted its first free election in December 1990, but nine months later the military reimposed authoritarian rule. Cuba is still under the control of an aging revolutionary and a single-party system. In the meantime, twelve English-speaking, parliamentary democracies have joined the group of independent governments. Of this group, only Grenada and Guyana departed from the democratic tradition, but the first returned after an invasion in 1983, and the second held free and fair elections in 1992, observed by the Council of Freely-Elected Heads of Government, chaired by Jimmy Carter, and a Commonwealth team.

With the exception of Haiti, and with a caveat for the Dominican Republic, most of these countries have made substantial social progress. Education and health standards are among the highest in the developing world; in terms of economics, however, the region has failed to find a path toward sustainable, equitable growth. Some have done better than others, and there are lessons to be learned in the differences, but generally, economic development has proven elusive.

Historically, Puerto Rico and the Latin countries (Cuba, the Dominican Republic, and Haiti) were at the center of U.S. considerations, and the English-speaking nations on the periphery. In this chapter, we reverse the traditional emphasis. CARICOM, the thirteen-member group of English-speaking islands and states, is smaller in size and population but has an increasingly influential voice in the world. A sign of CARICOM's centrality is that the non-English-speaking Caribbean is gravitating toward some association with CARICOM, rather than the other way around. Similarly, although we do not neglect the Latin Caribbean, our preliminary focus is on CARICOM.

We begin from the premise that the region is prepared to accept a candid and difficult self-critique and to consider a range of very provocative recommendations. The strength of the region has always been its people and their adaptability. The region's democratic leaders have absorbed recent changes in the world and modified their views, from a philosophy based on Third World state-directed economic management to one that relies more on the market's ability to allocate resources. The region has evolved from a time when many feared foreign investment to the present, when people have become anxious about the lack of foreign investment. Many of its leaders previously viewed the Cuban model as the solution and the United States as the problem; now there is a widespread recognition that Cuba's path is of limited, if any, relevance for the future, while the United States is viewed more pragmatically as a vital market, a source of support, and a possible partner.

The United States has also evolved in a way that permits it to have a more mature relationship with the region. Large-scale emigration from the region has already influenced the United States in important ways; one example is that a son of the Caribbean is the senior U.S. military officer, the chairman of the Joint Chiefs of Staff. Articulate leaders of the region have demonstrated an ability to influence U.S. foreign policy in positive and important ways. Jamaican Prime Minister Edward Seaga persuaded President Ronald Reagan to undertake a dramatic trade initiative, the Caribbean Basin Initiative (CBI), while his counterpart Prime Minister Michael Manley exerted similar influence on President Jimmy Carter to establish the Caribbean Group for Cooperation in Economic Development and on George Bush to modify his position on bilateral debt. Driven primarily by security interests, the United States has often oscillated between intervention to preclude a foreign rival from gaining a foothold to neglect when the threat passed, but the new human bonds connecting the democracies of the region offer hope for a steadier, more balanced, and long-term relationship.

The time has come to consider a new stage in the region's development and its relationship with the United States. We recommend that the region shift toward a new economic strategy based fundamentally on self-reliance that is outward-, not inward-, oriented. Provided the region makes the appropriate macroeconomic decisions, the United States should offer a bold economic initiative, opening its markets wider to the region's exports, perhaps as part of a broader extension of a North American Free Trade Area. U.S. aid and financing should supplement and complement, not substitute for, such a program.

Aspirations and Realities

Politically and socially, Caribbean hopes have been commendable. The region has wanted democracy, independence, and stability for its nations and justice and equality of opportunity for its citizens. Although the English-speaking Caribbean has serious social and economic problems, by and large, it has retained its independence within a democratic framework that has permitted peaceful change. This is a remarkable achievement in the developing world. Culturally, the region is justly proud of its separate identity, and its reggae and calypso have enhanced the global cultural fabric.

The base of the region's problem is that its large economic aspirations have been beyond the reach of the islands' small scale. Influenced by proximity and the demonstration effect of the United States, the Caribbean people have naturally wanted the same "sporting life." Caribbean labor has been unwilling to accept lower living standards than those achieved by relatives who have migrated to North America, particularly when the Caribbean elites surpass the standards they see on American television programs. Democratic leaders of the region have not wanted to tell their constituents that such aspirations are unreal. The region's businessmen have preferred to sell American and European goods at home in protected markets rather than try to manufacture Caribbean goods for export.

The region suffers chronic balance of payments deficits, overdependence on a few agricultural or mineral commodities (sugar, bananas, bauxite, oil), and increasing dependence on tourism. Tourism, however, may prove to be a greater source of vulnerability in the long term rather than a benefit due to increased foreign exchange. Revenues are greatly affected by developments that are totally unrelated to the tourist industry in a particular country. Tourism plummets as a result of rumors, such as the spread of AIDS in Haiti, or violence in a neighboring country, or recession in the United States or Europe—all factors beyond the influence of hoteliers. The region suffers from other problems, including the exodus of skilled labor and professionals. Foreign investment has preferred Mexico or Costa Rica to the Caribbean. While the region has largely maintained its democratic system, political and drug-related threats have increased; the attempted coup in Trinidad in July 1990 underscored the vulnerability of all of the islands.

The entire CARICOM population numbers 5 million people, fewer than in each of the three largest Latin states—Haiti, Cuba, and the Dominican Republic. Even if one adds these, the total population is less than 30 million, and the gross domestic product is probably less than that of Dade County, Florida. The air traffic in Miami exceeds that of the entire region. These nations simply do not have as large a margin for choice as they would like.

Most of the Caribbean has lost two decades of economic progress. This has led to high unemployment levels (20 percent on average, 50 percent among youth) and increasing frustration. The Caribbean is not in danger of exploding or becoming communist; rather, the prospect is for continued deterioration, growing social delinquency (crime, drugs), out-migration, and sporadic attempted coups by radicals, drug traffickers, or both.

In 1952, Puerto Ricans asked themselves whether they should become independent, and the island of 3.2 million people decided that it was just too small and underpopulated to consider independence as a viable option. Ten years later, Puerto Rico's much smaller and poorer English-speaking neighbors began to declare their independence, not bothering to ask the question Puerto Ricans had agonized over. That question of economic viability remains unanswered.

A Time for Choice

We believe that the Caribbean can seek and attain economic growth, more jobs, and a more equitable income distribution. After a decade of economic regression, in which the gross domestic product per capita in Jamaica and Guyana fell to levels of the early 1960s, the immediate prospects are not good. Nevertheless, within five years the region can begin a turnaround.

The conventional wisdom is that the only solution for the Caribbean is massive and continuous resource transfers—aid—from outside combined with the "safety valve" of out-migration. The Caribbean has been remarkably successful in obtaining more aid on a per capita basis than any region in the world. However, the tragic irony is that those countries that received the largest amount of outside aid in the 1970s and 1980s (Jamaica and Guyana) and foreign exchange (Trinidad, due to oil) had the worst performance. Far from solving the problem, massive outside resources compounded these nations' problems by fostering dependency. By creating a burden of annual debt service without development, foreign aid actually reduced the autonomy of the "fortunate." And conversely, those nations that used internal savings rather than foreign aid to develop, such as Barbados, achieved a good rate of growth.

Those nations that experienced the largest out-migration of talented, skilled labor—Guyana, Jamaica in the late 1970s—have suffered the worst administrative bottlenecks, hampering development efforts. Emigration has long been viewed as a right, a necessary "safety valve," and a source of valuable foreign exchange through remittances. In fact, it has denuded nations of the very entrepreneurial, upwardly mobile people who tend to pull countries up as they climb the ladder to self-improvement. Remittances help dependent families to survive, but in many cases the communities would be better off if the enterprising youth that are sending checks home had not left. The communities that have experienced heavy out-migration are generally stagnant.

Two lessons emerge from these experiences of the last twenty years. First, economic performance depends not on the amount of resources a nation receives but on how it uses them. Second, the most effective policies in the region were those that put greatest emphasis on the use of a country's own material and human resources, that is, on *self-reliance*. Self-reliance has two components:

1. Economic policy reform should be driven by a process of local consultation and consensus formation rather than by foreign or International Monetary Fund officials, because that will ensure the commitment necessary for the reforms to be sustained.
2. Countries must limit their external borrowing to within about 2 percent of gross national product. Imports should be paid mostly with export revenues; budgets should be financed by taxation and not by printing money.

In recent years, a new consensus has emerged among economists regarding those economic policies that are more likely to produce positive economic growth.[1] Those macroeconomic policies are described in some detail below, but briefly, the package includes the following: trade liberalization with a bias toward export; fiscal self-reliance with an effective tax system; a policy favoring investment over consumption; and deregulation and privatization. A number of countries, notably the "Asian tigers," have demonstrated that this policy mix can produce excellent results. Those who think that Asian culture is the cause of the "tigers"' success need only consider that among the smallest countries in the Caribbean with the least resources, two utilized the same mix of economic policies that the Asians used, with the same positive effect—Barbados from 1960 to 1980 and the Bahamas from 1970 to 1990.

If the recipe is so clear, then why have more countries not used it? The reason is that implementing the correct policy mix and sustaining it long enough to see results is difficult politically. Among the political obstacles that have to be overcome are the following:

1. Local oligarchies, bureaucrats, and labor unions all prefer the certainty of the status quo or of slow deterioration to the uncertain but considerable risk of policy reform, for example, of privatization.
2. Policy reforms produce painful dislocations and often unemployment and high prices in the short term; the benefits take longer. Politicians run for office in the short term; if they lose, they will have paid the price while their rivals will secure the benefits.
3. There is a risky tradeoff: capital accumulation, which is essential to growth, leads to cuts in consumption and often excessive concentration of wealth and power. If the state intervenes to compensate for the growing inequalities, it might very well discourage capital accumulation. If it does not intervene, then exploitation could worsen. The hard part is to get the right mix—to use market forces to achieve growth and create jobs while transferring revenues to those who have not shared in the profits.[2]

TRADE POLICIES. Import substitution as an engine of growth has exhausted its possibilities for the Caribbean. To grow, the region now needs to expand its imports, but given the limits to future capital flows, the only way to pay for these imports is to expand and diversify exports. The traditional exports—bauxite, sugar, bananas, and even tourism—cannot grow fast enough. To develop new lines of exports—for example, apparel, light manufacturing, assembly operations, data entry, agro-industry, services—will require a fundamental shift in policy orientation from an antiexport to a proexport bias. Such a change involves policies such as flexible exchange rates, tariff reduction, deregulation, and tax incentives for investment. These policies are very unpopular, which is why they have seldom been implemented and even more rarely sustained for any period of time.

FISCAL POLICIES. To be self-sustaining, the Caribbean must learn to live within its means, with perhaps a modest current account deficit. (So should the United States.) Fiscal policy must be oriented toward increasing the level of domestic savings and ensuring that budgetary expenditures are financed in a sustainable fashion (i.e., without resort to excessive borrowing or printing of money). The tradition of dependence on external finance in the 1980s unfortunately has been both the cause and the effect of extremely low savings rates, chronic budget deficits, and periodic debt crises in most Caribbean countries. Adjustment in these areas will require reducing public employment, increasing taxes and reforming the tax codes, reducing subsidies, increasing utility rates, and other very difficult measures.

INVESTMENT POLICIES. Growth and job creation are not possible without capital accumulation. The tough questions are: Who will invest? In what areas should they invest? How should the government privatize most efficiently? What other steps should the government take to encourage investment?

It is widely recognized that few states have been efficient investors or manufacturers, particularly in the export sector. Therefore, export diversification programs will depend mainly on local and foreign private investors. Governments will need to provide infrastructure and human resource development (education, training) and should establish an environment conducive to private investment. Governments have options for judging where they want to encourage investment, and the experience in East Asia suggests that close collaboration between the government and the private sector works better than a laissez-faire or an adversarial system. Caribbean governments have not begun to develop mechanisms for collaboration yet, but they need to begin to do that.

If implemented properly, privatization can generate new investment and innovation in bloated, inefficient industries. National governments can also compel these large companies to respond more to the market by measuring their performance according to private standards. But privatization entails some risks if it is not handled correctly, or if the public monopoly is transferred to private hands with no public accountability or increase in competitiveness.

TRADE UNIONS. Traditionally, Caribbean trade unions have bargained for higher wages and benefits in capital-intensive industries (oil, bauxite, cement). These could afford high wages but have generated little additional employment. Trade union wage push has contributed to the antiexport bias and to inefficiencies, which have made Caribbean workers uncompetitive compared with their Mexican and Dominican Republic counterparts. Trade unions will need to reexamine and broaden their role so that they participate in and take responsibility for macroeconomic decisions, such as the tradeoff between high wages and job creation.

SOCIAL POLICIES. The transformation of import-driven economies to export-oriented engines for growth will require a massive effort in education, not just in schools but also in on-the-job training. The universities will also have to be adapted to the computer and technological needs of the twenty-first century, since the labor force of the next millennium is already in school.

Health programs are essential not only because of their inherent worth but because they are related directly to productivity, and tourists are attracted more to a country that maintains high health standards. Indeed, Costa Rica has shown that a small country with a high level of education and health can attract large numbers of Americans who have retired. Retirement communities represent an important potential area for development for the smaller islands or for local areas on the larger islands.

If the region changes the role of the state in the economies and becomes more export-oriented, it will soon see the emergence of a new class of entrepreneurs climbing up the economic ladder. Nevertheless, there will remain a large number of people who cannot find the first rung. There will be increasing needs for programs aimed specifically at relieving the distress of society's poorest. The most effective remedies are education, job creation, and price stability, but specific programs will need to be targeted to those who are dislocated by the changes.

Regionalism

Self-reliance does not mean isolationism, an end to regionalism, or the cessation of external assistance. It does suggest a different set of priorities in approaching economic problems, and it does raise some new and difficult questions. Since the early 1960s, when Jamaica and Trinidad discarded the idea of a West Indies Federation in favor of a Caribbean Free Trade Area (CARIFTA), all the leaders in the region have made eloquent statements about the necessity of regionalism but have been very reluctant to agree to any plan that could limit their autonomous decision-making authority. Indeed, despite frequent ringing endorsements of Caribbean integration, the failure by the region's governments to take steps to ensure compliance with the CARICOM Multilateral Clearing Facility (CMCF) has harmed intraregional trade and proven a much more telling indication of the *actual* priorities of the individual governments.

Some of the leaders of the small Eastern Caribbean nations are contemplating unification, but in practice, it appears that they may only be considering adding another layer—an Eastern Caribbean parliament—on the already burdensome bureaucratic and political duplication of these small town-states. It verges on the bizarre that nations with fewer than 100,000 people have embassies throughout the world, security forces, numerous ministries, and what is more important, ministers. Any outsider would conclude that there is a compelling need to unify the bureaucracies and political leadership, but the gap between defining a problem and executing its solution is the sovereign divide, and crossing that has not been possible thus far.

Rather than rehearse the old questions related to unification, it might be more productive to ask how a regional approach today could be more productive. The truth is that only a small portion of each nation's trade is within the Caribbean; the major part is with the United States and to lesser degrees with Great Britain and Canada. Therefore, CARICOM should be viewed, not as an alternative to an economic relationship with a wider group such as the United States or Europe, but as a necessary complement. Given the importance of the global market but the increasing trend toward regional blocs in world trade, the Caribbean needs to decide its trading priorities. Some have suggested that the region should turn to Europe,[3] and while we agree that it is an important market for the region, *we recommend that the highest priority be to complete the integration of CARICOM as an essential steppingstone toward eventual entry to a wider North American Free Trade Area (NAFTA).*

One preliminary issue in need of some hard thinking concerns the currency. A stable economy is a precondition for a stable currency, but to maintain a stable economy, a country also needs a stable currency. The region has three options. First, weak and volatile national currencies can coexist alongside trade in U.S. dollars. The irony is that the region's most vociferously nationalistic regimes—Sandinista Nicaragua, Guyana, Jamaica—were forced to rely increasingly on the dollar as their own currency lost its credibility or value. A second option is a Caribbean-wide currency that is printed and distributed by a single central bank. If Europe can move in this direction, the Caribbean could too. A regional currency may be facilitated by establishing a single CARICOM central bank. (The OECS has a single central bank, though CARICOM does not.) A third option is to formally adopt the dollar as the region's currency. From the perspective of the Caribbean, this option is not desirable politically, but it could be inevitable economically. If the first option fails, or if the region cannot agree to a regional currency, which we view as the best path, then this third option might be reconsidered by default.

U.S. Policies

Self-reliance does not mean that there is no room for external assistance. Rather, external aid should *not* be used as a substitute for domestic efforts, *nor* should it precede or reduce the incentive for the necessary but difficult domestic policies that we have described above. The first step is to change mind-sets. There is a tendency in the region to look for answers abroad and a tendency by the United States to deal with the regime's problems by fits and starts. We recommend a compact that begins by a determination of individual Caribbean leaders to help themselves because it is in their interest to do so. Then, the United States and others should offer their help because it is in their interests and because it could reinforce the correct policies.

From the perspective of the United States, the Caribbean is insignificant economically, accounting for a small fraction of U.S. trade. Nonetheless, for strategic reasons, the United States modified the multilateral trade policy that it had pursued consistently in the post–Second World War period in favor of a regional trade policy aimed at fostering development in the Caribbean. The policy was the Caribbean Basin Initiative. Passed by Congress in August 1983 and made permanent seven years later, the CBI aimed to stimulate investment, create jobs, and promote economic development through increasing trading opportunities. Congress, however, excluded from the program many of the products with the greatest potential for growth because local U.S. producers feared the competition.

The U.S. International Trade Commission evaluated the program's effect from 1983 to 1988 and concluded that "over all, levels of new investment in beneficiary countries in the region remain disappointingly low."[4] The CBI stimulated nontraditional exports and had a net positive impact on the economies of the region, but the overall impact was quite small. Two economists estimated that the annual trade creation due to the CBI ranged from $164 million to $267 million, but this was less than the annual cost of the simultaneous reduction in sugar exports from the region.[5]

The effect of U.S. sugar policy on the region has been comparable to that of the most ferocious natural or political disasters. In the 1890s, an increase in the U.S. tariff on Cuban sugar imports precipitated the Cuban war for independence. More recently, the end of the U.S. sugar quota system in 1975 led to a deep decline in the sugar industry, a mainstay of the region's economy. A new quota system was approved by Congress in 1981.

Imported sugar received a higher price, but the reduction in quotas for the Caribbean region was severe—from an annual average of 1.7 million tons of sugar imported per year from 1975 to 1981 to only 442,200 tons in 1989. From 1982 to 1989 the countries in the region lost about $1.8 billion in potential revenue as a result of sugar quotas. The CBI hardly made a dent in that loss. In the Dominican Republic alone, five sugar mills have closed since 1982. Throughout the Caribbean Basin, about 400,000 jobs were lost because of the diminished sugar quotas, and these were mostly jobs in rural areas with the worst poverty and the highest unemployment. In contrast, the CBI created about 136,000 jobs in manufacturing from 1983 to 1988. This net loss in jobs should be juxtaposed with the increase in the entire region's labor force during that period of 2.3 million. The region, like sugar's value, has been falling.

The decision by Congress in 1990 to make the CBI permanent without expanding its provisions or coverage is a mixed blessing.[6] It is marginally useful for promoting development, but the region is in need of a more potent stimulus. If the Caribbean is willing to consider the steps discussed above, then the United States should consider a similarly bold initiative in the region. Such an initiative should include the following: (1) the expansion of the U.S.-Canadian-Mexican free trade talks to include the Caribbean soon after the agreement is completed; (2) an interim series of steps to open the U.S. market for sugar, textiles and apparel, and steel; (3) a coordinated debt and aid strategy; (4) a new dialogue on immigration; (5) strengthening the tourist industry; (6) a disaster relief program; and (7) a coordinated approach to political and security issues, including drugs.

A North American Free Trade Area (NAFTA)

Official negotiations began on June 1, 1991, to create a North American Free Trade Area, comprising the United States, Canada, and Mexico. The issue for the United States and the Caribbean is whether, and if so, when, to expand that area to include the Caribbean. The CARICOM countries can approach the United States one at a time or as a group to become part of NAFTA or to try to conclude a bilateral trade agreement. To be excluded from NAFTA would mean declining competitiveness. "Mexico," in the words of one of the region's leaders, "will have the Caribbean for lunch."

In the interim, there are steps that the United States should take to ease the transition toward a freer trade area and to offer opportunities for the region. Such steps are consistent with U.S. national interests in freer and fairer trade and would benefit U.S. consumers. The adverse effect on U.S. producers would be minimal. The step that could have the most rapid and most positive impact would be to loosen quota systems on sugar and textiles. Of course, the two U.S. lobbies are very strong. The sugar lobby beat back any liberalization when CBI was extended; and the textile lobby came within a few votes of imposing the first protectionist bill on a president in over fifty years. Any change in trade policy will require strong presidential leadership.

OPTIONS FOR SUGAR POLICY. If the president is willing to bear the political consequences, there are a host of alternatives. He could (1) directly subsidize domestic farmers in a free market; (2) change quotas to outright tariffs and reduce them; (3) expand quotas for the region gradually; or (4) guarantee quantity and price on a multiyear basis, which would permit greater stability and predictability for the region. Whatever option is chosen, it should be implemented in a gradual and predictable manner that would permit long-term planning.

OPTIONS FOR TEXTILES AND APPAREL. Expanding access to the U.S. market for Caribbean textiles and apparel is another area where asymmetry could be used to assist the region. The effect on the region would be substantial, with little adverse effect on the United States. In general, it might be easier politically for the United States to negotiate an expansion of the free trade agreement to include the Caribbean than it would be to modify the sugar or textile policies.

REGIONAL CONTEXT. Mexico and Venezuela have continued to renew the San Jose Pact of 1980, which provides credit for oil purchases, and while this has been useful in the past, important questions have been raised about the program's real benefit. The changing of payments into long-term loans in many ways postpones the unavoidable adjustment. Mexico agreed to open its market to Central America, and it has begun talks with the Caribbean that could eventually lead toward the same end. Venezuela might try to steer the Andean Pact in a similar direction.

Aid and Debt

The Caribbean has a two-sided problem regarding financial flows: on the one hand, it needs a substantial infusion of new capital to finance the modernization of its economy to become more competitive and export-oriented; on the other hand, it cannot service the debt it contracted in the past. These two sides, of course, are related not only in the past—past aid is current debt—but in the future—new aid or financing is infeasible unless the region demonstrates that it can use the new money more effectively than it did the old. We recommend that new financing and debt relief must follow, not precede, reforms and self-reliance, but such financing cannot be delayed for long without jeopardizing the reforms.

The Caribbean has been the recipient of some of the largest aid flows on a per capita basis in the developing world. The Caribbean Group for Cooperation in Economic Development, established at the initiative of the Carter administration in 1977 and under the auspices of the World Bank, succeeded in coordinating and rationalizing external aid flows and increasing aid quite substantially—net official transfers in 1982 were almost three times the 1978 level. Since then, aid has gradually declined, though it still remains high by global standards for a middle-income region.[7]

The region's debt problem is different from that of Latin America's, whose debt is primarily contracted with private banks. From 1980 to 1988, Caribbean debt doubled, to nearly $10 billion.[8] Some of that new debt stemmed from the loans generated by the Caribbean Group. In 1991, Jamaica had to use 31 percent of its $2.4 billion in exports of goods and services to service its debt. For the whole Caribbean, with the exception of Trinidad and Tobago, 36 percent of total debt is owed to the multilateral financial institutions (IFIs), 27 percent to donor governments, and 37 percent to commercial banks. For Jamaica, 47 percent of total debt is owed to governments and 31 percent to multilateral agencies.[9]

U.S. Secretary of the Treasury Nicholas Brady offered an important proposal on March 10, 1989, to reduce privately contracted debt, but his initiative made little progress because no single entity was placed in charge of the negotiations. Thus far, there has been no effort to negotiate this proposal in the Caribbean. We recommend that the World Bank take the lead in negotiating the Brady Initiative and begin doing so in the Caribbean immediately.

Even if the Brady Initiative is applied vigorously to the Caribbean, its overall effect on the economies will be small, since most of the region's debt is official, not private. With regard to the official debt, the then prime minister, Michael Manley, made a proposal to Brady, and on June 27, 1990, in the context of his Enterprise for the Americas initiative, President Bush responded with a promise of official debt relief.

Jamaica (with 47 percent of its total debt owed to individual governments) and Guyana (with 53 percent of its total debt owed to governments) would benefit most from this relief. The Caribbean owed the U.S. government more than $2 billion. A sizable reduction of that amount would permit the region to shift scarce foreign exchange from servicing its debt to long-term investments. U.S. bilateral loans represent about one-quarter of the total. Canada announced in early 1990 that it intended to cancel all outstanding development aid debt owed by eleven CARICOM countries. That amounts to a total of $182 million. We recommend that other governments follow the spirit of the U.S. and Canadian initiatives and implement across-the-board official debt relief.

Another idea suggested by Richard Bernal and Tony Bogues is to have all bilateral debt repaid in local currency and recycled through local governments as grants applied to approved development projects or programs. This would deal with the problem noted above on aid; donors would be able to see that this money would be used effectively.

An additional problem is that the region has begun to have a negative transfer of resources *to* the IFIs. Write-offs of official IFI debt are infeasible, but it is possible to consider several alternative approaches. The maturities of existing loans could be lengthened. This is already being done with new loans, but it should also be applied to older ones. The banks could also refinance loans coming due and capitalize the interest, as well as provide new loans with mixed credits.

Immigration

Immigration remains a powerful factor affecting the region's development, but few have bothered to incorporate that variable into the development equation. Already, about one-fourth of the population of the English-speaking Caribbean has emigrated to the United States, Great Britain, and Canada.[10] The loss of skilled and entrepreneurial manpower remains a significant cost to the region's development, probably exceeding the positive effect of remittances.[11] The 1990 U.S. immigration law, which makes it much easier for people with skills to immigrate, will undoubtedly hurt the region even as it contributes to the economic development of the United States. Despite these facts, immigration is such a central characteristic of the psychology of the region, and particularly of its elite, that its leaders seek more access to the U.S. labor market, not less.

We recommend a change. It is time to create incentives for the region's talented population to return home. The first place to start is at the international development banks, where so many talented Caribbean economists work. We recommend that the banks adopt a new rule that permits Caribbean technocrats to work there for a fixed term and then to return to their countries. Perhaps, more than any single initiative this would create a new psychology for the region and permit the accumulation of human capital needed to manage both private enterprises and public projects. Moreover, since so many of these individuals will have returned with great experience in the IFIs, they would serve as effective interlocutors with these institutions.

Tourism

Tourism has replaced sugar in many islands as the principal source of foreign exchange, but too much of that foreign exchange leaves the region, because too few linkages have been developed with local economies. Few hotels use local food or products. Private-sector leaders in the region need to find ways to increase the backward and forward linkages of these hotels and to bring the costs down or risk losing the tourists. Other ideas for expanding tourism include preclearance facilities in more countries. The Bahamas and Bermuda already have such facilities whereby U.S. customs and immigration handle tourists before they leave the island. Tourists prefer this arrangement, as it permits them to exit to their destination rapidly.

Disaster Relief

In the course of reviewing a range of policies, it is worth recalling that the islands rest in a very turbulent sea, and nature has had a much more potent effect on the islands than has man. Hurricanes strike periodically with devastating force—hurricane David in the fall of 1988, Hugo the next year. Jamaica, Puerto Rico, the Virgin Islands, Montserrat, St. Kitts and Nevis—none of these has fully recovered from the force of these winds.

The United States has established a Federal Emergency Management Administration (FEMA) to deal with natural disasters at home, and international agencies have helped the Caribbean to dig out from their disasters. The U.S. Army Corps of Engineers has often played a useful role, but as yet there is no central mechanism or fund to which all in the region should contribute. We recommend that CARICOM leaders invite the United States and Canada to join them in developing a permanent region-wide plan to manage the relief assistance on an emergency basis to cope with natural disasters.

Political and Security Cooperation in the Caribbean

The region's strength and vulnerability is its democracy. There is no better framework for peaceful change or for meeting the needs of the people. The region's democracies have not experienced the Latin American problem of coup d'états, in part because they have kept their armed forces small and professional. Some have criticized the region's "creeping militarization," but we agree with Neville Linton and Vaughan Lewis that the bigger problem may be that people cannot find the police. The attempted coup in Trinidad shows that security remains a serious problem, and the CARICOM leaders agreed in July 1990 to study the security issue. The question is, what will be done?

The region needs to begin by addressing some hard questions and accepting that there have been some important moments when the lack of a collective decision was costly. In the case of Grenada, such moments occurred in 1974 when Gairy's thugs beat Bishop, in 1979 when Bishop toppled Gairy, and in 1983 when the OECS countries turned to the United States rather than to CARICOM to restore democracy and order. In 1982, CARICOM began debating the issue of whether to transform the Chagua-ramas Treaty into a collective agreement to secure democracy, but Trini-dad's Prime Minister George Chambers sidestepped the issue by negotiat-ing a private understanding with Grenada's Bishop. Similarly, in the case of Guyana, Eric Williams turned to direct mediation between Burnham and Jagan rather than a collective effort, and when he failed, CARICOM ignored the issue.

To build the appropriate mechanism to defend the region, we need to start with a more precise definition of the nature of the threats faced by the region and the most appropriate responses. There are four kinds of threats:

1. *Rogue or pariah states:* What should be done when a rogue regime that threatens its people and its neighbors takes power?
2. *Coups by mercenaries or minorities (bandits or radicals):* What should the region do when a small minority subverts the constitution and takes over a neighboring government?
3. *Subversion or corruption by drug or criminal elements:* What should be done about arms smuggling, drug trafficking, and money laundering?
4. *Oil spills, foreign fishing in territorial waters:* How should the region re-spond to intrusions or effluents in the Caribbean?

To deal with the more conventional threats, several of the larger nations in the region have military forces. Six smaller nations established the Regional Security System (RSS), with a combined force of about 60 specially trained policemen from each country. While this is an improve-ment on the past, it is inadequate or inappropriate for dealing with these threats.

What more is needed? The region should pool intelligence and coop-erate more with the French in the area. Annual military exercises involv-ing the United States, Canada, France, and maybe the British might help to give a greater sense of security. But there is a more effective way to deter threats without increasing the defense capabilities of the islands. We rec-ommend amending the CARICOM treaty to spell out in detail the steps that the region would take in the event of a coup, a threat of a takeover by drug traffickers, or the emergence of a rogue state. The first step should be to convoke an immediate summit meeting to discuss the timing and se-quence for diplomatic, economic, and ultimately military sanctions. Such

a treaty provision would deter a large military and would be the best substitute for it. The treaty also ought to include a provision whereby CARI-
COM can call on non-Caribbean nations or international organizations to
reinforce their security forces. If it is clear that the region can count on
outside support, that will strengthen the regime's deterrent capability. The
size of local forces does not matter if there is a credible deterrent; only a
major power can provide that.

Also, as Linton notes, one needs to deal with the side of the problem
that gives rise to pariah regimes. The region should try to gain wide acceptance for stronger human rights provisions and groups, such as the CARI-
COM Commission of Human Rights and a CARICOM court of appeals.

International election observers may also play a key role, as they did in
Haiti and Guyana. As Anthony Maingot writes: "The defense of democracy in the region can only be made possible when *all* the democracies in
the [Caribbean] sea decide to secure democracy for themselves and for
their neighbors. That situation has not yet been achieved in the region." [12]

David Coore, Jamaica's minister of foreign affairs, told the United
Nations in October 1989: "There is no doubt that the drug problem has
today assumed proportions which are far beyond the capacity of individual
states to control." [13] A recognition of the transnational dimension of the
drug problem is the first step toward managing it better. We recommend
more regional collection and sharing of intelligence; more cooperation on
interdicting drug traffickers and arresting money launderers; a training facility for antinarcotics agents in both investigative and interdiction activities; and more cooperation involving the U.S. Coast Guard, a better model
for the region than the U.S. Navy. Former Prime Minister Manley's idea for
a multinational drug force was tabled by the United Nations; it merits re-
consideration for the Caribbean alone. A big problem in pursuing drug
traffickers relates to the reliability of sensitive information. The small
nations of the Caribbean were justifiably frightened when agents from the
U.S. Drug Enforcement Agency (DEA) arrested a Caribbean premier in
Miami. To ensure that such sensitive information is accurate rather than
used for political purposes to destroy a person's career, we recommend that
CARICOM and the United States establish a high-level, trustworthy special
court to consider the evidence and decide. Trinidad's former Prime Minister A. N. R. Robinson suggested an international criminal court, an idea
that might be worth pursuing.

In addition, the region needs, according to Ron Sanders, stringent legislation providing for heavy fines and long terms of imprisonment for drug
traffickers.[14] Their property ought to be held when they are arrested and

confiscated if they are found guilty. Only four Caribbean nations have such stringent legislation. Consideration ought to be given to strengthening extradition treaties to cope with international drug traffickers.

The United States is a growing source of arms trafficking, and Caribbean countries have a right to demand changes in U.S. laws on local arms sales if the United States is going to demand changes in banking laws in the Caribbean. Miami, as Maingot points out, has replaced Havana and Moscow as the principal source of subversion in the region, but it is a special kind of nongovernmental transnational subversion involving illicit arms sales, money laundering, and drugs.[15] The United States has a responsibility to address this side of the problem if it wants the Caribbean to address its side.

The Non-English-speaking Caribbean

While the entire region contemplates the significance and implications of the North American Free Trade Agreement, CARICOM remains the main club to which the non-English-speaking Caribbean seeks entry. Haiti, the Dominican Republic, Suriname, and Puerto Rico have all requested observer status, and the first two nations clearly would like to become full members. The language barrier, however, might represent as formidable a challenge as the fact that each of the nations on the island of Hispaniola is more populous than the rest of CARICOM combined.

Jonathan Hartlyn describes the Dominican Republic as an unusual double paradox (see above, chapter 8). Its conspiratorial politics is still defined by octogenarians of another age, and yet it also has one of the most durable democracies in Latin America. Since at least 1978, well-organized parties have participated in relatively free elections. And while the country suffers from serious problems of unemployment, inefficiency, and a bloated state bureaucracy, its social and economic progress during the last three decades has been spectacular, transforming the nation from a primitive, rural nation of 3 million to a "vibrant, internationally connected, mostly urban country of some 7 million" who are "better educated and better off materially."[16] In brief, the Dominican Republic is beginning to appear more like the members of CARICOM.

Puerto Rico has the highest standard of living in the Caribbean, and its dilemma is of a different nature. As Juan García-Passalacqua describes, Puerto Rico is an island in search of its identity, caught between its Latin heritage and its growing economic and social ties to the United States. In the last two decades, the statehood movement has grown stronger, and a thin majority might now favor that status. But the decision on status remains a paralyzing one, with many in Puerto Rico still waiting for the United States to decide, while the United States waits for Puerto Rico. Divisions on the island cause and are affected by the ambivalence on the mainland.[17]

The Caribbean and Puerto Rico have had a long, mutually ambivalent relationship stemming from the ambiguousness of Puerto Rico's status. If and when a plebiscite occurs, and if Puerto Ricans clearly choose one option, then special attention will be needed to develop more enduring relationships between the new Puerto Rico and the Caribbean. In the meantime, it would be desirable for CARICOM to permit Puerto Rico observer status even while Puerto Rico works to accelerate its 936 program aimed at providing financing for Caribbean area projects.

Puerto Rico has been stuck on the issue of status, but the island has made remarkable social and economic progress. Haiti's problem is the reverse. Populating the first independent nation in Latin America and the Caribbean, and the first black republic in the world, Haitians remain secure in their pride as a people, even while the nation's economy is practically moribund and the illiteracy rate is the highest in the Western Hemisphere. Three decades of Duvalierist rule brought relative stability at the price of terror and without the benefit of development.

In February 1986 the young Duvalier went into exile. After that, Haiti struggled under several military governments until finally, on December 16, 1990, with the help of international observers, the interim government of Madame Ertha Pascal-Trouillot oversaw Haiti's first real free election. Father Jean Bertrand-Aristide, a radical priest with a gift for speaking for the vast majority of Haiti's poor, literally swept away the field of eleven presidential candidates with a *lavelas* (landslide) and two-thirds of the vote. Between his election and the inauguration on February 7, 1991, the fifth anniversary of "Baby Doc" Duvalier's departure, the country nervously awaited the rightist reaction, and it came.

In early January, Roger LaFontant, Duvalier's minister of the interior and chief of the dreaded Tonton Macoutes, the paramilitary forces of the dictator, seized the presidential palace, forced Trouillot to resign, and demanded that the military support him. Aristide's supporters mobbed the palace, and General Herard Abraham, the shrewd leader of the armed forces, threw his support to the people and sent the army to arrest LaFontant. It was a decisive moment, and Aristide had the good sense to capitalize on it.

Although many had feared that he would arm a popular militia and try to intimidate Abraham and the armed forces, Aristide chose instead to embrace Abraham and the military and to tell his people on inauguration day that the military were now their protectors. With the Macoutes beaten, the military under Abraham defending Aristide, and wellsprings of international support from the United States, Venezuela, France, and the international development banks, the new president had the best opportunity in Haiti's history to build the country. On September 30 the Haitian military overthrew Aristide and sent him into exile. The Organization of American States (OAS) responded quickly by demanding the reinstatement of Aristide and imposing stiff diplomatic and economic sanctions, but the military and the elite were unresponsive.

After the military overthrew the Suriname government in December 1990, CARICOM forthrightly suspended Suriname's observer status. This, plus an OAS condemnation, troubled the military government, and it decided to call for new elections on May 25, 1991. The elections were judged free and fair by OAS observers and representatives of the Council of Freely-Elected Heads of Government. The challenge in Suriname was for the new government under President Ronald Venetiaan to structure a framework that would assure civilian control of the military. The Dutch government plays a key role in Suriname, and the issue is whether the two governments will construct a new "Commonwealth-type" association or whether Suriname will move closer to CARICOM, which remains a potentially important democratic magnet for the region.

Cuba is too big to ignore, although it has become less of a player since the collapse of the Soviet Union. The Caribbean may be forgiven for some ambivalence toward its big neighbor. If the island moves in the direction of the hemisphere—toward democracy and free markets—it will become a potent competitor, particularly for tourists. If the United States imports sugar from Cuba, then the rest of the Caribbean will suffer. Still, there might not be any way to avoid that. The issue in Cuba is when it will change, and the answer to that question will have to await either a heart attack or a change of heart by Fidel Castro.

A North American Commonwealth

If the Caribbean joins Mexico, Canada, and the United States in a North American Free Trade Area, then political and social issues will become regional in scope. Greater economic integration will inevitably lead to questions about the freer movement of population and social policies, and these, in turn, will lead to an inquiry into political association. At the present time, however, parts of the region are still moving in the opposite direction. The premier of Nevis, an island of thirty-six square miles and ten thousand people, announced in the fall of 1990 that he will ask his people to vote on independence from St. Kitts.

From the other direction, the prime ministers of Grenada, St. Vincent, St. Lucia, and Dominica decided to call for a referendum on political unification. It is unclear, however, whether that will lead to unity or just to an additional bureaucratic layer. If the leaders want to establish an Eastern Caribbean parliament separate from the other parliaments, then this effort seems to be more fiction than fact.[18] In the summer of 1990, CARICOM decided to intensify its efforts to establish a single unified market by 1993, the twentieth anniversary of its establishment, beginning with the establishment of a common external tariff (CET) in January 1991.[19] Since that date came and went without a CET, it is fair to ask again, how real? Are the leaders willing to reduce their sovereignty for a more effective regional autonomy, or are they just trying to create new chairs for the region's elite?

Nonetheless, if the movement toward Caribbean-wide integration continues, the leaders of the region will face the same kinds of questions that the European Community has addressed.[20] First, should there be a Caribbean-wide currency with a single central bank? Should the region seek a political association with the United States or restrict its relations to an economic compact? Should the region consider a North American commonwealth, a grouping of sovereign states that coordinate foreign and defense policies in addition to economic and welfare policies? Should there be a freer movement of people? What about citizenship?

As the walls of the old world are tumbling down, it is time to begin some regionwide thinking of new ways to rearrange the "new world." To begin the process, we recommend the establishment of an informal group of North Americans with interests in the Caribbean Basin. This includes Canada, the United States, Mexico, Venezuela, Colombia, the Caribbean, and Central America. Such a group could be modeled on the Inter-American Dialogue, a group of leaders from all of the Americas, but it should focus much more on the dynamics of the Caribbean Basin. Such an informal group might eventually propose the establishment of a Caribbean Basin parliament or assembly.

The Caribbean is small in size and population but of large importance to the people of the region and, for different reasons, to the United States. If the region is to fulfill its potential, the answers must come first from the region. We therefore recommend a compact between the United States and the region to begin only after the region's leaders demonstrate a commitment to new economic policies aimed at promoting exports, expanding investment, minimizing fiscal and current account deficits, and providing incentives for return migration by skilled labor.

Such a plan of self-reliance is not autarchical; it is not intended to shield the region from the competition of the world. Quite the contrary, the plan is designed to make the region more competitive. Such a plan does not rely solely on the market; it is premised on the idea that governments have a crucial role to play in fomenting development, not in production but in regulating and ensuring that those who are disadvantaged by the market system are compensated by those who gain.

The United States should take a long view of the region and realize that a relatively small investment can yield a bountiful dividend in assuring a democratic and prosperous neighborhood. By opening its markets and providing financing, the United States would be helping these countries to provide jobs for restless youth who might otherwise consider illegal migration or drugs.

The time has also come for both the United States and the Caribbean to contemplate new forms of economic and political association. In considering such options, the only guideline should be to rule out nothing. Haiti has presented the opportunity to move toward a new horizon. CARICOM and the United States ought to embrace this fragile state and devise a political framework that will bring it back from dictatorship while at the same time guaranteeing the democracies of the entire region. The steps to deter such an adverse swing of the pendulum need to be clear and uniformly accepted by all and should run the gamut from diplomatic to economic to military sanctions. Their goal is to ensure the vitality and permanence of democracy for the entire Caribbean Basin.

Notes

Foreword

1. U.S. Census Bureau, 1990.
2. The source for all figures relating to the population numbers of Caribbean-born peoples residing in the United States is the U.S. Immigration & Naturalization Service, 1990.
3. Haitian Advocacy Associates of Central Boston, 1990.

1 The Caribbean Question: Why Has Liberal Democracy (Surprisingly) Flourished?

This is not a freestanding chapter. Instead, it calls attention to and, to some degree, summarizes themes that emerge in the chapters that follow and in other papers prepared for the World Peace Foundation's Caribbean Project. Because the chapters and other papers are rich and diverse, and because the concluding chapter by Robert Pastor and Richard Fletcher focuses on domestic and international policy issues with special attention to economic matters, this chapter concentrates on exploring the fate of liberal democratic politics in the Caribbean. As a result, this chapter overlaps rather more with those written by Evelyne Huber and Anthony Payne, though it treats the subject somewhat differently. The chapter relies on textual references when it calls attention to the other chapters; at other times a few bibliographic references are given, including references to the project's other papers. This somewhat unorthodox approach to a rapporteur's task has two additional advantages: the World Peace Foundation will find it easier to assert that the views expressed here are mine alone, and the authors will be free to claim, accurately, that all the errors in this draft are mine and that all the insights are theirs. An earlier draft was prepared for discussion at the World Peace Foundation's conference, "The Caribbean Prepares for the Twenty-first Century," Kingston, Jamaica, 10–13 January 1991.

1. Ralf Dahrendorf, *Society and Democracy in Germany* (Munich, 1965; New York: W. W. Norton, 1979).

2. This project chose not to include Cuba; except for an occasional point, this report likewise excludes Cuba. Obviously, Cuba's political regime is not liberal democratic.

3. Myron Weiner and Samuel P. Huntington, eds., *Understanding Political Development* (Boston: Little, Brown, 1987), chap. 2.

4. World Bank, *World Development Report, 1990* (New York: Oxford University Press, 1990), tables 1 and A.1.

5. Data are from Inter-American Development Bank, *Economic and Social Progress in Latin America, 1989 Report* (Washington, D.C., 1989), p. 463.

6. See also United Nations, Economic Commission for Latin American and the Caribbean, *Preliminary Overview of the Economy of Latin America and the Caribbean, 1989,* LC/G. 1586 (New York, 1989), p. 18.

7. Samuel P. Huntington, "Will More Countries Become Democratic?" *Political Science Quarterly* 99, no. 2 (Summer 1984): 201.

8. U.S. Arms Control and Disarmament Agency, *World Military Expenditures and Arms Transfers, 1987* (Washington, D.C.: GPO, 1988), table 1.

9. Dion E. Phillips, "Defense Policy in Barbados, 1966–88," *Journal of Interamerican Studies and World Affairs* 32, no. 2 (Summer 1990): 69–102.

10. See Anthony P. Maingot, "The Visions of Elites since Independence" (Paper prepared for the World Peace Foundation's Caribbean Project, Boston, October 1990); see also his "The Caribbean: The Structure of Modern-Conservative Societies," in *Latin America, Its Problems and Its Promise: A Multidisciplinary Introduction,* ed. Jan Knippers Black (Boulder: Westview, 1984).

11. Robert A. Dahl, *Polyarchy: Participation and Opposition* (New Haven: Yale University Press, 1971), pp. 110–11.

12. See also Selwyn Ryan, *Race and Nationalism in Trinidad and Tobago: A Study of Decolonization in a Multiracial Society* (Toronto: University of Toronto Press, 1972).

13. For a discussion of efforts to manage such cleavages in the Netherlands Antilles and in Suriname by means of consociational pacts, see Arend Lijphart, *Democracy in Plural Societies* (New Haven: Yale University Press, 1977), chap. 6.

14. See Claus Offe, "Competitive Party Democracies and the Keynesian Welfare State," in his *Contradictions of the Welfare State* (Cambridge, Mass.: MIT Press, 1984).

15. Data from World Bank, *World Development Report, 1990,* tables 1, 28, and A.1.

16. I am grateful to Javier Corrales for provoking this thought. See also Peter J. Katzenstein, *Small States in World Markets: Industrial Policy in Europe* (Ithaca: Cornell University Press, 1985).

17. See, e.g., Carl Stone, "Political Aspects of Postwar Agricultural Policies in Jamaica (1945–1970)," *Social and Economic Studies* 23, no. 2 (June 1974): 145–76.

18. See Charles Skeete, "Performance and Prospects of the Caribbean Group for Cooperation in Economic Development" (Paper prepared for the World Peace Foundation's Caribbean Project, Boston, October 1990).

19. See Courtney Blackman, "CARICOM Private Sector Enterprise in the Global Marketplace" (Paper prepared for the World Peace Foundation's Caribbean Project, 15 November 1990). See also Stephen A. Quick, "The International Economy and the Caribbean: The 1990s and Beyond," chapter 11 in this volume.

20. Maingot, "Visions of Elites since Independence."

21. Lijphart, *Democracy in Plural Societies*.

22. Maingot, "Visions of Elites since Independence."

23. Henry Wells, *The Modernization of Puerto Rico: A Political Study of Changing Values and Institutions* (Cambridge, Mass.: Harvard University Press, 1969), p. 315.

24. Maingot, "The Caribbean," p. 365.

25. Skeete, "Performance and Prospects of the Caribbean Group."

26. Blackman, "CARICOM Private Sector Enterprise."

27. I am indebted to Professor Frances Hagopian at Tufts University for calling to my attention aspects of the complex relationship between patronage, parties, democratic regimes, and new economic strategies such as the one under consideration.

28. Carl Stone, *Politics versus Economics: The 1989 Elections in Jamaica* (Kingston: Heinemann, 1989).

29. Blackman, "CARICOM Private Sector Enterprise"; Swinburne Lestrade, "Considerations Relating to the Promotion of Foreign Investment in the Caribbean" (Paper prepared for the World Peace Foundation's Caribbean Project, August 1990).

30. The expression is C. E. Lindblom's in *Politics and Markets* (New York: Basic Books, 1977), chap. 13.

2 The Societies of the Caribbean since Independence

1. For the best analysis of the changes in Cuba, see Jorge I. Domínguez, *Cuba: Order and Revolution* (Cambridge, Mass.: Harvard University Press, 1978).

2. For the political scene during and after the Muñoz period, see Arturo Morales Carrión, *Puerto Rico: A Political and Cultural History* (New York: W. W. Norton, 1983), pp. 256–316; Roberta Ann Johnson, *Puerto Rico: Commonwealth or Colony?* (New York: Praeger, 1980); and Robert Anderson, "The Party System: Change or Stagnation," in *Time for Decision: The United States and Puerto Rico*, ed. Jorge Heine (Lanham, Md.: North-South, 1983), pp. 3–26.

3. The French and Dutch Antilles tend to be largely overlooked when the considerations are not narrowly touristic, for example, in the otherwise comprehensive and fine treatment of the contemporary scene offered in Richard Millett and W. Marvin Will, eds., *The Restless Caribbean: Changing Patterns of International Relations* (New York: Praeger, 1979). They are, however, included in Catherine A. Sunshine, *The Caribbean: Survival, Struggle, and Sovereignty* (Washington, D.C.: EPICA, 1985), pp. 164–70.

4. David Geggus, "The Haitian Revolution," in *The Modern Caribbean*, ed. Franklin W. Knight and Colin A. Palmer (Chapel Hill: University of North Carolina Press, 1989), pp. 21–50.

5. The per capita incomes are calculated from *Caribbean and Central American Databook, 1987* (Washington, D.C.: Caribbean and Central American Action, 1987). See also Franklin W. Knight, *The Caribbean: The Genesis of a Fragmented Nationalism*, 2d ed. (New York: Oxford University Press, 1990), p. 374.

6. I have developed this theme more fully in *The Caribbean*, pp. 66–87.

7. Inter-American Development Bank, *April/May 1989 Report* (Washington, D.C., 1989), p. 3. Cuba is not currently a member of the Inter-American Development Bank and so is not included in its reports, but there is no reason to expect any better economic performance there (see Carmelo Mesa-Lago, "The Economy: Caution, Frugality, and Resilient Ideology," in *Cuba: Internal and International Affairs*, ed. Jorge I. Domínguez [Beverly Hills: Sage, 1982], pp. 113–66).

8. See Dawn Marshall, "The International Politics of Migration," in Millett and Will, *The Restless Caribbean,* pp. 42–50; Roy S. Bryce-Laporte and Dolores Mortimer, eds., *Caribbean Immigration to the United States* (Washington, D.C.: RIIES, 1976); William F. Stinner, Klaus de Albuquerque, and Roy S. Bryce-Laporte, eds., *Return Migration and Remittances: Developing a Caribbean Perspective* (Washington, D.C.: RIIES, 1982); Bonham Richardson, *Caribbean Migrants: Environment and Human Survival on St. Kitts and Nevis* (Knoxville: University of Tennessee Press, 1983); and idem, *Panama Money in Barbados, 1900–1920* (Knoxville: University of Tennessee Press, 1985).

9. See Juan Pérez de la Riva, "Cuba y la migración antillana, 1900–1931," in *Anuario de estudios cubanos,* vol. 2, *La republica neocolonial* (Havana: Editorial Ciencias Sociales, 1979), pp. 1–76; Dawn Marshall, *The Haitian Problem: Illegal Migration to the Bahamas* (Mona, Jamaica: ISER, 1979); *The Caribbean Exodus,* special issue of *Caribbean Review,* 11, no. 1 (Winter 1982); and Franklin W. Knight, "Jamaican Migrants and the Cuban Sugar Industry, 1900–1934," in *Between Slavery and Free Labor: The Spanish-Speaking Caribbean in the Nineteenth Century,* ed. Manuel Moreno Fraginals, Frank Moya Pons, and Stanley L. Engerman (Baltimore: Johns Hopkins University Press, 1985).

10. Stinner, De Albuquerque, and Bryce-Laporte, *Return Migration and Remittances.*

11. This is certainly one of the most controversial aspects of Caribbean (or any) migration. Two excellent articles dealing with this are Dawn Marshall, "Migration and Development in the Eastern Caribbean," and Patricia Y. Anderson, "Migration and Development in Jamaica," in *Migration and Development in the Caribbean: The Unexplored Connection,* ed. Robert A. Pastor (Boulder: Westview, 1985), 91–116 and 117–39. For the Eastern Caribbean states (Antigua, Barbados, Dominica, Grenada, Montserrat, St. Christopher-Nevis, St. Lucia, and St. Vincent) Marshall found the consequences of migration "mixed. Emigration has definitely controlled the growth of population . . . and . . . alleviates unemployment . . . at the same time that the loss of actual or potential administrative and managerial skills is quite high" (p. 107). Anderson, after looking at Jamaica, states that "there is little reason to believe that most manpower lost through out-migration would have added to net employment rather than unemployment" (p. 136).

12. The information here and in the following paragraphs is based, unless otherwise stated, on data published in Inter-American Development Bank, *Economic and Social Progress in Latin America, 1987 Report* (Washington, D.C., 1987).

13. "1988 World Population Data Sheet," cited in *Latin America Today: An Atlas of Reproducible Pages* (Massachusetts: World Eagle, 1989), p. 101.

14. See *Caribbean Update,* October 1990, p. 16.

15. Ransford W. Palmer, *Caribbean Dependence on the United States Economy* (New York: Praeger, 1979), pp. 90–105.

16. The figures for education that appear here and subsequently are taken from Sandra W. Meditz and Denis Hanratty, eds., *Islands of the Commonwealth Caribbean: A Regional Study* (Washington, D.C.: Department of the Army, 1989). Enrollment figures, of course, may or may not be consistent with attendance figures. For some school enrollment figures see also Inter-American Development Bank, "Labor Force and Employment," *Economic and Social Progress in Latin America, 1987 Report,* p. 65.

17. Meditz and Hanratty, *Islands of the Commonwealth Caribbean,* p. 66.

18. The 1982–83 figures are taken from Director of Statistics, *Pocketbook of Statistics: Jamaica 1983* (Kingston, 1984).

19. Meditz and Hanratty, *Islands of the Commonwealth Caribbean,* pp. 181–82, 394–95.

20. *The University of the West Indies: Vice Chancellor's Report to Council*, March 1989 (Jamaica: University School of Printing, 1989), p. 2.

21. Inter-American Development Bank, "Labor Force and Employment," p. 88.

22. See, e.g., B. W. Higman, "Domestic Service in Jamaica since 1750," in Higman's *Trade, Government, and Society in Caribbean History, 1700–1920* (Kingston: Heinemann, 1983), pp. 117–38; and Michele Johnson, "The Ultimate Sale: Domestic Service in Jamaica, 1920–1970" (Paper prepared for a seminar, Johns Hopkins University, Department of History, 1990).

23. See Paul Goodwin, *Global Studies: Latin America*, 3d ed. (Guilford, Conn.: Dushkin, 1988), p. 96.

24. Raymond W. Mack, "Race, Class, and Power in Barbados," in *The Democratic Revolution in the West Indies*, ed. Wendell Bell (Cambridge, Mass.: Schenkman, 1967), pp. 140–64.

25. See Trevor Munroe, *The Politics of Constitutional Decolonization: Jamaica, 1944–1962* (Mona, Jamaica: ISER, 1972); Carol S. Holzberg, *Minorities and Power in a Black Society: The Jewish Community of Jamaica* (Lanham, Md.: North-South, 1987); and Carl Stone, *Democracy and Clientelism in Jamaica* (New Brunswick: Transaction Books, 1980).

26. M. G. Smith, F. R. Augier, and Rex Nettleford, *Report on the Ras Tafari in Kingston* (Mona, Jamaica: ISER, 1960); Rex Nettleford, *Identity, Race, and Protest in Jamaica* (New York: Morrow, 1972), pp. 39–112; Leonard Barrett, *The Rastafarians: Sounds of Cultural Dissonance* (Boston: Beacon, 1977), pp. 92–102.

3 The Internationalization of Corruption and Violence: Threats to the Caribbean in the Post–Cold War World

1. *El Nuevo Herald*, 30 December 1990.

2. Michael Manley, speech to the United Nations, New York, 9 June 1989, transcript made available by the Office of the Prime Minister, Kingston, Jamaica.

3. *Miami Herald*, 10 June 1989.

4. Walter Lippmann, "A Theory about Corruption," *Vanity Fair*, November 1930, p. 61.

5. Alfonso Lopez Michelsen, "Is Colombia to Blame?" *Hemisphere* 1, no. 1 (Fall 1988): 35.

6. Cf. Steven R. David, *Third World Coups d'Etat and International Security* (Baltimore: Johns Hopkins University Press, 1987).

7. Wade Parrish Hinkle, "The Security of Very Small States" (Ph.D. diss., University of Maryland, 1990), pp. 99, 138.

8. Peter Calvert, "Problems and Policies: An Agenda for the 1990's," in *The Central American Security System: North-South or East-West?* ed. Calvert (Cambridge: Cambridge University Press, 1988), p. 195.

9. U.S. Congress, Senate Subcommittee on Terrorism, Narcotics and International Operations, Hearings, 100th Cong., 2d sess., pt. 4, 11–14 July 1988, p. 196.

10. Robert E. Fenton, *Illegal Immigration to the United States: A Growing Problem of Law Enforcement* (Newport, R.I.: Center for Advanced Research, The Naval War College, March 1983), pp. 85–88.

11. *The Maritime Smuggling of Aliens*, El Paso Intelligence Center Report no. SR-09-81 (El Paso, Tex., 31 August 1981).

12. See these and many other approaches to the issue of corruption in Arnold T. Heidenheimer, ed., *Political Corruption* (New York: Holt, Rinehart & Winston, 1970).

13. Robert Klitgaard, "Incentive Myopia," *World Development* 17, no. 4 (1989): 447–59.

14. Cf. Frederick Kempe, *Divorcing the Dictator: America's Bungled Affair with Noriega* (New York: Putnam, 1990); John Dinges, *Our Man in Panama: How General Noriega Used the United States and Made Millions in Drugs and Arms* (New York: Random House, 1990).

15. Note Gary Brana-Shute's questions in a recent essay on Desi Bouterse: "What exactly is the agenda of the military? Would they again call upon Libyan assistance or strike financial deals with drug cartels? Clearly they have abandoned ideology and now maintain power through pragmatic thuggery" ("Suriname: Years of Living Dangerously," *Times of the Americas*, 28 November 1990, p. 11). For an essay on the Dutch "pandering" of Bouterse's corruption, see Peter Meel, "Money Talks, Morals Vex," *European Review of Latin American and Caribbean Studies*, June 1990, pp. 75–98.

16. *White Paper on Public Participation in Industrial and Commercial Activities* (Washington, D.C.: GPO, 1972), pp. 7–8.

17. Cf. F. A. Hoyos, *Tom Adams: A Biography* (London: Macmillan Caribbean, 1988), p. 110.

18. James F. Mitchell, *Caribbean Crusade* (Waitsfield, Vt.: Concepts, 1989), pp. 155, 159.

19. On 7 March 1991 the newly appointed financial secretary to the government of Montserrat revoked over three hundred bank licenses on that island (*Financial Times*, 7 March 1991). For an account of the role of such "offshore" operations, see A. P. Maingot, "Laundering Drug Profits: Miami and Caribbean Tax Havens," *Journal of Interamerican Studies and World Affairs* 30, nos. 2 and 3 (Summer and Fall 1988): 167–88; and idem, "'Offshore' Development: A High Risk Strategy," in *Modern Caribbean Politics*, ed. Anthony Payne and Paul Sutton (Baltimore: Johns Hopkins University Press, 1993).

20. Michael Manley, *The Politics of Change* (London: Andre Deutsch, 1973); idem, *A Voice in the Workplace* (London: Andre Deutsch, 1975).

21. Michael Manley, *Jamaica: Struggle in the Periphery* (London: Writers and Readers Cooperative Society, 1982); idem, *Up the Down Escalator* (London: Andre Deutsch, 1987).

22. *Jamaican Weekly Gleaner*, 18 April 1988. For a similar attitude by the then minister of labor, see ibid., 18 July 1988.

23. Ibid., 17 April 1989.

24. Cf. A. P. Maingot, "The Drug Menace to the Caribbean," *The World and I*, July 1989, pp. 128–35.

25. *Jamaican Weekly Gleaner*, 16 January 1989.

26. Dr. Edward C. Ezell's testimony, U.S. Congress, Permanent Subcommittee on Investigations of the Senate Governmental Affairs Committee, Hearings, 103d Cong., 1st sess., 28 February 1991.

27. "Informe Oral del Fiscal," *Granma* (Havana), 5 July 1989.

28. Ibid., 3 July 1989.

29. Enrique Baloyra (Paper on the trial presented to the American University Research Group of Civil-Military Relations, Working session, Miami, Fla., 26 July 1990).

30. For a serious legal analysis of the trial, see "Cuba Situation Report," *Radio Martí Transcripts (May–August 1989)* (Washington, D.C., February 1990).

31. The first story linking Cuba to the drug trade appeared in the *Miami Herald* on 24 January 1982. Between that date and 6 April 1983 the *Herald* published nine more stories on the subject.

32. There were so many congressional hearings on the drug trade in the Caribbean

Basin that a special bibliography has been produced: Edith Sutterlin, *Narcotics and Illicit Drug Trafficking: Selected References, 1986–1988* (Washington, D.C.: Congressional Research Service, August 1988).

33. A good assessment of the U.S. lack of preparation and totally inadequate intelligence prior to the invasions of the Dominican Republic in 1965 and Grenada in 1983 is provided by Bruce Palmer, Jr., in *Intervention in the Caribbean* (Lexington: University Press of Kentucky, 1989). General Palmer's startling conclusion is that the United States is in a weaker position in the late 1980s than it was in the 1960s (p. 179).

34. See *Trinidad Guardian*, 15 August and 3 September 1983.

35. See the account of John Babb in ibid., 12 August 1990.

36. These events are compiled from *United States* v. *Louis Hanee, Yasin Abu Bakr, Bilaal Abdullah, and Riad Alithe*, criminal complaint, U.S. District Court, Southern District, Florida, 13 September 1990.

37. Dr. Dion E. Phillips, coeditor of *Militarization in the Non-Hispanic Caribbean* (Boulder: Lynne Rienner, 1986), gave this definition of "repression" at meetings in Venezuela and Barbados: "Repression occurs when legitimization fails or is peeled away. It involves preventing people from taking actions that would harm or are perceived as having the potential to harm the state in major ways." The preceding quote is extracted from "Defense Policy and Planning in the Caribbean: The Case of Barbados" (Paper presented to the Caribbean Studies Association annual meeting, Port-of-Spain, Trinidad, 23–26 May 1989, p. 36).

38. Louis Blom-Cooper, Q.C., *Guns for Antigua: Report of the Commission of Inquiry into the Circumstances surrounding the Shipment of Arms from Israel to Antigua and Transshipment on 24 April 1989 en route to Colombia commissioner* (London: Duckworth, 1990).

39. The extent of the Italian Mafia's reach into the Caribbean and Latin America is documented by Claire Sterling in *Octopus: The Long Reach of the International Sicilian Mafia* (New York: W. W. Norton, 1990). Sterling maintains that Caracas, Venezuela, is the Latin American "headquarters" of the Mafia (pp. 130–44).

40. U.S. Congress, Senate Caucus on International Narcotics Control, *Report on the Status of the Draft Convention, the U.S. Negotiating Position, and Issues for the Senate*, 100th Cong., 1st sess., October 1987, p. 10, emphasis added.

4 Westminster Adapted: The Political Order of the Commonwealth Caribbean

1. M. G. Smith, "Short Range Prospects in the British Caribbean," *Social and Economic Studies* 11, no. 4 (1962): 393, as cited in Patrick Emmanuel, "Approaches to the Comparative Study of Caribbean Politics: Some Comments," ibid. 30, no. 3 (1981): 125.

2. Emmanuel, "Approaches to the Comparative Study of Caribbean Politics," p. 125.

3. I recognize that the system should more accurately be labeled the Westminster-Whitehall system, and the ensuing discussion reflects the administrative dimension, but generally I adopt the shorthand label.

4. I use this term in spite of the view of James Manor, who in a recent discussion of Indian politics since independence argued that it was best to avoid "the use of the more loaded word 'democracy.'" He took this to imply "very widespread participation by people with at least a rough understanding of the logic of the political and electoral systems and of the implications of their actions," as well as "participation which is reasonably free of constraints by the more powerful elements in society" (James Manor, "How and Why Liberal and Representative Politics Emerged in India," *Political Studies*

38, no. 1 [March 1990]: 20). The point is well taken in terms of political theory, but in the real world it seems churlish to deny the Commonwealth Caribbean its claim to democracy.

5. See esp. Anthony P. Maingot, "The Caribbean: The Structure of Modern-Conservative Societies," in *Latin America, Its Problems and Its Promise: A Multidisciplinary Introduction,* ed. Jan Knippers Black (Boulder: Westview, 1984), pp. 362–78.

6. See, among others, Hume Wrong, *Government of the West Indies* (Oxford: Oxford University Press, 1923); and D. J. Murray, *The West Indies and the Development of Colonial Government* (Oxford: Oxford University Press, 1965).

7. See esp. Trevor Munroe, *The Politics of Constitutional Decolonization: Jamaica, 1944–1962* (Mona, Jamaica: ISER, 1972).

8. Report of the Hon. E. F. L. Wood, M.P., on his visit to the West Indies and British Guiana, Cmnd. 1679, 1922, cited in extract in Ann Spackman, *Constitutional Development of the West Indies, 1922–1968: A Selection from the Major Documents* (Bridgetown, Barbados: Caribbean Universities Press, 1975), p. 76.

9. See Ken Post, *Arise Ye Starvelings: The Jamaican Labour Rebellion of 1938 and Its Aftermath* (The Hague: Martinus Nijhoff, 1978).

10. The details of this process are described in Elisabeth Wallace, *The British Caribbean: From the Decline of Colonialism to the End of Federation* (Toronto: University of Toronto Press, 1977).

11. Anthony Payne, *Politics in Jamaica* (London: Christopher Hurst; Kingston: Heinemann; New York: St. Martin's, 1988), p. 4.

12. Sir Fred Philips, *West Indian Constitutions: Post-independence Reform* (New York: Oceana, 1985).

13. For an account of these efforts, see Evelyne Huber Stephens and John D. Stephens, *Democratic Socialism in Jamaica: The Political Movement and Social Transformation in Dependent Capitalism* (London: Macmillan, 1986), pp. 154–55, 314–15, 357–58.

14. Paul Sutton, "Constancy, Change, and Accommodation: The Distinct Tradition of the Commonwealth Caribbean," in *The Fallacies of Hope: The Post-colonial Record of the Commonwealth Third World,* ed. James Mayall and Anthony Payne (Manchester: Manchester University Press, 1991), p. 108.

15. Eric Williams, in *Forged from the Love of Liberty: Selected Speeches of Dr. Eric Williams,* comp. Paul Sutton (Port-of-Spain: Longman Caribbean, 1981), p. 425, as cited in Mayall and Payne, *Fallacies of Hope,* pp. 108–9.

16. See Anthony Payne, Paul Sutton, and Tony Thorndike, *Grenada: Revolution and Invasion* (London: Croom Helm; New York: St. Martin's, 1984), pp. 35–36.

17. See Clive Y. Thomas, *The Rise of the Authoritarian State in Peripheral Societies* (London: Heinemann; New York: Monthly Review, 1984).

18. See, e.g., Leslie Manigat, "Grenada: Revolutionary Shockwave, Crisis, and Intervention," in *The Caribbean and World Politics: Cross Currents and Cleavages,* ed. Jorge Heine and Leslie Manigat (New York: Holmes & Meier, 1988), p. 182.

19. For an extended discussion, see Payne, Sutton, and Thorndike, *Grenada,* pp. 105–47.

20. The figures are taken from George K. Danns, "The Role of the Military in the National Security of Guyana," in *Militarization in the Non-Hispanic Caribbean,* ed. Alma H. Young and Dion E. Phillips (Boulder: Lynne Rienner, 1986), pp. 112–38.

21. See, e.g., David Simmons, "Militarization of the Caribbean: Concerns for National and Regional Security," *International Journal* 40, no. 2 (Spring 1985): 348–76; Tony Thorndike, "The Militarization of the Commonwealth Caribbean," in *The Central*

American Security System: North-South or East-West? ed. Peter Calvert (Cambridge: Cambridge University Press, 1988), pp. 135–54; and esp. Young and Phillips, *Militarization in the Non-Hispanic Caribbean.*

22. See Paul Sutton and Anthony Payne, "Size and Survival: The Security Problems of Small Island and Enclave Developing States" (1992, manuscript).

23. See Michael Manley, *Jamaica: Struggle in the Periphery* (London: Writers and Readers Cooperative Society, 1982), p. 155.

24. This literature is extensive. See, e.g., G. E. Mills and Paul Robertson, "The Attitudes and Behaviour of the Senior Civil Service in Jamaica," *Social and Economic Studies* 23, no. 2 (1974): 311–43; Edwin Jones and G. E. Mills, "Institutional Innovation and Change in the Commonwealth Caribbean," ibid. 25, no. 4 (1976): 323–46; and Edwin Jones, "Role of the State in Public Enterprise," ibid. 30, no. 1 (1981): 17–44.

25. For a classic account, see A. W. Singham, *The Hero and the Crown in a Colonial Polity* (New Haven: Yale University Press, 1968). It is worth noting that the politician in question in this study was Eric Gairy.

26. Mills and Robertson, "Senior Civil Service in Jamaica."

27. Ron Sanders, "Narcotics, Corruption, and Development: The Problems in the Smaller Islands," *Caribbean Affairs* 3, no. 1 (1990): 79–92.

28. Again, the literature here is vast. Here I cite only key examples: Carl Stone, *Democracy and Clientelism in Jamaica* (New Brunswick: Transaction Books, 1980); Selwyn Ryan, *Race and Nationalism in Trinidad and Tobago: A Study of Decolonization in a Multiracial Society* (Toronto: University of Toronto Press, 1972); and Patrick Emmanuel, *General Elections in the Eastern Caribbean: A Handbook* (Cave Hill, Barbados: ISER, 1979).

29. A neat account of this process is given in *Guyana: Fraudulent Revolution* (London: Latin America Bureau, 1984).

30. Maurice Bishop, interview, in *Advocate-News* (Bridgetown), 14 March 1981.

31. Maurice Bishop, *Maurice Bishop Speaks: The Grenada Revolution, 1979–1983,* ed. Bruce Marcus and Michael Taber (New York: Pathfinder, 1983), pp. 187–88.

32. The most informed discussion of its attempt is to be found in Tony Thorndike, *Grenada: Politics, Economics, and Society* (London: Frances Pinter; Boulder: Lynne Rienner, 1985).

33. See G. E. Mills, "The Electoral System and the Parish Council Elections," *Sunday Gleaner,* 17 August 1986; and Carl Stone, "An Open Letter to Michael Manley," *Daily Gleaner,* 27 March 1990.

34. Bernard Coard, quoted in *To Construct from Morning: Making the People's Budget in Grenada* (St. George's, Grenada: Fedon, 1982), p. 150.

35. Gordon K. Lewis, *The Growth of the Modern West Indies* (London: Monthly Review, 1968), p. 25.

36. I am grateful to Jorge Domínguez for making this point to me in conversation.

37. Anthony P. Maingot, "Citizenship and Parliamentary Politics in the English-speaking Caribbean," in *Dual Legacies in the Contemporary Caribbean: Continuing Aspects of British and French Dominion,* ed. Paul Sutton (London: Frank Cass, 1986), pp. 120–40.

38. See Cheddi Jagan, *The West on Trial* (London: Michael Joseph, 1966).

39. For a discussion, see Anthony Payne, "Full Bellies in Freedom House: Universal Human Rights, Cultural Relativism, and the Commonwealth Third World," in Mayall and Payne, *Fallacies of Hope,* pp. 191–211.

40. Payne, *Politics in Jamaica,* p. 186.

41. As revealed in the pages of *Caribbean Contact,* the monthly regional newspaper of the Caribbean Conference of Churches.

42. Singham, *The Hero and the Crowd;* Lloyd Best, "Options Facing Williams, the Ruling Party, and the Country," *Trinidad Express,* 31 May 1969.

43. Sutton in Mayall and Payne, *Fallacies of Hope,* pp. 113–14.

5 The Future of Democracy in the Caribbean

1. This section is an extremely compressed summary of the main theoretical and empirical points of a research project that covers the emergence, consolidation, and breakdown of democracy in Western Europe; North, South and Central America; and the Caribbean (see Dietrich Rueschemeyer, Evelyne Huber Stephens, and John D. Stephens, *Capitalist Development and Democracy* [Cambridge: Polity Press; and Chicago: University of Chicago Press, 1992]. Parts of the research have been published in Evelyne Huber Stephens, "Capitalist Development and Democracy in South America," *Politics and Society* 17, no. 3 [1989], and John D. Stephens, "Democratic Transition and Breakdown in Western Europe," *American Journal of Sociology* 94, no. 5 [1989]).

2. See, e.g., the contributions to the four-volume collection edited by Guillermo O'Donnell, Philippe Schmitter, and Laurence Whitehead, *Transitions from Authoritarian Rule* (Baltimore: Johns Hopkins University Press, 1986). A mixture of structural and process- and actor-centered approaches can be found in the contributions to James M. Malloy and Mitchell A. Seligson, eds., *Authoritarians and Democrats* (Pittsburgh: University of Pittsburgh Press, 1987). Robert A. Dahl, *Democracy and Its Critics* (New Haven: Yale University Press, 1989), offers a thoughtful treatment of conditions for the emergence and consolidation of formal democracy, as well as of the limits and possibilities for the realization of democracy's substantive dimensions.

3. See, e.g., Seymour Martin Lipset, *Political Man* (Garden City, N.Y.: Anchor Books, 1960; rev. ed., Baltimore: Johns Hopkins University Press, 1980); Samuel P. Huntington, "Will More Countries Become Democratic?" *Political Science Quarterly* 99, no. 2 (Summer 1984): 193–218; and Larry Diamond, Juan J. Linz, and Seymour Martin Lipset, eds., *Democracy in Developing Countries* (Boulder: Lynne Rienner, 1989).

4. The fractionalization of political parties and their consequent loss of the ability to absorb pressures from below played an important part in the demise of democracy in, for instance, Colombia in the late 1940s and Uruguay in the late 1960s (see, e.g., Alexander Wilde, "Conversations among Gentlemen: Oligarchical Democracy in Colombia," in *The Breakdown of Democratic Regimes: Latin America,* ed. Alfred C. Stepan and Juan J. Linz [Baltimore: Johns Hopkins University Press, 1978]; and Juan Rial, *Partidos políticos, democracia y autoritarismo* [Montevideo: Centro de Informaciones y Estudios del Uruguay, Ediciones de la Banda Oriental, 1984]).

5. See, e.g., Lipset, *Political Man;* Philips Cutright, "National Political Development: Measurement and Analysis," *American Sociological Review* 28 (April 1963); Philips Cutright and James A. Wiley, "Modernization and Political Representation: 1927–1966," *Studies in Comparative International Development* 5 (1969); Kenneth A. Bollen, "Political Democracy and the Timing of Development," *American Sociological Review* 44, no. 4 (1979). The quantitative literature on determinants of democracy is reviewed in Rueschemeyer, Stephens, and Stephens, *Capitalist Development,* chap. 2.

6. For instance, Rainer M. Lepsius, "From Fragmented Party Democracy to Government by Emergency Decree and National Socialist Takeover: Germany," in *The Breakdown of Democratic Regimes: Europe,* ed. Juan J. Linz and Alfred C. Stepan (Baltimore: Johns Hopkins University Press, 1978), argues that the economic crisis was an important contributor to the demise of the Weimar Republic. The importance of the economic

problems of the fifties and sixties for the breakdown of democracies in the sixties and seventies in Latin America is stressed in the contributions to David Collier, ed., *The New Authoritarianism in Latin America* (Princeton: Princeton University Press, 1979).

7. Juan J. Linz and Alfred C. Stepan, "Political Crafting of Democratic Consolidation or Destruction: European and South American Comparisons," in *Democracy in the Americas: Stopping the Pendulum*, ed. Robert A. Pastor (New York: Holmes & Meier, 1989).

8. The calls for military intervention by Brazilian economic elites in the early sixties and the behavior of Chilean economic elites under Allende are cases in point (see, e.g., Alfred C. Stepan, *The Military in Politics: Changing Patterns in Brazil* [Princeton: Princeton University Press, 1971]; amongst the voluminous literature on the Allende period Sergio Bitar, *Chile: Experiment in Democracy* [Philadelphia: Institute for the Study of Human Issues, 1979], provides particularly insightful analyses of the breakdown). In contrast, the strength of parties representing elite interests, which lasted until the late fifties, was important for the consolidation of Chilean democracy in the earlier period (see, e.g., J. Samuel Valenzuela, *Democratización vía reforma: La expansión del sufragio en Chile* [Buenos Aires: Ediciones del Ides, 1985]).

9. Linz and Stepan, "Political Crafting," p. 57.

10. See Abraham F. Lowenthal and Samuel Fitch, eds., *Armies and Politics in Latin America*, rev. ed. (New York: Holmes & Meier, 1986); and Louis W. Goodman, Johanna S. R. Mendelson, and Juan Rial, eds., *The Military and Democracy: The Future of Civil-Military Relations in Latin America* (New York: Lexington Books, 1990).

11. Huntington's "Will More Countries Become Democratic?" makes this argument and calls this group the "zone of transition."

12. For a more elaborate version of such analysis see Rueschemeyer, Stephens, and Stephens, *Capitalist Development*, chap. 6.

13. The contrast, for instance, between the appointment by the British government of the Moyne Commission in response to labor unrest in the Caribbean and the slaughter by the Salvadoran government and military of some thirty thousand people in retaliation for the 1932 attempted popular uprising could not be starker (see, e.g., Ken Post, *Arise Ye Starvelings: The Jamaican Labour Rebellion of 1938 and Its Aftermath* [The Hague: Martinus Nijhoff, 1978]; and Thomas P. Anderson, *Matanza: El Salvador's Communist Revolt of 1932* [Lincoln: University of Nebraska Press, 1971]. For a historical background analysis of politics in Central America see Walter LaFeber, *Inevitable Revolutions: The United States and Central America*, rev. ed. [New York: W. W. Norton, 1984]).

14. For Jamaica, see, e.g., Trevor Munroe, *The Politics of Constitutional Decolonization: Jamaica, 1944–1962* (Mona, Jamaica: ISER, 1972); for Trinidad and Tobago, see, e.g., Selwyn Ryan, *Race and Nationalism in Trinidad and Tobago: A Study of Decolonization in a Multiracial Society* (Toronto: University of Toronto Press, 1972); for Barbados, see, e.g., F. A. Hoyos, *Barbados: A History from the Amerindians to Independence* (London: Macmillan, 1978).

15. Evelyne Huber Stephens and John D. Stephens, "Capitalists, Socialism, and Democracy: An Analysis of Business Attitudes towards Political Democracy in Jamaica," in *Comparative Social Research* 12 (Summer 1990), traces the change in the attitudes toward democracy of economic elites in the Jamaican case on the basis of interview data.

16. Percy C. Hintzen, *The Costs of Regime Survival: Racial Mobilization, Elite Domination, and Control of the State in Guyana and Trinidad*, Rose Monograph Series (Cambridge: Cambridge University Press, 1989), pp. 90–100, discusses the importance of the buildup of the military apparatus for the strengthening of the authoritarian regime in Guyana. There is an extensive literature documenting the antidemocratic role of the military in

Central America; for an overview see, e.g., LaFeber, *Inevitable Revolutions;* John A. Booth and Thomas W. Walker, *Understanding Central America* (Boulder: Westview, 1989); and Giuseppe Di Palma and Laurence Whitehead, eds., *The Central American Impasse* (New York: St. Martin's, 1986).

17. Anthony Payne in his contribution to this volume (chapter 4) emphasizes the adaptation of British institutions to the Caribbean and the resilience of the resulting political institutions.

18. This is visible, for instance, in the decreasing proportion of loyal party voters. In Jamaica they decreased from 83 percent in 1972 to 48 percent in 1986 (see Carl Stone, *Politics versus Economics: The 1989 Elections in Jamaica* [Kingston: Heinemann, 1989], p. 108).

19. The looting and arson surrounding the attempted coup in Trinidad and Tobago in July 1990 constituted a dramatic manifestation of the potential for anomic mass action.

20. The informal economy is defined as comprising those economic activities that are outside the reach of state controls designed to regulate such activities; for instance, they are not licensed, do not observe labor laws, and do not pay any taxes (see Manuel Castells and Alejandro Portes, "World Underneath: The Origins, Dynamics, and Effects of the Informal Economy," in *The Informal Economy: Studies in Advanced and Less Developed Countries,* ed. Alejandro Portes, Manuel Castells, and Lauren A. Benton [Baltimore: Johns Hopkins University Press, 1989]). Thus, the informal economy is not to be equated with small business per se.

21. See Hintzen, *Costs of Regime Survival,* on this point.

22. For an analysis of party politics in the 1970s, see Selwyn Ryan, *Revolution and Reaction: Parties and Politics in Trinidad and Tobago, 1970–1981* (St. Augustine, Trinidad: Institute of Social and Economic Research, University of the West Indies, 1989); the more recent period is discussed by Selwyn Ryan in chapter 7 in this volume.

23. For background information on the development of democratic politics in the Dominican Republic, see Jonathan Hartlyn, chapter 8 in this volume; and Rosario Espinal, *Autoritarismo y democracia en la política dominicana* (Costa Rica: Ediciones Capel, 1987).

24. Tony Thorndike, *Grenada: Politics, Economics, and Society* (London: Frances Pinter; Boulder: Lynne Rienner, 1985), offers essential background analysis for an understanding of Grenadian politics.

25. Michel-Rolph Trouillot, *Haiti, State against Nation: The Origins and Legacy of Duvalierism* (New York: Monthly Review, 1990), emphasizes the severity of the obstacles to democratization.

26. See Guillermo O'Donnell and Philippe Schmitter, *Transitions from Authoritarian Rule: Tentative Conclusions about Uncertain Democracies* (Baltimore: Johns Hopkins University Press, 1986), pp. 62–64, on the advantages for democratic consolidation of having the founding elections won by centrist and rightist parties.

27. See Hintzen, *Costs of Regime Survival,* and Leo A. Despres, *Cultural Pluralism and National Politics in British Guyana* (Chicago: Rand McNally, 1967) for analysis of the forces behind the breakdown of democracy in Guyana.

28. The Council of Freely-Elected Heads of Government is a group of eighteen current and former heads of government from throughout the hemisphere. It is based at the Carter Center of Emory University in Atlanta, Georgia.

29. The literature on politics in Suriname is extremely scarce. The comments here

are based in part on information provided by Edward M. Dew, "Suriname," in *Latin America and Caribbean Contemporary Record: Volume VI, 1986–1987*, ed. Abraham F. Lowenthal (New York: Holmes & Meier, 1989). See also Gary Brana-Shute, "Back to the Barracks? Five Years of 'Revo' in Suriname," *Journal of Interamerican Studies and World Affairs* 28, no. 1 (Spring 1986).

30. See *Times of the Americas*, 28 November 1990, pp. 10–11.

31. Though multilateral institutions so far have been the most resistant to any debt relief or renegotiation, basing this resistance on their charters, these charters need not be immutable.

32. See, e.g., Robert A. Dahl, *Polyarchy: Participation and Opposition* (New Haven: Yale University Press, 1971); idem, *Democracy and Its Critics;* and Edward N. Muller, "Democracy, Economic Development, and Income Inequality," *American Sociological Review* 53 (1988). There are other reasons why state intervention is necessary for development in the region. As the development literature of the 1960s and 1970s amply demonstrated, the private sector in the Caribbean is not strong enough to compete with foreign capital in strategic sectors, and only the state can ensure an adequate return to the local economy from foreign investment.

33. For an analysis of economic developments in Jamaica under Seaga, see Anthony Payne, "Liberal Economics vs. Electoral Politics in Jamaica," in *Modern Caribbean Politics*, ed. Anthony Payne and Paul Sutton (Baltimore: Johns Hopkins University Press, forthcoming); and Evelyne Huber Stephens and John D. Stephens, "The Political Economy of Jamaican Development: From Manley to Seaga to Manley" (Paper delivered at the annual meeting of the Latin American Studies Association, Miami, Fla., December 1989).

34. If CARICOM were really strengthened such that membership could bring substantial economic benefits, then the threat of expulsion itself might become quite an effective tool for pressuring governments into respecting democratic principles. The effects of pressure from the European Economic Community for democratization in Spain show how effective regional economic groupings can be in such matters if their cooperation is successful and consequently offers high incentives for aspiring members.

35. The buildup of the Regional Security System promoted by the Reagan administration caused considerable concern and critique (see, e.g., Alma H. Young and Dion E. Phillips, eds., *Militarization in the Non-Hispanic Caribbean* [Boulder: Lynne Rienner, 1986]). There clearly were some reasons for concern insofar as the initiative and design were too heavily external, emanating from the United States, and involved the buildup of permanent national security forces. The threatening example of El Salvador demonstrates how military apparatuses built up and sustained by heavy foreign support can become independent of civil society and of civilian political authority and impose their rule directly or act with impunity behind the facade of a formally democratic regime.

6 The Eastern Caribbean States: Fledgling Sovereignties in the Global Environment

This paper was prepared for the World Peace Foundation. It does not necessarily reflect the views of the institution to which the writer belongs.

1. For an early discussion, see E. A. G. Robinson, ed., *Economic Consequences of the Size of Nations* (London: Macmillan, 1960).

2. For some discussion of this growing relationship, see Vaughan A. Lewis, "Carib-

bean State Systems and the Contemporary World Order," in *The Newer Caribbean,* ed. Paget Henry and Carl Stone (Philadelphia: Institute for the Study of Human Issues, 1983).

3. DeLisle Worrell, "Economic Management in the English-speaking Caribbean since 1970," in Central Bank of Barbados, *Working Papers, 1987* (Barbados, 1988).

4. I discussed some aspects of the relationship between the OECS and CARICOM systems in "Then and Now: Future Relations among the States of the Caribbean Community," *Caribbean Affairs* 1, no. 1 (1988).

5. For a recent discussion of the particular problems of small island states, see B. Legarda, "Small Island Economies," *Finance and Development* 21 (June 1984).

6. See Vaughan A. Lewis, "International, National, and Regional Security Arrangements in the Caribbean," in *Peace, Development, and Security in the Caribbean,* ed. A. Bryan, J. E. Greene, and T. Shaw (New York: Macmillan, 1990). This writer joined the OECS as its director-general in July 1982 and thus was involved in some of the events and decision making leading to the intervention.

7. Lewis, "Then and Now."

8. Commonwealth Secretariat, *Vulnerability: Small States in the Global Society* (London: Marlborough House, 1985).

9. See "Statement Issued by the Heads of Government of the Caribbean Community" (Press release, CARICOM Secretariat, Georgetown, Guyana, July 1990).

10. I draw in what immediately follows on Lewis, "Then and Now."

11. The government of the small British colony of Anguilla, which had seceded from the then colony of St. Kitts, Nevis, and Anguilla, was in fact subsequently to reenter the ECCB, though it is not a member of the OECS.

7 Structural Adjustment and the Ethnic Factor in Caribbean Societies

1. *Budget Speech and Taxation Measures,* 12 December 1988 (Port-of-Spain: Government Printery, 1989).

2. Ibid.

3. "Sociological Impact of Changes at Caroni (1975) Ltd.," *The Future of Caroni (1975) Ltd.,* Position Document, Sanatan Dharma Maha Sabha, 1989, pp. 35–40.

4. Ibid.

5. *Budget Speech and Taxation Measures,* 22 December 1989 (Port-of-Spain: Government Printery, 1990).

6. Courtney Blackman, in *Cana Business* (Port-of-Spain: Caribbean News Agency, August 1990).

7. Dennis Pantin, *Into the Valley of Debt: An Alternative Road to the IMF/World Bank Path* (Port-of-Spain: ISER, 1989).

8. Lloyd Best, in *Trinidad and Tobago Review,* February 1990, p. 5.

9. IBRD, *Report and Recommendations of the President of the International Bank for Reconstruction and Development to the Executive Directors on a Proposed Structural Adjustment Loan to Trinidad and Tobago* (Washington, D.C., 21 November 1989).

10. Ralph Henry, "Putting the Poor Back on Their Feet," *Trinidad Express,* 22 September 1990.

11. Steve Solomon, "Will Poverty Always Exist?" ibid.

12. *Trinidad Express,* 16 February 1989.

13. Norma Abdulah, *The Youth of Trinidad and Tobago: A Statistical Profile* (Port-of-Spain: ISER, 1988).

14. *Daily Express,* 11 August 1990.

15. Ibid., 18 August 1990.

16. Tim Hector, "Is Abu Bakr Coming Here?" *Outlet,* Antigua, 24 August 1990.

17. Ralph Premdas, "Guyana: Violence and Democracy in a Communal State," *Plural Societies* 12, nos. 3 and 4 (Autumn and Winter 1981): 41.

18. Commonwealth Secretariat, "Guyana: The Economic Recovery Program and Beyond," *Report of a Commonwealth Advisory Group* (London, August 1989), pp. 15–16.

19. *Contribution to the McIntyre Report,* University of Guyana, p. 41.

20. Ibid., p. 20.

21. *Instituto Latino Americano e del Caribe de Planificacion Economica e Sociale: External Insertion, Development, and Planning,* no. 476, May 1989.

22. IBRD, *Report on Trinidad and Tobago.*

23. *Budget Speech and Taxation Measures,* 1989.

24. Hedrick Smith, *The Power Game: How Washington Works* (New York: Ballantine Books), pp. 679–80.

8 The Dominican Republic: Contemporary Problems and Challenges

1. A small indicator is that after the 1982 campaign, many observers wrote off both Balaguer and Bosch. For example, one analysis noted: "They called the elections the 'great caudillos' last stand. It was the final face-off between the old presidents—an aging and deteriorating Balaguer, and a forceful, irreverent Juan Bosch" (Adrian Rodríguez and Deborah Huntington, "Dominican Republic—The Launching of Democracy," *NACLA Report on the Americas* 16, no. 6 [November–December 1982]: 32).

2. See Henrik Hoetink, "The Dominican Republic, c. 1870–1930," in *The Cambridge History of Latin America,* ed. Leslie Bethell, vol. 5, *c. 1870 to 1930* (Cambridge: Cambridge University Press, 1986), pp. 287–98; see also Frank Moya Pons, *Manual de Historia Dominicana,* 7th ed. (Santo Domingo: Universidad Católica Madre y Maestra, 1983), pp. 281–426, passim.

3. For a fascinating fictional dialogue between Ulises Heureaux and Rafael Trujillo, see Bernardo Vega, *Domini Canes: Los perros del señor* (Santo Domingo: Fundación Cultural Dominicana, 1988).

4. Moya Pons, *Manual,* pp. 468–70.

5. Abraham F. Lowenthal, "The Politics of Chaos," in *Reform and Revolution,* ed. Arpad Lazar and Robert Kaufman (Boston: Allyn & Bacon, 1969), p. 53.

6. Frank Moya Pons, "The Dominican Republic since 1930," in *The Cambridge History of Latin America,* ed. Leslie Bethell, vol. 7, *Latin America since 1930: Mexico, Central America, and the Caribbean* (Cambridge: Cambridge University Press, 1990), p. 515.

7. Jerome Slater, *Intervention and Negotiation: The United States and the Dominican Revolution* (New York: Harper & Row, 1970), p. 7.

8. See Arthur Schlesinger, Jr., *A Thousand Days: John F. Kennedy in the White House* (Boston: Houghton Mifflin, 1965), p. 769.

9. For authors of varying perspectives who generally agree on this point, see Piero Gleijeses, *The Dominican Crisis: The 1965 Constitutionalist Revolt and American Intervention* (Baltimore: Johns Hopkins University Press, 1978); Abraham F. Lowenthal, *The Dominican Intervention* (Cambridge, Mass.: Harvard University Press, 1972); Howard Wiarda, *The Dominican Republic: Nation in Transition* (New York: Praeger, 1969); Theodore Draper, *The Dominican Revolt* (New York: Commentary, 1968); and Slater, *Intervention and Negotiation.*

10. For a more extensive analysis of U.S.-Dominican relations and of the multiple objectives behind U.S. involvement in Dominican affairs, including its efforts to promote democracy in the country, see Jonathan Hartlyn, "The Dominican Republic: The Legacy of Intermittent Engagement," in *Exporting Democracy: The United States and Latin America,* ed. Abraham F. Lowenthal (Baltimore: Johns Hopkins University Press, 1991).

11. See also Rosario Espinal, "An Interpretation of the Democratic Transition in the Dominican Republic," in *The Central American Impasse,* ed. Giuseppe Di Palma and Laurence Whitehead (New York: St. Martin's, 1986).

12. This discussion of corruption is taken from Jonathan Hartlyn, "The Dominican Republic," in *Latin America and Caribbean Contemporary Record: Volume VI, 1986–1987,* ed. Abraham F. Lowenthal (New York: Holmes & Meier, 1989), pp. B481–B485.

13. However, the executive can threaten members of the private sector with potential prosecution if he so desires, in this way limiting the ability of private-sector groups to pressure the government. This was widely reported to be the case with regard to one prominent member of the board of the CNHE and the Balaguer administration.

9 The Role of the Puerto Rican People in the Caribbean

1. Edgardo Rodríguez Juliá, "Puerto Rico y el Caribe," *El nuevo día–domingo,* 20 November 1988, summarizing a lecture delivered a year earlier at the Wilson Center of the Smithsonian Institution. For my answer to his position, see "Puerto Rico y el Caribe," *El mundo,* 7 April 1987.

2. Eric Williams, *From Columbus to Castro: The History of the Caribbean* (New York: Vintage, 1984), pp. 514–15.

3. *San Juan Star,* 20 July 1986.

4. See Richard J. Bloomfield, ed., *Puerto Rico: The Search for a National Policy* (Boulder: Westview, 1985).

5. See my *Puerto Rico: Equality and Freedom at Issue* (New York: Praeger, 1984).

6. J. H. Parry, Phillip Sherlock, and Anthony P. Maingot, *A Short History of the West Indies* (New York: St. Martin's, 1987), p. 150; See my "La literatura como fuente histórica del Caribe," *Revista talleres* (Puerto Rico Junior College) 4, no. 1 (1986): 19–40, reviewing the works on the region by Frantz Fanon, V. S. Naipaul, and José Luis González.

7. The annexationist movement had been a forgotten theme in Puerto Rican historiography. Its becoming a majoritarian sentiment has unleashed several new analytical books on the subject. The best is Edgardo Meléndez, *Puerto Rico's Statehood Movement* (New York: Greenwood, 1988). See also Aarón Gamaliel Ramos, *Las ideas anexionistas en Puerto Rico bajo la dominación norteamericana* (San Juan: Huracán, 1987).

8. See, e.g., Jesse Helms, "Puerto Rico――51st State?" *Congressional Record,* 22 March 1990, p. S3052; Patrick Buchanan, "Future State or Nation?" *Washington Times,* 16 May 1990; "Altered States," *New Republic,* 28 May 1990; "Taking Puerto Rico Seriously," *Washington Post,* 13 July 1990; Georgie Anne Geyer, "Statehood Is Wrong for Puerto Ricans," *Columbus Dispatch,* 17 July 1990; James J. Kilpatrick, "Discuss Puerto Rico Plebiscite Fully; Joining the Union Is Irreversible," *Miami Herald,* 3 December 1990; Tom Wicker, "The 51st State?" *New York Times,* 9 February 1990; and *San Juan Star,* 12 February 1991.

9. The commonality of origin and destiny has been elaborated in a brilliant manner by Antonio Benítez Rojo, *La isla que se repite: El Caribe y la perspectiva posmoderna* (New Hampshire: Ediciones del Norte, 1989).

10. See my "La diálectica del Ser y del Temer," in my *La alternativa liberal* (Río Piedras: Editorial Universitaria, 1974). See also Luis Nieves Falcón, "The Social Pathology of Dependence," in Bloomfield, *Puerto Rico*.

11. Sidney W. Mintz, "Africa en la América Latina: Una reflexión desprevenida," in *Africa en América Latina*, ed. Manuel Moreno Fraginals (Mexico City: Siglo XXI, 1987).

12. Juan Manuel García-Passalacqua, "Dignidad y jaibería: Los paradigmas políticos puertorriqueños," in *Anales, revista de ciencias sociales e historia de la Universidad Interamericana de Puerto Rico* 1, no. 1 (1984): 9.

13. Parry, Sherlock, and Maingot, *Short History of the West Indies*, chap. 12. See also Franklin W. Knight's seminal work, *The Caribbean: The Genesis of a Fragmented Nationalism* (New York: Oxford University Press, 1978).

14. Manuel Moreno Fraginals, "Plantaciones en el Caribe: El caso de Cuba–Puerto Rico–Santo Domingo (1860–1940)," in his *La historia como arma y otros estudios sobre esclavos, ingenios y plantaciones* (Barcelona: Editorial Crítica, 1983).

15. Parry, Sherlock, and Maingot, *Short History of the West Indies*, chap. 17.

16. The issue of American citizenship of the Puerto Ricans is crucial. See Arturo Morales Carrión, *Puerto Rico: A Political and Cultural History* (New York: W. W. Norton, 1983), pp. 197–99. Cf. José Cabranes, *Citizenship and the American Empire* (New Haven: Yale University Press, 1979). Above all, see Johnny H. Killian, "Discretion of Congress Respecting Citizenship Status of Puerto Ricans," memorandum, 9 March 1989, Congressional Research Service, Washington, D.C.

17. The public records of U.S. efforts to crush the nationalist tendencies of the Puerto Rican elite are varied and numerous. Suffice it to mention Aida Negrón de Montilla, *Americanization in Puerto Rico and the Public School System, 1900–1930* (Río Piedras: Edil, 1971); Carmiña Gautier and Teresa Blanco, "COINTELPRO en Puerto Rico (1960–1971)," *Pensamiento crítico*, Summer 1979; and the important Report of the Civil Rights Commission of Puerto Rico of 1989, *Revista del Colegio de Abogados de Puerto Rico* 51–52 (October 1990–January 1991).

18. Parry, Sherlock, and Maingot, *Short History of the West Indies*, chap. 18.

19. Carlos R. Zapata Oliveras, *Nuevos caminos hacia viejos objetivos: Estados Unidos y el establecimento del Estado Libre Asociado de Puerto Rico* (Río Piedras: Edil, 1991), pp. 175–78. Intimates report that Muñoz cried when he was informed.

20. Gerard Pierre Charles, *El pensamiento sociopolítico, moderno en el Caribe* (Mexico City: Fondo de Cultura Económica, 1985), chap. 4.

21. Jorge Rodríguez Beruff, *Política militar y dominación: Puerto Rico en el contexto latinoamericano* (Río Piedras: Huracán, 1988).

22. For a vivid example, see the testimony of a Central Intelligence Agency agent in the *San Juan Star*, 23 November 1991; and Juan Manuel García-Passalacqua, *Vengador del silencio: Crónica de mis tiempos* (San Juan: Editorial Cultural, 1991).

23. Ivonne Acosta, *La mordaza* (San Juan: Edil, 1988), esp. pp. 13–59.

24. See my "Caribbean Alternatives: Cuba and Puerto Rico," in *Central America and the Caribbean: Today and Tomorrow*, ed. Barbara A. Lafford (Tempe: Arizona State University, 1987).

25. Gerard Pierre Charles, *El Caribe contemporáneo* (Mexico City: Siglo XXI, 1981).

26. Proyecto Caribeño de Justicia y Paz, *Puerto Rico and Nuclear War* (San Juan, December 1988), reproduces a report by the Special Committee of the House of Representatives, Commonwealth of Puerto Rico, on the issue.

27. Message to the Congress, 9 February 1989, quoted in *New York Times*, 10 February 1989.

28. This drastic ideological change by the Popular Democratic Party is an untold and unnecessarily secret part of modern Puerto Rican history. Its main architect, Teodoro Moscoso, has refused to testify about the real reasons for the decision in a fateful late-evening meeting with Luis Muñoz Marín (see Roberto Rexach Benítez, "El día de la noche larga," *El nuevo día,* 28 March 1976).

29. James L. Dietz, *Economic History of Puerto Rico: Institutional Change and Capitalist Development* (Princeton: Princeton University Press, 1986).

30. See Joaquín Villamil, "Puerto Rico, 1948–1976: The Limits of Dependent Growth," in his *Transnational Capitalism and National Development: New Perspectives on Dependence* (Sussex: Harvester, 1979).

31. United States Department of Commerce, *Economic Study of Puerto Rico,* Report to the President prepared by the Interagency Task Force, 2 vols. (Washington, D.C.: GPO, December 1979).

32. A Yankelovich poll showed that 50 percent of those saying they had decided how they would vote in a plebiscite favored statehood (see *El nuevo día,* 2 October 1989). The poll was repeated six months later, with 51 percent for statehood. Still other polls showed a dead heat in February 1991 and 1992.

33. Robert W. Anderson, "El papel de Puerto Rico en el Caribe," in *Puerto Rico en el Caribe hoy,* ed. Carmen Gautier Mayoral, Angel I. Rivera Ortiz, and Idsa Alegría Ortega (Río Piedras: CLACSO-CEREP, 1987), p. 11.

34. See Rafael Hernández Colón, "Puerto Rico's Role in the Caribbean—The Next Century" (Yale University, New Haven, March 1989, Mimeographed), which ends with a skeptical view of "the uncertain days ahead" (p. 11).

35. See Jorge Heine, "Cruising Uncharted Waters: Puerto Rico's Foreign Policy, 1986–1987," in *Latin America and Caribbean Contemporary Record: Vol. VI, 1986–1987,* ed. Abraham F. Lowenthal (New York: Holmes & Meier, 1989), p. A131. See also Heraldo Muñoz, comp., *Las políticas exteriores de América Latina y el Caribe: Continuidad en la crisis* (Buenos Aires: Prospel, 1987), p. 109; and my article "Puerto Rico," in *Latin America and Caribbean Contemporary Record: Vol. V,* ed. Abraham F. Lowenthal (New York: Holmes & Meier, 1988), p. B581.

36. A simple, useful description is found in Caribbean Development Program, Economic Development Administration, Commonwealth of Puerto Rico, *Some Common Questions on CBI/936 Financing* (San Juan, April 1989). For the background of the program see Leslie Cook, "Section 936 Has Roots in Operation Bootstrap Started in 1947," *Caribbean Business,* 15 March 1990.

37. See Consultant's Group/Latin America, *The 936 Program: Manufacturing in Puerto Rico and the Caribbean Basin* (Washington, D.C., 1989). The countries attracting most twin-plant investment are the Dominican Republic, with twenty-four projects, and Costa Rica, with five projects. Westinghouse was the firm that most used the project. The report recognizes that "the program is off to a slow start" (p. 6).

38. *San Juan Star,* 20 February 1990; *Vocero,* 20 February 1990, p. 23. The source was from the Puerto Rico Economic Development Administration.

39. *San Juan Star,* 25 January 1990.

40. Under S. 712, Section 936 benefits would no longer be available to U.S. corporations. Puerto Rico could, however, offer several tax-related advantages, which might effectively replace those available under its current status. First, the republic could offer advantages of a low-tax foreign jurisdiction to U.S. firms. Further, the new nation would have the opportunity, unavailable under its current status, to negotiate tax-sparing trea-

ties making investments by corporations of third countries more attractive. Finally, the Independence Party of Puerto Rico has described a new set of provisions intended to duplicate the effects of Section 936 (see Congressional Budget Office, *Potential Economic Impacts of Changes in Puerto Rico's Status under S. 712* [Washington, D.C., April 1990], esp. p. 24 and n. 18; see also *Puerto Rico Chamber of Commerce in the U.S.* 17, no. 1 [January–February 1990], and *New York Times*, 7 April 1990).

41. Byron Blake, CARICOM director of economics, *San Juan Star*, 1 February 1990.

42. *El mundo*, 18 February, 5 March 1990; *San Juan Star*, 25 March 1990. Objections to statehood by neighboring countries have indeed been so blunt that the statehood movement has prompted visits to the regional neighbors to "dispel misconceptions" (see *Caribbean Business*, 1 February 1990).

43. See *An Alternative Policy for Central America and the Caribbean*, Summary and Conclusions of a Policy Workshop held by the Institute of Social Studies, The Hague, 6–25 June 1983. See also PACCA, *The Caribbean: Alternative Visions* (Washington, D.C., August 1989).

44. See Gordon K. Lewis, *Puerto Rico: Libertad y poder en el Caribe* (Río Piedras: Edil, 1970).

45. Ana Lydia Vega, "De cómo fue descubierto el Caribe y no precisamente por Cristóbal Colón," in *Diálogo* (University of Puerto Rico, San Juan), May 1989, pp. 22–23.

46. Congressional Budget Office, *Potential Economic Impacts*.

47. Both conservatives and liberals in the United States seem to share the aversion to admitting Puerto Rico as a state. See, e.g., Speaker Thomas Foley's Statement on Puerto Rican Legislation to the National Press Club, 24 July 1989; and Senator Jesse Helms, *Congressional Record*, 22 March 1990.

48. See Robert Pastor, "Puerto Rico as an International Issue: A Motive for Movement?" in Bloomfield, *Puerto Rico*.

49. See Marco Antonio Rigau and Juan Manuel García-Passalacqua, *Replica asociada y libre asociación: Documentación de un debate* (San Juan: Editorial Atlántico, 1987), esp. pp. 46–80. See also Marco Antonio Rigau, "Free Association: Certain Future for Puerto Rico," *Revista del Colegio de Abogados de Puerto Rico* 48, no. 4 (October–December 1987): 119.

11   The International Economy and the Caribbean: The 1990s and Beyond

The views expressed in this chapter are those of the author and do not necessarily reflect the views of the chairman or the members of the Joint Economic Committee.

1. Japan, for example, now uses less than 60 percent of the raw materials it required in 1973 to produce a unit of output (Peter F. Drucker, "The Changed World Economy," *Foreign Affairs* 64 [Spring 1986]: 773).

2. This tendency was first noted by Kenichi Ohmae in *Triad Power: The Coming Shape of Global Competition* (London: Macmillan, 1985). It has recently been considerably refined and elaborated by Alfred Chandler in his monumental *Scale and Scope: The Dynamics of Industrial Capitalism* (Cambridge, Mass.: Harvard University Press, 1990).

3. DeAnne Julius, *Global Companies and Public Policy* (London: Royal Institute of International Affairs, 1990), p. 6.

4. *Economist*, 23 June 1990, p. 67.

5. According to a recent IMF estimate, prices for commodities other than oil in 1990 will be nearly 20 percent below their levels in 1980, compared with an average *annual* rate of increase of 11.6 percent per year during the 1970s.

6. John Williamson, *Latin American Adjustment: How Much Has Happened* (Washington, D.C.: Institute for International Economics, 1990), p. 1.

7. This aggregate picture of the region's financial balance obscures some important differences among the countries. Jamaica and Guyana were by far the largest borrowers from official creditors, while Grenada received heavy inflows of aid from Cuba during the late 1970s and early 1980s. Trinidad and Tobago borrowed very little initially, owing to strong oil exports, but became a significant borrower in the mid 1980s as oil prices collapsed. Barbados and many of the OECS countries were generally able to finance their external deficits with modest official borrowing supplemented by private capital flows and managed to avoid serious overindebtedness.

8. See Kempe Ronald Hope, "Private Direct Investment and Development Policy in the Caribbean," *American Journal of Economics and Sociology* 48 (January 1989): 69–78.

9. John Oneal, "Foreign Investments in Less Developed Regions," *Political Science Quarterly* 103 (Spring 1988): 143.

10. World Bank, "Caribbean Region: Current Economic Situation, Regional Issues and Capital Flows," Report no. 8246-CRG (Washington, D.C., 22 February 1990, Mimeographed), p. 3.

11. For a quantitative analysis of the benefits of CBI, see Joseph Pelzman and Gregory Schoepfle, "The Impact of the Caribbean Basin Economic Recovery Act on Caribbean Nations' Exports and Development," *Economic Development and Cultural Change* 36 (July 1988): 753–96.

12. Both the United States and the EC subsidize sugar production but then permit some imports from the Caribbean into their markets. The EC subsidizes sugar directly, while the United States uses imports as a device for regulating domestic supply and demand conditions so that "the market" sets a high price for sugar without the need of direct government subsidy. As a result, EC sugar quotas for the Caribbean are fixed, while U.S. quotas are variable. Under heavy pressure from subsidized European sugar production, the world sugar price collapsed in the 1980s, forcing the United States to cut back on imports sharply in order to maintain domestic prices. As a result, Caribbean countries saw their sugar quota cut from over 5 million tons in 1981 to less than 1 million in 1987.

13. U.S. International Trade Commission, *Annual Report on the Impact of the Caribbean Basin Economic Recovery Act on U.S. Industries and Consumers,* Publication 2225 (Washington, D.C., 1989).

14. Of the European Currency Unit (ECU) 10.4 billion of tropical agricultural imports to the EC, some ECU 7.7 billion are now affected by specific trade preferences. The EC offer would eliminate most of these preferences (see *Financial Times* [London], 20 March 1990).

15. Recent World Bank projections show that an elimination of banana subsidies would result in a 49 percent drop in the prices paid to "protected" exporters in Africa, the Caribbean, and Pacific regions (see World Bank, *World Development Report, 1990* [New York: Oxford University Press, 1990], p. 22).

16. The case of sugar is particularly interesting. The World Bank is forecasting a generally positive environment for sugar in world markets because of tight world supplies, but in a recent report it noted that Brazil may be a lower-cost sugar producer than

most Caribbean islands. Brazil has recently scrapped an ethanol fuel program that absorbed much of its sugar production in the domestic market. If the United States liberalizes sugar imports, Brazil could well displace many Caribbean producers now benefiting from the quota system.

17. See Richard Fletcher, "Undervaluation, Adjustment, and Growth," in *Debt Disaster? Banks, Governments, and Multilaterals Confront the Crisis,* ed. John Weeks (New York: New York University Press, 1989).

18. Recent case studies of firms investing in the free zones found "domestic customs procedures" to be among the most frequently cited impediments to business activity, despite the goal of such zones to eliminate government interference (see Susan Kramer, *Incentives and Impediments to U.S. Foreign Direct Investment in the Caribbean,* Commission for the Study of International Migration and Cooperative Economic Development, Working Paper, no. 14 [Washington, D.C., January 1990]).

19. Lawrence Krause, "Industrialization of an Advanced Global City," in *The Singapore Economy Reconsidered,* ed. Lawrence Krause et al. (Singapore: Institute of Southeast Asian Studies, 1987), p. 56.

20. World Bank, *World Development Report, 1990,* p. 16.

21. The World Bank notes that while roughly 5–8 percent of total island exports are sold within the CARICOM market, over 50 percent of manufactures exports are sold within the region (see World Bank, "Caribbean Region"). An official of the Planning Institute of Jamaica referred to his country as "a nation of samples," where manufacturers produced goods in tiny lots at high cost and low quality (see *Economist,* 6 August 1988).

22. A recent study discussed the general problem facing developing countries seeking to expand manufacturing in the following terms: "Countries are able to attract industrial investment not so much because of their comparative advantage in labor costs but because of their market potential and their technological capacity. . . . A few countries in the Third World have been able to achieve the required technological capacity after competing in the world economy for at least two decades, mainly on the basis of lower production costs in traditional manufacturing. But the large majority of Third World countries do not have the potential to attain a significant level of technological upgrading by themselves; hence they seem destined to lag increasingly behind the OECD countries" (Manuel Castells and Laura D'Andrea Tyson, "High Technology and the Changing International Division of Production," in *The Newly Industrializing Countries in the World Economy,* ed. Randall Purcell [Boulder: Lynne Rienner, 1989], p. 21).

23. OECD, *Trade in Services and Developing Countries* (Paris, 1989).

24. On the high capital intensity see Robert Erbes, *International Tourism and the Economy of Developing Countries* (Paris: OECD, June 1973); on the heavy import demands see U.N. Economic and Social Council, *Impact of International Tourism on the Economic Development of Developing Countries* (New York, May 1975).

25. Jamaican Prime Minister Michael Manley recently announced that tourism is "the strategic industry for Jamaica's immediate future and the sector which could improve the island's balance of payments and pull it out of the clutches of the International Monetary Fund" (see *Inter Press Service,* 5 February 1990).

26. "The Largest Locally Owned Businesses in Puerto Rico," in *The Caribbean Business Book of Lists, 1990* (San Juan: Caribbean Business Publications, 1990).

27. George Danns, "The Role of the Entrepreneur in the Development Strategy of the Caribbean," *Caribbean Affairs* 2 (July–September 1989): 152.

28. William Demas, "Perspectives on the Future of the Caribbean in the World Economy," ibid. 1 (October–December 1988): 9.

29. William H. Davidson, "The Location of Foreign Direct Investment Activity," *Journal of International Business Studies*, Fall 1980, pp. 9–22.

30. To the extent that trade tensions continue between the United States and the Asian NICs, a strategy of expanding investment inside the U.S. tariff wall may make sense to Asian firms.

31. Theodore Moran, "Shaping a Future for Foreign Direct Investment in the Third World," *Washington Quarterly* 11 (Winter 1988): 119–30.

32. The OECS countries have generally had a more stable macroeconomic environment than have other Caribbean countries, owing partly to their decision to adopt an umbrella central bank that separated control of fiscal and monetary policy.

33. Throughout the 1980s, the process of European integration convinced most of the nations of Europe to abandon national monetary autonomy, first by linking their currencies together in the European Monetary System and more recently by endorsing the concept of a European Monetary Union managed by a single "Euro-Fed." They have apparently decided that encouraging investment through regional monetary harmonization was worth the costs of diminished national flexibility in responding to external shocks. Singapore, a highly successful NIC, also abandoned monetary autonomy by electing to set a firm external exchange-rate target and sticking with it despite domestic distress (see Lee Tsao Yuan, "The Government in Macro-economic Management," in Krause et al., *Singapore Economy Reconsidered*, p. 132).

34. A recent article on international taxation observed: "In the world today, some forms of incentives are necessary in order to match those offered by competing host countries in attracting capital investments. In the tax area, such incentives should reduce the level of taxation in the host country to its average level in the home countries of the investors, and preferably across the board as part of a comprehensive tax reform plan available to all taxpayers" (see Yitzhak Hadari, "The Role of Tax Incentives in Attracting Foreign Investments in Selected Developing Countries," *International Lawyer* 24 [Spring 1990]: 152).

35. The new U.S. policy of "zero tolerance" for drugs on any ship or airline has resulted in heavy fines on shippers operating in the Caribbean. Some shipping lines have withdrawn from direct Caribbean-to-U.S. shipping, raising the specter of rising freight rates and diminished service (Helen Richardson, "Troubled Growth for Caribbean Sourcing," *Transportation and Distribution* 18 [February 1989]).

36. See Kramer, "Incentives and Impediments."

37. W. G. Huff, "Patterns in the Economic Development of Singapore," *Journal of Developing Areas* 21 (April 1987): 311.

12   The Drug Problem: Policy Options for Caribbean Countries

1. See Ron Sanders, "Narcotics, Corruption, and Development: The Problems in the Smaller Islands," *Caribbean Affairs* 3, no. 1 (1990): 79–92.

2. *Commission of Inquiry Report: Commission of Inquiry into the Illegal Use of the Bahamas for the Transshipment of Dangerous Drugs Destined for the United States of America*, 2 vols. (Nassau, Bahamas, December 1984), 1:109–28.

3. Louis Blom-Cooper, Q.C., *Guns for Antigua: Report of the Commission of Inquiry into the Circumstances surrounding the Shipment of Arms from Israel to Antigua and Transshipment on 24 April 1989 en route to Colombia* (London: Duckworth, 1990), p. 117.

4. Ibid., pp. 120–31.

5. Television statement by the prime minister of Trinidad and Tobago, Rt. Hon. Mr. A. N. R. Robinson, on 25 June 1988, to launch the First International Day Against Drug Abuse and Illicit Trafficking, observed on 26 June 1988 (typescript).

6. See "Drug Addicts on the Rise," *Barbados Advocate*, 20 September 1989, p. 32.

7. Central Statistical Office of Trinidad and Tobago, *Annual Statistical Digest, 1987* and *1988* (Port-of-Spain, December 1987 and December 1988), and updated figures, June 1990.

8. West Indian Commission Secretariat, *Let All Ideas Contend* (St. James, Barbados, July 1990), pp. 11–12.

9. *Caribbean Affairs* 2, no. 4 (1989): 141–45.

10. Statement of Second Encounter of Bishops, Pastors, and Consultants of Latin America and the Caribbean at a meeting in Jamaica in June 1990, *Caribbean Contact*, July–August 1990, pp. 10–11.

11. Rt. Hon. Mr. V.C. Bird to President Ronald Reagan, 8 July 1988.

12. Sanders, "Narcotics, Corruption, and Development."

13. *Caribbean Contact*, July–August 1990.

14. Kenneth McNeil, "Development of Cocaine Trafficking in Jamaica," keynote address at World Ministerial Summit to Reduce the Demand for Drugs and to Combat the Cocaine Threat, London, 9–11 April 1990, p. 8.

15. For Prime Minister Manley's original proposal, see communiqué of Tenth CARICOM Heads of Government Conference, Grenada, 7 July 1989, typescript. For the General Assembly's response, see U.N., General Assembly, Resolution A/RES/44/141, 12 January 1990.

16. See *Caribbean Insight* 12, no. 8 (August 1989): 15 and no. 9 (September 1989): 14.

17. See U.N., General Assembly, Resolution A/RES/44/141.

13 The Future of Regional Security in the Caribbean

1. See Alma H. Young and Dion E. Phillips, eds., *Militarization in the Non-Hispanic Caribbean* (Boulder: Lynne Rienner, 1986).

2. Regional Security System, Headquarters Staff, "The Roles of the RSS in the East Caribbean," *Bulletin of Eastern Caribbean Affairs* 11, no. 6 (1986).

3. Trinidad and Tobago signed the 1974 Inter-American Treaty on Reciprocal Assistance (Rio Treaty); the Bahamas signed it but did not ratify.

4. See J. Scott Davidson, *Grenada: A Study in Politics and International Law* (Aldershot: Avebury, 1987).

5. See Vaughan A. Lewis, "International, National, and Regional Security Arrangements in the Caribbean," in *Peace, Development, and Security in the Caribbean*, ed. A. Bryant, J. E. Greene, and T. Shaw (New York: Macmillan, 1990).

6. Training has been provided by both the United States and the United Kingdom. At RSS headquarters in Barbados, U.K. personnel are a part of the command structure; there is a gradual training of regional officers to replace these. The U.S. sends ad hoc teams to participate as trainers in RSS-run training courses.

7. See RSS, "Roles of the RSS," p. 7.

8. See Alister McIntyre, "Whither CARICOM?" *CARICOM Perspective* 25 (May–June 1984): 11.

9. See Lewis, "International, National and Regional Security Arrangements."

10. See Commonwealth Secretariat, *Vulnerability: Small States in the Global Society*

(London: Marlborough House, 1985). In that study a small state was defined as essentially being a state of up to one million population, but a few states with larger populations were included in the study when they were part of a regional security grouping wherein the majority of member states had populations of under one million.

11. In both recent cases of domestic political crisis in Trinidad and Tobago, Venezuela offered military help, which, however, was not accepted.

12. See Anselm Francis, "The New Law of the Sea and the Security Interests of the CARICOM States," *Journal of Interamerican Studies and World Affairs* 31, no. 3 (Fall 1989).

13. The RSS was used after the coup collapsed to assist in maintaining law and order under the continuing state of emergency as well as to permit the strained national forces adequate rest breaks.

14. This RSS training includes some training, specifically in negotiating techniques, for cases in which there are hostages at risk. For a comprehensive survey of the RSS, see Brig. Gen. R. Lewis, "Eastern Caribbean RSS as a Model for UN Action in Relation to the Security of Small States" (Course paper, Royal College of Defence Studies, London, 1990).

15. Particularly after the Grenada crisis in 1983, there was little possibility of inviting the U.S. forces; apart from the political aspects, there are strong doubts in the region about both their efficiency and their techniques in these situations.

16. See Steven Baranyi and Edgar Dosman, "Canada and the Security of the Commonwealth Caribbean," in Bryant, Greene, and Shaw, *Peace, Development, and Security*.

17. U.N., General Assembly, Resolution 45/51, 8 December 1989.

18. U.N., Secretary-General, "Study on Concepts of Security," Document A/46/553, 26 August 1985, which makes a passing reference to the problems of small states.

19. Independent Commission on Disarmament and Security Issues, *Common Security* (London: Pan Books, 1982), pp. 162–67. The essence of the commission's proposal for implementing this modified version of the Charter collective security system is for a political partnership between the permanent members of the Security Council and Third World countries in order to prevent conflicts' being settled by armed force. The commission had specific proposals on organization of standby forces. See also Sheila Harden, ed., *Small Is Dangerous* (London: Pinter, 1985), chap. 5, for suggestions for peacekeeping forces through the United Nations and the Commonwealth.

20. Commonwealth emphasis both in bilateral and multilateral programs has been on economic assistance and cooperation.

21. See Humberto García Muñiz, *Boots, Boots, Boots: Intervention, Regional Security, and Militarization in the Caribbean,* Caribbean Project for Justice and Peace, Occasional Paper (Rio Piedras, Puerto Rico, 1986); Dion Phillips, "Barbados and the Militarisation of the Eastern Caribbean," *Bulletin of Eastern Caribbean Affairs* 11, no. 6 (1986); and David Simmons, "Militarization of the Caribbean: Concern for National and Regional Security," *International Journal* 40, no. 2 (Spring 1985).

22. Security cooperation is a new concept for the region and needs fostering. Whereas intelligence cooperation seems to flow smoothly between the RSS states and Jamaica, to date the links with Trinidad and Tobago have not been satisfactory in practice.

23. See Commonwealth Secretariat, *Vulnerability*, pp. 47–51.

24. Small states in such situations are particularly vulnerable to the phenomenon of prestigious international media getting access to sensitive areas to which the government

might itself not have access. Such media intervention itself sometimes leads to further complications.

25. The U.S. foreign presence in the region, apart from that of France, the Netherlands, Britain, and Venezuela, has meant that the 1979 OAS proposal to declare the Caribbean a "zone of peace" has had little chance of getting off the ground.

14   Twenty-first Century Challenges for the Caribbean and the United States: Toward a New Horizon

We would like to thank Peter Hakim and Richard Bloomfield for comments on an earlier draft.

1. John Williamson, *The Progress of Policy Reform in Latin America* (Washington, D.C.: Institute for International Economics, 1990).

2. Joan Nelson, *Fragile Coalitions: The Politics of Economic Adjustment* (Washington, D.C.: Overseas Development Council, 1989).

3. Carl Stone, "A Unified Regional European Market and Its Implications and Challenges for the Caribbean," *Caribbean Affairs* 3, no. 3 (1990): 57–65.

4. U.S. International Trade Commission, *Annual Report on the Impact of the Caribbean Basin Economic Recovery Act on U.S. Industries and Consumers*, Fourth Report (Washington, D.C.: GPO, September 1989), p. vi.

5. Joseph Pelzman and Gregory K. Schoepfle, cited in Stuart K. Tucker and Maiko Chambers, *U.S. Sugar Quotas and the Caribbean Basin*, Policy Focus #6 (Washington, D.C.: Overseas Development Council, December 1989), p. 4.

6. Dory Owens, "Caribbean Basin Bill Passes," *Miami Herald*, 5 August 1990.

7. World Bank, *Caribbean Region: Current Economic Situation, Regional Issues, and Capital Flows* (Washington, D.C., 22 February 1990), p. 15.

8. According to World Bank tables, the total amount in 1988 was $9.792 billion (cited by Richard Bernal and Tony Bogues, "Caribbean Debt" [Paper prepared for the World Peace Foundation's Caribbean Project, Boston, October 1990], p. 3).

9. Ibid., p. 4.

10. David S. North and Judy A. Whitehead, "Policy Recommendations for Improving the Utilization of Emigrant Resources in the Nations of the Eastern Caribbean" (Report prepared for the U.S. Commission for the Study of International Migration and Cooperative Economic Development, Washington, D.C., 1989), p. 5.

11. See Robert A. Pastor, ed., *Migration and Development in the Caribbean: The Unexplored Connection* (Boulder: Westview, 1985).

12. Anthony P. Maingot, "U.S. Geopolitical Perceptions and Caribbean Elite Ideologies: Three Watersheds" (Paper prepared for the World Peace Foundation's Caribbean Project, Boston, October 1990), p. 51.

13. U.N., General Assembly, statement by the Honourable David Coore, Q.C., Minister of foreign affairs and foreign trade of Jamaica, 4 October 1989, p. 11.

14. Ron Sanders, "The Drug Problem: Policy Options for Caribbean Countries" (Paper prepared for the World Peace Foundation's Caribbean Project, Boston, October 1990).

15. Maingot, "U.S. Geopolitical Perceptions and Caribbean Elite Ideologies," p. 50.

16. Jonathan Hartlyn, "The Dominican Republic" (Paper prepared for the World Peace Foundation's Caribbean Project, February 1990), p. 2.

17. García-Passalacqua superbly explores the frustration in chapter 9, above.

18. Latin American Weekly Report, 4 October 1990, p. 12.

19. "CARICOM Aiming for Unified Market by '93," *Carib News*, 29 May 1990, p. 4.

20. See Sahadeo Basdeo, "The Single European Act: A CARICOM Perspective," *Journal of Interamerican Studies and World Affairs* 32, no. 2 (Summer 1990): 103–20.

Contributors

Richard J. Bloomfield, executive director, World Peace Foundation; former career diplomat: ambassador to Ecuador, 1976–78, and to Portugal, 1978–82.

Jorge I. Domínguez, professor of government and chairman of the Committee on Latin American and Iberian Studies, Harvard University; former president, Latin American Studies Association.

Richard D. Fletcher, deputy manager of the Plans and Programs Department, Inter-American Development Bank; former minister of state for finance and planning, Jamaica; former executive president of the Sugar Institute of Jamaica.

Juan Manuel García-Passalacqua, president of Analisis, Inc., and political analyst for newspapers, radio, and television in San Juan, Puerto Rico; former visiting lecturer at Yale University.

Jonathan Hartlyn, associate professor of political science, University of North Carolina at Chapel Hill; author of *The Politics of Coalition Rule in Colombia* and coeditor of *Latin American Political Economy.*

Evelyne Huber, professor of political science and sociology and director of Latin American and Caribbean Studies Program, Northwestern University; coauthor of *Capitalist Development and Democracy* and *Democratic Socialism in Jamaica.*

Franklin W. Knight, Leonard and Helen R. Stulman Professor of History and director of Latin American Studies, The Johns Hopkins University; author of *The Caribbean: The Genesis of a Fragmented Nationalism* and coeditor of *Atlantic Port Cities.*

Vaughan A. Lewis, director-general of the Organization of Eastern Caribbean States; former director, Institute of Social and Economic Research, University of the West Indies.

Neville Linton, assistant director of the International Affairs Division, Commonwealth Secretariat, England; former senior fellow at the Institute of International Relations, University of the West Indies.

Anthony P. Maingot, professor of sociology and editor of *Hemisphere,* Florida International University; former president, Caribbean Studies Association; editor of *Small Country Development and International Labor Flows: Experiences in the Caribbean.*

Robert A. Pastor, professor of political science and director of the Carter Center's Latin American and Caribbean Program, Emory University; former director of Latin America Affairs of the National Security Council, 1977–81; author of *Whirlpool: U.S. Foreign Policy toward Latin America and the Caribbean* (1992) and *Condemned to Repetition: The United States and Nicaragua* (1988), both published by Princeton University Press.

Anthony Payne, reader in politics and director of the graduate program in International Studies, University of Sheffield, England.

Stephen A. Quick, executive director, Joint Economic Committee, U.S. Congress.

Selwyn Ryan, director, Institute of Social and Economic Research, University of the West Indies, Trinidad and Tobago.

Ron Sanders, consultant to the West Indies Commission; former ambassador to UNESCO for Antigua and Barbuda.

R. DeLisle Worrell, deputy governor, Central Bank of Barbados; author of *Small Island Economies: Structure and Performance in the English-speaking Caribbean since 1970.*

Index